WINTERTHUR
STYLE SOURCEBOOK

Traditional American Rooms

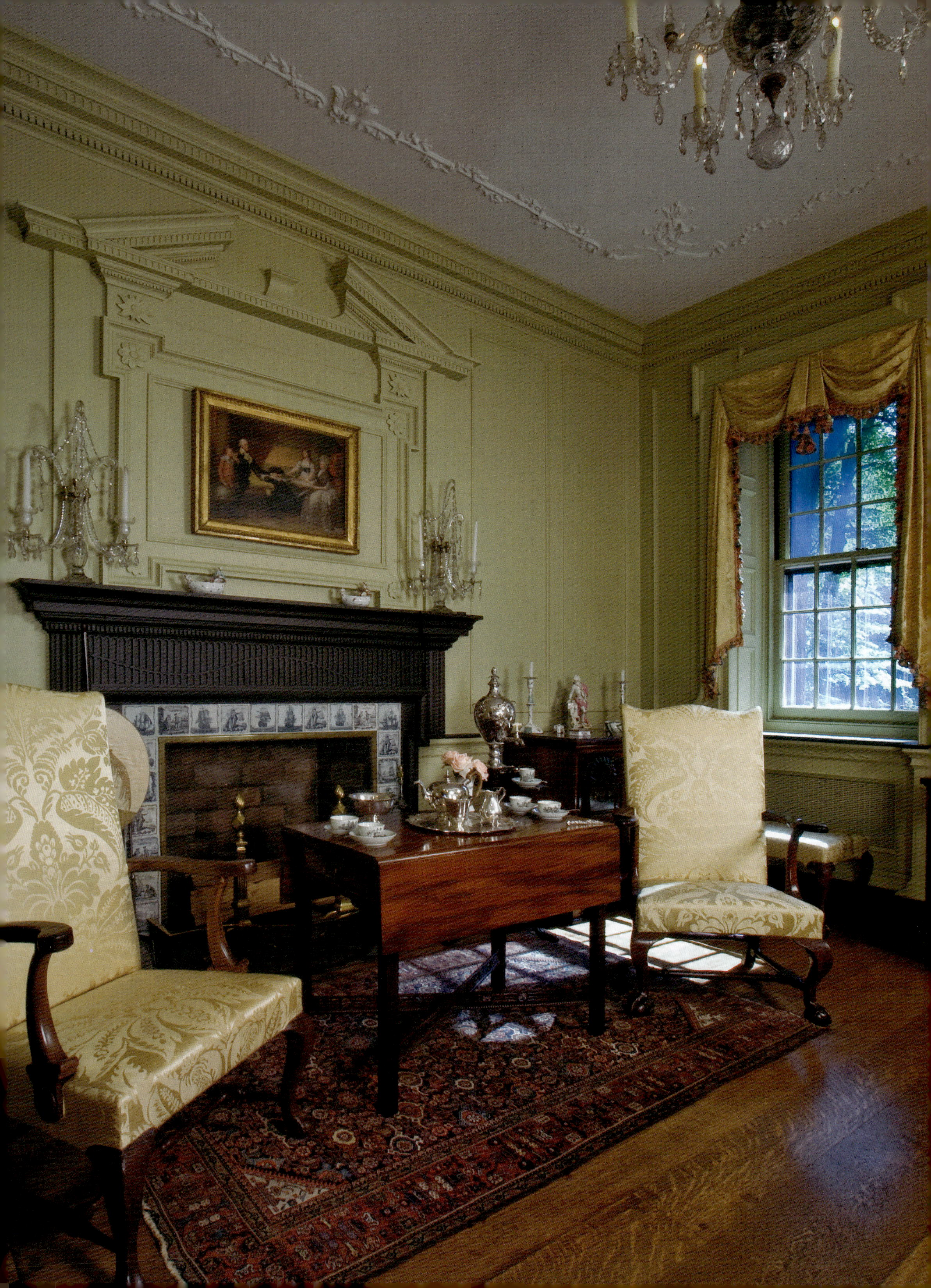

WINTERTHUR
STYLE SOURCEBOOK

Traditional American Rooms

Celebrating Style, Craftsmanship, and Historic Woodwork

Brent Hull
Christine G.H. Franck
Preface by Maggie Lidz
Foreword by Barbra Streisand

WINTERTHUR

FOX CHAPEL
PUBLISHING

WINTERTHUR

Published under license to Winterthur Museum & County Estate.

ISBN 978-1-56523-322-5

Library of Congress Control Number: 2008

To learn more about the other great books from Fox Chapel Publishing, or to find a retailer near you, call toll-free 800-457-9112 or visit us at *www.FoxChapelPublishing.com*.

We are always looking for talented authors. To submit an idea, please send a brief inquiry to acquisitions@foxchapelpublishing.com.

Printed in China
Second Printing

Previous page: Chestertown Room, from Chestertown, Md., circa 1790. See page 58.

About Winterthur

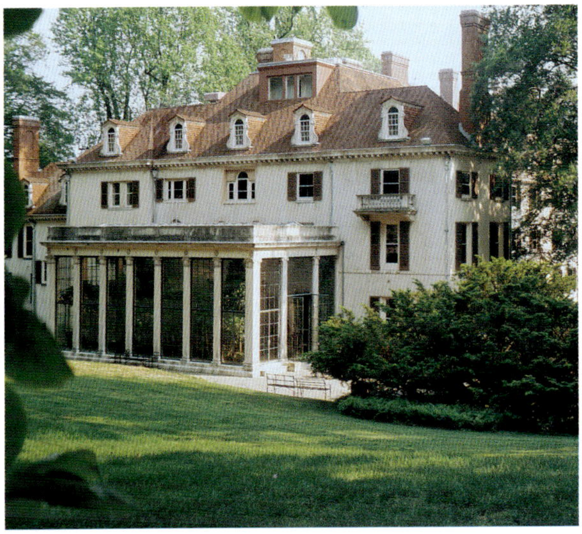

In the early 20th century, collector and horticulturist Henry Francis du Pont (1880–1969) created a grand country estate at Winterthur, his ancestral home in Delaware's scenic Brandywine Valley. An avid collector of American art and antiques, a devoted gardener and horticulturist, and a keen student of American history, du Pont furnished his house with exquisite antiques representing the best craftsmanship and styles of early America. In 1951, he opened the 175-room house and surrounding 60-acre garden to the public.

Today, Winterthur's collection of more than 85,000 early American decorative arts objects is without equal. The brilliantly conceived naturalistic garden is set amid 1,000 acres of rolling pasture and woodlands, a landscape of quiet grandeur. The research library serves as an important center for the study of American art and culture, and the museum is home to groundbreaking exhibitions, research, and art conservation laboratories.

Winterthur is a unique national treasure, offering a rare combination of beauty, history, art, and learning. H. F. du Pont's legacy at Winterthur continues to inspire, enlighten, and delight our visitors. We invite you to experience our unique history, tour our impressive museum of decorative arts, and stroll our lovely garden.

Table of Contents

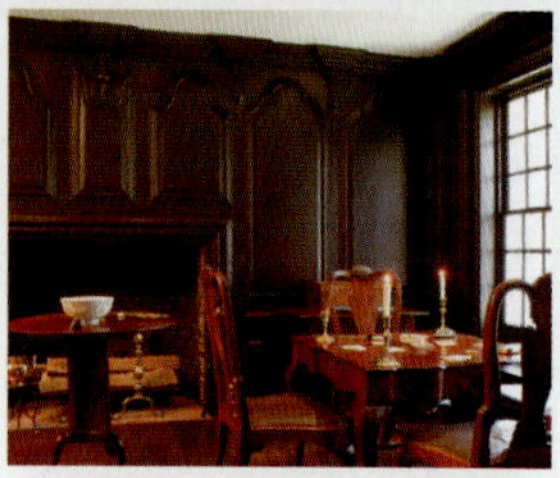

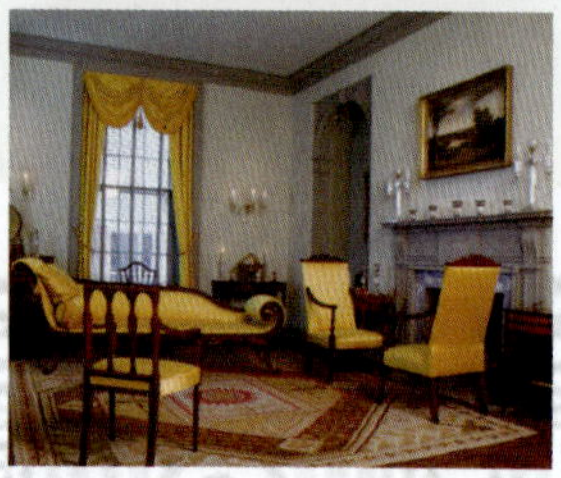

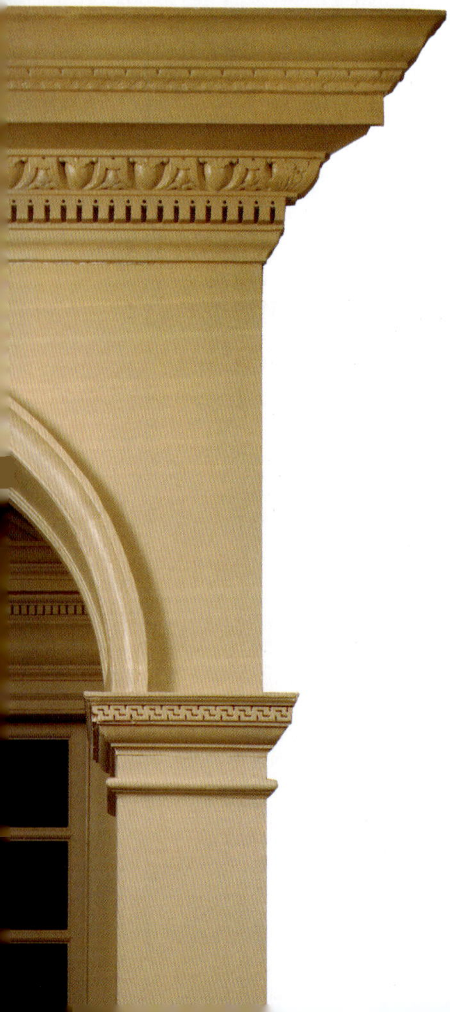

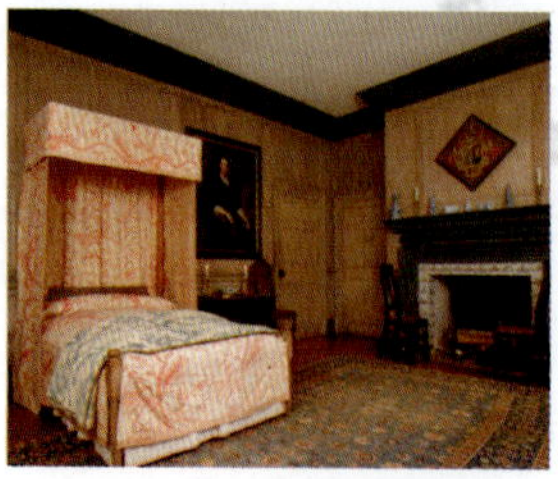

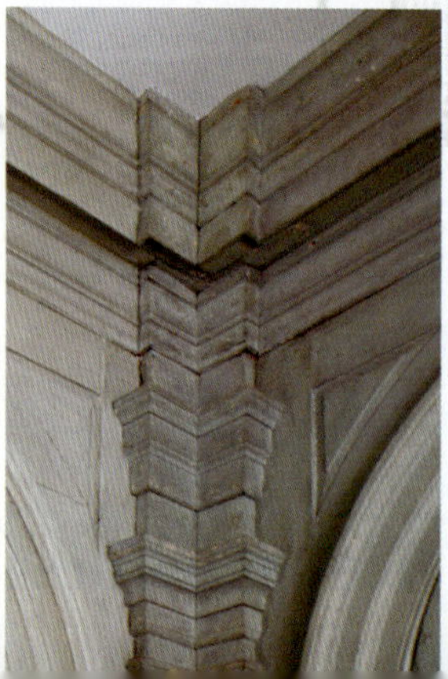

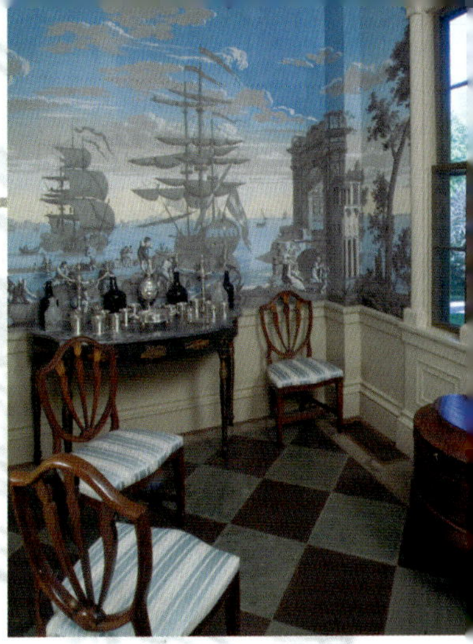

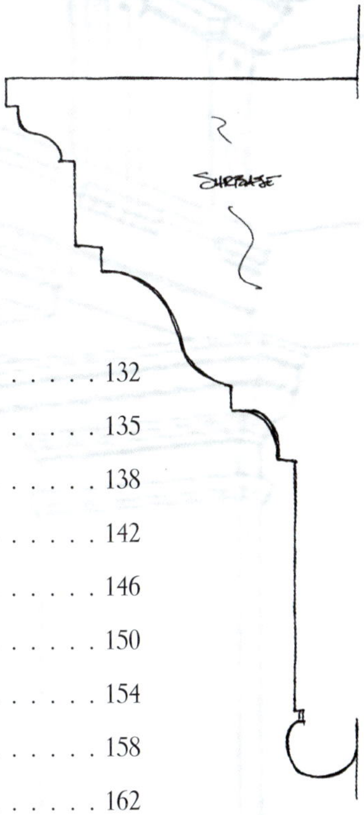

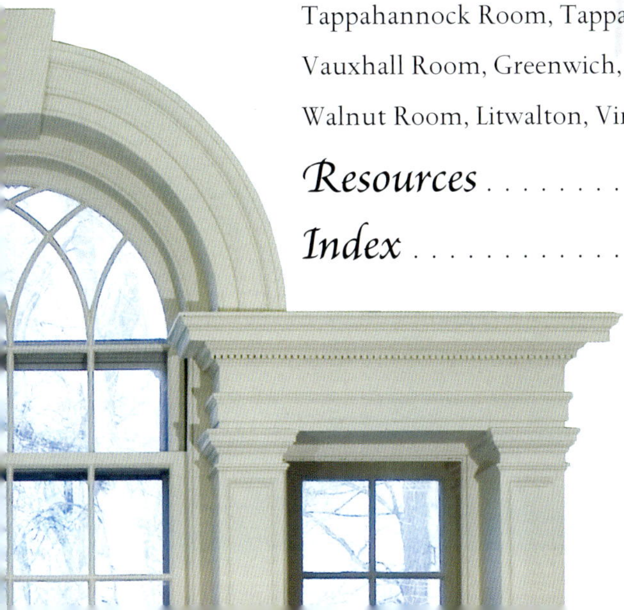

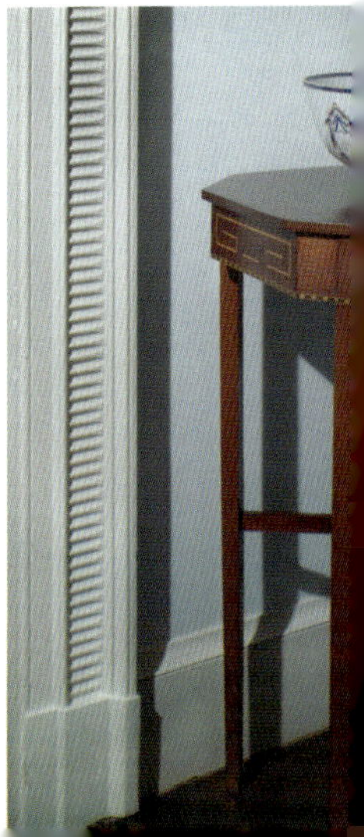

Foreword

I was so happy to read this book. It shows exactly what you and your builder need to know to create traditional American rooms with grace and style. A few years ago, when I was designing and about to build my own home to house my collection of eighteenth century American furniture and early twentieth century decorative arts, I had the pleasure of spending two days at the Winterthur Museum. Their indoor street inspired me to build my own. Mr. du Pont focused on American antiques and furnishings, something in which I take great interest, at a time when many of his peers were collecting European objects. His eye for detail and style is demonstrated not only by Winterthur, but also by his work for Jackie Kennedy at the White House in the 1960s. That gave me great direction as to the authentic moldings I required.

What makes Mr. du Pont unique is his passion for collecting American culture, and the extent of his collections: not only the objects but the very rooms themselves, 175 of them. The rooms date from 1640 to 1860 and come from twelve of the thirteen original American colonies. These architectural interiors represent a beautiful cross section of American interiors, from the very highest style rooms of Newport and Philadelphia to the simple taverns of New Hampshire, from the houses of rich merchants to those of simple tradesmen. It is a remarkable window on the history of our people, and of the material culture that enabled and enriched their lives.

It is these architectural interiors that my friend, Brent Hull, celebrates in his book, *Traditional American Rooms*. The beauty of these historic rooms resides in the principles of classical scale and proportion, as Brent demonstrates with his careful measurements and lovely drawings. These rooms feel right because they are right: they are based on the Classical structure of American interior architecture, the ancient truths discovered in Greece and Rome. A study of these rooms gives us insight into how the ancient master-builders designed and planned their homes, and of how we may plan and build ours.

Traditional American Rooms celebrates the things I love: beautiful architecture, authentic American furniture and art, and Classic style. I'm a great admirer of Winterthur and of Mr. du Pont's vision of decorating and design. I am delighted that this book celebrates these interiors in such a wonderful American fashion.

—Barbra Streisand,
Malibu, California

Marlboro Room, Patuxent Manor, Lower Marlboro, Md. This was the du Pont sitting room at Winterthur. See page 98.

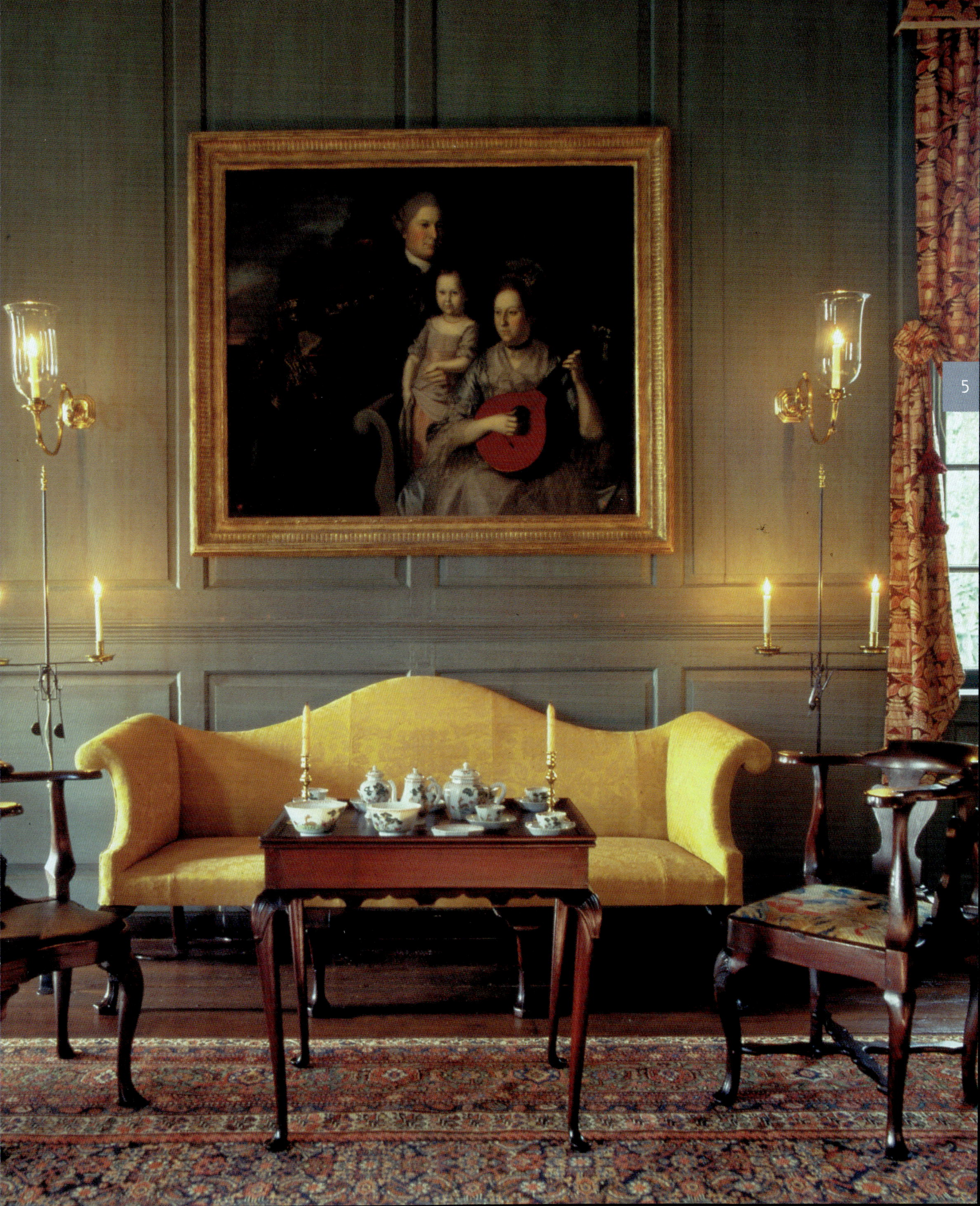

Preface

Henry Francis du Pont and His Collection of Historic Architecture

"A foremost drive of the collector is a love of his materials."
H. F. du Pont, 1952

Henry Francis du Pont's woodwork installations are some of the museum's greatest assets. Halls, rooms, alcoves, and stairwells—135 interior spaces—feature architecture from seventeenth-, eighteenth-, and nineteenth-century American buildings. Indeed, eminent architectural historian John Harris described Winterthur as the world's largest collection of architectural salvages in a private house.[1] The salvages range from a few feet of molding to entire house facades.

H. F. du Pont was already a seasoned buyer of American architecture when he began collecting it in 1924. The original Winterthur house in which he was reared was built in 1839 in Greek Revival style. In 1902, when he was twenty-two, du Pont saw the house transformed into a French Renaissance-style villa by his father and a local architectural firm. At the time, the young du Pont took on the task of changing the interiors to fit the new casing. He became an enthusiastic buyer of old European paneling and mantels, just one among many Americans hoping to achieve a look of age and culture in their new houses.[2]

A shift in his thinking occurred in 1923, however, when he and his wife, Ruth, considered building a summer house in Southampton, Long Island. Du Pont decided to make, as he called it, "an American House." In the early 1920s, American rooms "weren't correct at all," du Pont remembered later in his life, but he thought that some of the houses on the Eastern Shore of Maryland "were very nice." He began buying antique paneling from the Eastern Shore for use in the summer house, which was designed by the New York architectural firm of Cross and Cross and built between 1925 and 1926. The house was a great success. Du Pont called it Chestertown in honor of the town in Kent County, Maryland. The interiors, inspired by Beauport, Henry Davis Sleeper's masterpiece in Gloucester, Massachusetts, were filled with architecture from 18th- and early 19th-century Kent County houses, under Sleeper's supervision.

H. F. du Pont's collection of American architecture eventually expanded beyond the capacity of Chestertown, and after his father's death in 1926 he hired architect Albert Ely Ives to renovate Winterthur. Between 1929 and 1931 Ives added an enormous wing to the house and removed the French Renaissance trappings on the exterior. As at Chestertown, but on a much grander scale, the Winterthur interiors were constructed from salvaged materials: mantels, doors, pediments, moldings, paneling, flooring, and staircase balustrades. Ives worked with at least nine salvaged houses to create the interiors of the new addition. Of the nine houses, he made twenty-three rooms.[3]

Among the salvaged sources, Port Royal, an eighteenth-century Georgian house in the Frankford section of Philadelphia, became the central feature of the new wing. The once-grand country house, marooned and derelict, had been spotted from a train by antiques dealer J. Lloyd Hyde and brought to du Pont's attention. In addition, the Metropolitan Museum of Art sold du Pont the seventeenth-century Hart Room from Ipswich, Massachusetts, and interiors were also acquired from the Readbourne and Pickard houses in Maryland. However, the historic woodwork was not installed at Winterthur as it had been in its original location. The materials were reassembled and very much modified to fit modern needs and tastes.

Peter Mooz wrote in the 1970 *Guide to Winterthur Collections*, "To find, to acquire, to move, and to install rooms from old houses

. . . takes meticulous care, a well-filled purse, and the patience of Job." When du Pont began building his American wing at Winterthur, he hired Schleich Studios in New York, which specialized in historic room installations. By the end of the 1930s, he had assembled his own in-house team of carpenters, painters, and masons capable of taking a building apart and reassembling it to fit at Winterthur (and in at least one case, of fashioning a reproduction for the owner to replace the original). Du Pont's interest in period architecture never waned. By the time the house opened to the public as a museum in 1951, du Pont had moved out and nearly every available space had been fitted out with period architecture.

One day in the 1960s, as du Pont and museum curator Charles Hummel were walking through the old house kitchen, which was by then in disuse, Hummel remembers du Pont's comment that "we ought to put a period room in there." When reminded that Winterthur had interiors from all thirteen original colonies except Georgia, the decision was made. Unfortunately, du Pont died in April 1969, before work was completed on the 1837 dining room from Milledgeville, Georgia. Although there have been alterations to existing rooms, no new rooms have been added to Winterthur since his death.

The thirteen original colonies are represented, but the historic architecture collection at Winterthur is not comprehensive by any standard. It reflects the East Coast bias of H. F. du Pont as well as the type of material on the market from the time period during which he collected. It is a subject that is ripe for more in-depth research, and Winterthur is grateful to Brent Hull and Christine Franck for undertaking the publication of this volume.

Maggie Lidz
Estate Historian
Winterthur Museum & Country Estate

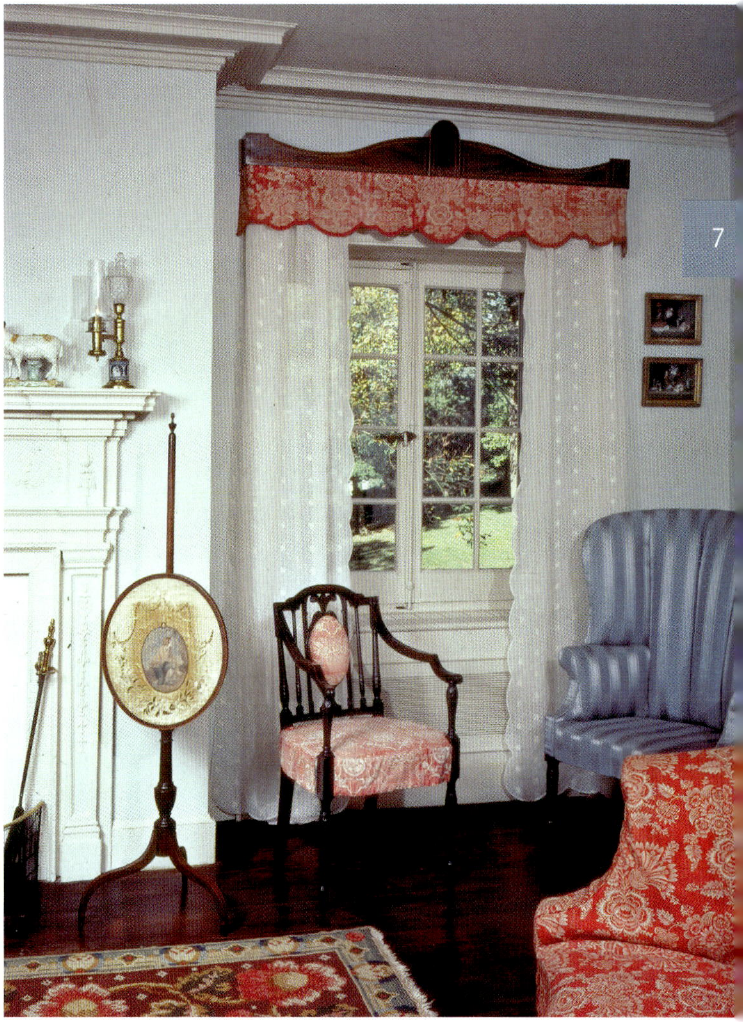

The Blue Room, Wilson House, Salem, N.J. The Blue Room was Mrs. du Pont's bedroom at Winterthur. See page 42.

1. John Harris, Moving Rooms: *The Trade in Architectural Salvages* (New Haven: Yale University Press, 2007), p. 217.

2. HA Box 1, Koopman Apr. 1, 1910; HF 158, Duveen Brothers, 1909 correspondence; HF 196, Little and Brown, correspondence with Aux Quatrième, Wanamaker Department Store, 1919–26.

3. The houses were Readbourne, Centreville, Md.; Belle Isle, Litwalton, Va.; Hampton Court, Elizabeth, N.J.; Mordington, Frederica, Del.; Pickard House, North East, Md.; Imlay House, Allentown, N.J.; Port Royal House, Frankford Pa.; Ritchie House, Tappahannock, Va.; Wentworth House, Portsmouth, N.H.

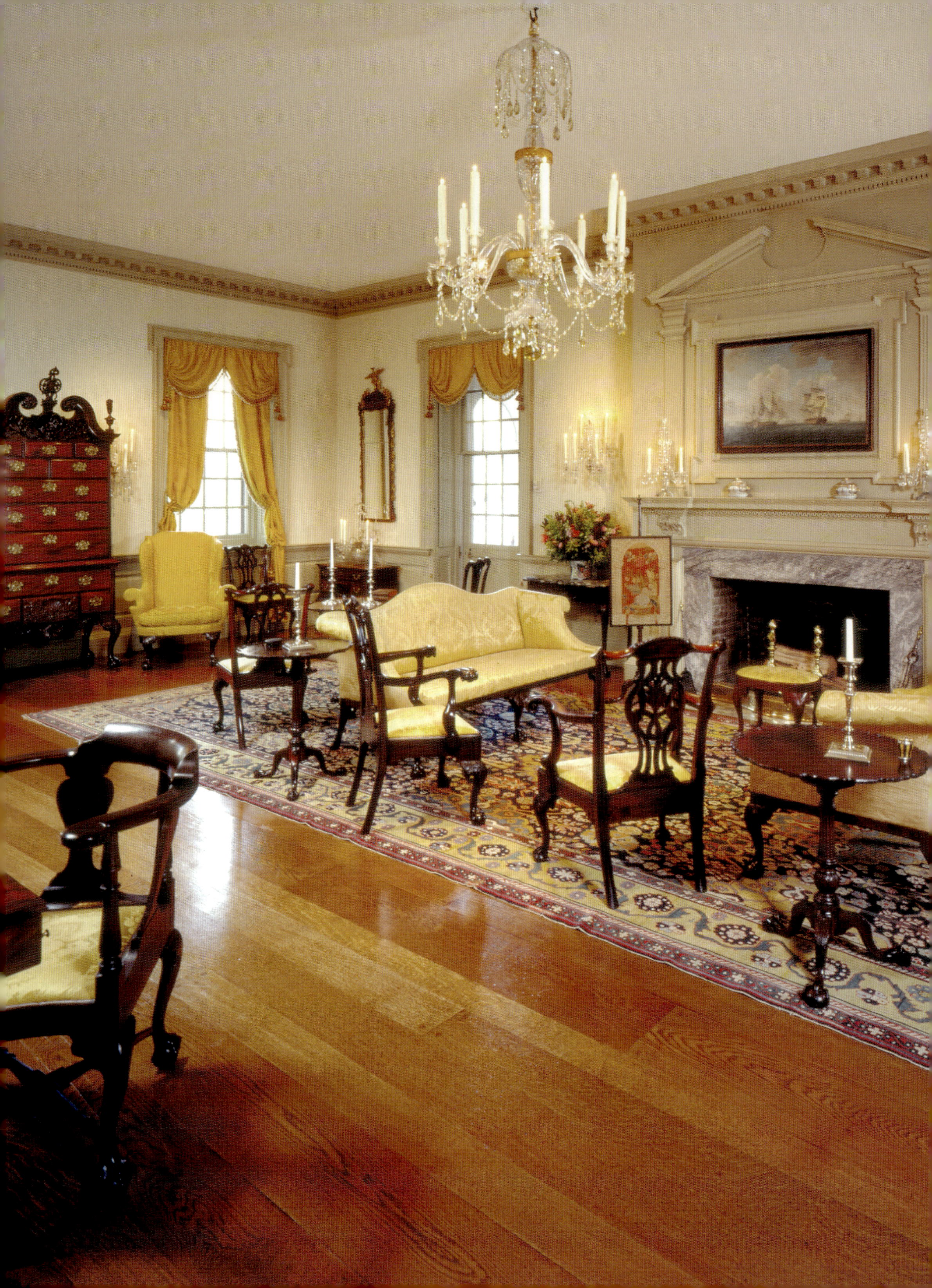

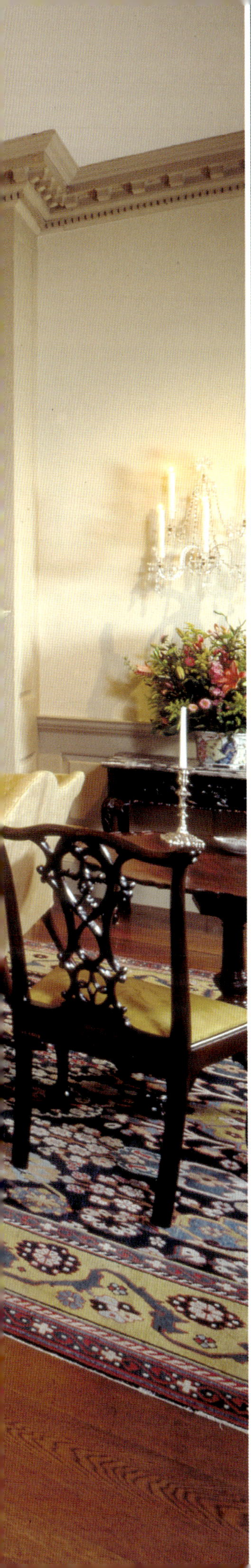

Introduction

Architectural Traditions of Early America

The architectural traditions of early America are but one chapter in the long story of the Classical tradition. This tale has its origins in the temples of ancient Greece and Rome. It was retold in Renaissance treatises, villas, and churches and passed on to a young America by English, Dutch, Spanish, French, and other colonists. Though it may seem unlikely, to better understand the collection of historic American rooms installed at Winterthur, one must first become familiar with the Classical architecture of Greece and Rome.

The Port Royal Parlor, circa 1762, is a fine example of a late-Georgian-style American house influenced by English traditions. See page 135.

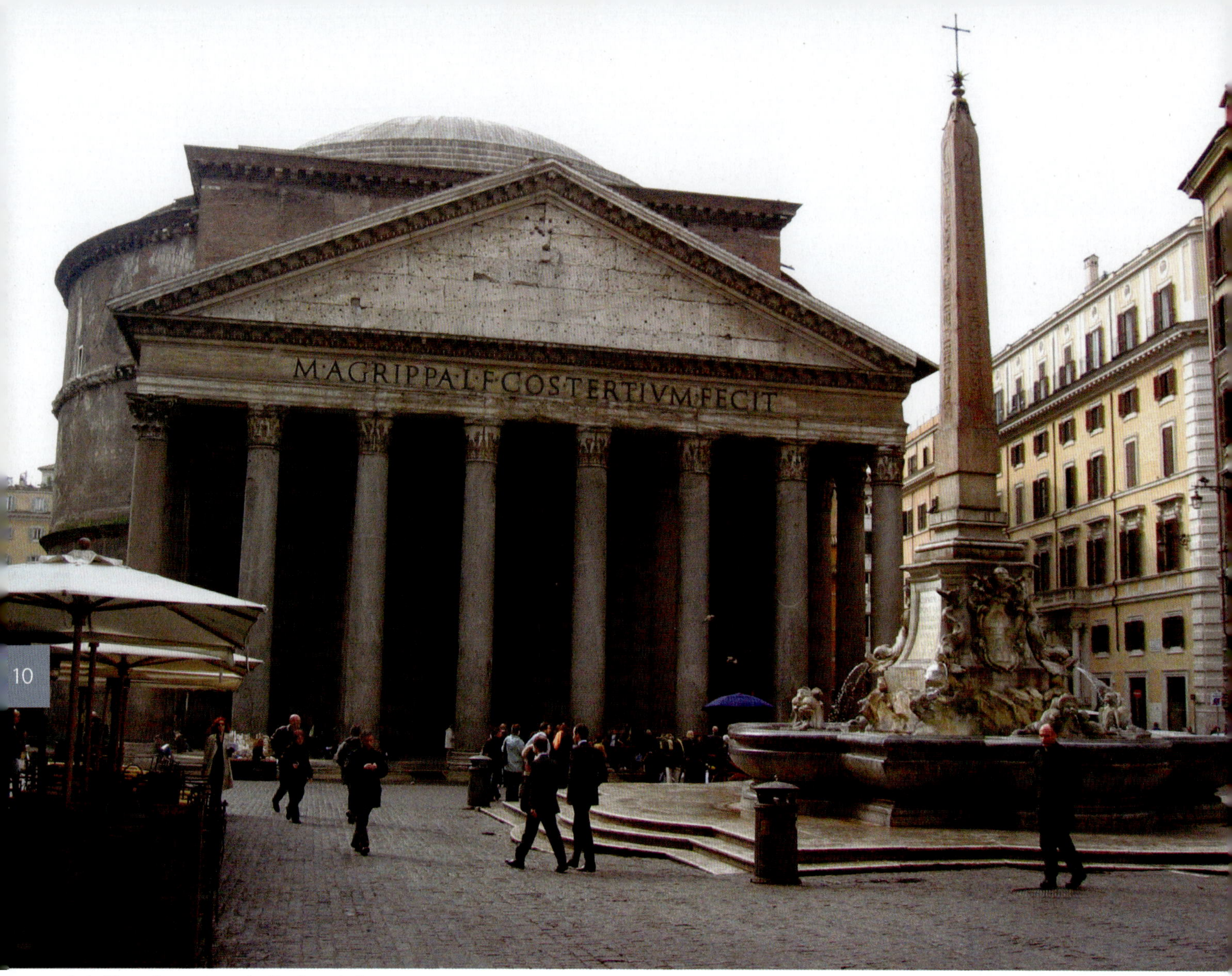

Corinthian columns grace the Pantheon in Rome.

Classical Origins

Ancient Greek and Roman architecture is recorded not only in the buildings and ruins that remain, but also in the only existing book on architecture from antiquity, *De Architectura*. Known as the *Ten Books on Architecture*, it was written by a Roman architect, Marcus Vitruvius Pollio, around 25 BCE. In it he describes "a complete system of architecture" covering a range of subjects including the origins of architecture, city planning, materials, and construction methods. He also presents principles for designing sacred, civic, and domestic buildings, and instructions on how to compose these buildings according to three types, or orders, of architecture: the Doric, Ionic, and Corinthian.

Though Vitruvius details these so-called rules, even a cursory look at Greek and Roman buildings shows that while there were normative principles, there was also rich variety. Likewise, while one imagines Classical architecture springing fully formed from Greece and Rome, related forms are found far earlier throughout Egypt and Mesopotamia. Classical architecture is a cumulative tradition of place- and building-making that has been formed through history, one that continues even today. It is a language, not an historic style, that reaches from Greece to Winterthur's rooms to create cities, buildings, and interiors.

Rebirth

Copies of Vitruvius' manuscript were known throughout the Middle Ages, though little attention was paid to it until the Florentine humanist Poggio Bracciolini found a copy in the Abbey of St. Gallen in Switzerland in 1414, a time when all things Classical were being dusted off and restudied. Of all of the Renaissance architects to grapple with this history, Andrea Palladio is one of the most important to American history. Apprenticed as a stonemason, he showed such aptitude he was mentored by the statesman Gian Giorgio Trissino, who in 1541 took him south from the Veneto for his first trip to Rome.

As Palladio struggled to understand Vitruvius' text and explored Roman buildings on his own, he claimed the Classical tradition for himself and transformed it for his time. Eventually he would create his own treatise, *I Quattro Libri del Architectura*, or *The Four Books of Architecture*, a book of great importance for western architecture. In direct text and clear drawings understandable to patron and builder alike, Palladio describes the orders of architecture, ancient buildings, and his own designs for urban palazzos, rural villas, churches, and civic buildings *all'antica*, or "in the ancient manner."

The built and written achievements of Palladio and other Renaissance architects like Alberti, Serlio, and Vignola revived the Classical tradition of architecture. They demonstrated its applicability for addressing building challenges of their day, and in turn transmitted it to the future.

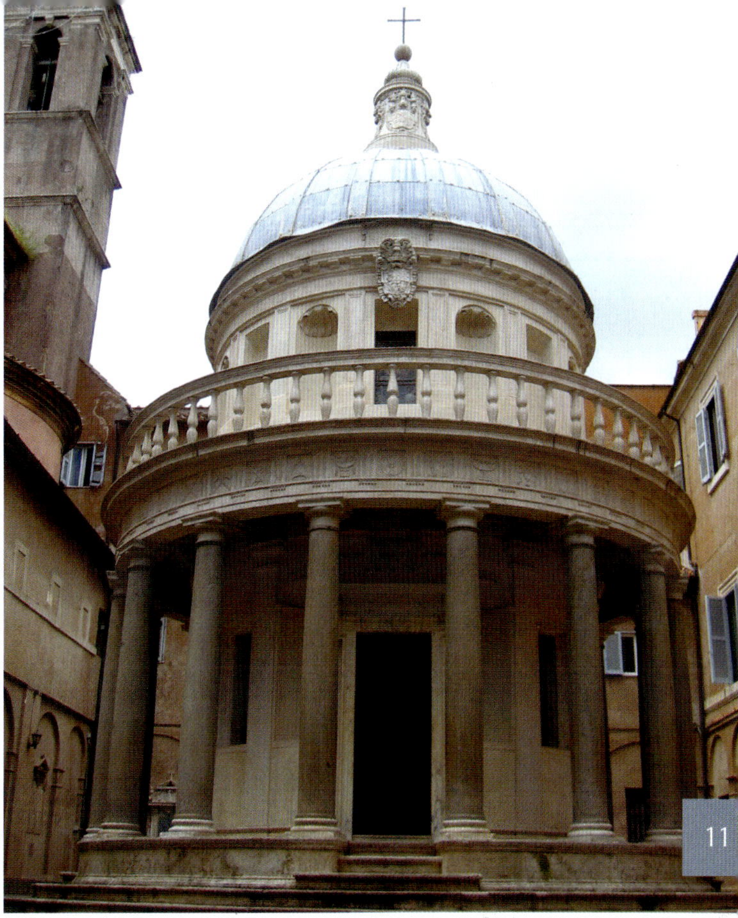

Brumante employed The Doric Order in his Tempietto at San Pietro in Montorio, Rome (1502). Below is Palladio's version of The Doric Order.

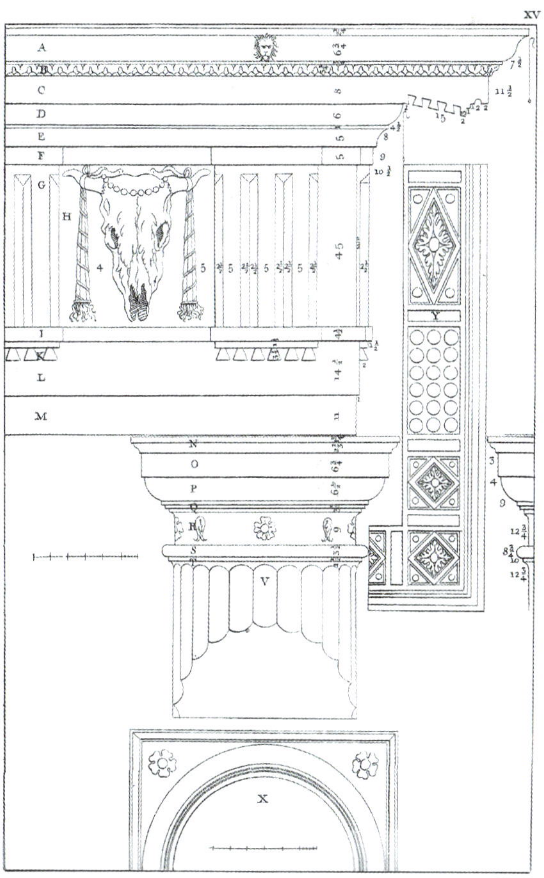

Transformation

As early as the first half of the seventeenth century, the influence of Palladio is seen in England in the work of Inigo Jones. Against a backdrop of Elizabethan architecture still largely medieval in character, Jones' Banqueting House on Whitehall was radical for its time, a literate essay in Classical design. Like Palladio before him, Inigo Jones studied the architecture of ancient Rome as well as that of the Italian Renaissance. He was one of the first English architects to travel to Italy, making two trips in the late-sixteenth and early seventeenth centuries with his copy of Palladio in hand. Returning to England, he applied the lessons he'd learned to new buildings with contemporary needs.

In the following decades, instead of Palladio, the baroque thrived in England in the works of Wren, Hawksmoor, and Vanbrugh. Wren's rather chaste Baroque style influenced domestic architecture. Simple, well-proportioned houses, generally made of brick with elaborate door surrounds topped by hipped roofs, were common. Such houses, like Coleshill (1662) by Sir Roger Pratt, were well-known precedents for English colonists settling in colonial America.

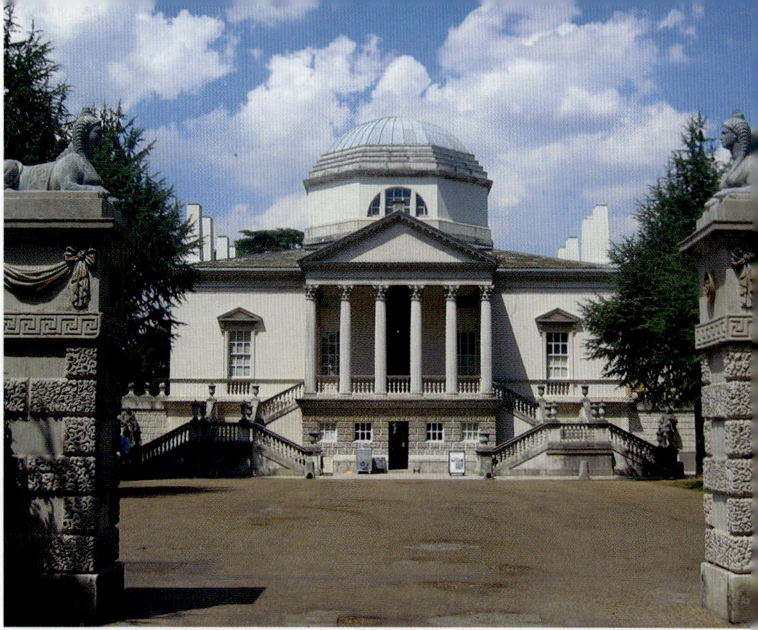

Completed in 1729, Chiswick House, an Anglo-Palladian villa in West London designed by Richard Boyle, the third Earl of Burlington, is modeled on Palladio's Villa Rotunda.

A detail of Chiswick House, which closely follows the Corinthian Order in architecture.

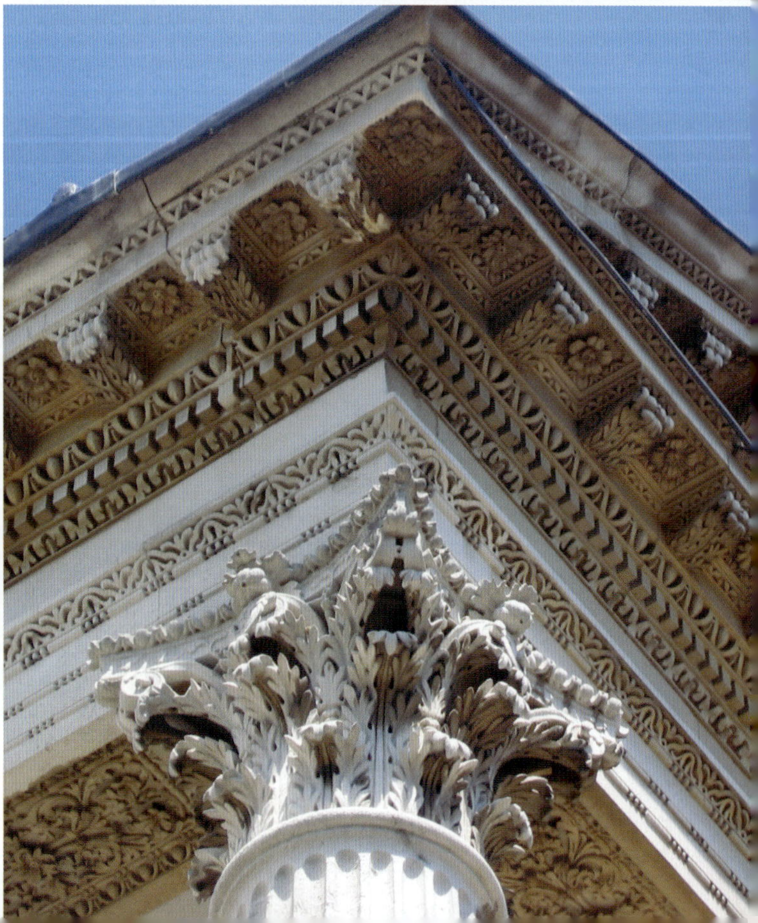

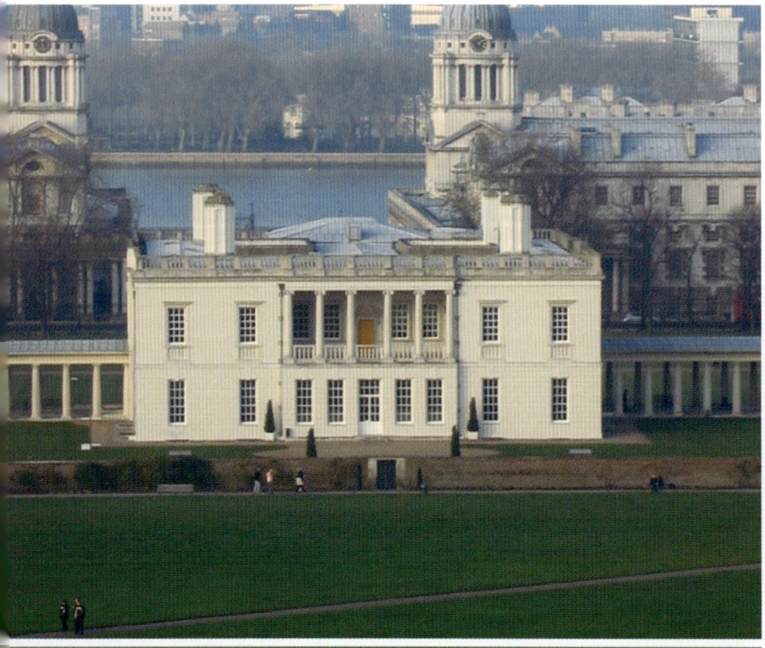

The Queen's House in Greenwich was designed by Imigo Jones and construction began in 1616. It marks the first wave of Palladianism in England.

As King George I ascended the throne in 1714, a second wave of Palladianism hit England. This movement away from the perceived licentiousness of the baroque toward Palladian rationality was led by Lord Burlington, who surrounded himself with architects like Colen Campbell and William Kent. For himself, Burlington built Chiswick House, modeled directly on Palladio's Villa Rotonda and closely following Palladio's Four Books.

Giacomo Leoni's first complete English translation of Palladio's *Four Books* (1715-1720) and Colen Campbell's concurrent *Vitruvius Brittanicus* provided guidance for achieving Palladian perfection. And while that perfection was admired, it also had a sobriety that left some cold. Rather than a strict Palladianism, architects like James Gibbs married the English Baroque work of Wren with the rigor of Palladio, creating some of the most beautiful architecture of the period.

Later in the eighteenth century, in the wake of the discovery of Pompeii and Herculaneum, English gentry made their way to Italy for the Grand Tour. Architects followed to study and draw the newly discovered ruins. It was soon obvious that neither Vitruvius nor Palladio had fully covered the rich, expressive variety of Classical architecture. These revelations sparked a wave of neoclassicism that in England was so closely associated with the architect Robert Adam that it was often called the Adam Style.

These three manifestations of the Classical tradition in English seventeenth- and eighteenth-century architecture—the ebullient baroque, the rigorous Anglo-Palladian, and the refined neoclassical—each have parallels in American colonial and post-revolutionary architecture, where the story of the Classical tradition continues.

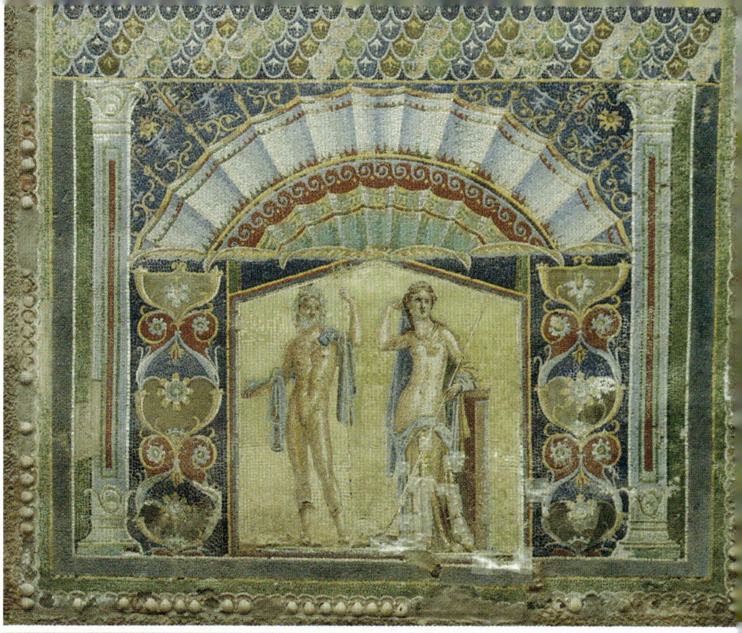

The discovery of Pompeii and Herculaneum, in the eighteenth century, inspired a new wave of neoclassical design in Europe. Motifs from mosaics such as this from Herculaneum inspired the work of architects such as Robert Adam.

Robert Adam designed this neoclassical fireplace surround and overmantel for Syon House outside London, the seat of the Duke of Northumberland.

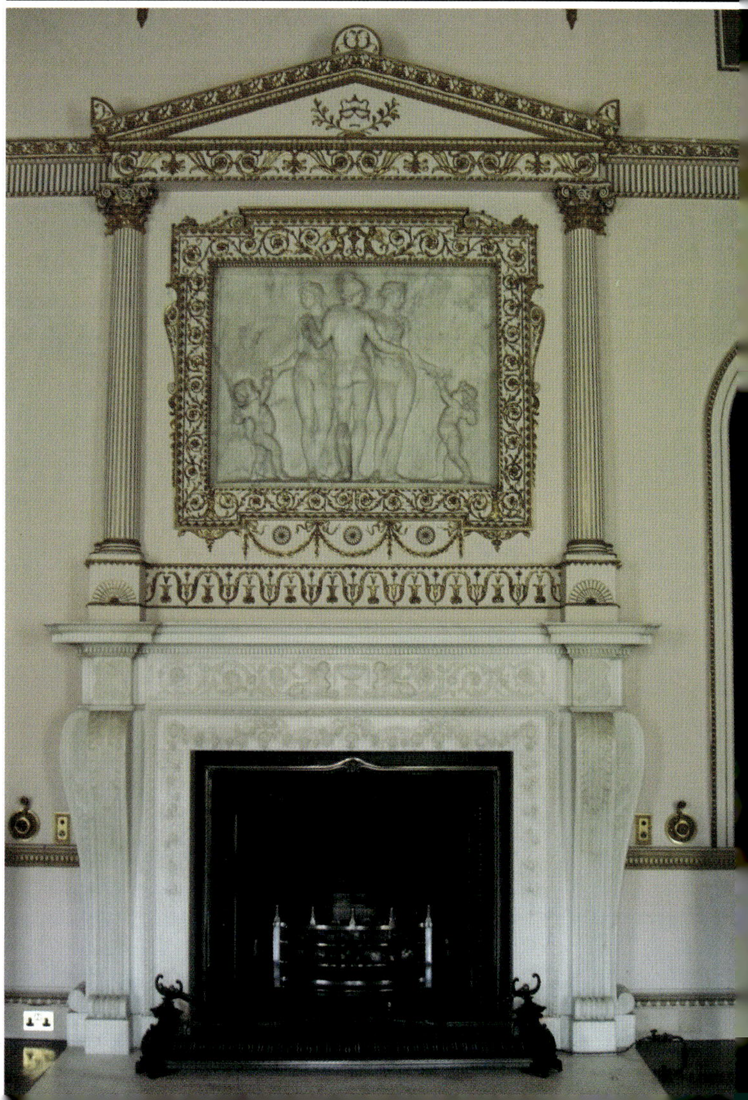

Continuity

The earliest built structures in the American colonies, apart from crude shelters, followed the medieval vernacular building traditions brought by early settlers: brick walls and steeply pitched roofs in the southeast, or wood clapboard and overhanging second floors in the northeast. These simple houses, with straightforward interiors similar to Winterthur's Vauxhall and Hardenbergh Rooms, were built throughout the colonies well into the eighteenth century. This early architecture is called colonial architecture. While English and Dutch building traditions of the thirteen original colonies form the core, other colonial traditions in early America include Swedish, Spanish, and French.

In the late-seventeenth century, as prosperity, population, and skilled labor increased, aesthetically conscious colonists from north to south along the East Coast built houses similar to the Baroque Wren-influenced houses they or their builders knew from England. Houses like Westover and the Governor's Palace in Williamsburg, with interiors like Winterthur's Gidley Room and Blackwell Parlor, continue the baroque traditions of English seventeenth century architecture in colonial America.

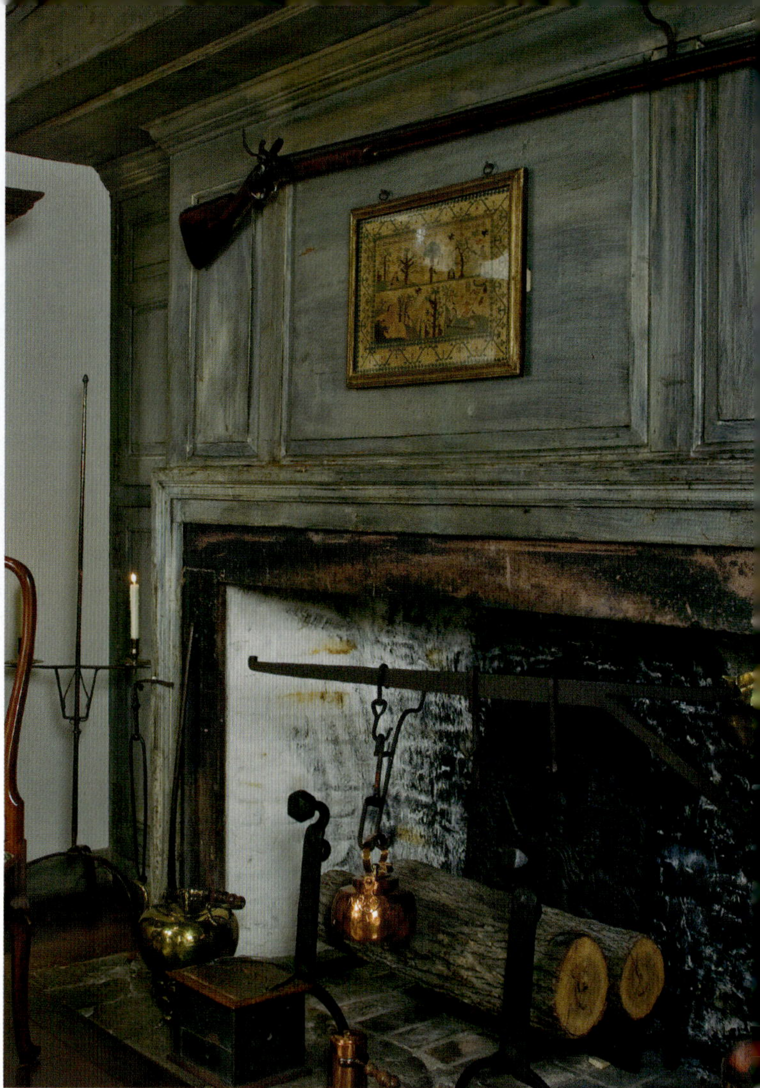

The Hardenbergh Parlor is representative of Colonial architecture in America. **See page 84.**

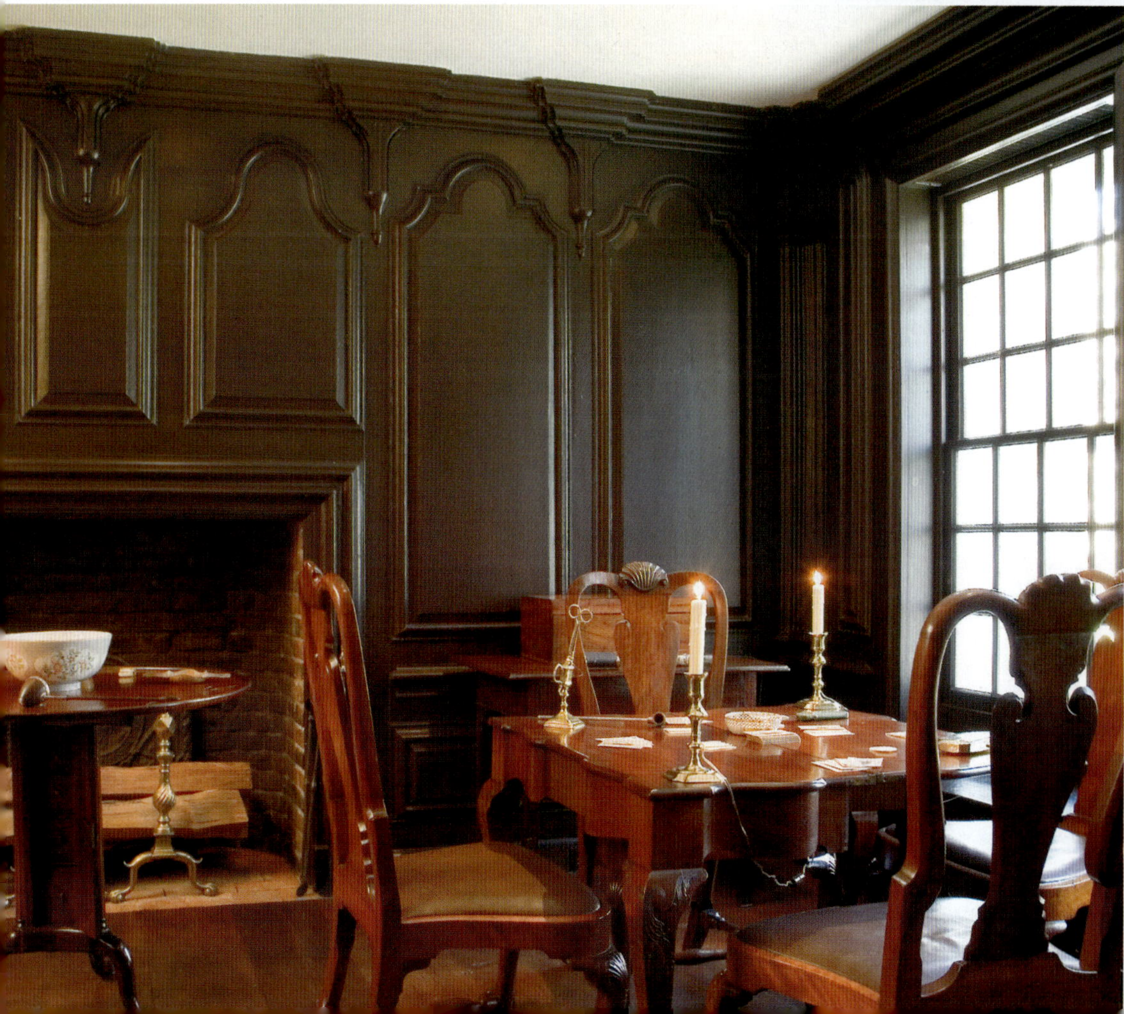

The Gidley Room at Winterthur continues the baroque traditions of English architecture. **See page 76.**

In the mid-eighteenth century, English architects like Batty Langley introduced exotic Chinese and Gothic references to English Georgian architecture. These motifs were also popular in colonial American rooms like Buckland's Chinese Parlor at Gunston Hall, and Winterthur's Philadelphia Hall.

Georgian-style architecture in colonial America (so called for its origins in English Georgian architecture) encompasses those first baroque houses as well as those with exotic influences. It also extends to sober Anglo-Palladian and Gibbs-inspired houses, like Mount Airy, Hammond-Harwood, and exceptional Winterthur interiors such as those from Port Royal, and the Hampton and Chestertown rooms.

As the eighteenth century drew to a close in America, newfound independence coincided with the arrival of a new fashion in architecture: the neoclassical. The fashionable designs of Robert Adam and associations with the Classical world held great appeal for a young America. While stylistic differences are never simple, the Federal style generally departs from the canonically classical Georgian by employing classical motifs decoratively and more delicate proportions. The Federal style seems an appropriate reflection of the early Republic.

Throughout the thirteen original colonies, various influences from the baroque to the Palladian to the neoclassical were transmitted through builders, craftsmen, books, built works, and the knowledge of patrons.

It is astonishing to recall that this tradition of America's architecture began as far away as ancient Greece and Rome. Yet from its origins in Antiquity, to its rediscovery in the Renaissance, to its transformation in Georgian England, to its continuity in colonial America and indeed today, the Classical tradition is one continuous conversation. It is expressed differently by different cultures, for different purposes, in different places, with different materials. With each new age, the underlying forms are enriched with layers of meaning.

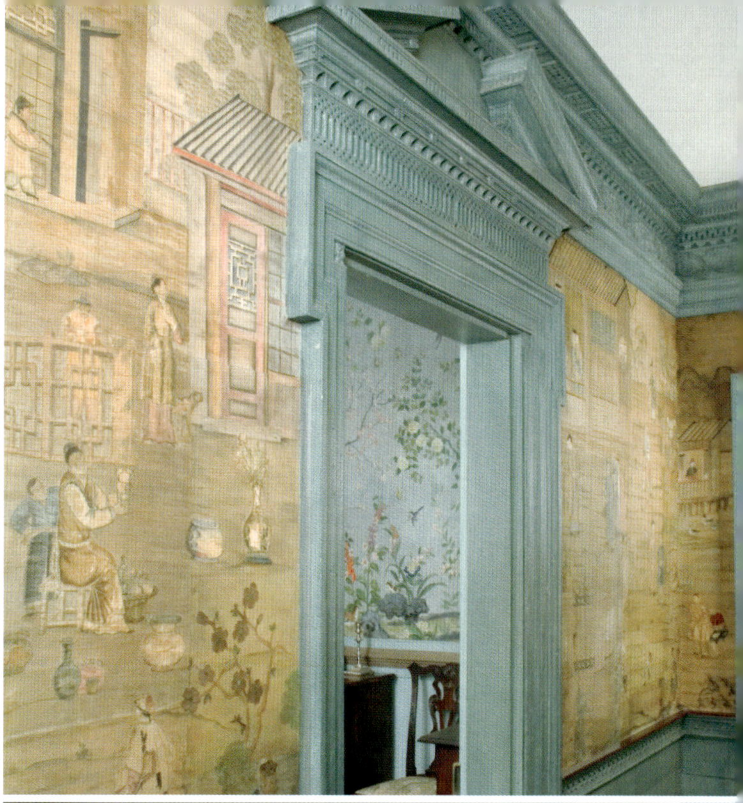

The Philadelphia Hall uses Chinese motifs decoratively. **See page 120.**

The Chestertown room, completed late in the eighteenth century, exemplifies sophisticated late-Georgian architecture. **See page 58.**

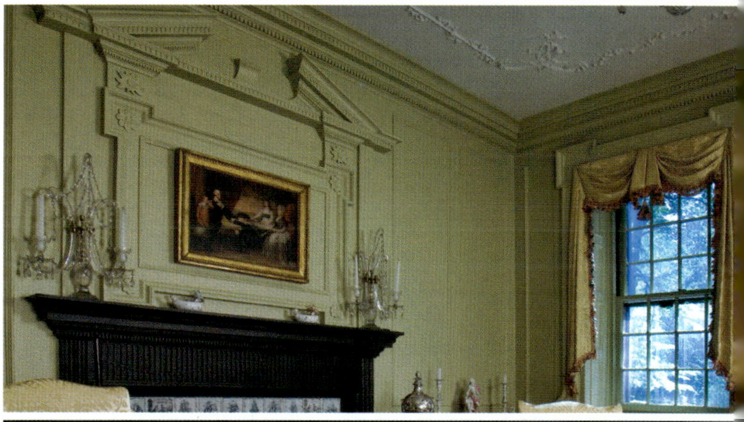

The Phyfe Room, completed early in the nineteenth century, showcases the then-fashionable Federal style. **See page 126.**

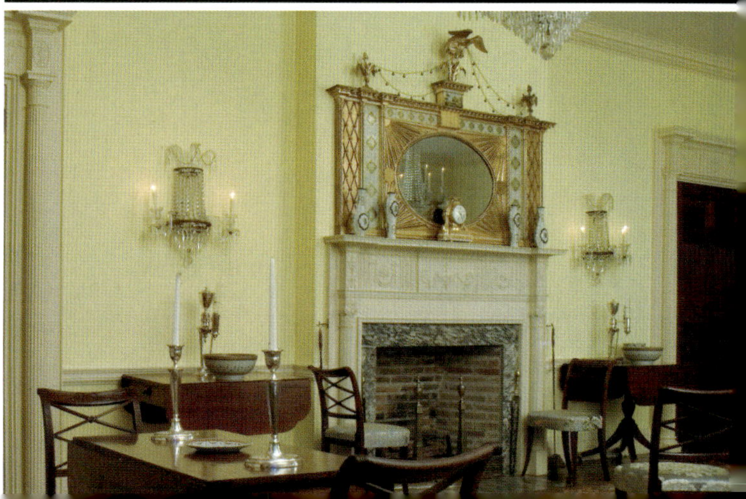

Publications

From the earliest days, books have been a primary mechanism for the transmission of taste and knowledge about architecture. Long after Vitruvius and Palladio, throughout the Georgian era in England (encompassing the reigns of King George I, II, III, and IV from 1714 to 1830), numerous books on architecture were published, including theoretical treatises, inspirational pattern books, and practical builder's books. Books such as these were essential to the development of the Classical tradition, both in England and America.

Books like Sir William Chambers' 1759 *Treatise on Civil Architecture*, Isaac Ware's 1731 *Designs of Inigo Jones*, Batty and Thomas Langley's various editions of *The City and Country Builder's and Workman's Treasury of Designs*, and many others were published in England, and sold in America. Likewise books such as Robert Woods *Ruins of Palmyra* (1753), and Stuart and Revett's *Antiquities of Athens* (1762-1818) opened wide the frame of reference toward the end of the eighteenth century.

The link between English architectural publications and American early architecture cannot be overstated. For example, it is known from the "Inventory of the Goods and Chattells of William Buckland" that one of America's first joiner-turned-architects owned copies of books including Gibbs' *Book of Architecture* (1728); Salmon's *Palladio Londonensis* (1734); Hoppus' *Practical Measuring* (1736); Langley's *Builder's Treasury* (1740); Swan's *British Architect* (1745), and Ware's *Complete Body of Architecture* (1756), among others.

Gibbs even writes in his introduction that his book will be useful to people involved in building especially "in remote parts of the Country, where little or no assistance for Design may be procured." Early American patrons, carpenters, joiners, and others without an existing building tradition or many skilled architects did indeed rely on these books for instruction in how to design and build correctly. In later years, American architects such as Asher Benjamin and Minard Lafever would publish their own pattern and builder's books.

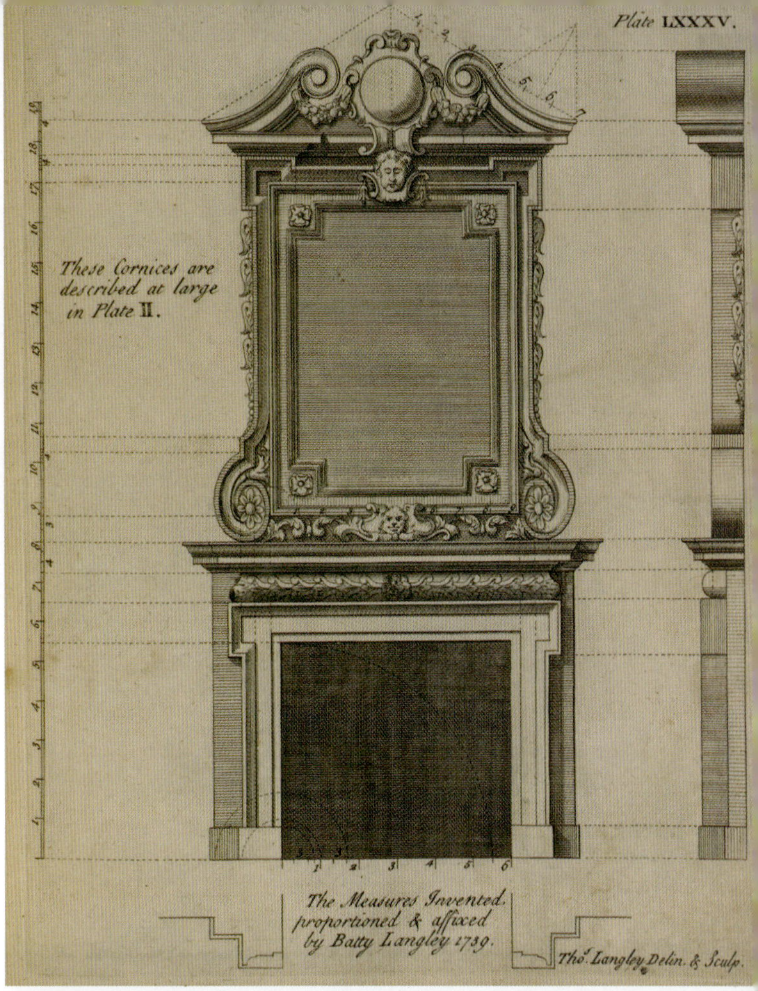

Plate LXXXV from Batty Langley's *Builder's Treasury* (1740) is thought to have inspired the fireplace wall in Winterthur's Hampton Room (page 80).

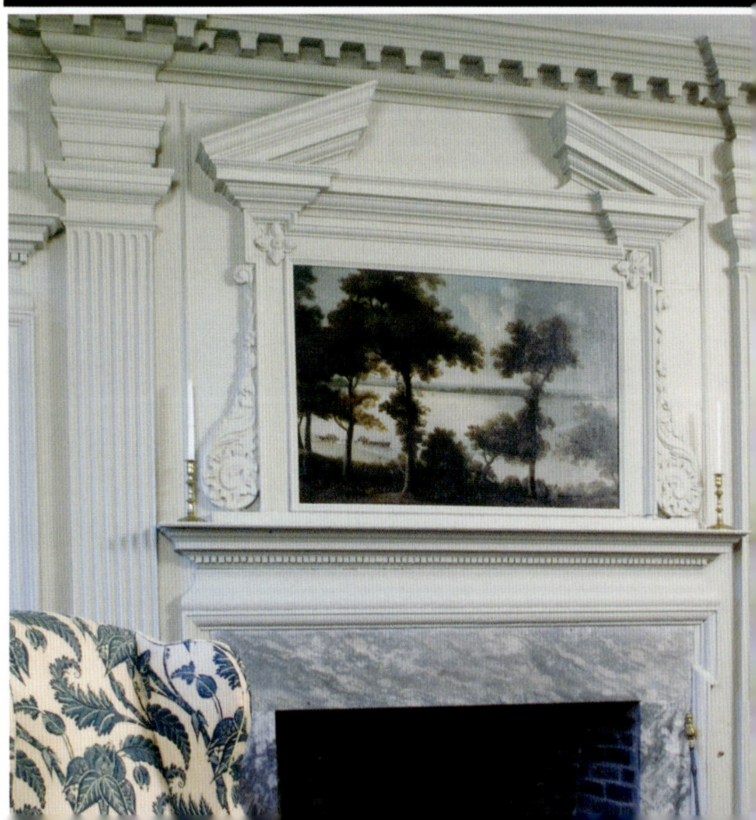

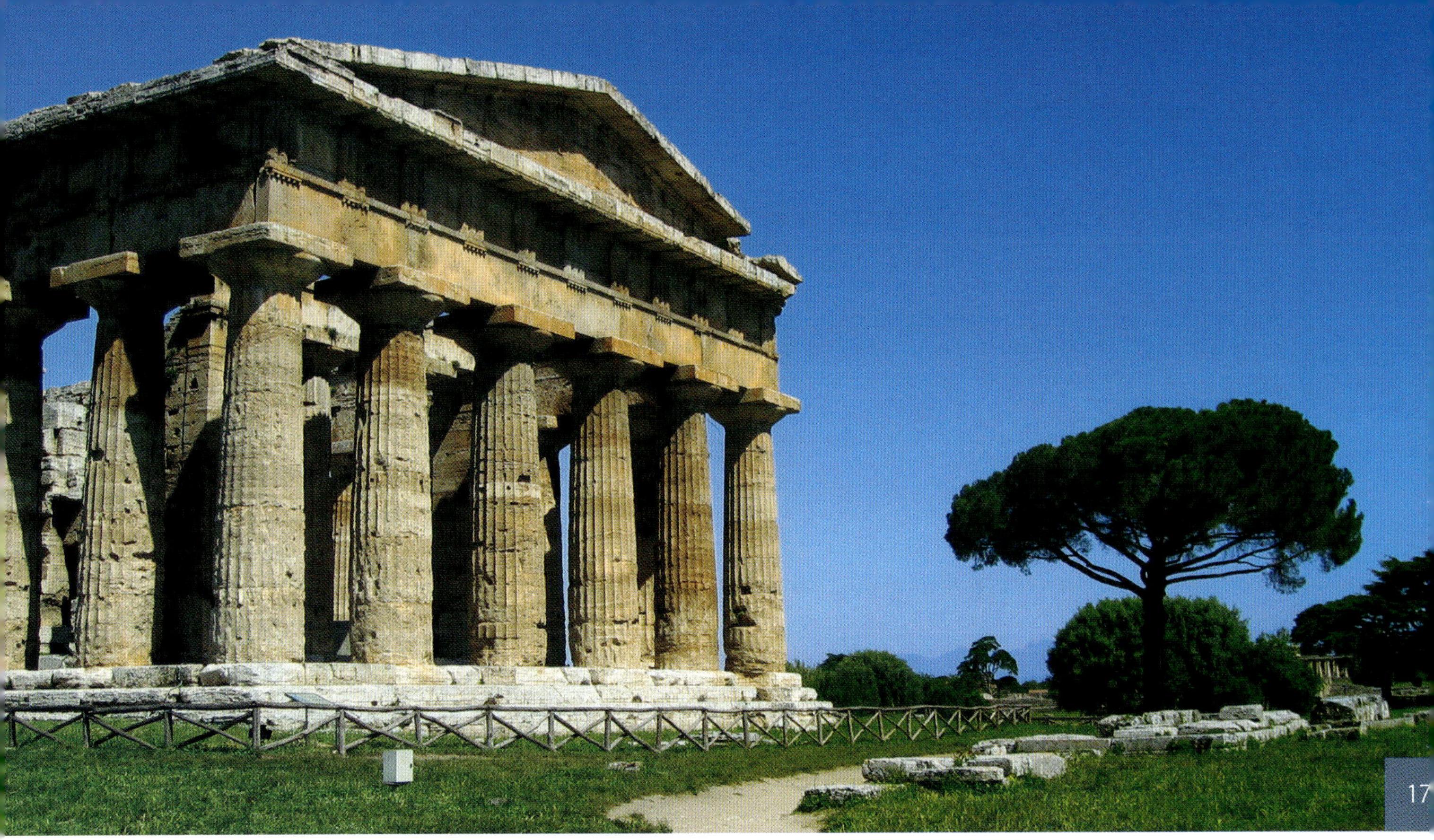

The Second Temple of Hera, built in the first half of the sixth century BCE at Paestum, Italy, is an early example of The Doric Order.

The Classical Orders

These architectural treatises, pattern, and builder books included the orders because they form the language of Classical architecture. The term "order" describes what the orders do: they order the design of things. Simply put, an order is an accepted way of assembling beams on top of columns. Each order is distinguished by its proportions, entablature, capital, column shaft, base, and related moldings and ornament. An order is not just a column, but an entire system of proportions and forms that generate and organize a building's composition.

The two principal orders that Vitruvius presents—the Doric and the Ionic—emerged centuries earlier than Vitruvius in ancient Greece. Each was associated with its respective culture. First was the Doric, associated with temples built by the Dorians on mainland Greece and throughout the Peloponnesus. The Ionic developed slightly later across the Aegean in Ionia, which stretched along the southwest coast of Asia Minor (modern-day Turkey) and nearby islands. These two orders are two different dialects of a common language of post-and-beam construction. Vitruvius describes the Doric and Ionic respectively as "one, manlike in appearance, bare, and unadorned; the other feminine," and as such, was proportioned according to the human form.

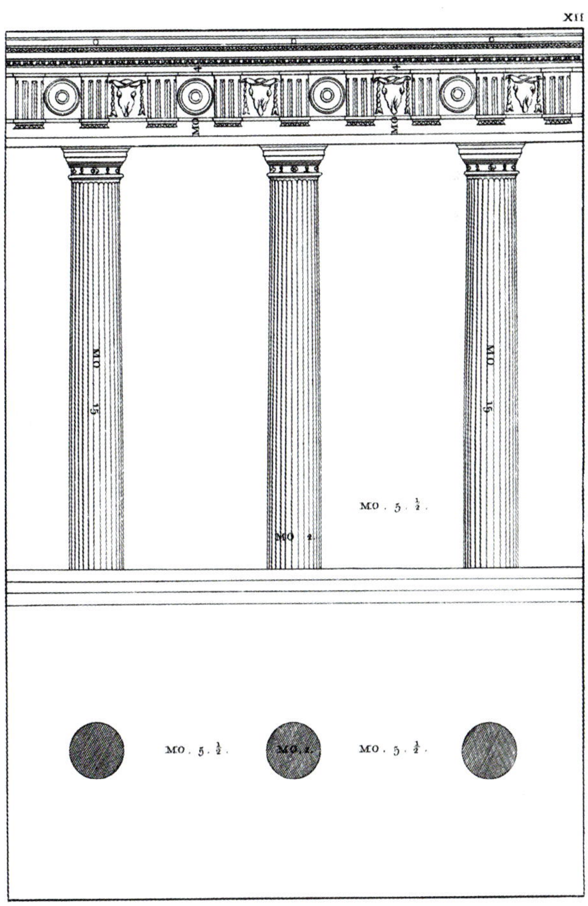

The Doric Order, according to Palladio.

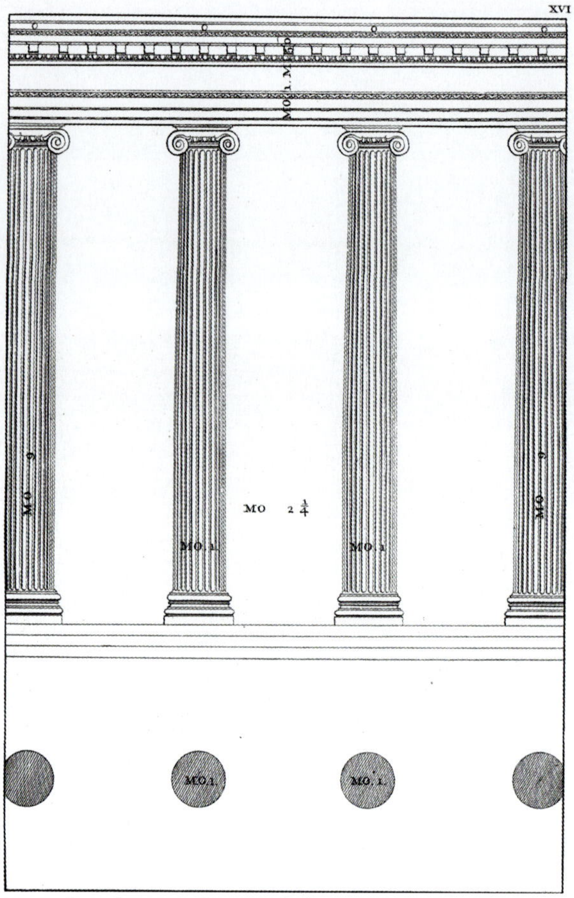

The Ionic Order, according to Palladio.

A third order developed later in Greece, the Corinthian. Vitruvius sees the Corinthian as similar to the Ionic, but with a different capital. In fact, he describes either the Doric or Ionic entablature as being acceptable atop the Corinthian capital. It was only later in Roman architecture that the Corinthian would become established as a separate order with its own associated entablature.

In anthropomorphic terms, the Corinthian is associated with the qualities of a young maiden. Vitruvius recounts the story of the first Corinthian capital: after a young woman of Corinth died, her nurse placed a basket of her favorite things atop her grave, and a tile above to protect them. In the spring the leaves and stalks of an acanthus plant grew around the basket, spreading under the tile. Seeing such a poignant sight, the Greek sculptor Callimachus was inspired to carve it in capitals for the Corinthians. This story establishes the Corinthian's associations with femininity and youth, as well as rebirth, and reinforces the harmony between nature and Classical architecture.

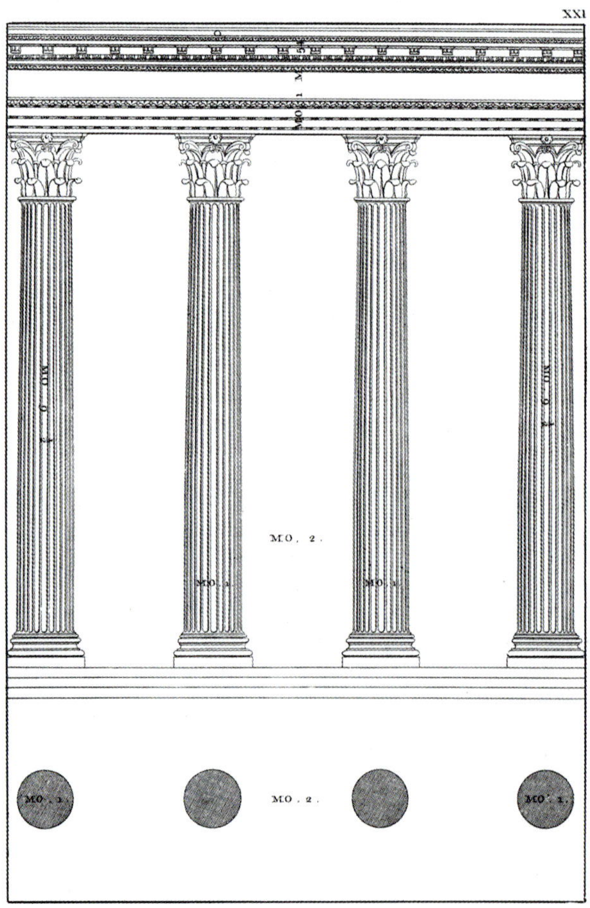

The Corinthian Order, according to Palladio.

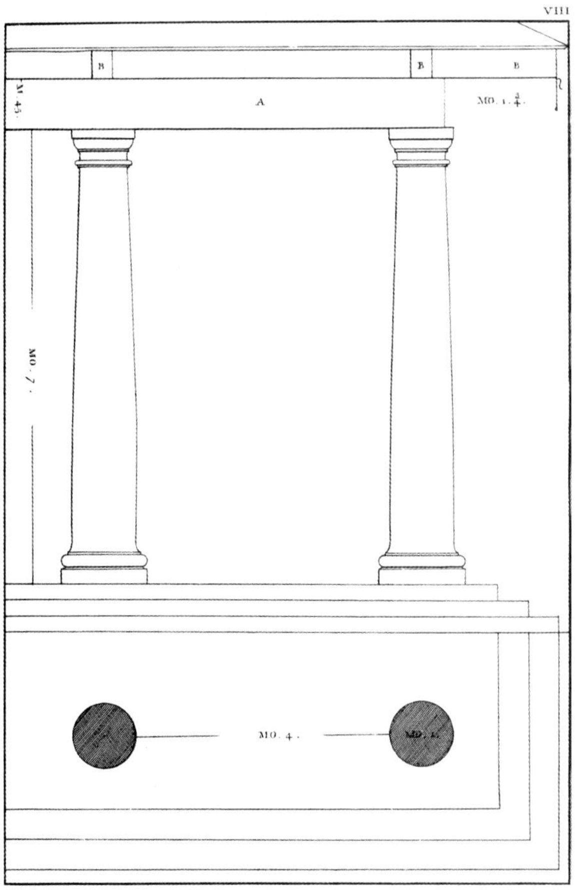

The Tuscan Order, according to Palladio.

Vitruvius also documents the architecture of the native Etruscans, the Tuscan style, though he is not fond of it, describing temples of this type as "straddling, top-heavy, low, broad." But it is not until the later Renaissance that five, rather than two or three, orders of architecture were defined: Tuscan, Doric, Ionic, Corinthian, and Composite.

In lieu of ancient buildings for examples of the Tuscan order, Renaissance architects had to rely on Vitruvius' written description and recommended its use for buildings of rural, functional, or defensive purposes. While related to the Doric, with its similar forms and stout proportions, the Tuscan Order was seen as less refined, or the lowest of the orders.

The Composite Order appears in later Roman architecture, after Vitruvius' time, and was perhaps then seen as a variation on the Corinthian. Renaissance architects set it apart as its own order formed by combining Ionic and Corinthian forms in its capital, and placed it at the top of the hierarchy. It is the most ornate of all of the orders.

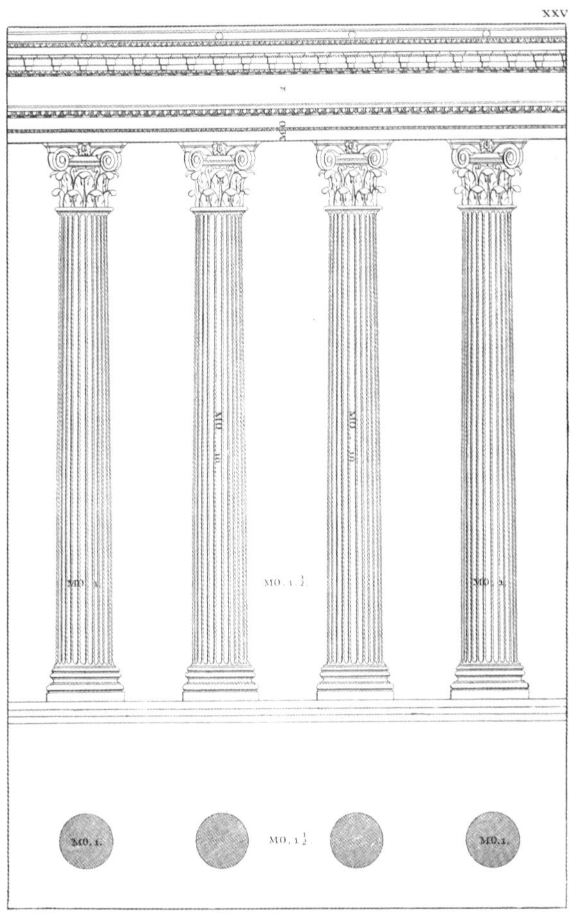

The Composite Order, according to Palladio.

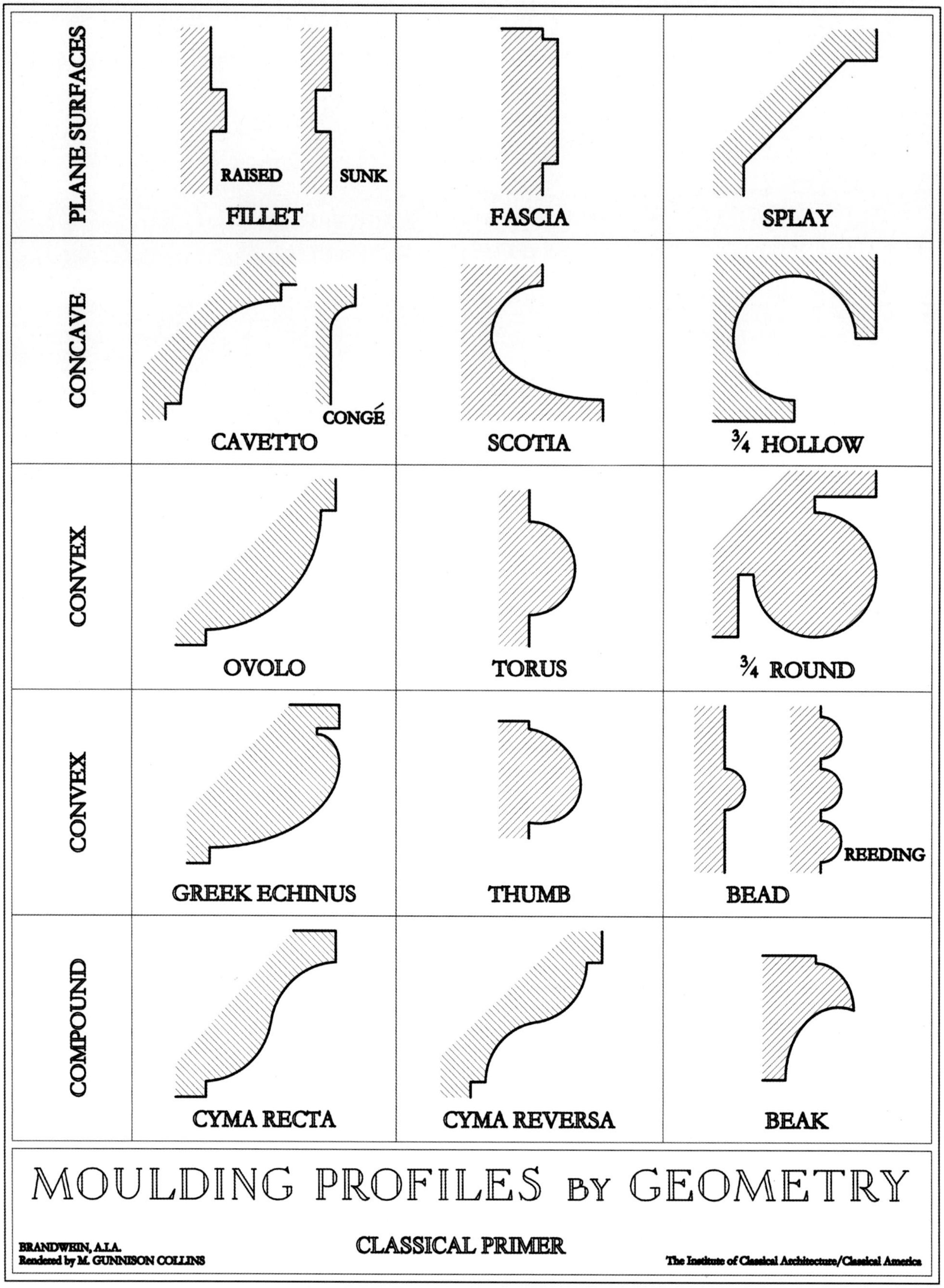

The orders are made up of different molding profiles shown above. Used with permission of The Institute of Classical Architecture & Classical America from its forthcoming publication, *A Handbook of Classical Architecture*, published by W. W. Norton.

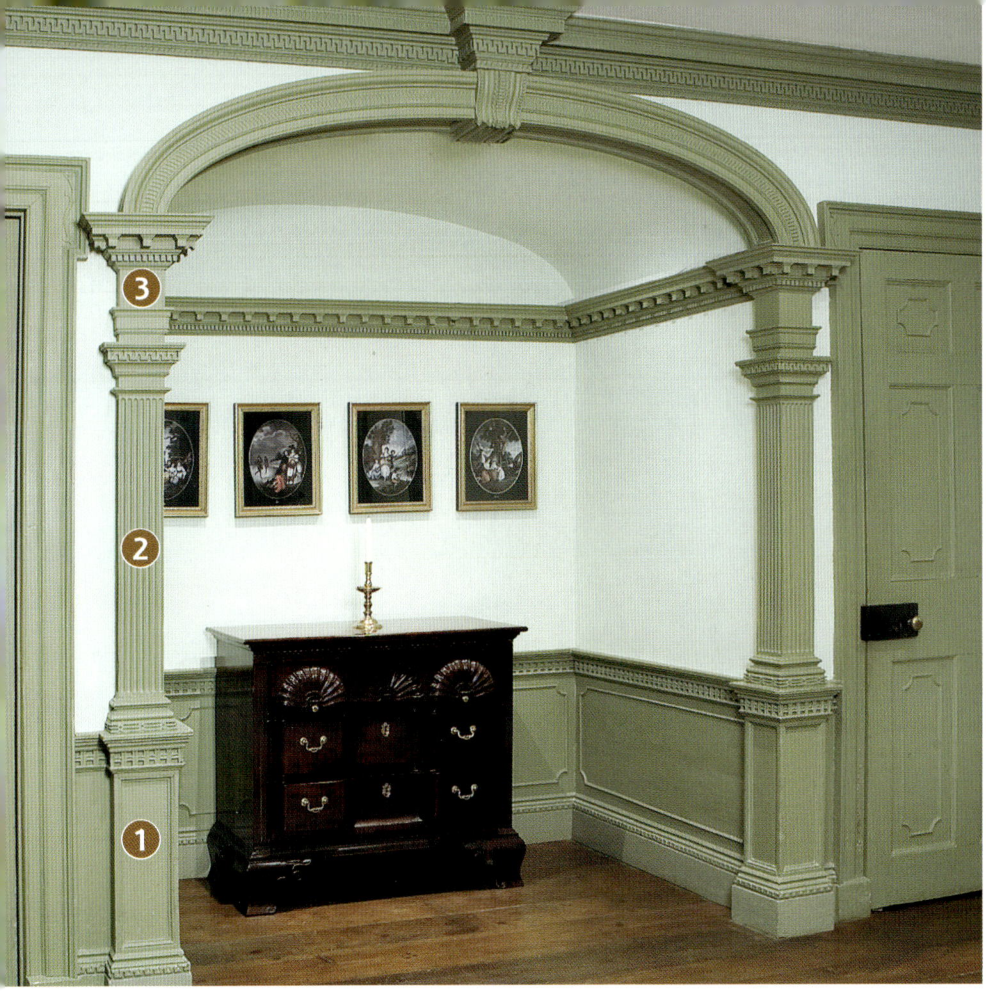

A full order is first divided into three parts, the pedestal (1), the column (2), and the entablature (3). The Somerset Room, page 158.

The Language of Classical Architecture in Interiors

While the language of Classical architecture may be spoken in five different dialects, or orders, each order has common pieces and parts. A full order is broken first into three parts: the supporting element of the pedestal (1), the vertical element of the column (2), and the horizontal spanning element of the entablature (3).

Each of these three parts is generally again subdivided into three similar parts. The pedestal is divided into a supporting base, upward-reaching block or dado, and crowning moldings. The column is divided into a base that transitions the load of the column shaft to the pedestal, a shaft spanning upward, and a capital bearing the load of the entablature above. The entablature is divided into an architrave or beam, spanning from support to support (or column to column), a frieze reaching upward, and a cornice transitioning to the projection of the roof.

An order is not only a column, but an entire system of forms abstractly describing a building's purpose from earth to sky. The poetry of Classical architecture is that the forms themselves express and celebrate what is happening in a building as it bears load and organizes space in a manner the inhabitant can understand.

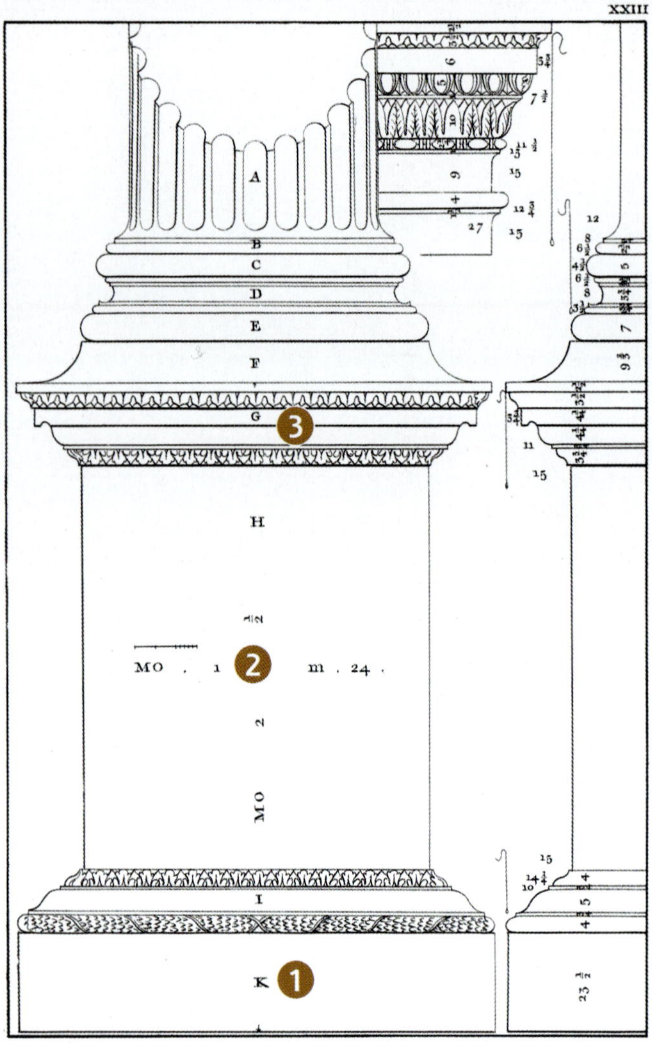

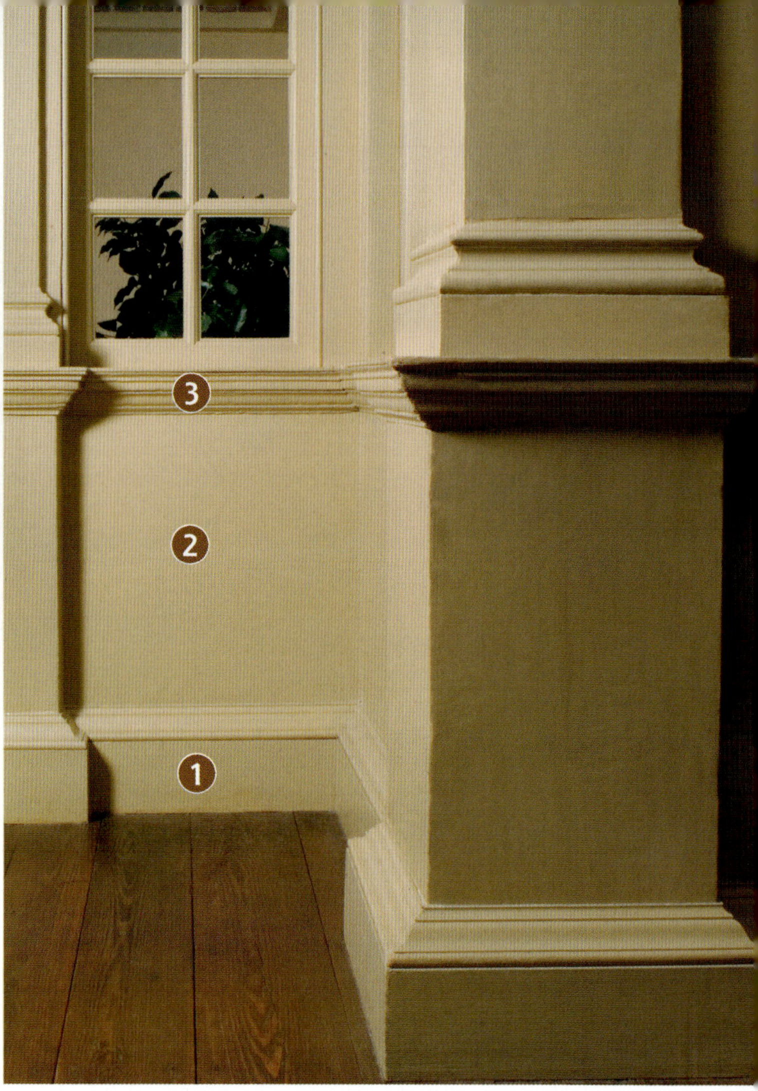

Taken from the pedestal, the wainscot is divided into three parts, the base (1), the dado (2), and the surbase or chair rail (3). The Charleston Dining Room, page 54.

When designing interiors, these same pieces and parts of an order are used to delineate spaces. Using the language of Classicism, the character of a room, its scale, its volume, and moments of transition are defined, making the room comprehensible, comfortable, and beautiful. To do so, Classical architecture relies on design tools like proportion (the correspondence of the ratio of parts), and scale (the apparent size of things), along with the orders.

Taking a wall from floor to ceiling, for example, and recalling the overall divisions of an order, one can see how an order is used to design a room. Beginning with the major divisions into pedestal, column, and entablature, the pedestal becomes the wainscot. The base of the pedestal becomes the baseboard of the room with its tall, flat plinth and moldings (1); the dado transforms into the paneled field of the wainscot (2); and the crowning moldings become the chair rail, or surbase (3), wrapping around the room and protecting the wall.

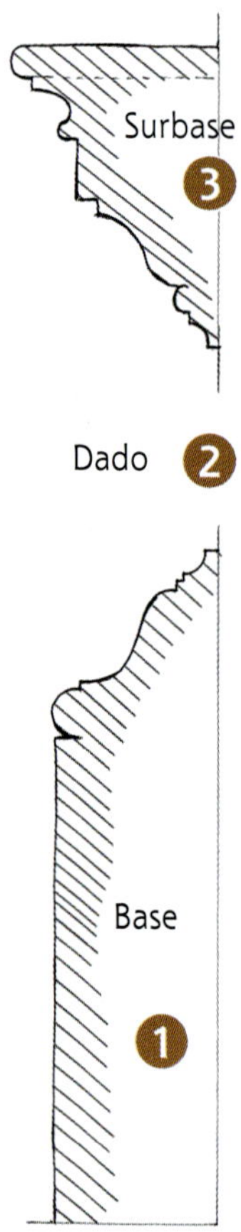

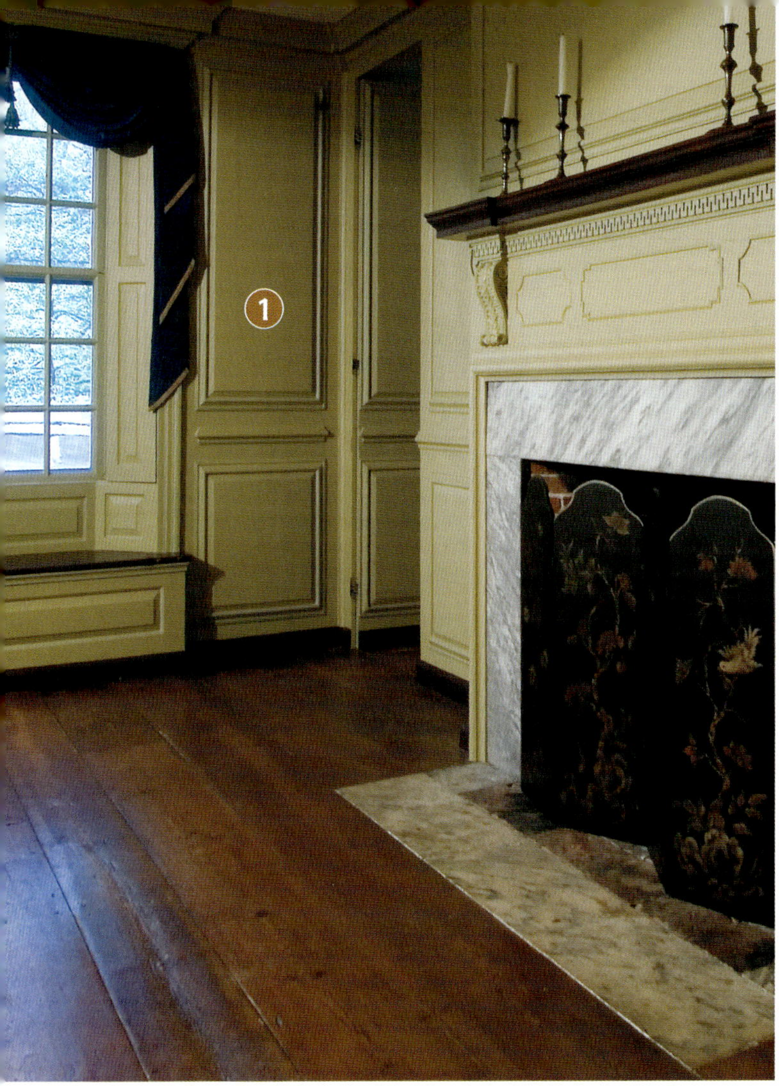

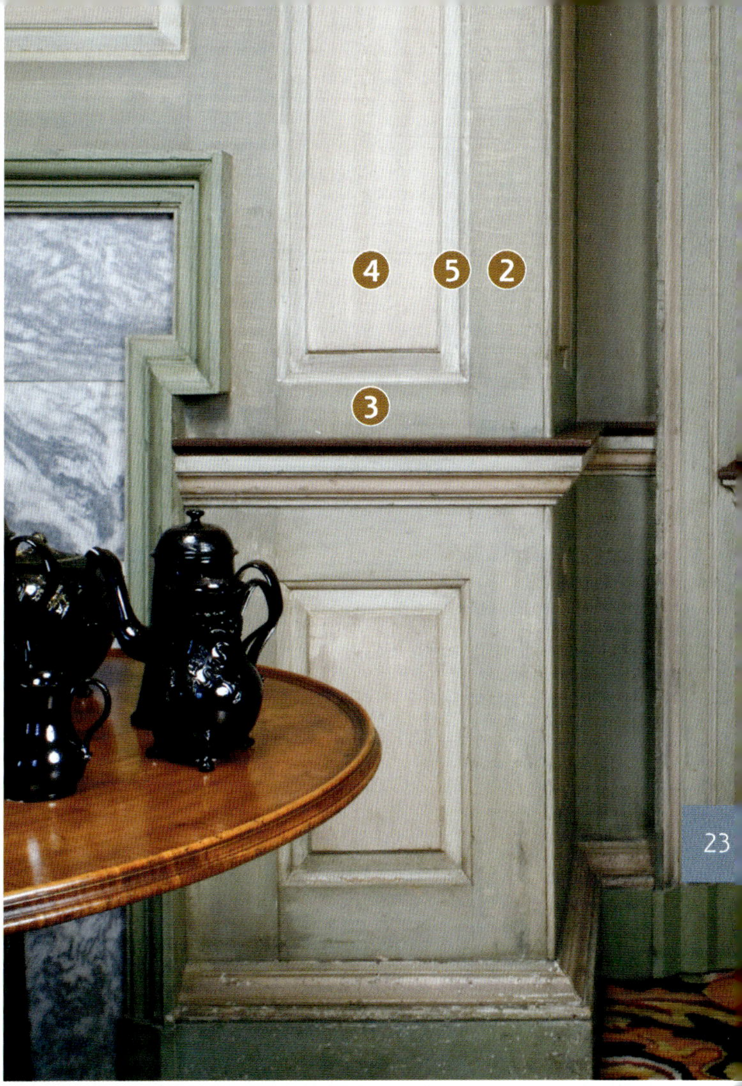

The flat panel above the chair rail (1) corresponds to the vertical element of a column in the Bowers Parlor, page 46.

Panels consist of vertical stiles (2), horizontal rails (3), and the field (4) they contain. Maple Bedroom, page 144.

Panel moldings (5) conceal joints and emphasize the panel design. Gidley Room, page 76.

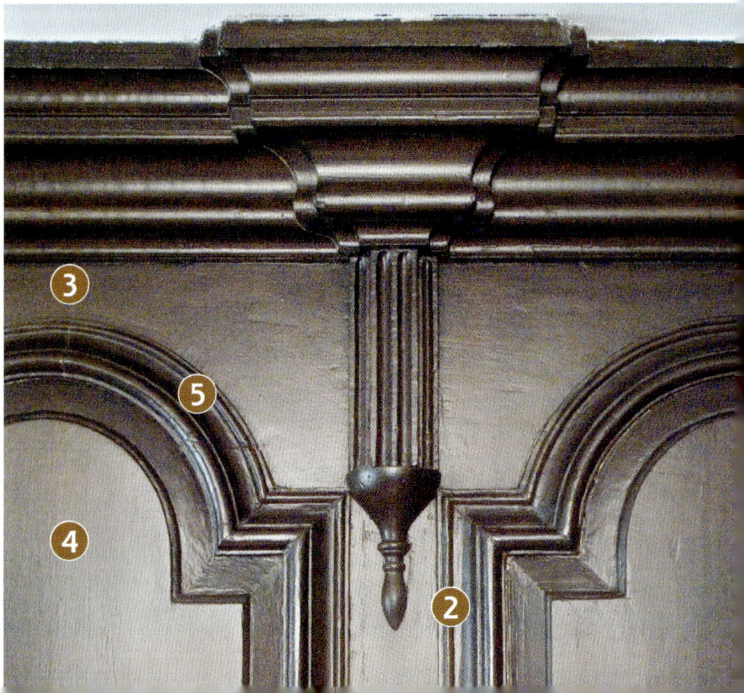

Above the wainscot, the wall spans upward like the column of an order. Sometimes this order may be fully expressed, or visible, through freestanding columns, engaged columns, or pilasters (flattened columns), and sometimes the order is invisible and disappears entirely into the wall (1).

The wall zone above the wainscot is often expressed with paneling in early American architecture. Wood paneling was a way of finishing interior rooms in lieu of plaster. The design of the size, shape, and rhythm of panels strongly affects one's perception of a room's scale. Paneling accounts for the natural expansion and contraction of wood. The stiles (vertical, 2) and rails (horizontal, 3) form a grid in which panel fields (4) can float, expanding and contracting as needed.

Usually moldings (5) are used around the panel fields, between the stiles and rails, to conceal joints and emphasize the panel design. Sometimes bolection moldings are used. These moldings grow increasingly larger as the molding moves inward to the panel field or opening of a fireplace or door, which is the reverse of normal moldings that increase in projection as they move away from an opening or panel.

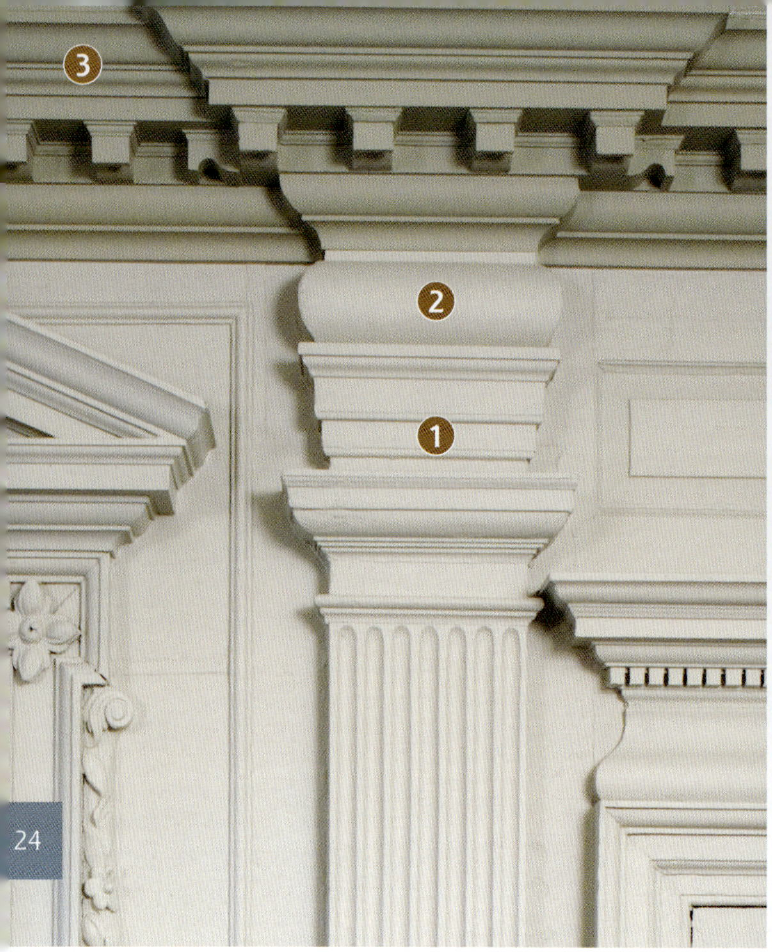

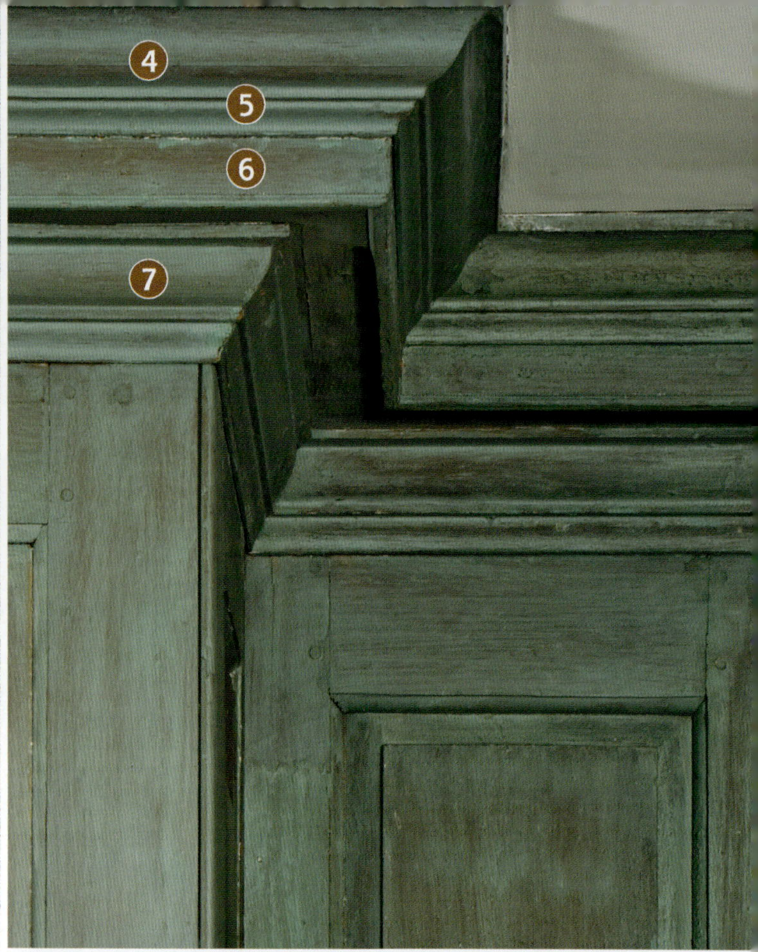

The entablature is divided into three parts: the architrave (1), frieze (2), and cornice (3). Hampton Room, page 80.

The cornice generally consists of a cymatium (4) atop moldings forming a bedmold (5), then a corona (6), supported by another bedmold (7) making the transition to the wall below. Marlboro Room, page 98.

Above the wall, transitioning to the ceiling, is the entablature that normally spans between column and roof. It is divided into three parts—an architrave (1), frieze (2), and cornice (3)—although it is uncommon to find a full entablature expressed in interiors, because it tends to appear too heavy. Instead, it is more common to find only the cornice (3) of the entablature used in interiors.

A cornice generally has an upper curved piece called the cymatium (4) atop a smaller series of moldings forming a bedmold (5) between the cymatium and the corona. The corona (6) is the tall, flat projecting element that also has smaller moldings forming a bedmold (7) and making the transition to the frieze below.

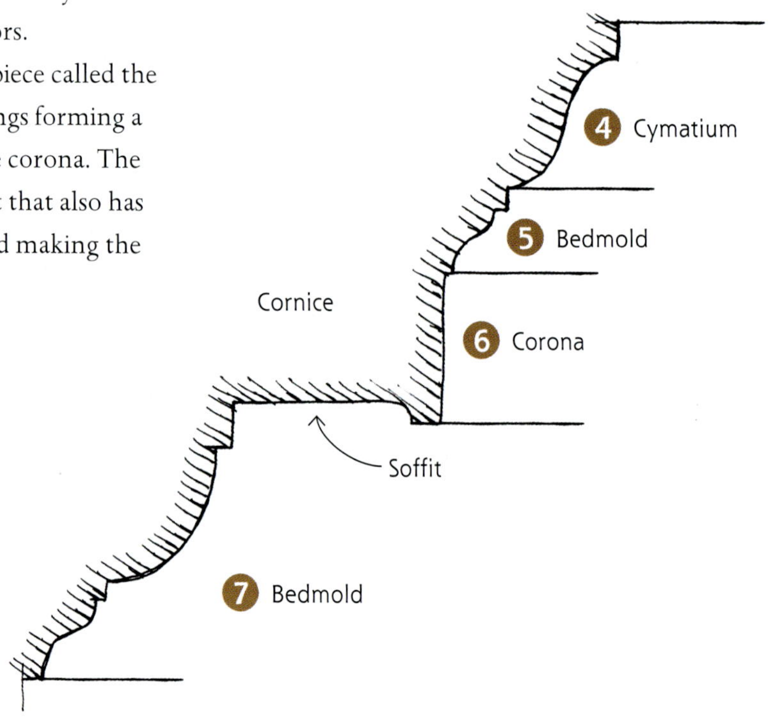

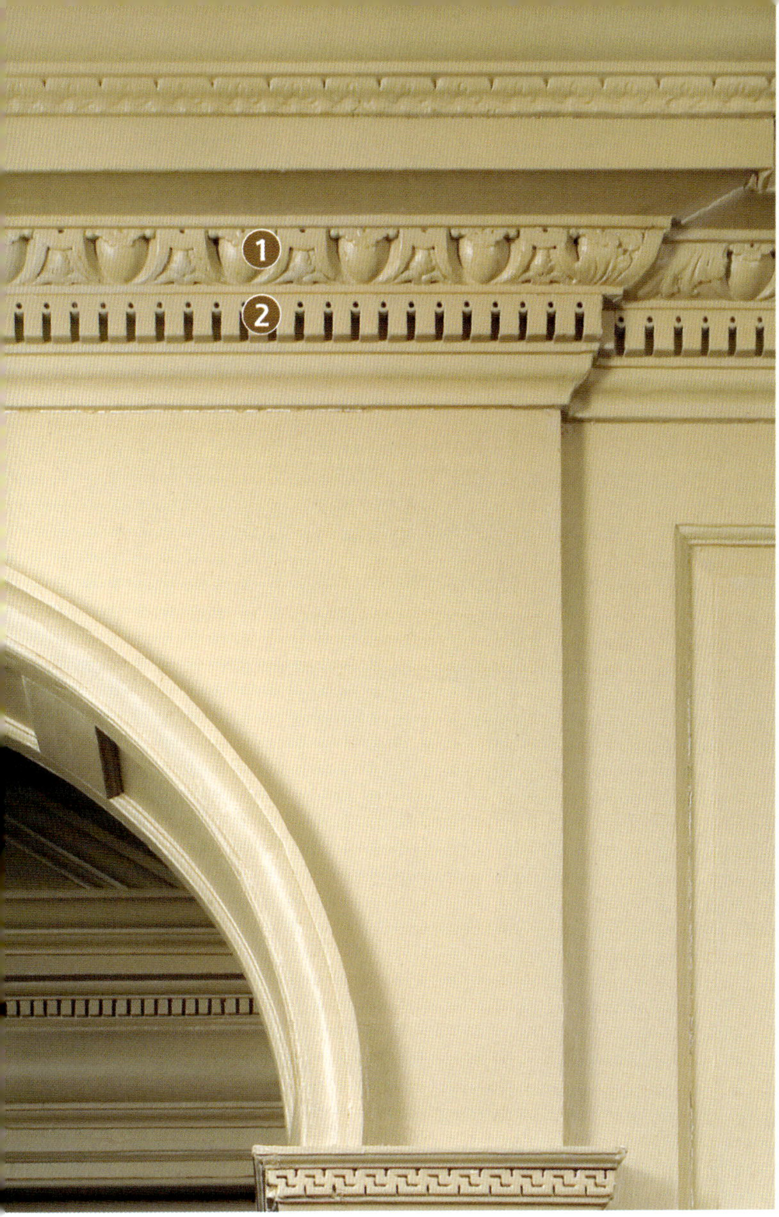

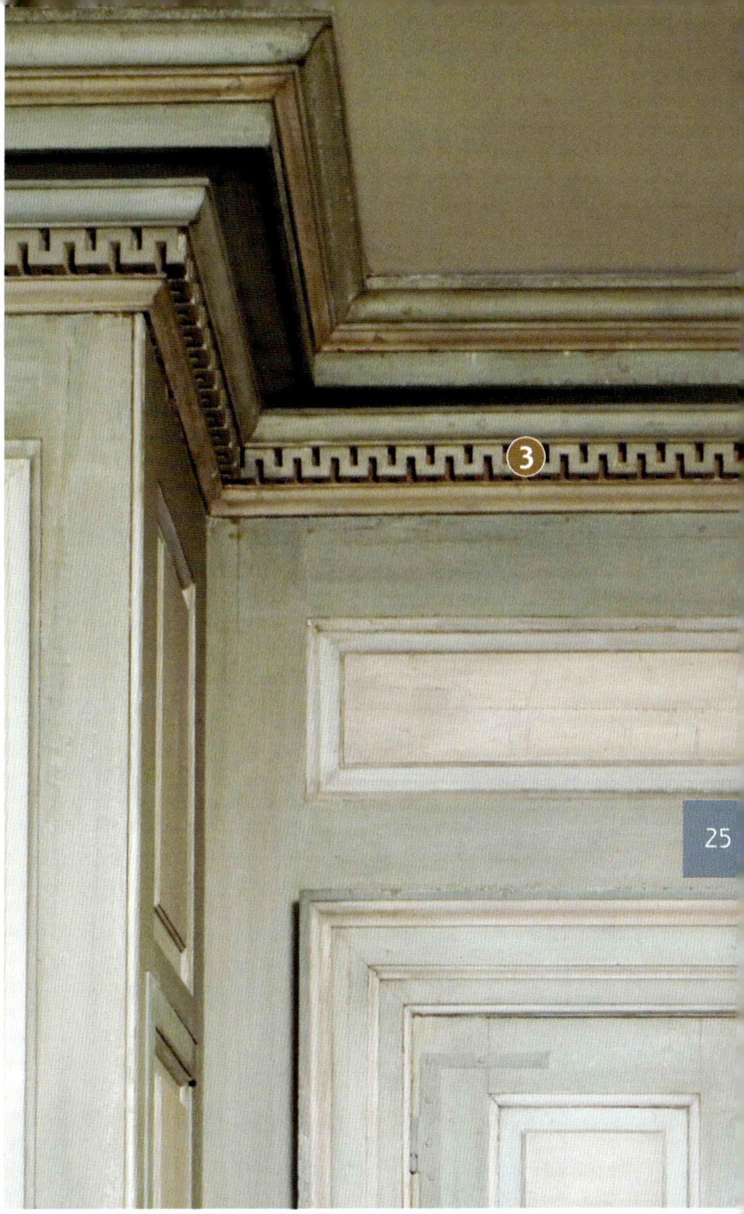

Some ornaments, such as the egg-and-dart (1), are associated with particular molding shapes like the ovolo. Others, such as the dentil, a linear strip of teeth-like moldings (2), are appropriate only to rectangular forms. Both the egg-and-dart and the dentil are ornaments seen often at Winterthur.

The egg-and-dart (1) and dentil (2) are commonly seen ornamenting moldings at Winterthur. The Charleston Dining Room, page 54.

"I" dentils (left) are so called because of the shape made by the swag and round hole between each tooth (2). Dentils also appear as a meander pattern, sometimes called a "Wall of Troy" molding (3), or just as simple blocks.

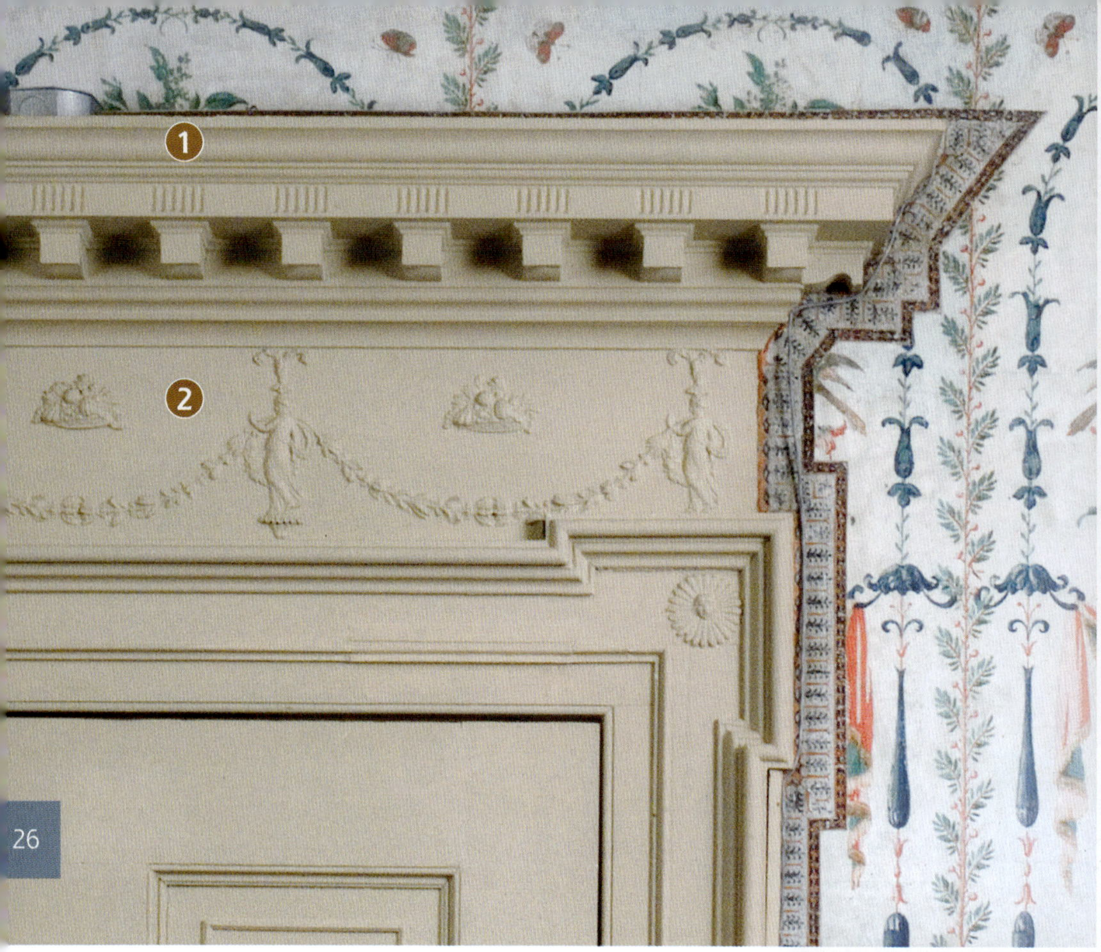

The frieze (2) is a flat area that may or may not be decorated, as in this detail from the Federal Parlor, page 68.

In the Doric Order the frieze is divided into triglyphs (3) separated by metopes (4). Port Royal Entrance Hall, page 132.

Below the cornice (1) is located the frieze (2), which is generally flat, but sometimes in the Ionic Order it is pulvinated, or curved outward. In the Doric Order, the frieze canonically contains triglyphs (3) and the spaces between them, metopes (4). The frieze is a flexible area where decoration may be applied and the character of the room can be emphasized. In Federal architecture in particular, plaster or composition decorations often were applied in the frieze. “Composition,” or “compo,” is a molded or cast mixture of glue, binders, and such aggregates as horsehair, hemp, and dried clay.

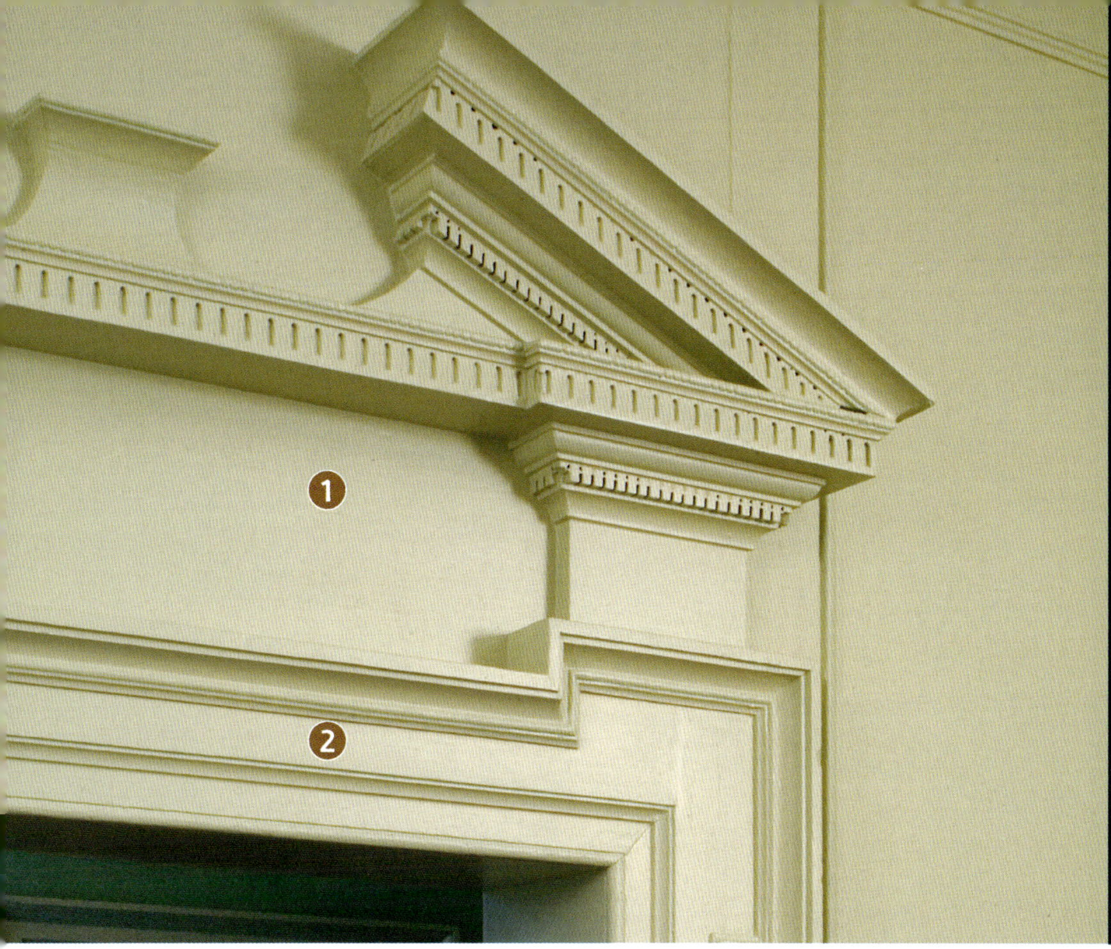

The architrave (1) spans the openings of windows and doors, as in this example from the Chestertown Room, page 58. The drawings below show the subdivision of the architrave into flat fascias (3) separated by smaller moldings (4) and finished by a backband (5).

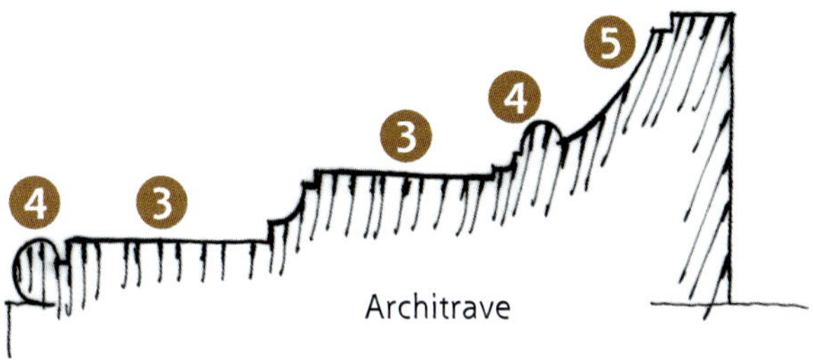

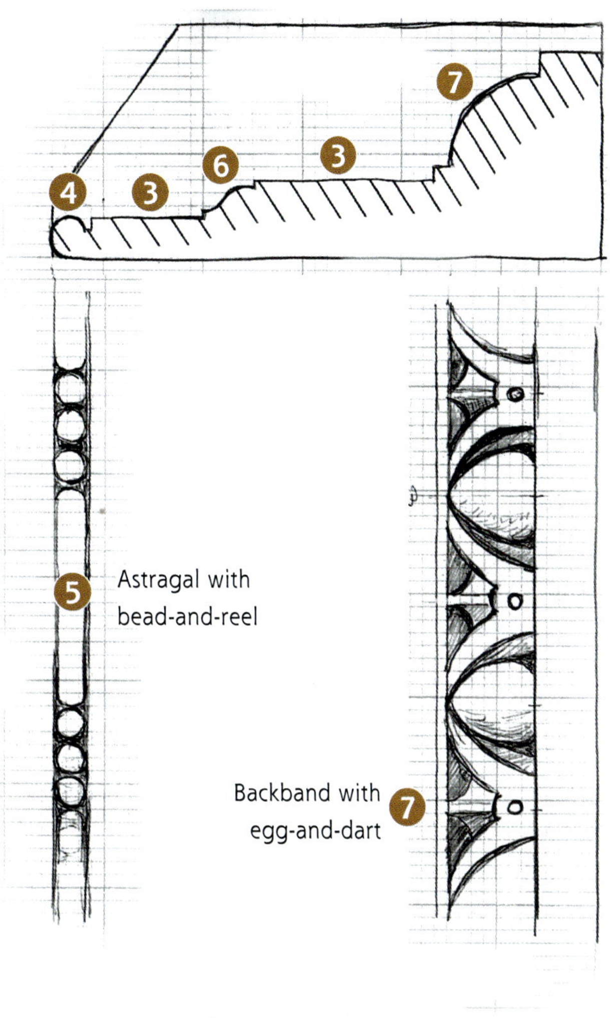

Supporting the frieze (1) is the architrave (2). An architrave is a beam and may be expressed as one flat piece, or subdivided into two or three fascias (3), or broad flat planes. These are often emphasized by smaller moldings like an astragal (4), or small round molding, which is often ornamented with a corresponding bead-and-reel (5) or cyma reversas (6). Because architraves are beams spanning openings, this element is used to articulate the span at window and door openings. A terminating molding, or backband (7), around door and window finishes the architrave. The reader will see all of these elements throughout the traditional rooms at Winterthur. They are the language of Classical architecture.

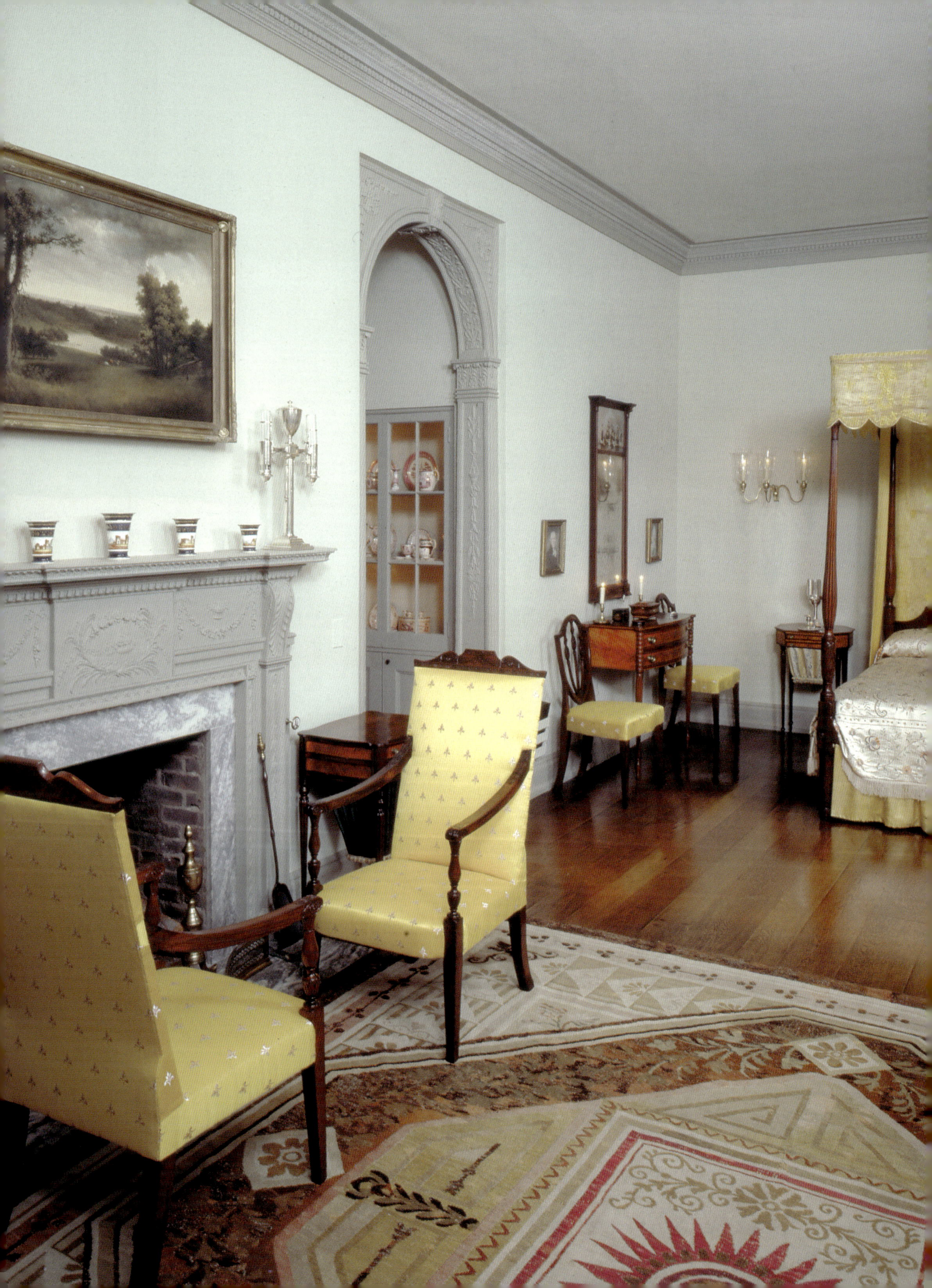

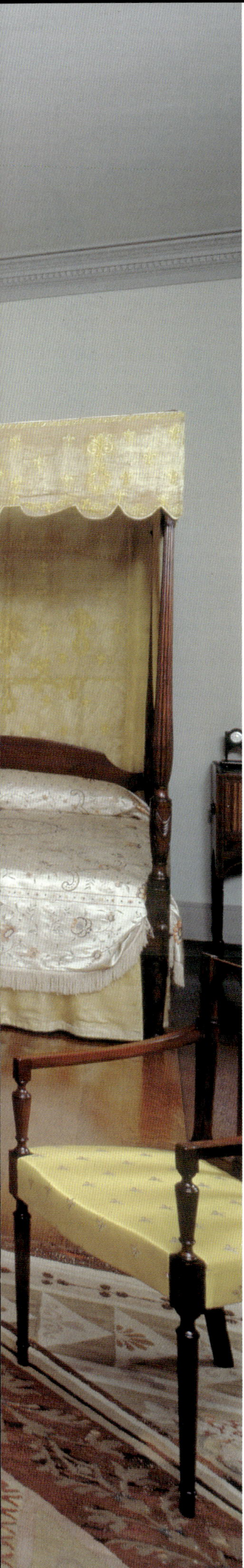

The Rooms of Winterthur

In the pages that follow, the reader is invited to enjoy thirty-three traditional American rooms at Winterthur. Each room is introduced with an overall photo that typically includes appropriate furnishings and fabrics. The architecture is then analyzed, with photographs of details supported by hand sketches taken directly from study of the moldings in each room. Graphic scales on each page or spread may be used to approximate the size of the moldings studied. Numbers key the drawings, photos, and text, enabling the reader to understand the architectural elements present in the room.

Architectural styles are never black and white, nor do they necessarily follow one another on a strict historical progression. For these reasons, the rooms from Winterthur included here are presented in alphabetical order.

The McIntire Bedroom is a quintessentially Federal-style room, with smooth walls, delicately proportioned moldings, and a mantelpiece with a tall frieze decorated with Classical motifs. See page 102.

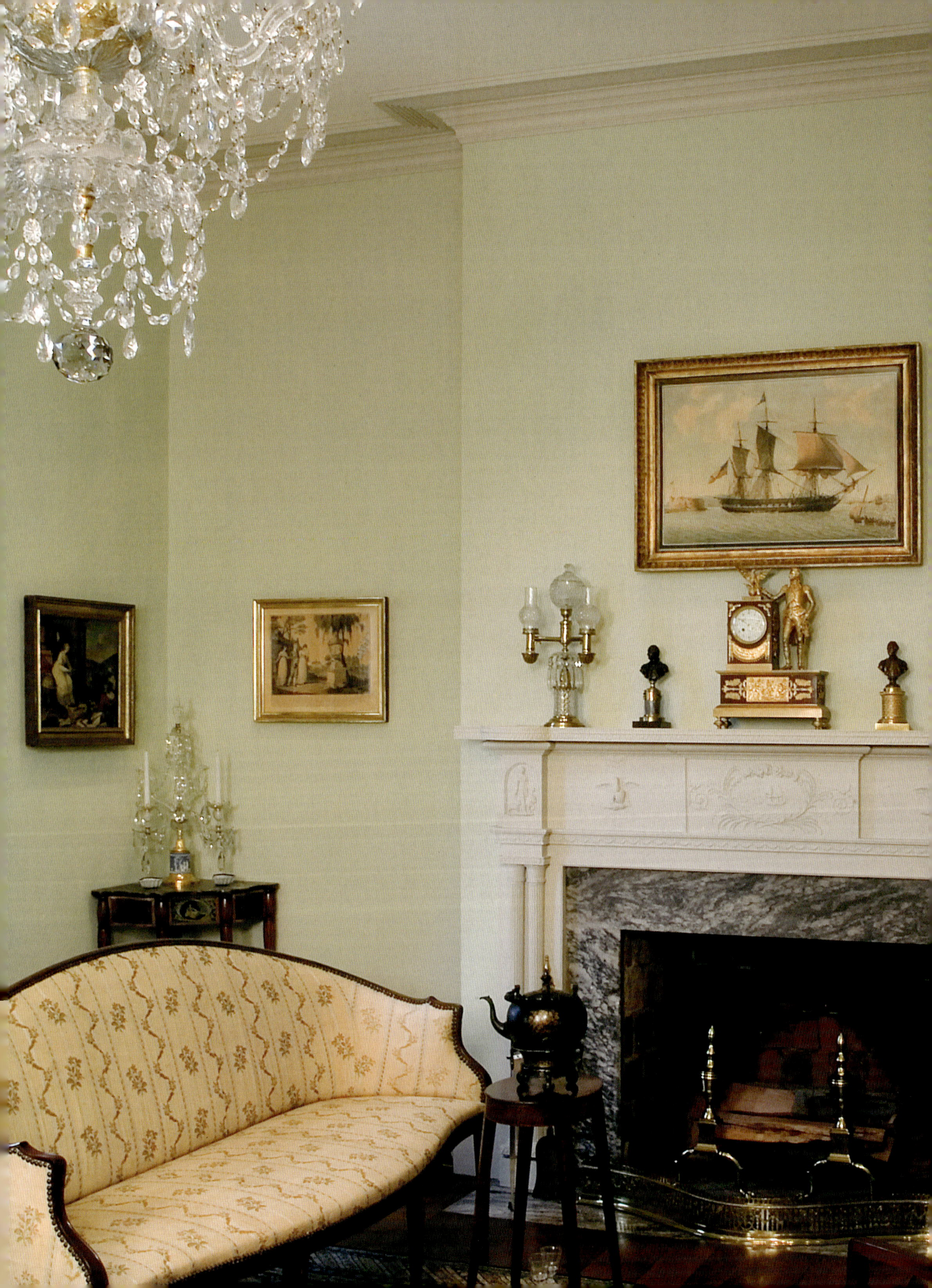

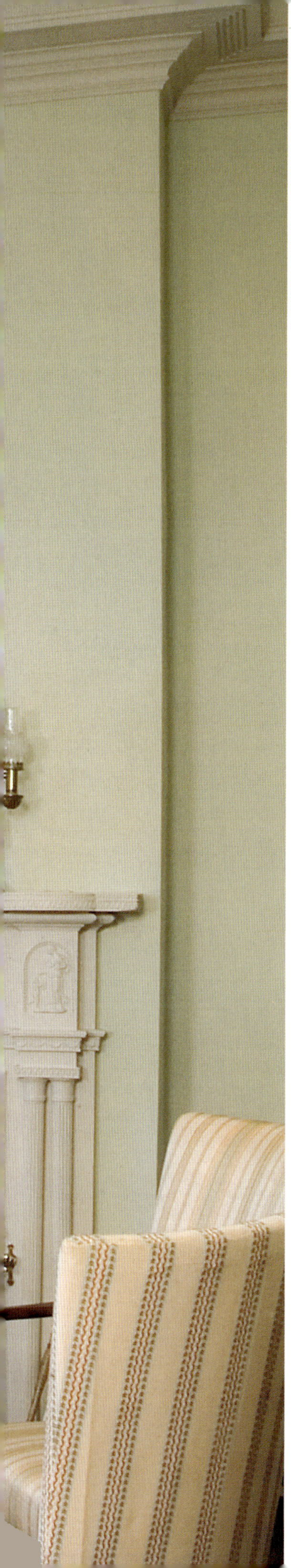

Baltimore Drawing Room

Peter Breen House, Philadelphia, Pennsylvania, circa 1812

11'6" high by 16' wide by 24' long

The Baltimore Drawing Room's woodwork came from the Peter Breen house in Philadelphia. Breen was a distiller and is listed in the Philadelphia city directories. The original Peter Breen house is attributed to Robert Wellford, who may have also lived in it for a short time.

Installed in the Baltimore Drawing Room are thin, attenuated moldings with ornamental motifs common to the Federal style. The door surrounds, for example, as well as the window architraves, are lightly proportioned and employ Classical motifs for ornamentation and decoration.

Fluted pilasters, in a modified Doric Order, frame the door openings and support an entablature over the door. Like many Federal-style door surrounds, the pilaster capital merges with the entablature's architrave, resulting in a proportionally tall frieze well suited for displaying a Grecian urn and foliated scroll, or *rinceau*.

The mantelpiece also has a compressed architrave and thin mantel shelf, again resulting in a broad frieze. Applied composition ornament reflecting Classical and Federal motifs decorates the expansive frieze. With its graceful moldings set off against a light wall, the Baltimore Drawing Room at Winterthur shows how delicate proportions can imbue a room with a sense of peace and calm.

The airy, beautifully proportioned Baltimore Drawing Room served as Mr. du Pont's morning room.

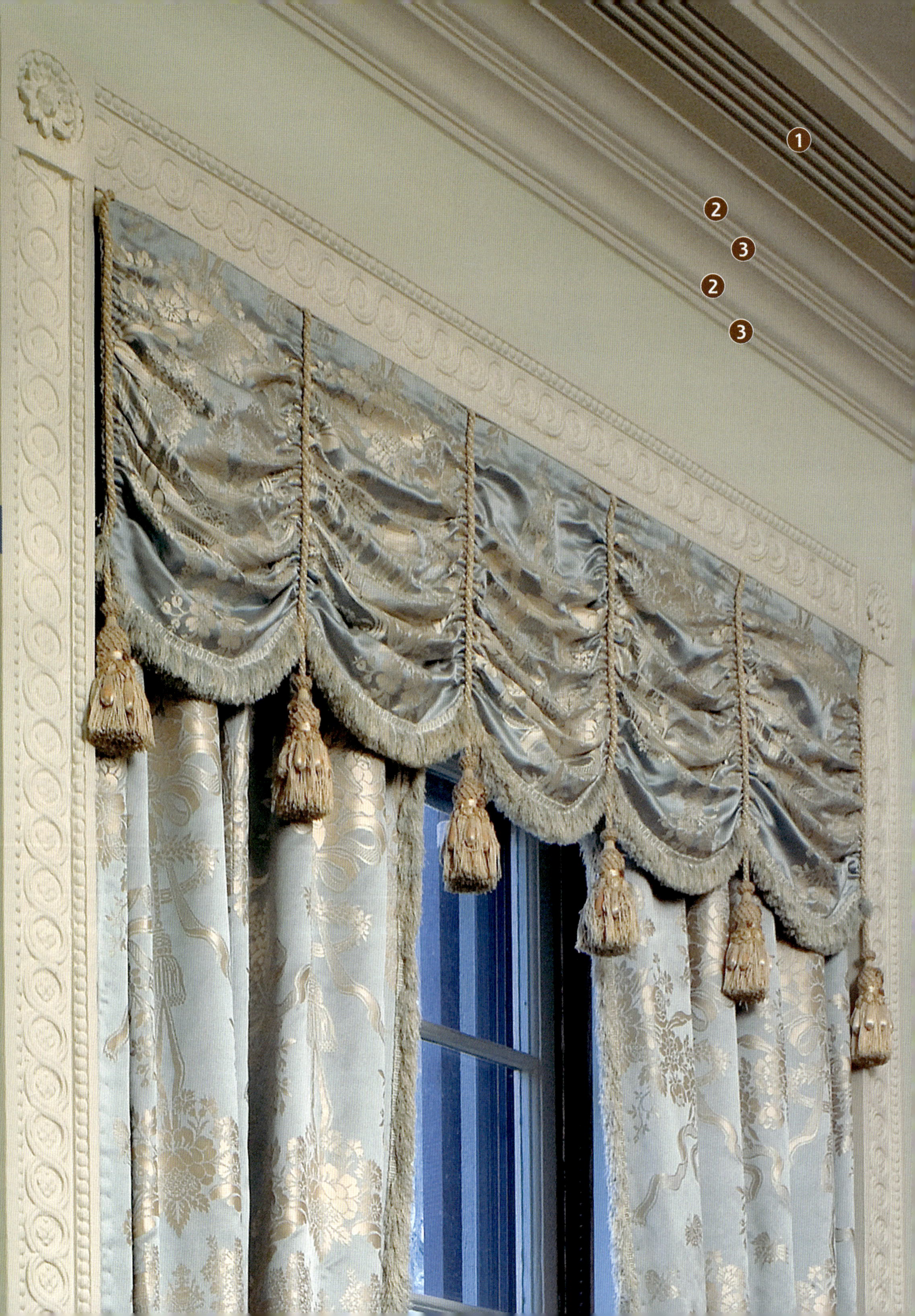
1
2
3
2
3

Cornice & Window Architraves

The cornice is simple and elegant in its refinement. It projects out nine inches across the ceiling, yet extends only four-and-one-half inches down the wall. The flutes, or grooves, found in the soffit (1), and the repetition of beads (2) and fillets (3), accentuate the sense of line and movement in the room as well as the lightly scaled proportions. Such proportions and the molding shapes themselves are similar to those in the Blue Room (page 42) and other Federal period cornices.

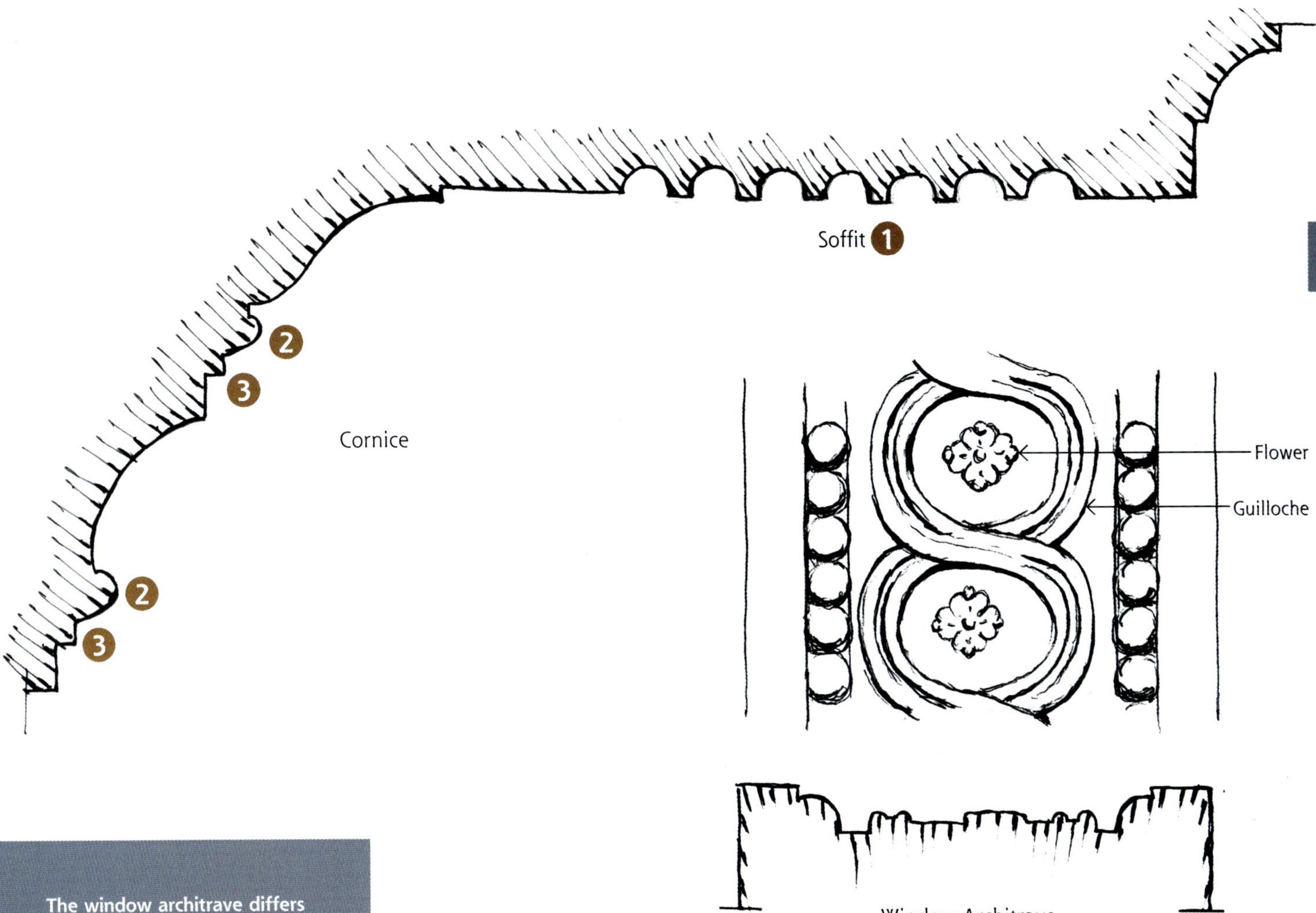

Cornice

Window Architrave

The window architrave differs from the door architrave (next page) and is similar to one seen in the Imlay Room, also from a Wellford-built home. Two rows of beads frame a *guilloche*, or interlacing ribbons, with flowers between the ribbon windings. This motif is borrowed from guilloche patterns in Classical Roman architectural elements and mosaics.

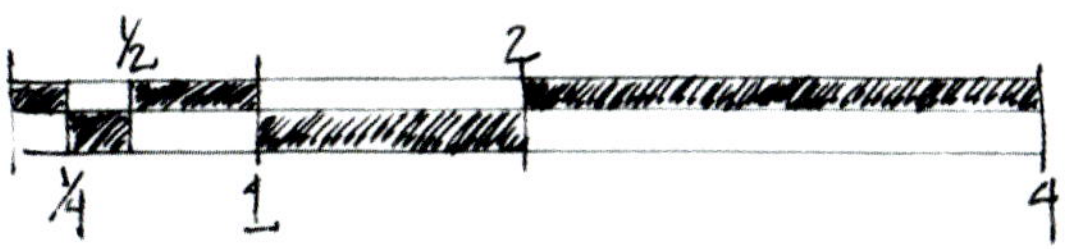

Door Architrave

The door architrave is similarly articulated with a series of gouges (1) that visually lighten the architrave around the door. These add a shimmering reflection of light and shadow to an otherwise plain surface.

The overdoor includes a tall frieze supported by a thin architrave decorated with gouged ribs and stars (2). The frieze itself becomes a landscape for a Grecian urn (3) with bellflower swags dropping from it and a foliated scroll in a Vitruvian wave pattern (4) expanding outward on either side, exquisite and delicate, like icing on a cake.

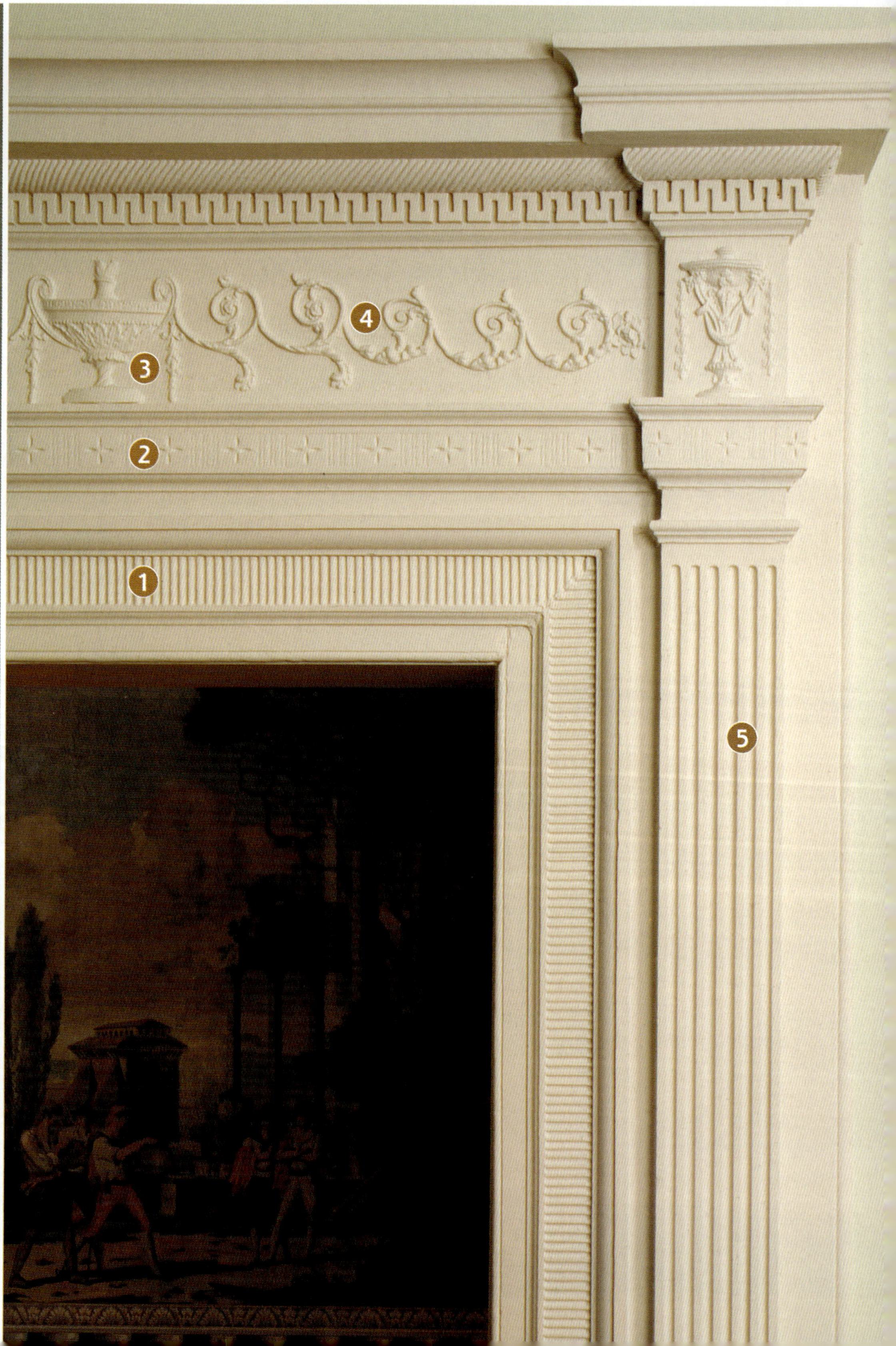

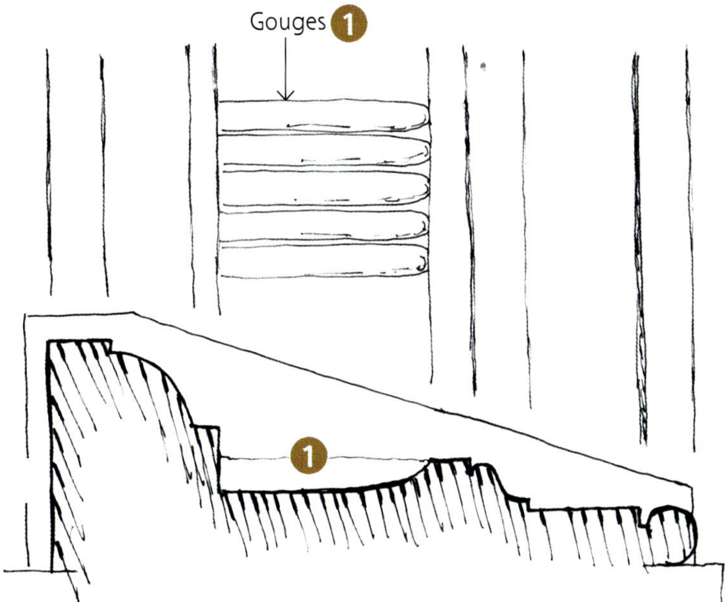

Architrave at Door

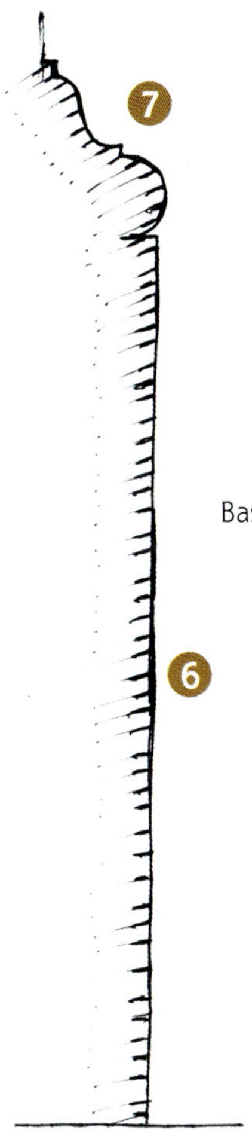

Base

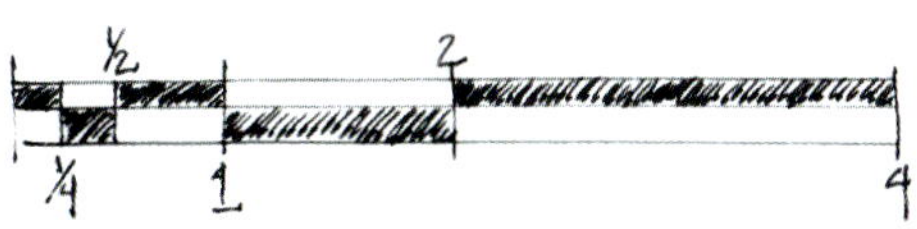

The gouged door architrave (1) and fluted pilasters (5) rest upon a flat base or plinth (6) capped by a simple molding (7).

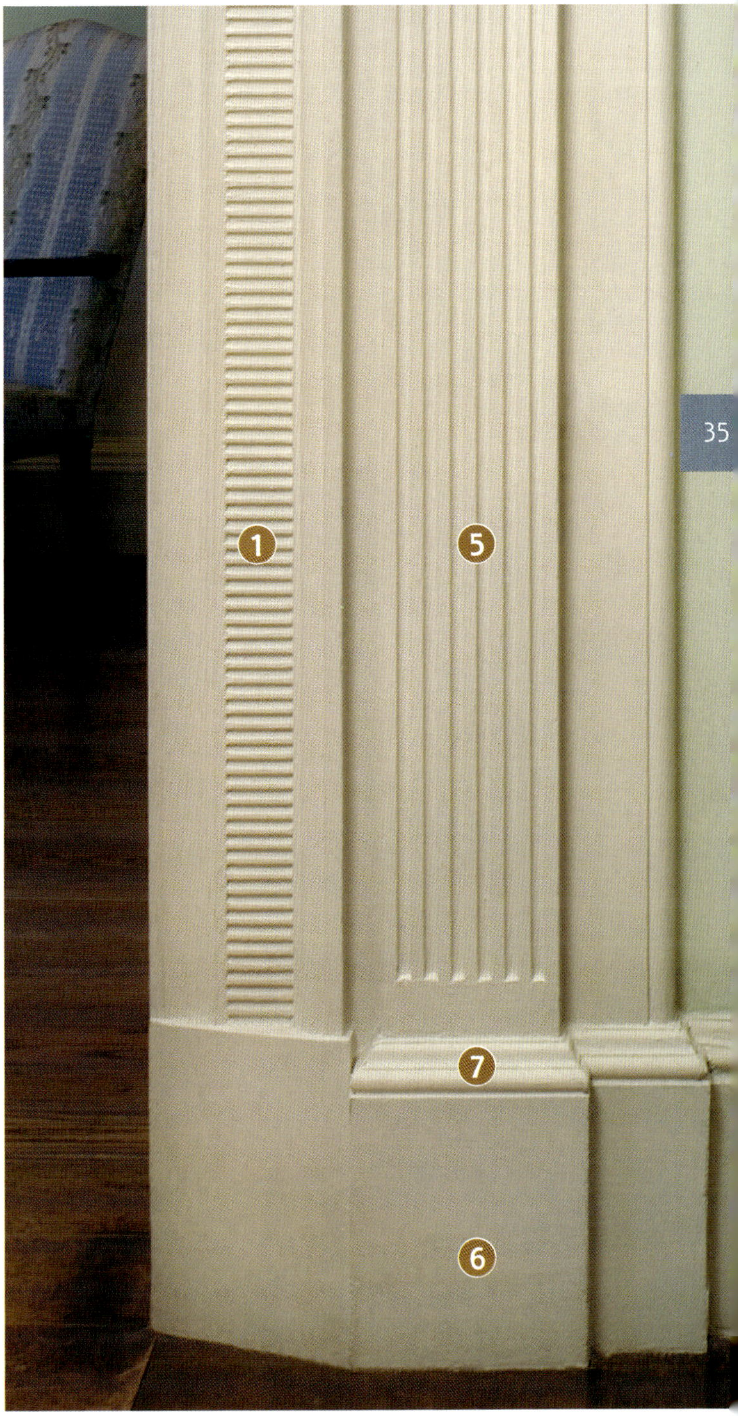

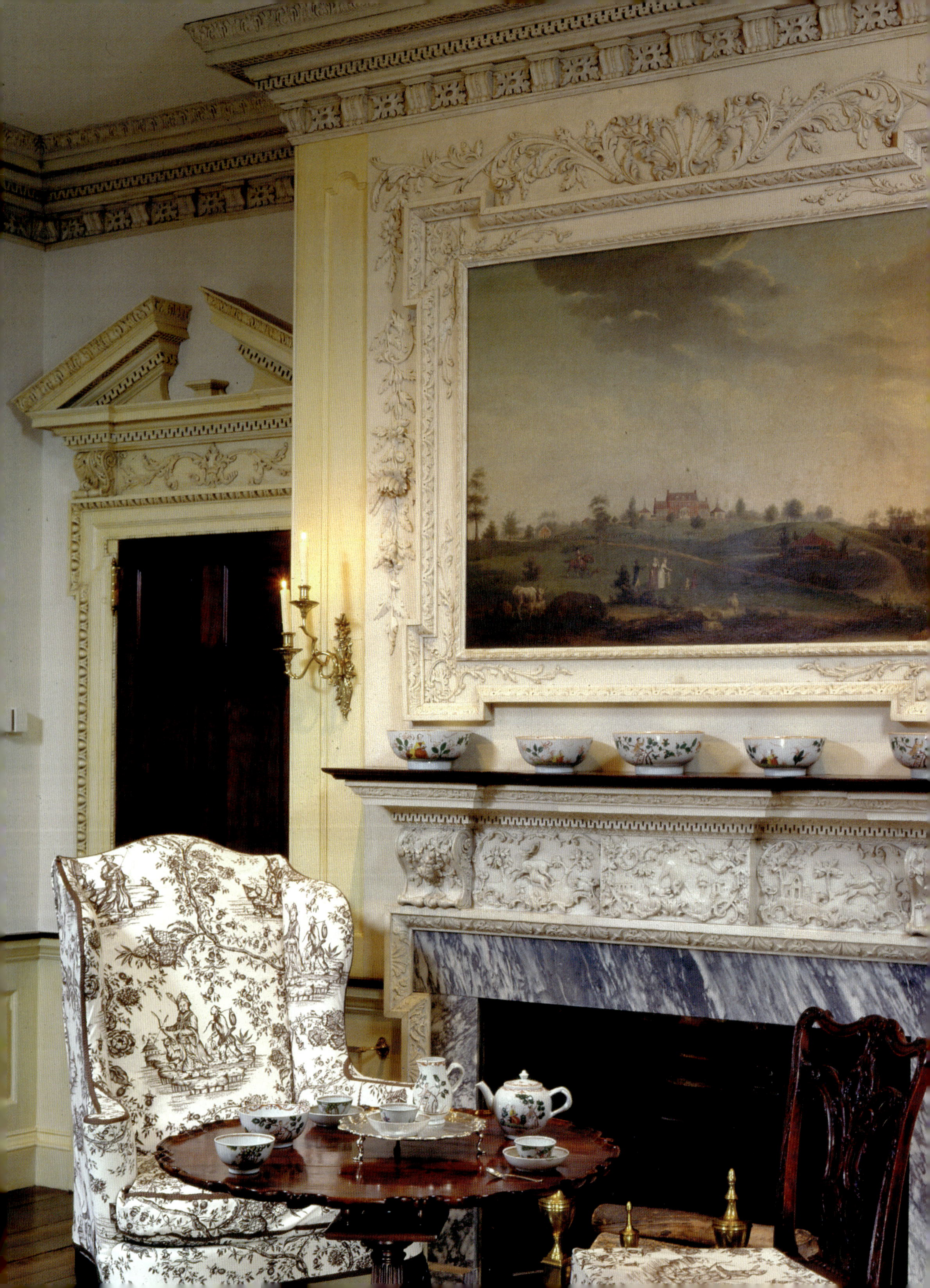

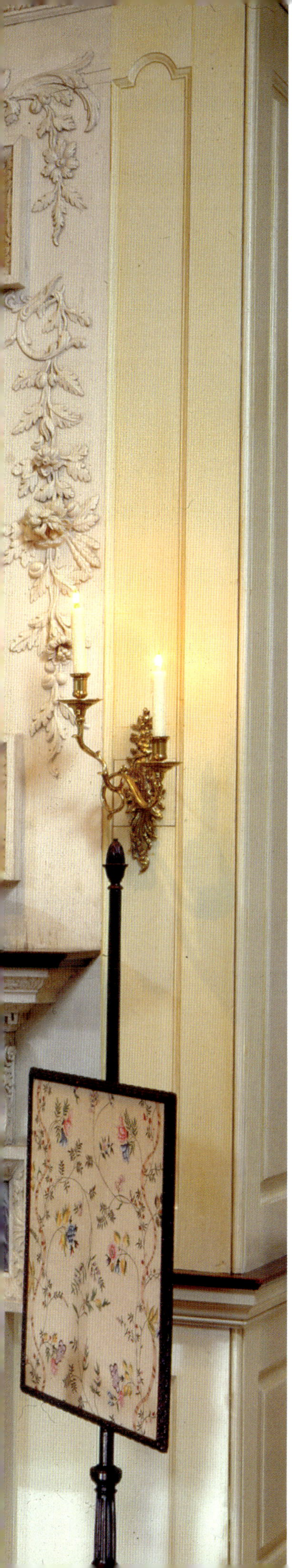

Blackwell Parlor

Stamper-Blackwell House, Philadelphia, Pennsylvania, 1764

11'1" high by 18'5" wide by 19'7" long

Reverend Robert Blackwell, a well-connected minister, inherited this house from his father-in-law, Philadelphia Mayor John Stamper, who bought the land from the Penn family.

The most striking elements of the parlor—the mantel, overmantel, cornice, and door surrounds—illustrate how ornamental moldings and decoration can be used to enhance a room. The room's decorative motifs are believed to have been inspired by Abraham Swan's 1758 *A Collection of Designs in Architecture*. Refined and lush, the ornamental carvings are similar to those carved by furniture makers, such as Thomas Chippendale, and to designs for interior elements shown in numerous pattern books of this period. With robust foliated patterns, the important elements of the room are given focus, and a rich, sculptural texture is created throughout.

Blackwell Parlor shows the level of craftsmanship present in America before the Revolution. Philadelphia was a large and wealthy colonial city and home to many talented craftsmen capable of such exquisite work.

An ornate interior, the Blackwell Parlor is known for the quality of its carvings.

Cornice

The cornice is inventive, combining a mixture of ornamental and decorative elements. The cymatium (1) features an acanthus leaf pattern. The soffit (2) has stylized mutules adapted from the Doric Order. Unlike the canonic Doric Order, here the mutules consist of a pattern of drilled holes, a good economical adaptation, rather than dropping guttae from the mutule blocks. Typically, dentils are used in the Ionic Order; however, there is a denticulated Doric Order that gives precedent for the fretwork dentils (3) used in the cornice. Beneath the dentils and their bedmold is an interesting band of scrolled brackets (4), which relate to the brackets found in the door surrounds (facing page).

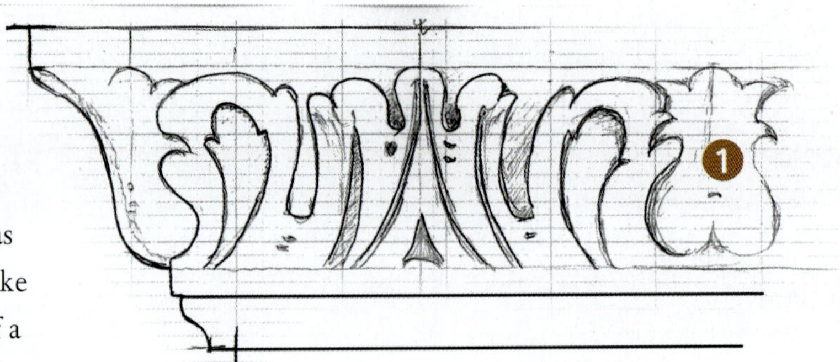

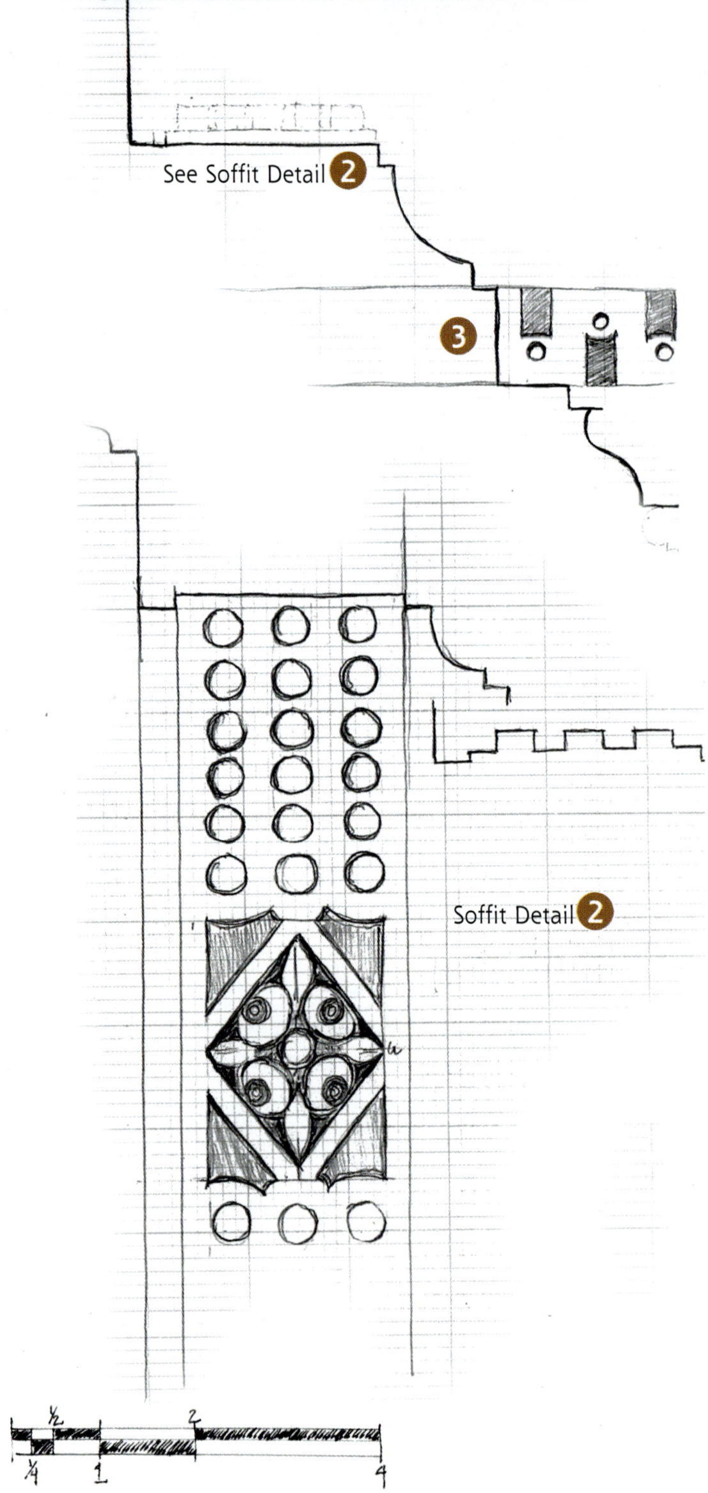

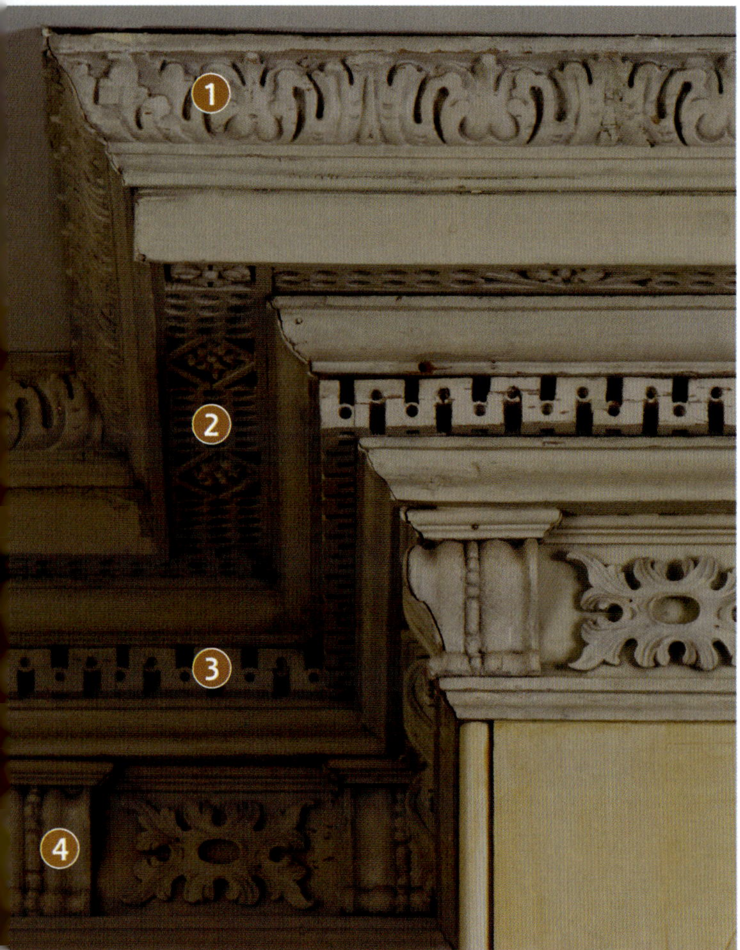

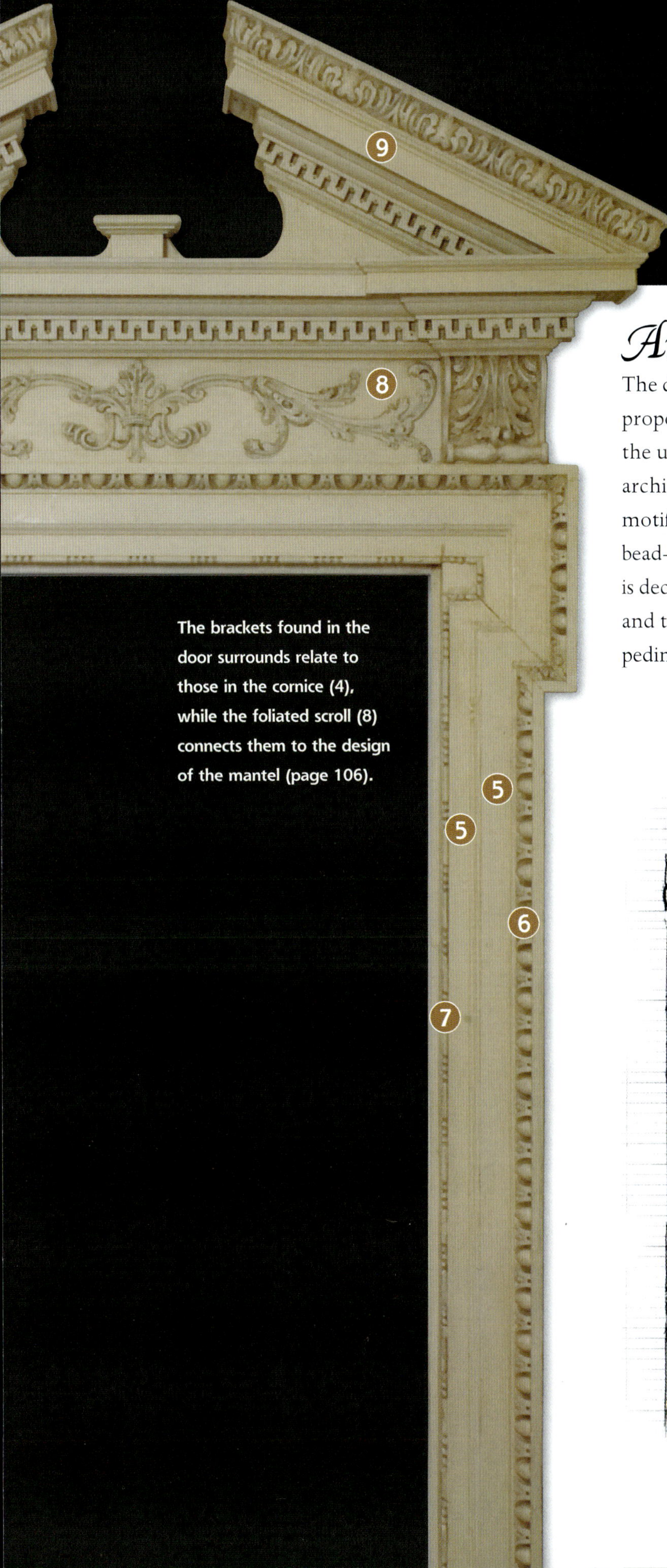

The brackets found in the door surrounds relate to those in the cornice (4), while the foliated scroll (8) connects them to the design of the mantel (page 106).

Architraves

The doorways are surrounded by beautifully proportioned and carved architraves. In contrast to the unornamented fascias (5) of the door surround's architrave, the ovolo is carved with an egg-and-dart motif (6) and the three-quarter round bead with a bead-and-reel motif (7). The frieze (8) over the door is decorated with a foliated scroll in the center panel, and two scrolled and carved brackets support a broken pediment (9) above.

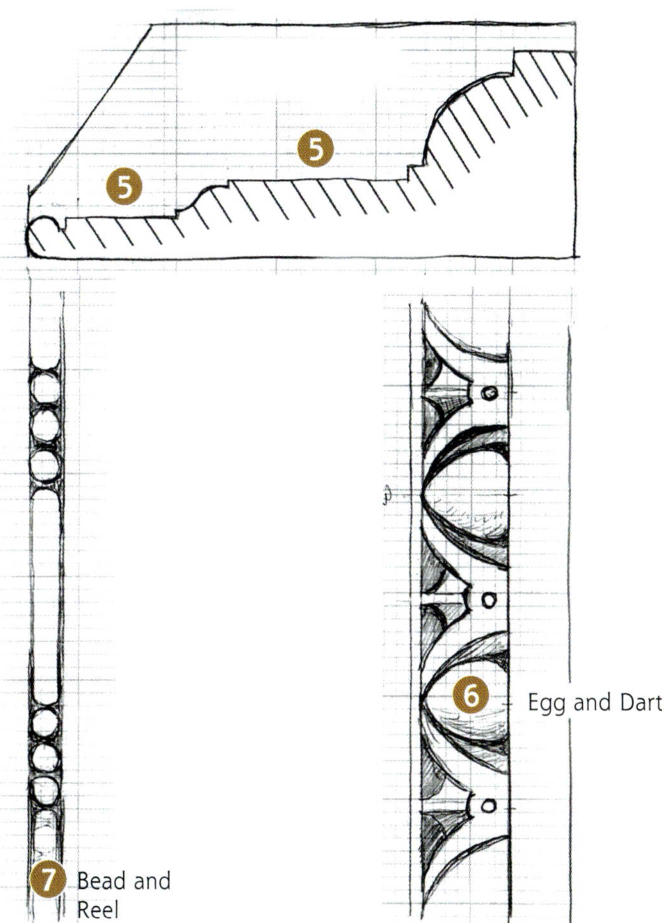

Panels

Rather than fully paneled walls, the Blackwell Parlor has only its dado, or wainscot, paneled with raised panels (2), allowing the ornamental elements of the room to stand out.

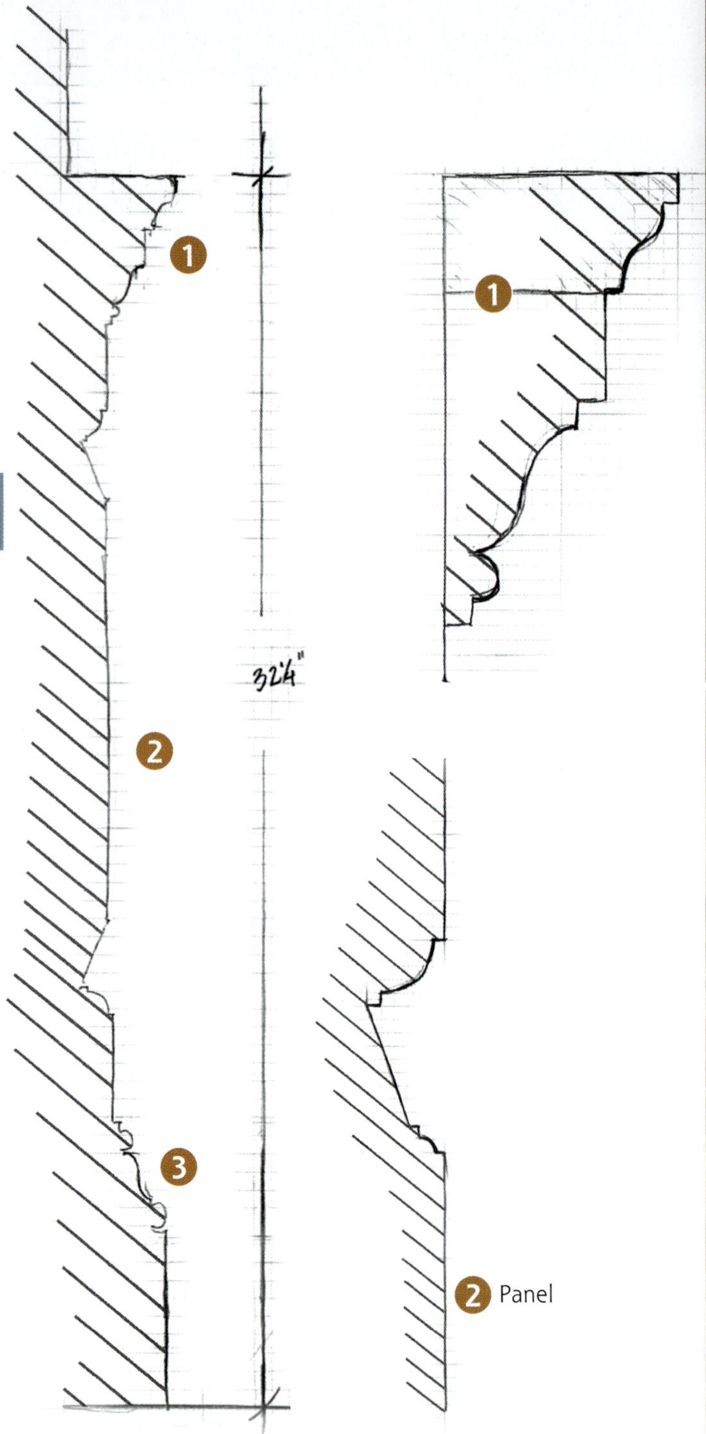

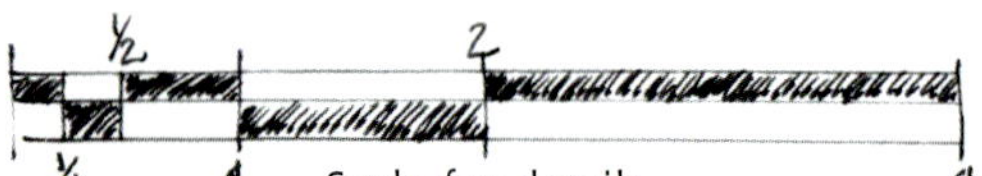

The paneled dado measures just over thirty-two inches high, and the ceiling eleven feet, one inch high, a nice proportional division between the dado and the overall room height.

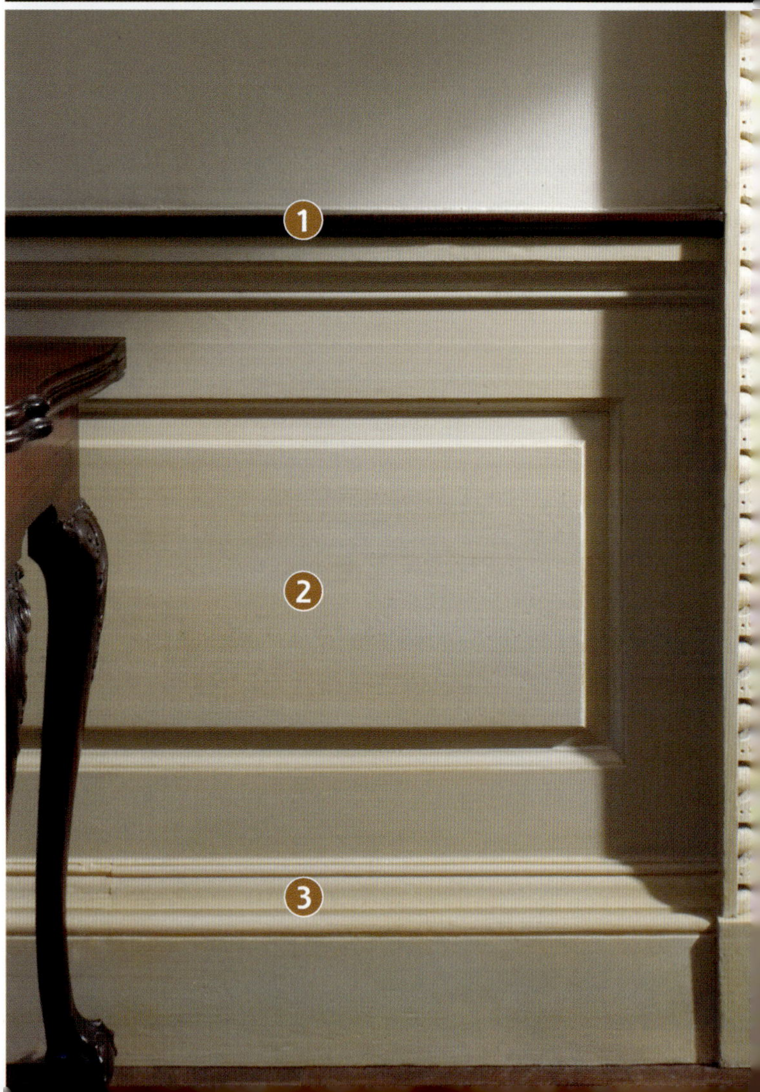

Mantel & Base

The mantel elements seen here are commonly found in late Georgian designs with a mantelshelf (5) supported by brackets (6) over a marble surround (7). The overmantel frieze (8) and brackets are elaborately carved, making this the central feature of the room.

The base moldings are bold by today's standards; the base plinth and base cap (3) project nearly two inches from the wall surface. The cap of the dado, or surbase (1), is equally bold. Neither is ornamented with additional carvings, highlighting the abundance of ornament elsewhere in the room.

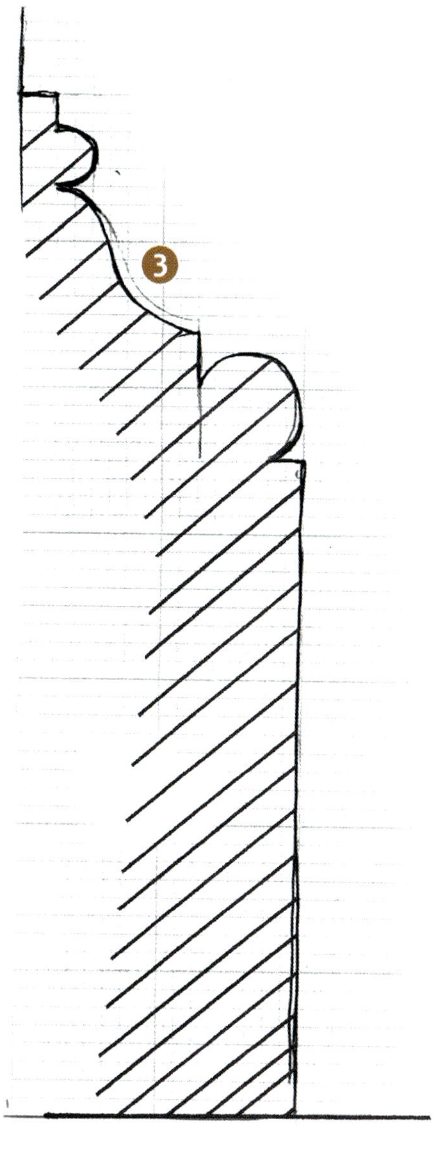

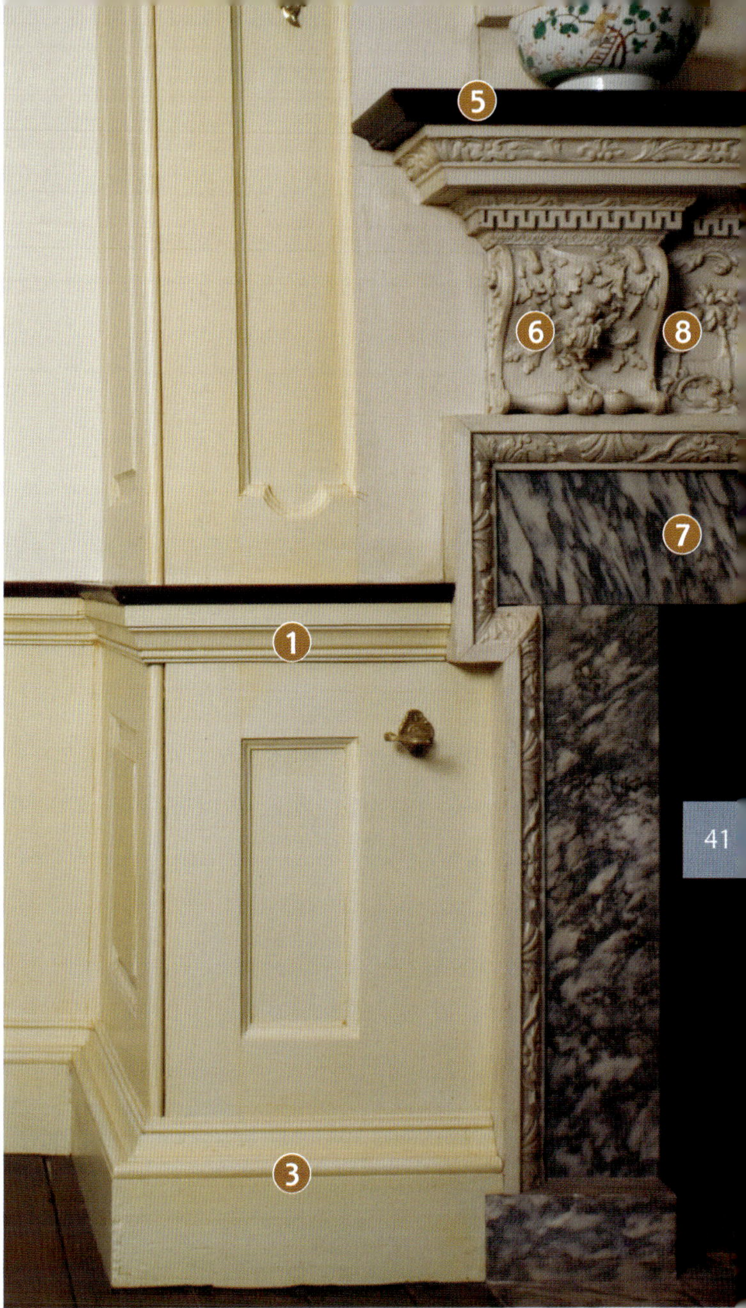

See the full mantel carvings on page 36. Mr. du Pont added the painting when the Blackwell Parlor was installed at Winterthur.

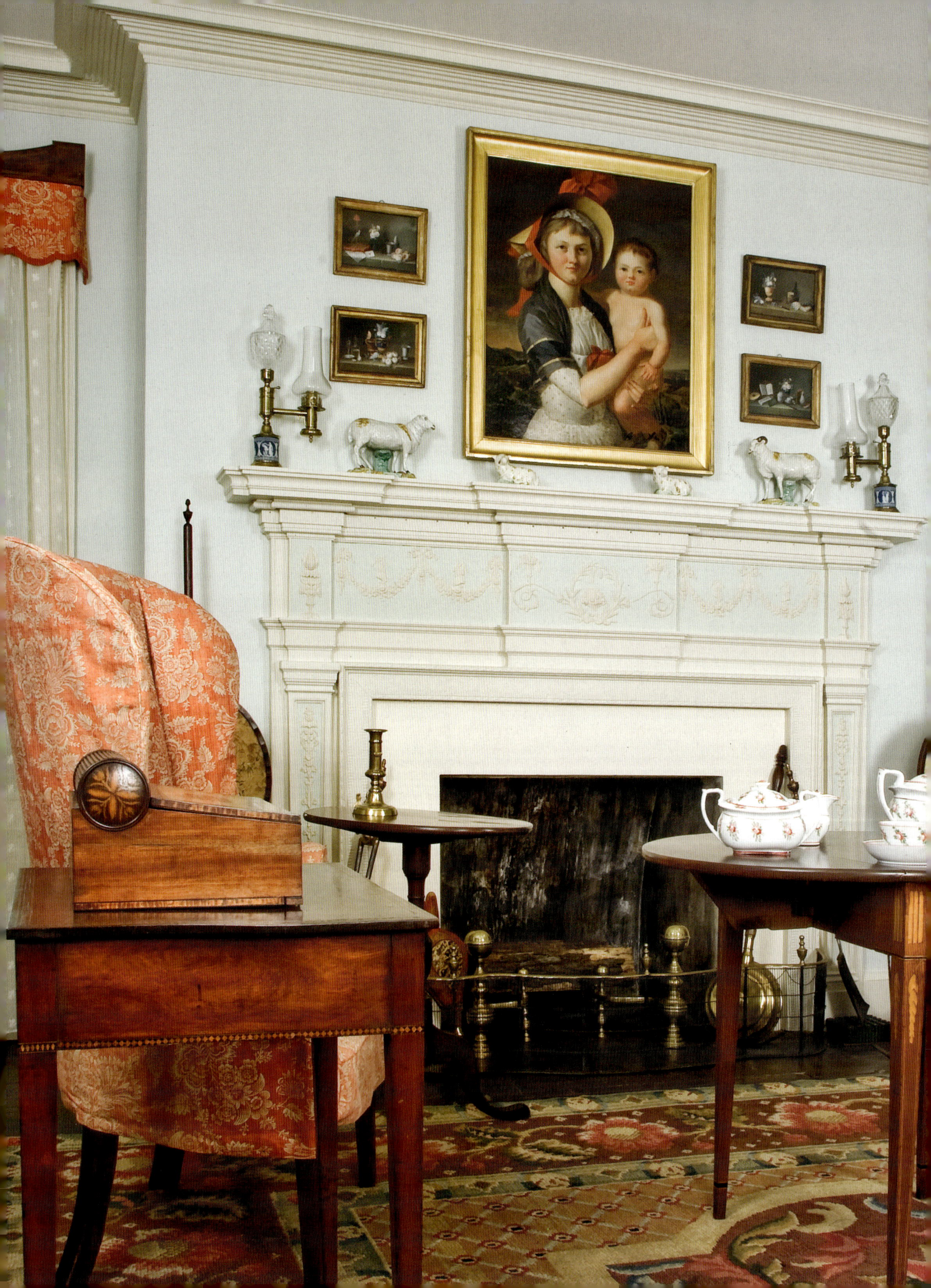

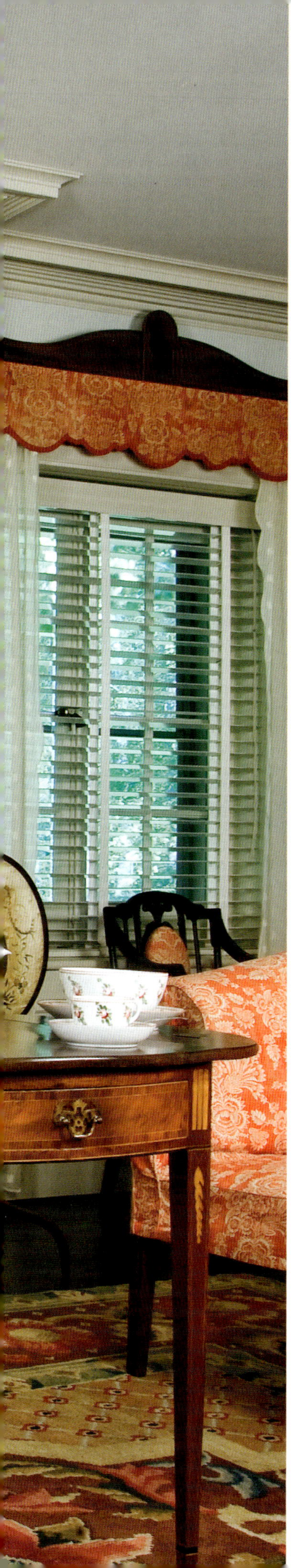

Blue Room

Wilson House, Salem, New Jersey, circa 1805

9′ high by 22′ 8″ wide by 22′ 6″ long

The Blue Room was designed for Mrs. du Pont using woodwork from the Wilson House in Salem, New Jersey. The delightful robin's-egg-blue walls give the room a restful serenity appropriate for a bedroom.

A central fireplace and windows on either side balance a pair of doors opposite. The mantel, with fine composition busts of Franklin and Washington, is thought to be a Robert Wellford design. Typical of Federal-style mantels, its frieze is filled with a dazzling array of swags, and floral elements.

Plain wall surfaces, without paneling or even a dado, are a quiet background balancing the highly decorative mantel and door surrounds. Against the blank sweep of the wall, the base and cornice are delicately proportioned.

Decorative composition, thought to be by Philadelphia craftsman Robert Wellford, adorns the graceful Blue Room.

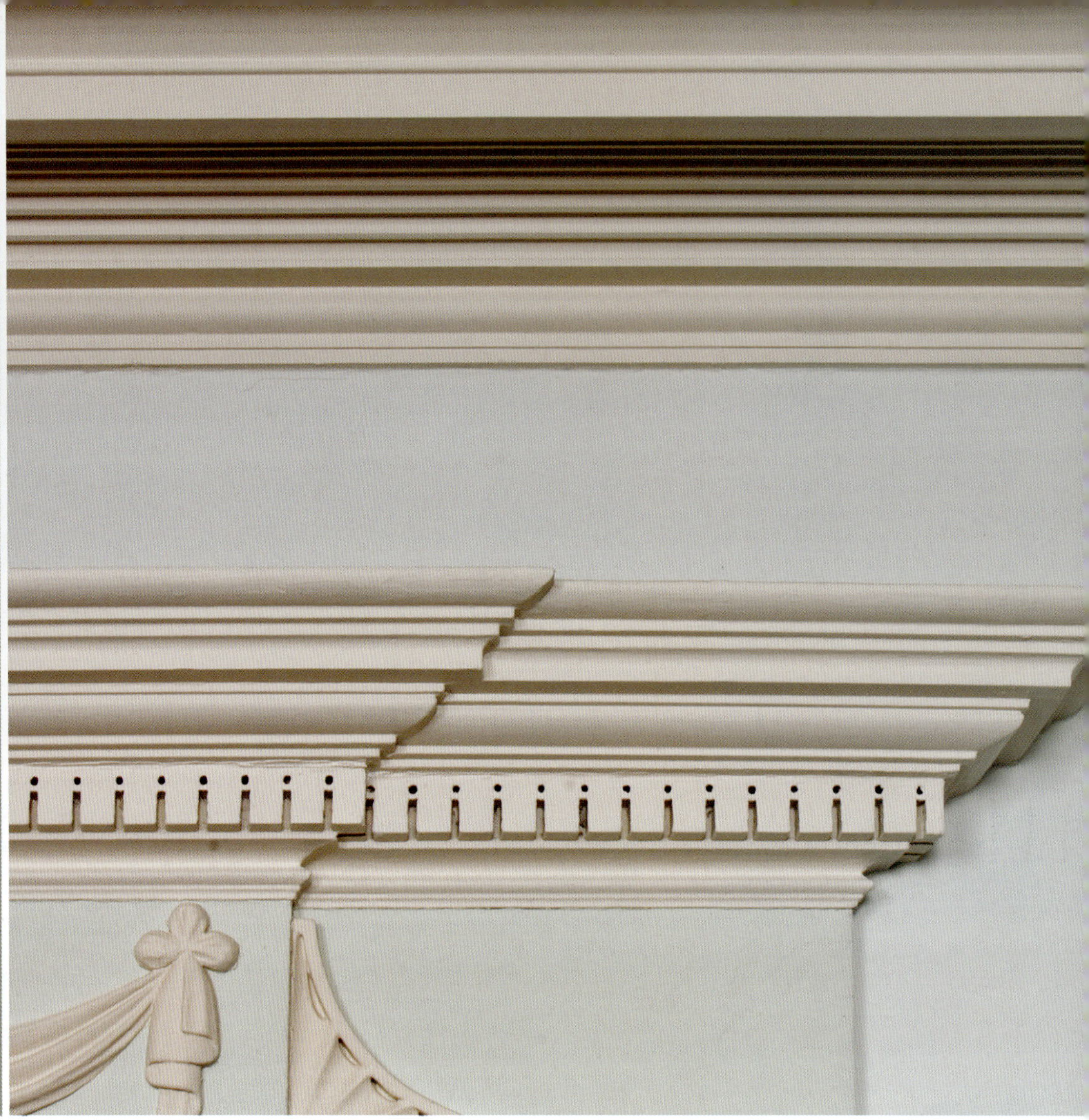

Cornice

The cornice, while different from a typical Georgian or Palladian-influenced cornice, is a common Federal-style cornice. It projects out along the ceiling with a concave soffit articulated with flutes that enhance the visual delicacy and sense of movement in the room.

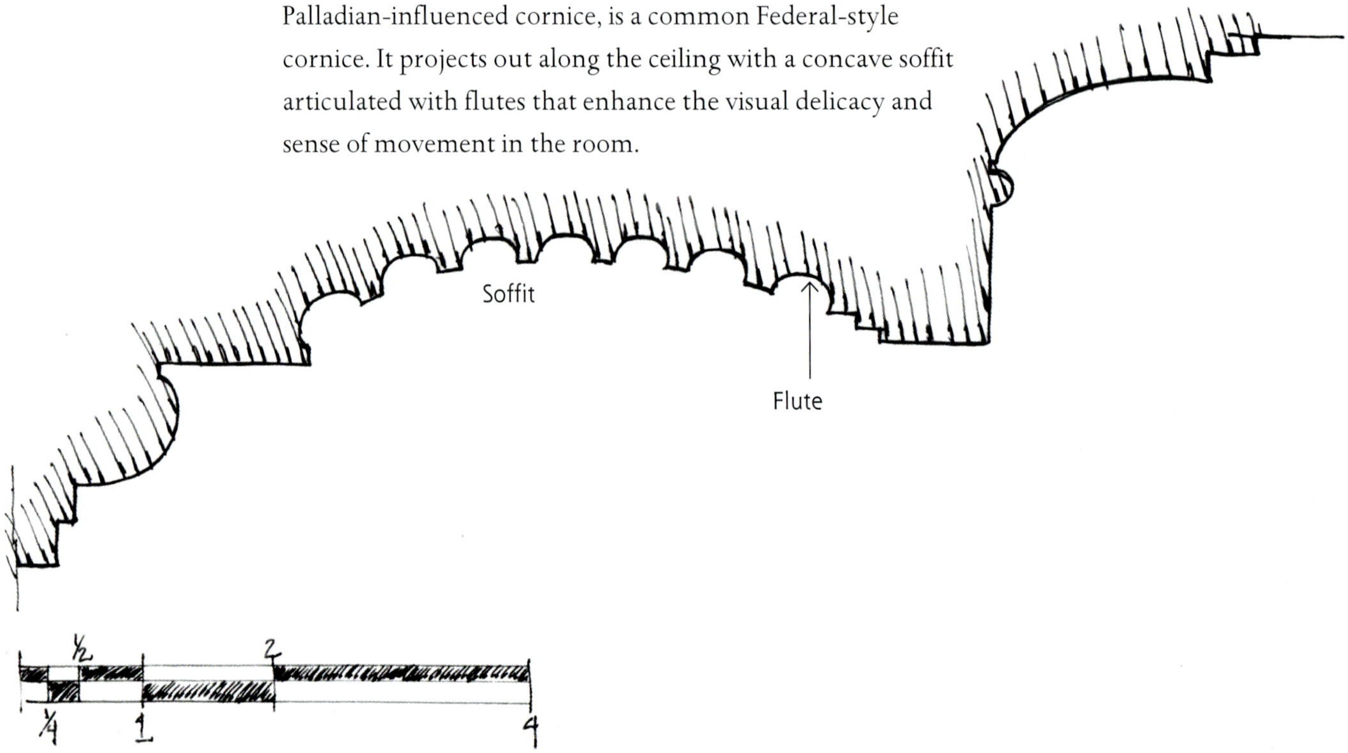

Architraves

Decorative composition, or compo, also appears over the doors on either side of the bed. The doors are surrounded by an architrave lightly gouged (1) with a flute-like detail that creates soft shadows and texture around the doors. Above, a graceful swag and fan detail (2) decorates the frieze, and small dentils (3) articulate the cornice of the overdoor. The door architrave has a small echinus-shaped molding (4) at its outside and dies onto a simple plinth block.

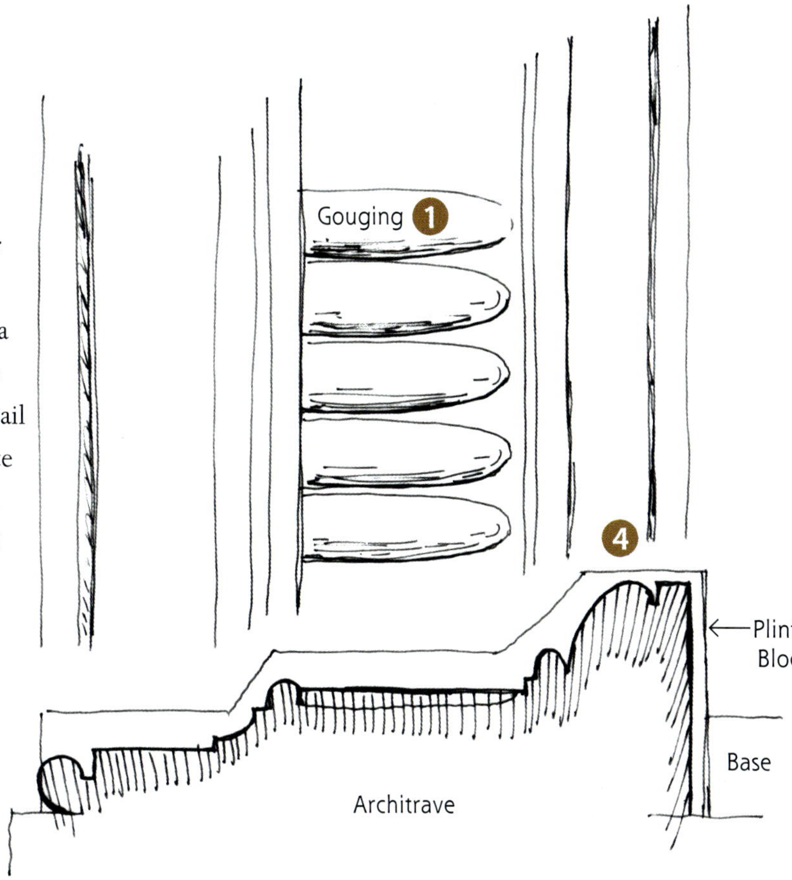

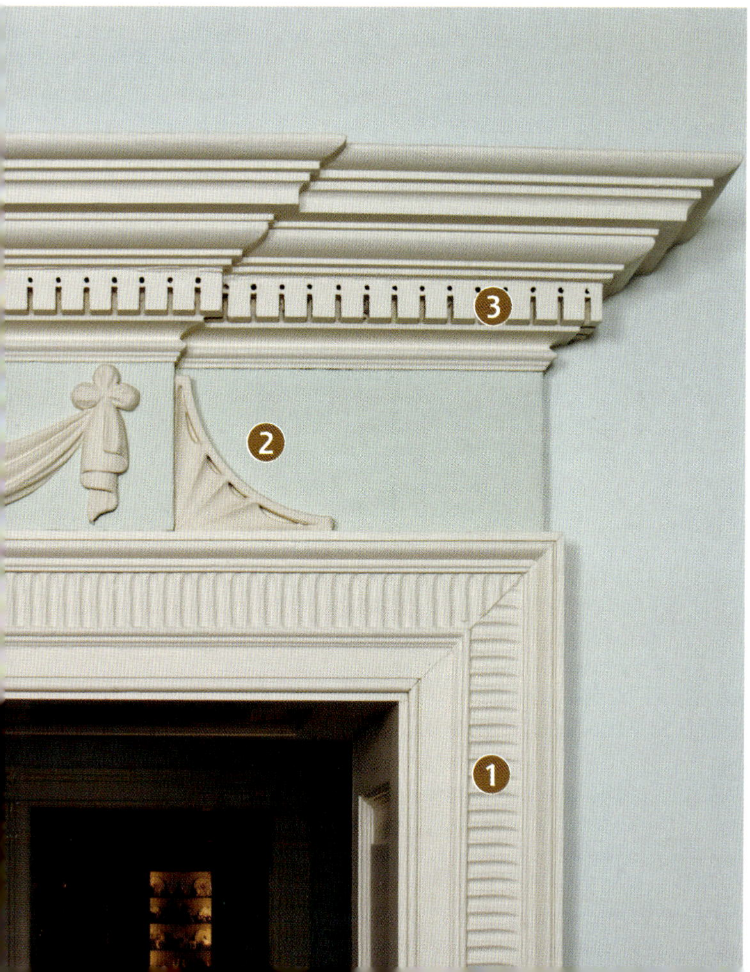

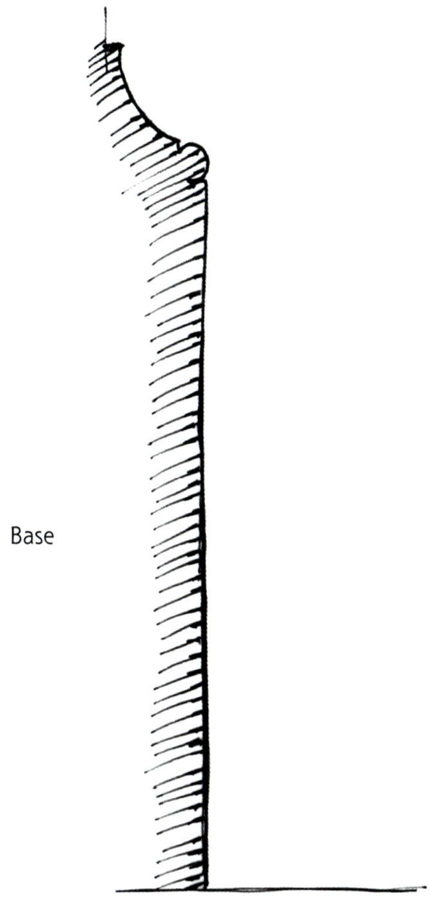

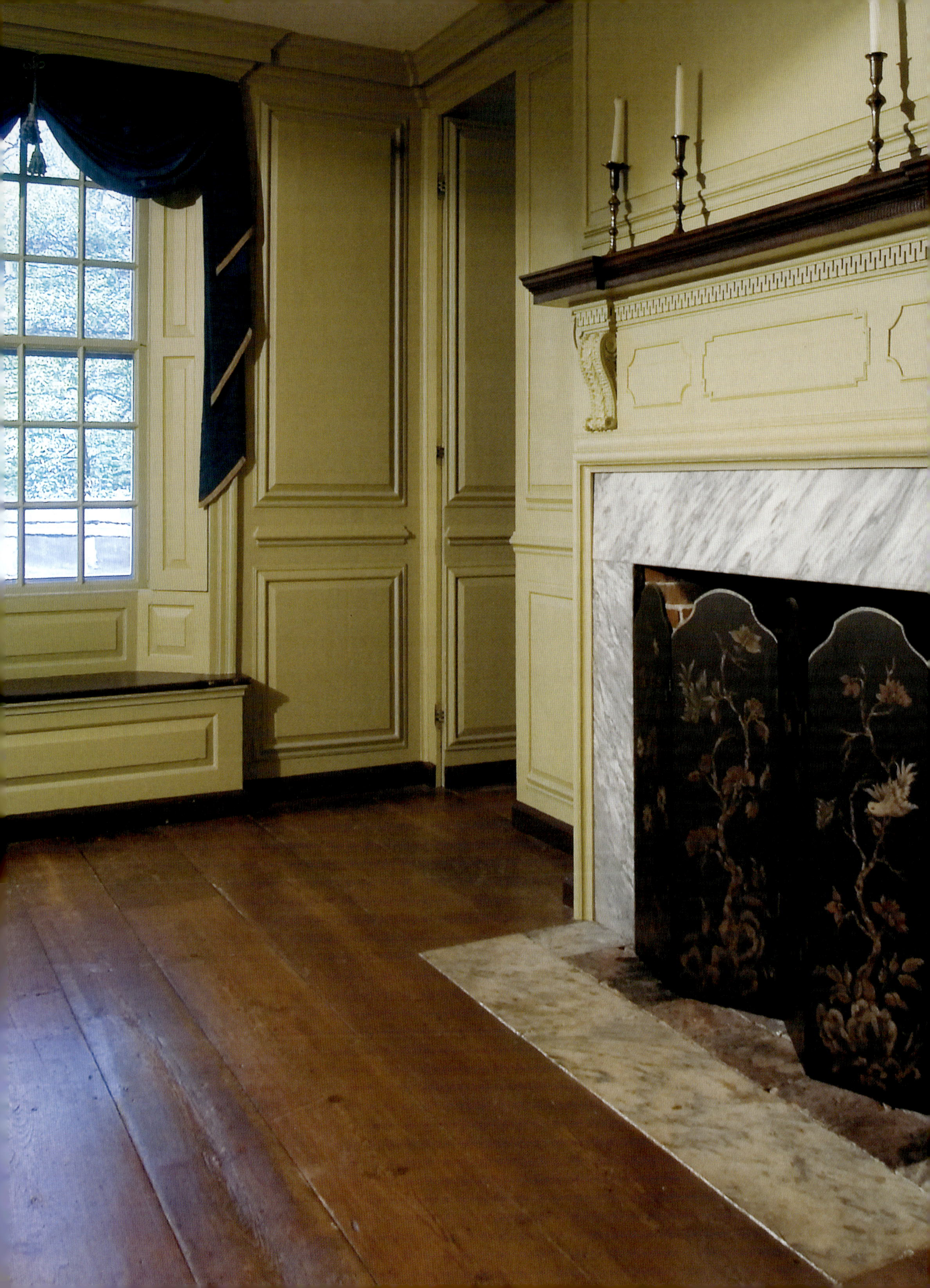

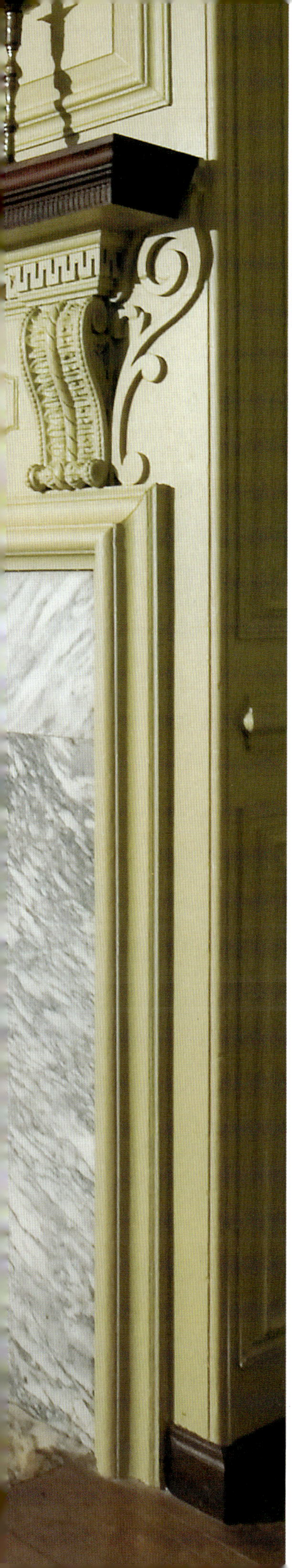

Bowers Parlor

Bowers House, Somerset, Massachusetts, 1763

8'6" high by 17'8" wide by 18'2" long

After Jerathmael Bowers amassed great wealth in commerce and speculative trade, he and his wife built a luxurious house near Somerset, Massachusetts, to suit their frequent entertaining. Two of the Bowers' rooms are at Winterthur, the Bowers Parlor and the Somerset Room (page 158).

The Bowers house was described as "the nicest ever built in Somerset," and indeed the Bowers Parlor is elegantly graceful and refined. Its fully paneled walls, hospitable and useful window seats, and simply ornamented mantel make this room well-suited for either living or dining.

The room's window jambs splay or angle out from the window, reflecting additional light into the room. They are fitted with pocketing paneled shutters.

Cornice

The cornice projects approximately six inches from the wall and is composed of a cymatium (6), bedmold (7), corona (8), and another bedmold (9) formed of an ovolo and a cyma reversa. Each curved molding is separated from the next with a fillet, which articulates and separates each shape with a shadow line.

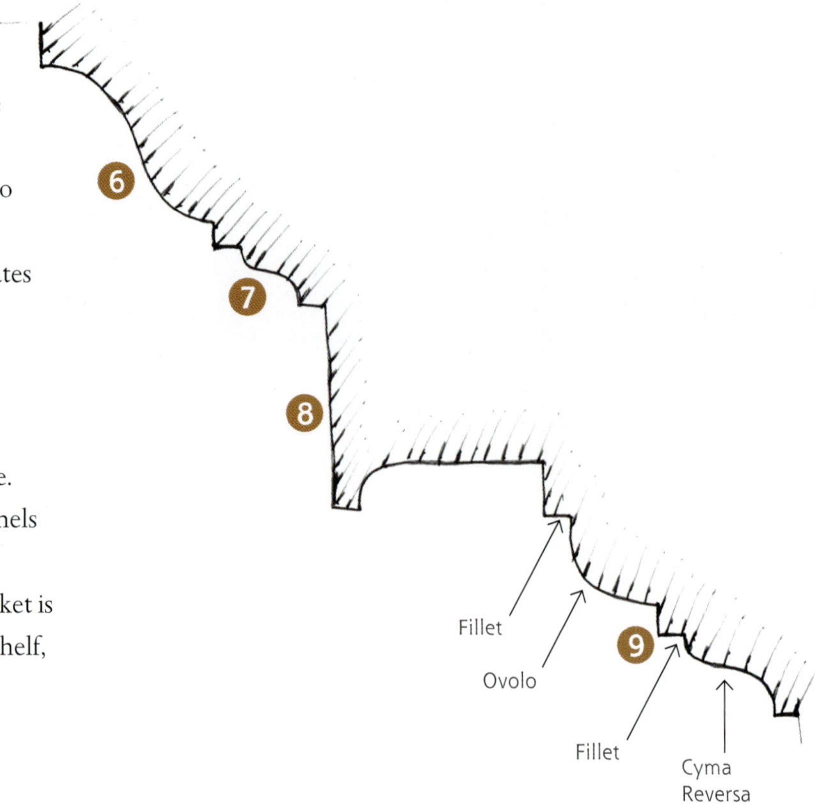

Fireplace Wall

The fireplace surround is the room's most ornate feature. Delicate applied moldings (1) are used to create three panels in the frieze under the mantelshelf. Scrolled brackets (2) support fretwork dentils (3), while another scrolled bracket is applied stencil-like (4) and visually supports the mantelshelf, which is lightened with a gouged pattern on its edge (5).

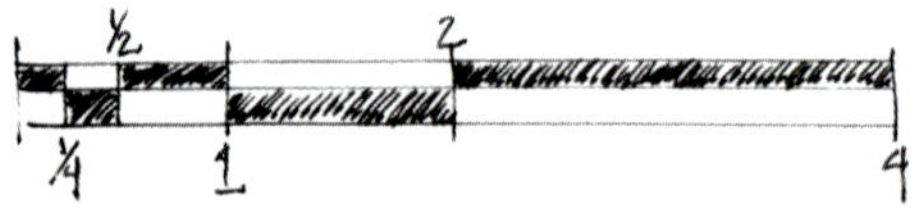

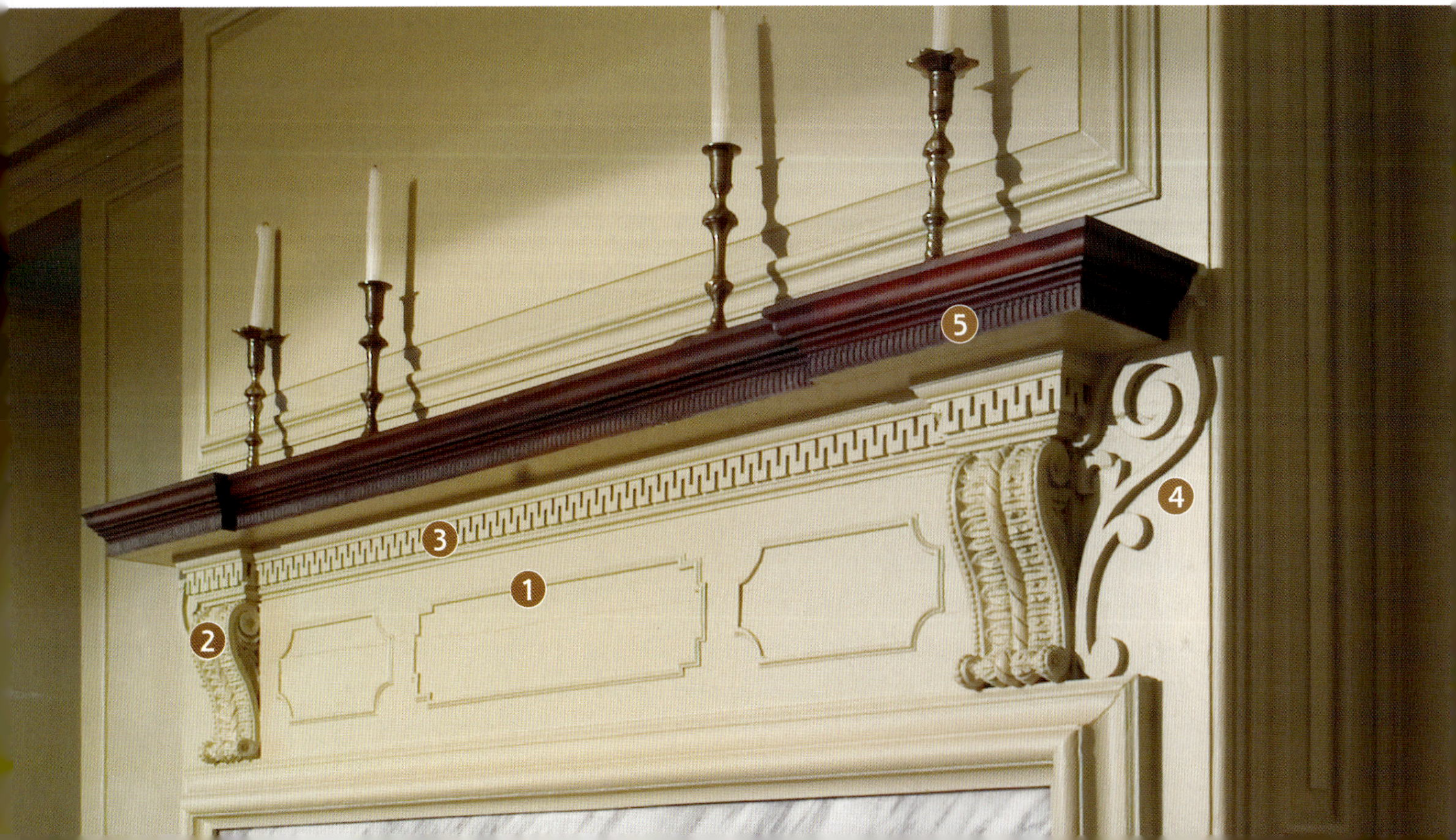

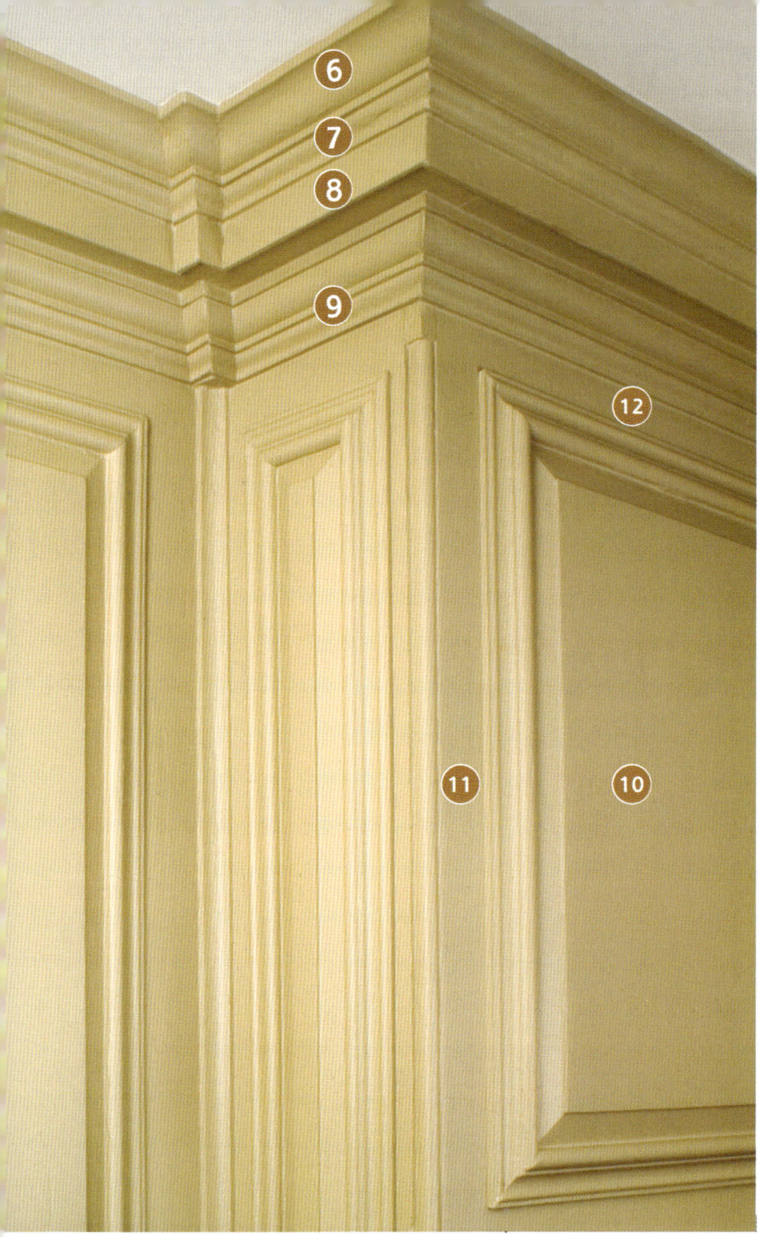

Panels

The Bowers Parlor has raised panels (10), the fields and moldings of which project beyond the surface of the stiles (11) and rails (12), similar to those in the Gidley Room (page 76). More commonly today, panel fields are flush with the surface of the stiles and rails, and panel moldings sit just below that plane. Panels such as these at Bowers, projecting from the wall plane, are bold and strong.

The dado, or wainscot, is also paneled and separated from the upper panels by a chair rail that wraps the room at about three feet above the floor.

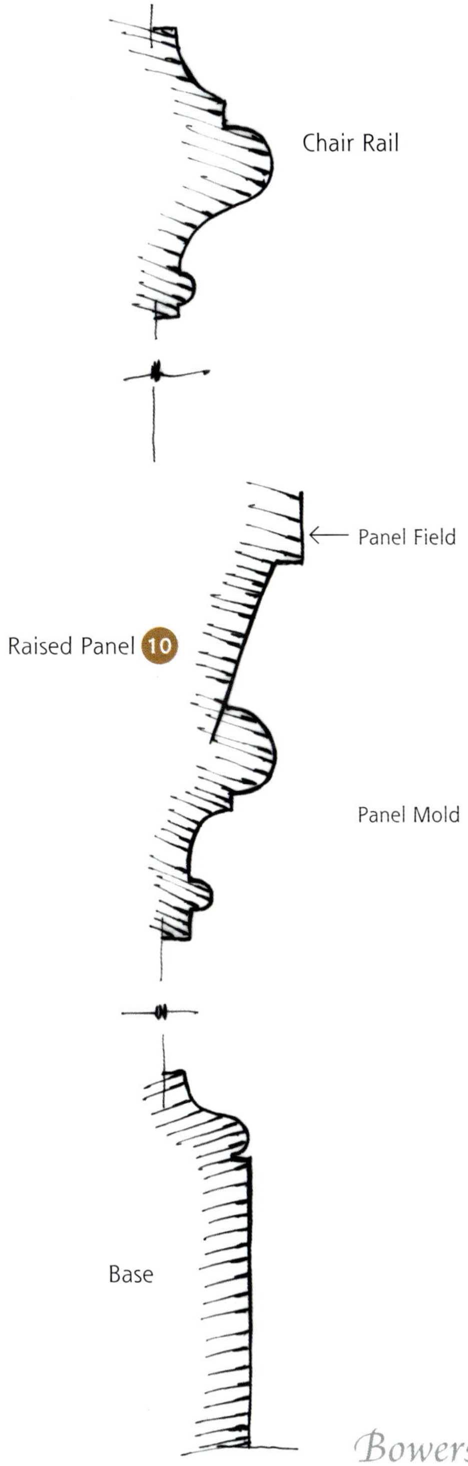

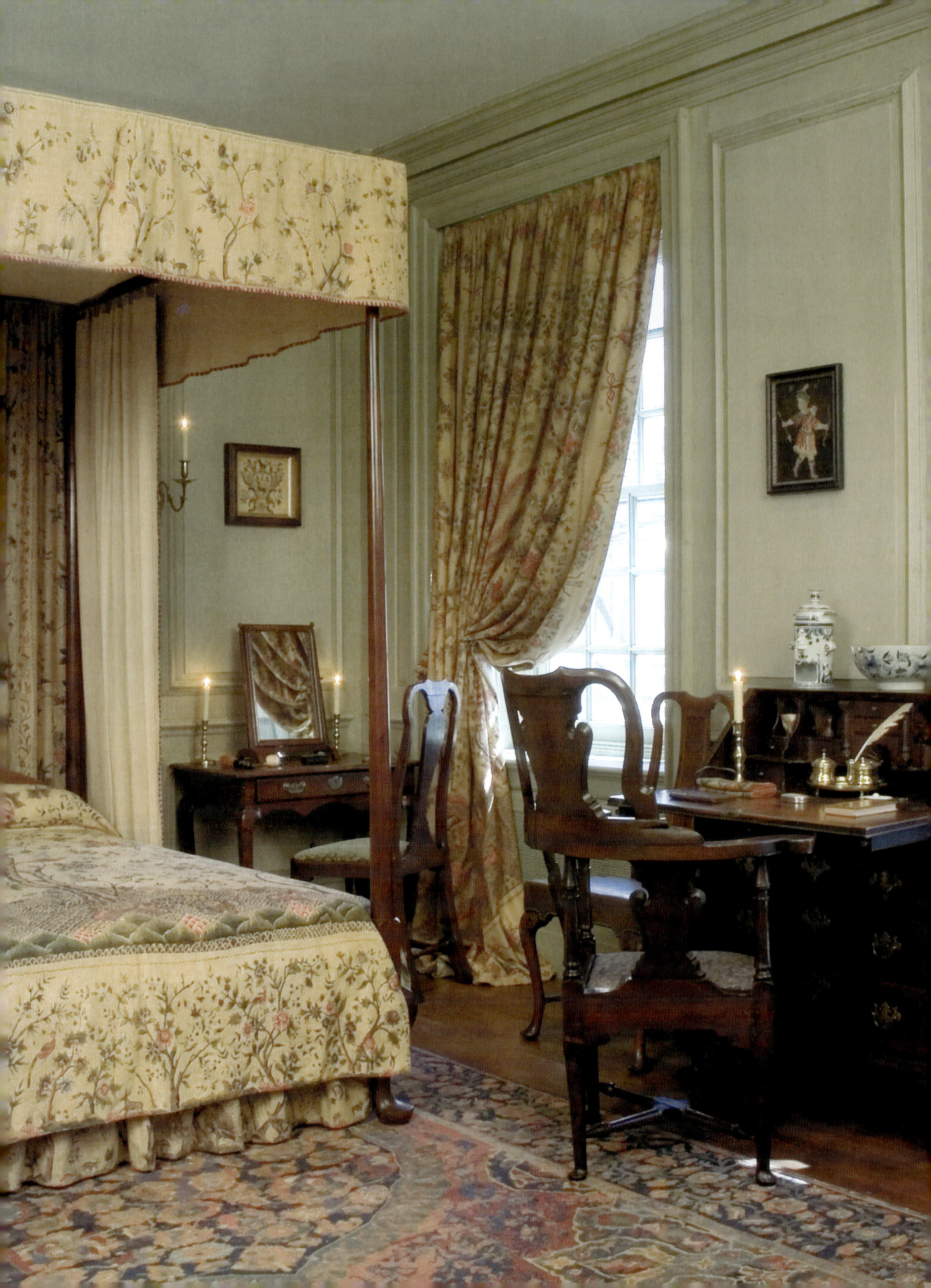

Cecil Bedroom

Cecil County, Maryland, circa 1740

9′ 11″ high by 18′ wide by 14′ 8″ long

The Cecil Bedroom was Mr. du Pont's bedroom, one of his favorite rooms, and a special place at Winterthur.

The splendid woodwork comes from a house situated on the northernmost point of the Chesapeake Bay, along the shipping route to Baltimore and Philadelphia. The original owner was a miller who evidently prospered from trade at this key juncture.

Built as a parlor addition to an existing house, the main wall as installed at Winterthur features a fireplace surrounded by a bolection molding and flanked with engaged fluted Doric pilasters. Two symmetrically disposed arched doorways and engaged fluted corner pilasters complete this elevation (not shown).

The Cecil Bedroom has fully paneled walls, creating a warm environment for a bedroom.

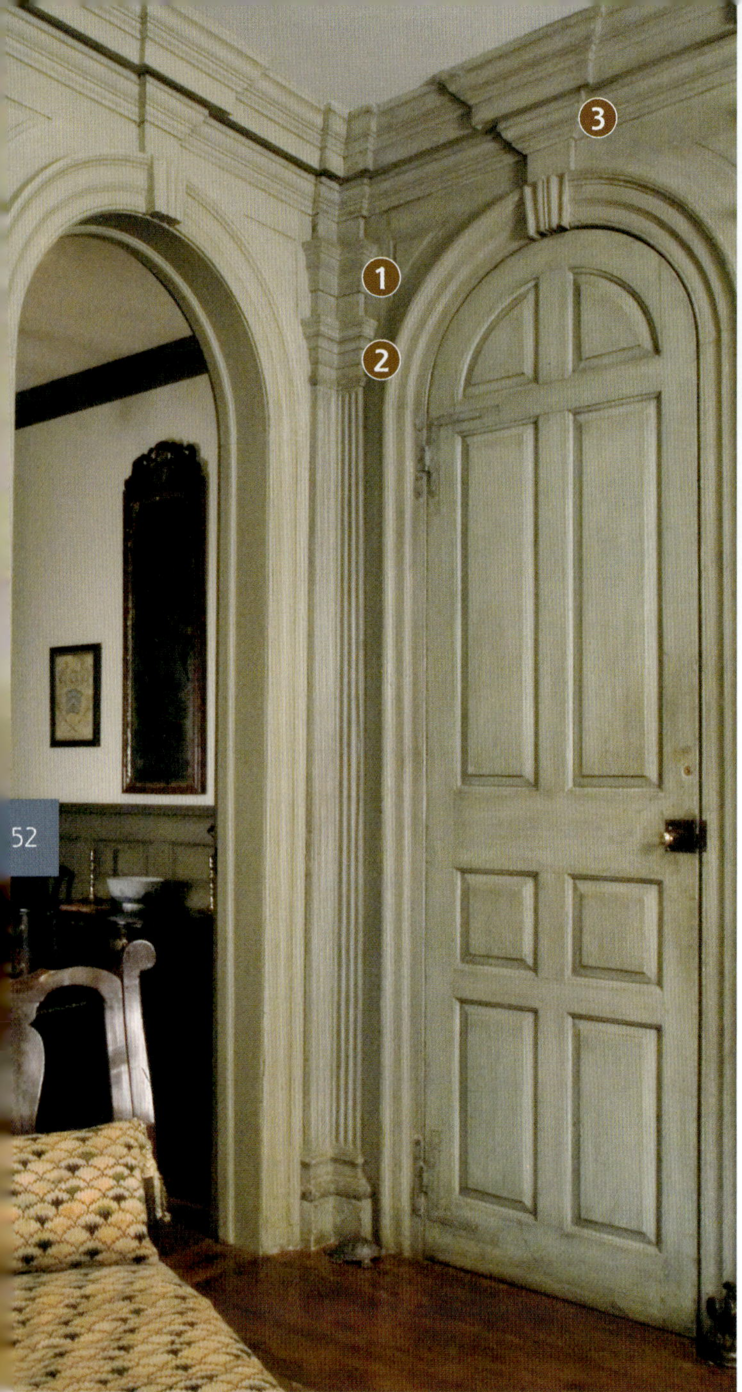

Cornice

The cornice projects six inches and is seven inches high. It breaks forward at each pilaster and keystone, tying all of the room's elements together. An interesting secondary architrave (1) is found above the pilaster capitals (2), allowing the architrave of the pilasters and that of the arched doors to align (detail on facing page).

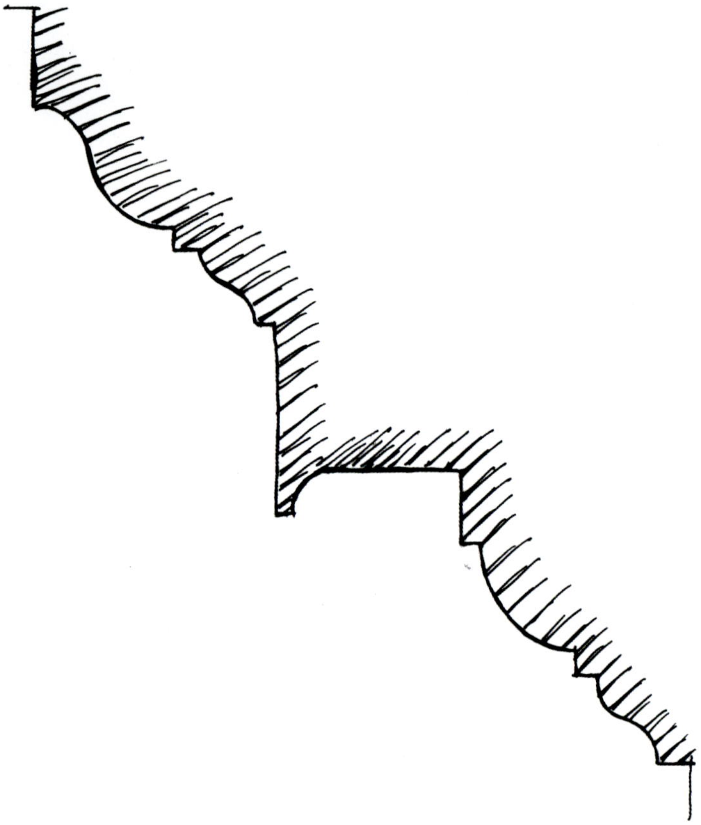

Architraves

The cupboard doors on either side of the fireplace are eight-panel doors with an arched top, left. The door architrave is scaled correctly for the doors, being about one-sixth of the width of the door opening and projecting about two inches from the wall surface. Over the doors, the arch is supported and connected to the cornice with a keystone (3).

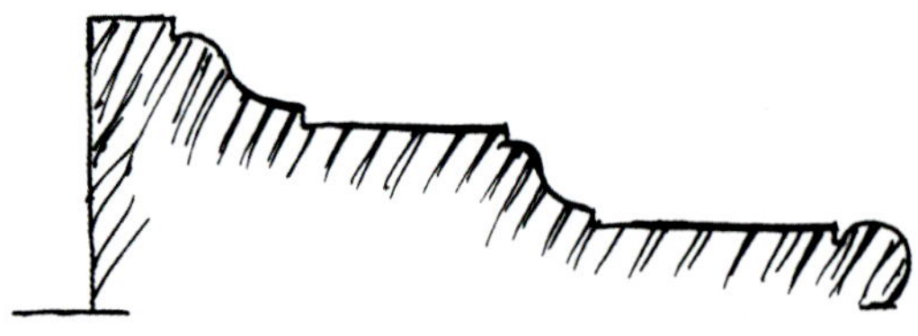

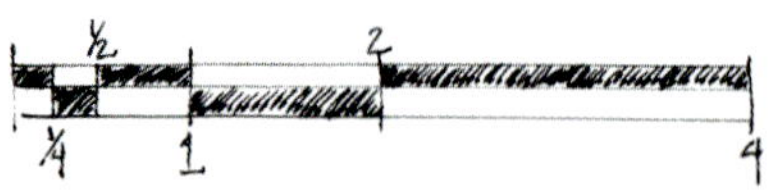

Panels

The wall panels are raised, similar to the paneling in the Gidley and Bowers rooms (pages 76, 46) and project from the surface of the stiles and rails. A chair rail wraps the room at a height of thirty-six inches and divides the upper and lower panel registers.

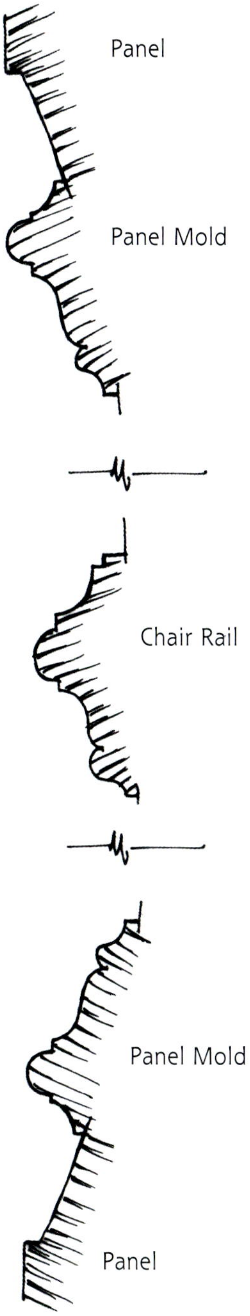

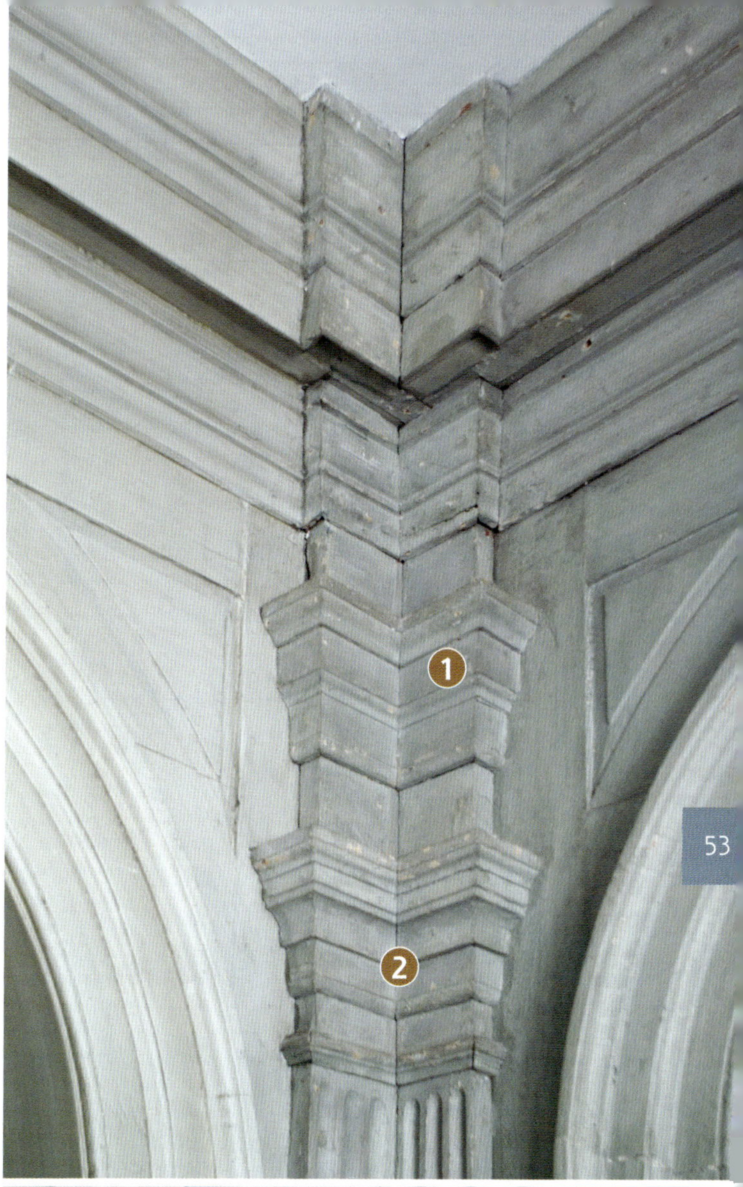

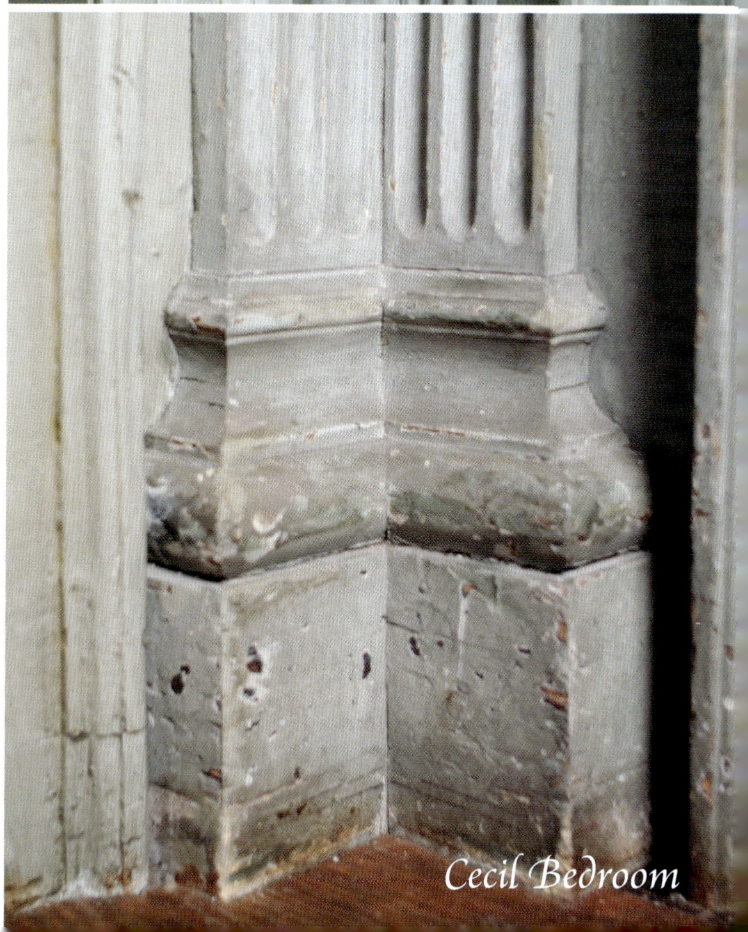

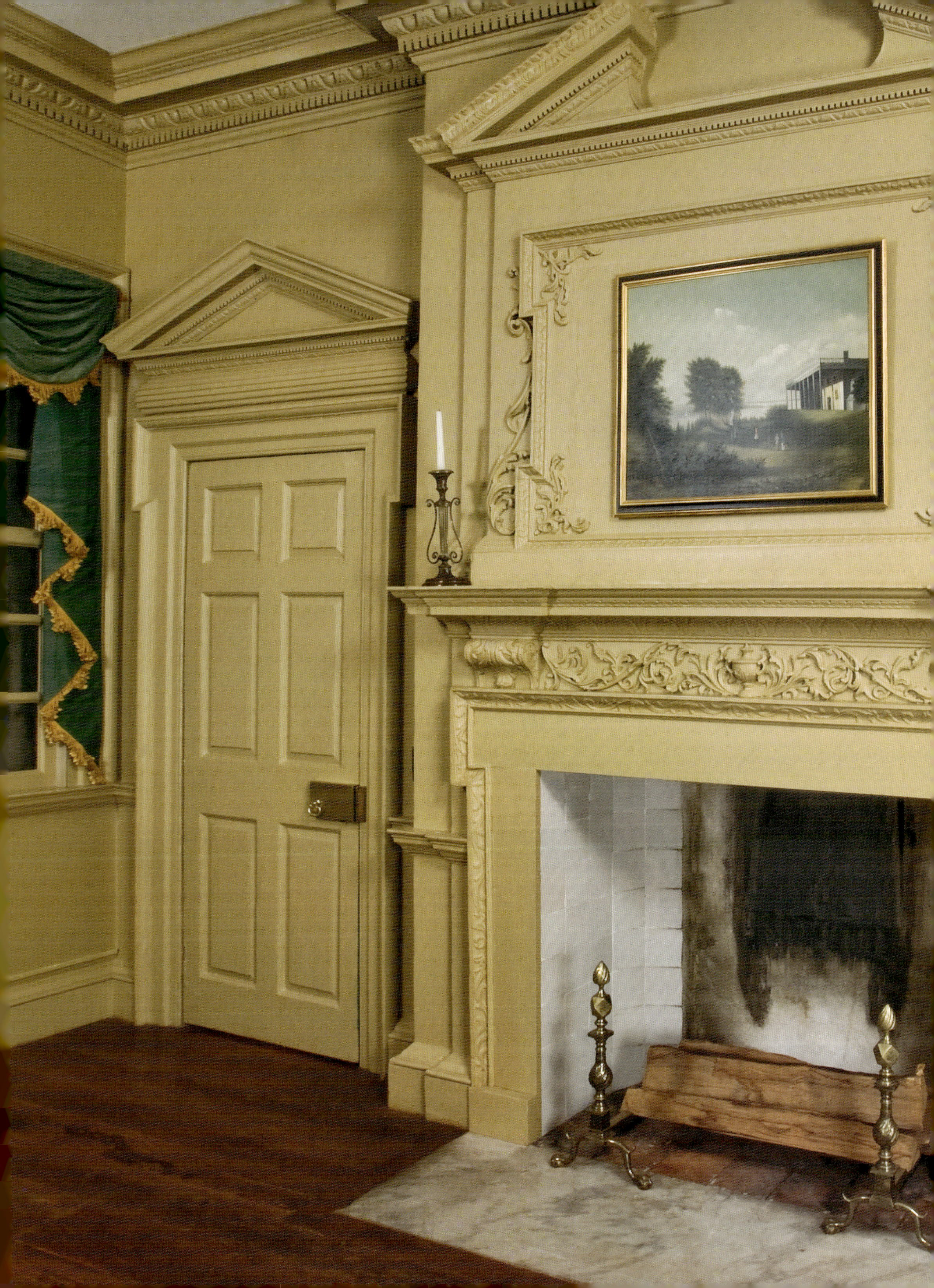

Charleston Dining Room

William Burrows House, Charleston, South Carolina, 1772

11'7" tall by 27'2" wide by 19'9" long

The Charleston Dining Room comes from the William Burrows House, a prominent residence on Broad Street in Charleston, South Carolina. Burrows, a judge and lawyer, was prosperous enough to afford the finely carved moldings and decorative elements ornamenting this room, which was probably his parlor. The three-story Burrows house was designed for hospitality and entertaining, important aspects of the southern lifestyle then as well as now.

The canonic details and sophisticated design reflect the influence or use of pattern or builder's books. The Palladian window, for example, is similar to one found in Isaac Ware's book, *A Complete Body of Architecture*, published in 1756.

Originally a parlor, the Charleston Dining Room is lavishly decorated with rich, carved details.

Fireplace Wall

The fireplace wall (previous page) is symmetrical, composed with a pedimented doorway on either side of the fireplace surround. These are Ionic with a pulvinated, or cushion-shaped, and fluted frieze. The mantel frieze is decorated with carvings of scrolls and natural forms. Above the mantel, a panel with crossetted corners is softened with more foliated scrolls and accentuated with a broken pediment. Exuberant and rich, the decorative carving is as fine as that of the Blackwell Parlor (page 36).

Entrance

Along one wall, a graceful elliptical arch frames a Palladian, or Serlian, window. Two pilasters (foreground) that rest on the dado support the elliptical arch in the wall. This dado, or wainscot, continues into the entryway, and two additional pilasters frame the Palladian window.

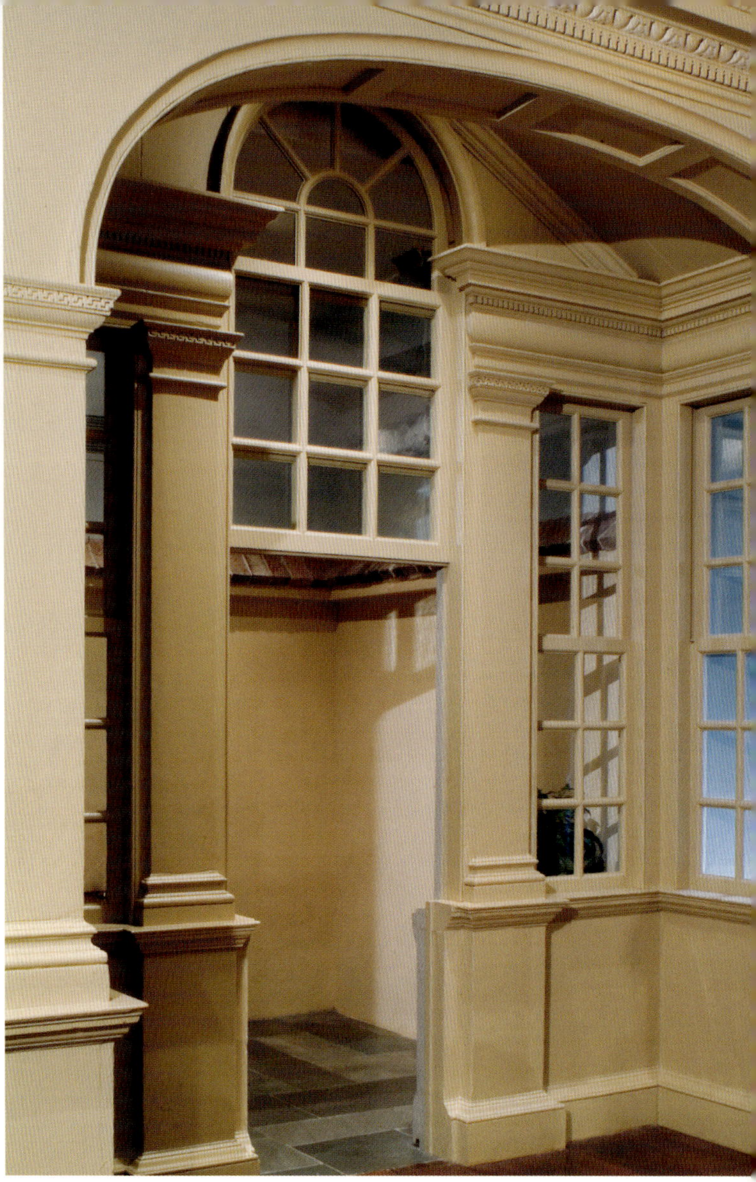

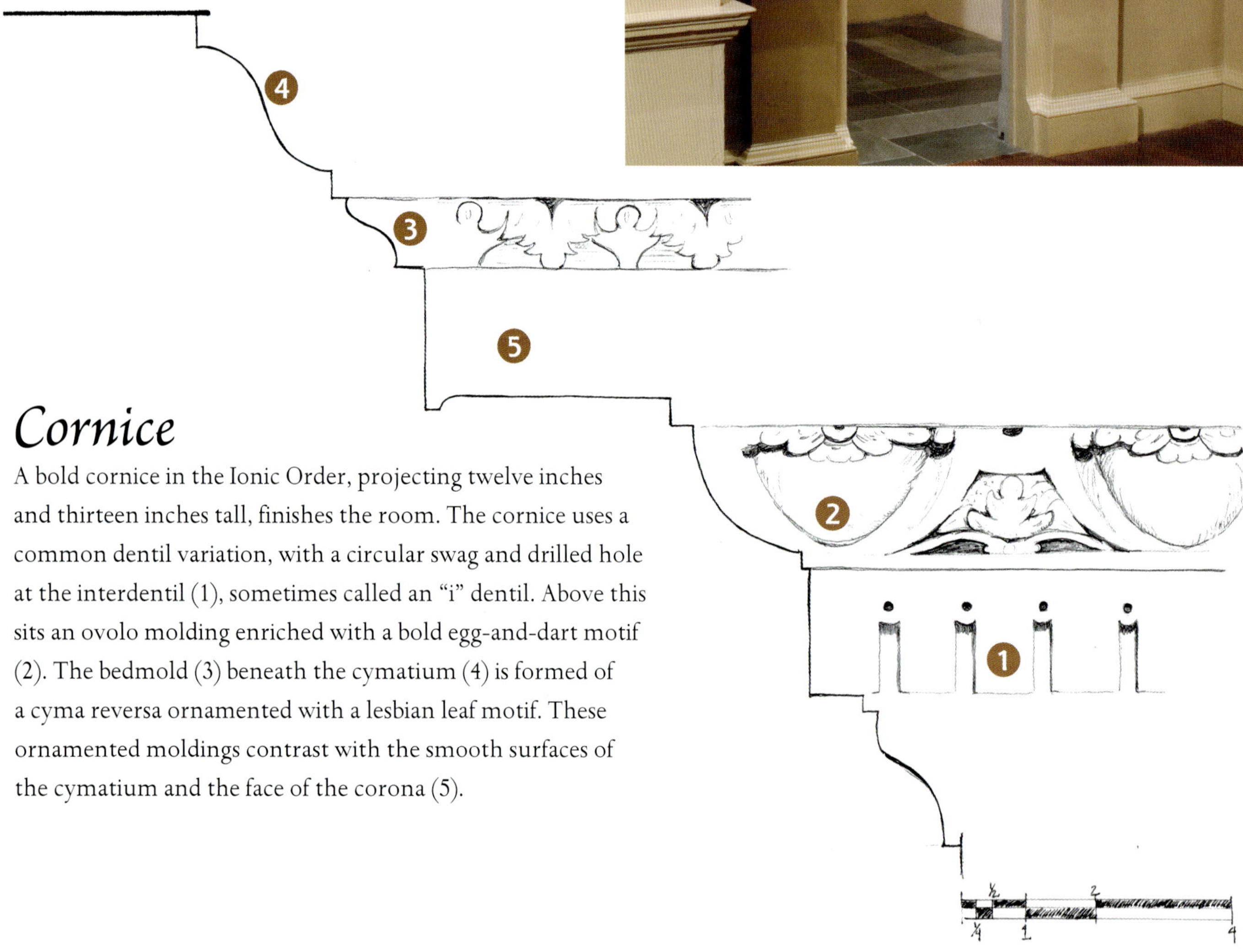

Cornice

A bold cornice in the Ionic Order, projecting twelve inches and thirteen inches tall, finishes the room. The cornice uses a common dentil variation, with a circular swag and drilled hole at the interdentil (1), sometimes called an "i" dentil. Above this sits an ovolo molding enriched with a bold egg-and-dart motif (2). The bedmold (3) beneath the cymatium (4) is formed of a cyma reversa ornamented with a lesbian leaf motif. These ornamented moldings contrast with the smooth surfaces of the cymatium and the face of the corona (5).

Panels

Upper panels and a large chair rail and base molding articulate the room. Such strongly projecting moldings at the base of the room support the equally bold cornice moldings at the top of the room.

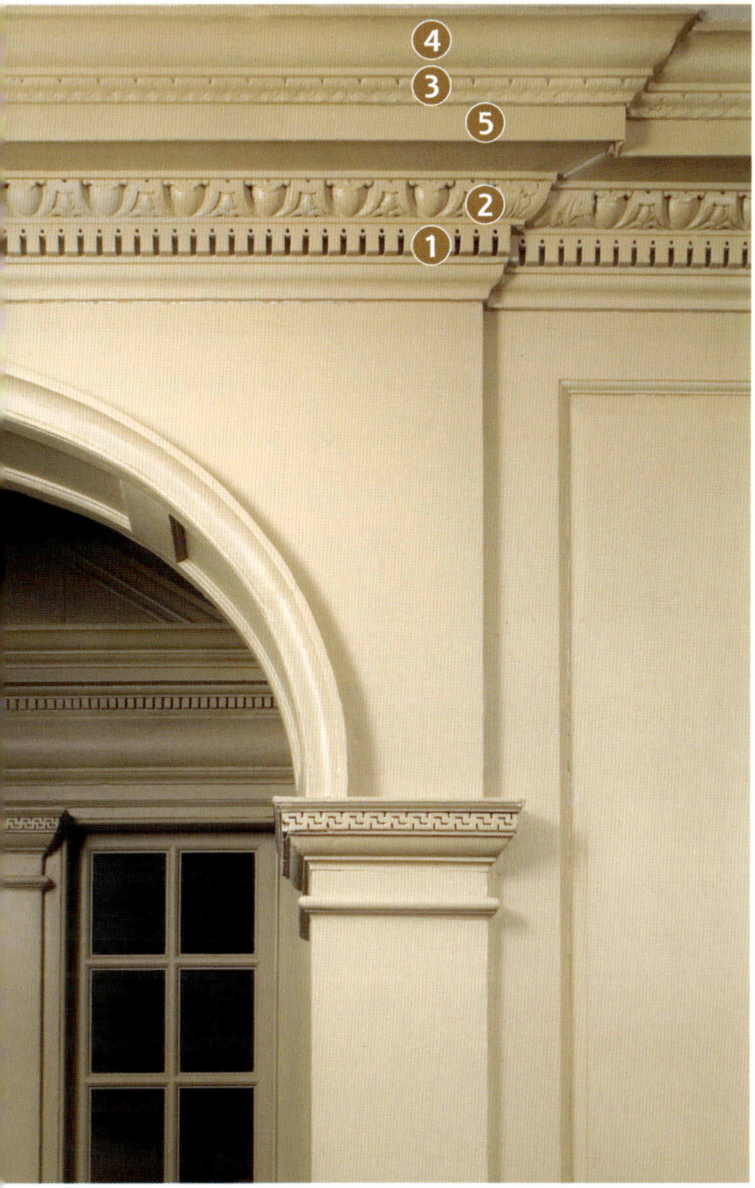

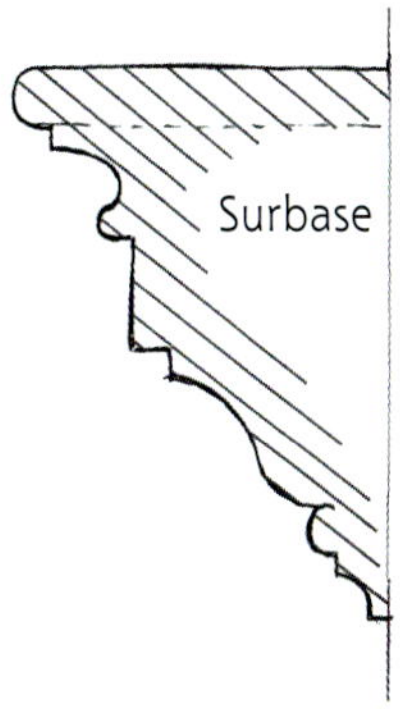

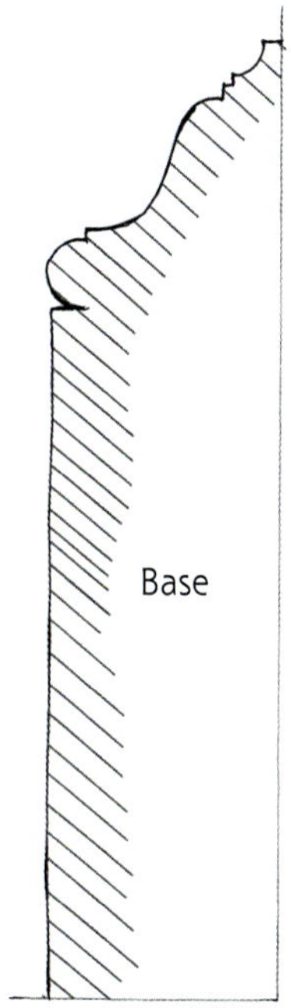

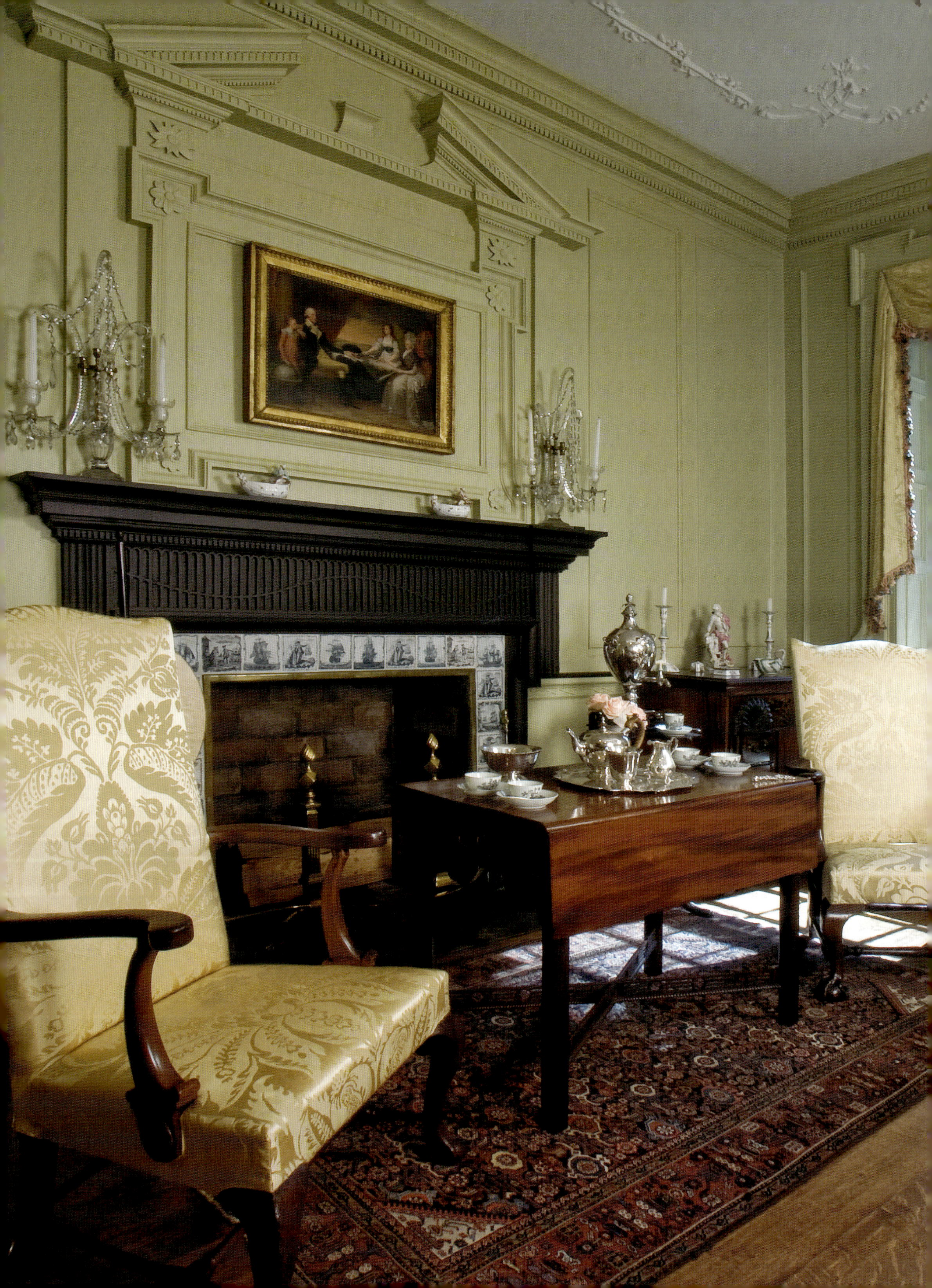

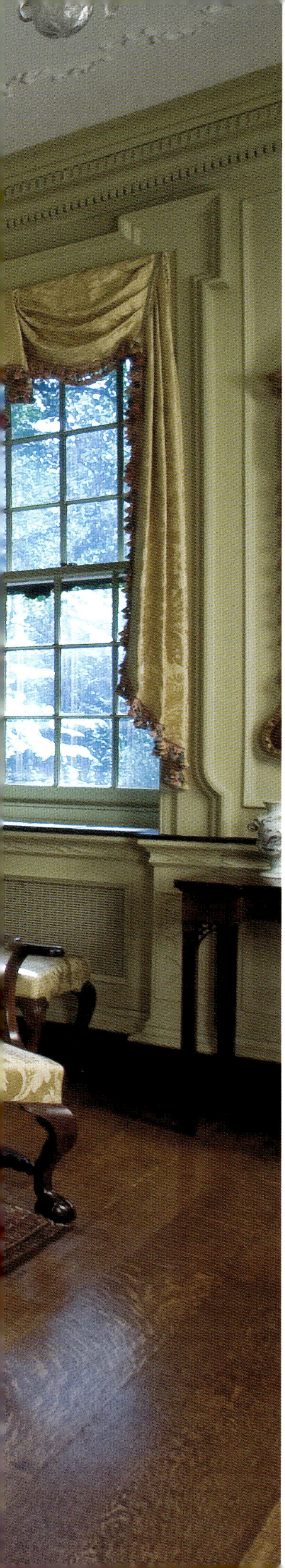

Chestertown Room

Chestertown, Maryland, circa 1790

10' 7" high by 14' 4" wide by 15' 3" long

By the mid-eighteenth century, Chestertown was one of Maryland's leading ports and home to many prosperous merchants and lawyers. The Chestertown Room at Winterthur comes from the second floor of a house built along the Chester River at 107 Water Street. According to the Historic American Buildings Survey's documentation of this house, construction was likely begun between 1784 and 1787 and may have incorporated an older structure. Thomas Smyth purchased this property in 1784 and sold it to his son, Robert Smyth, who in turn sold it in 1787 to Peregrine Letherbury, who commenced or completed construction. In later years, this house came to be known as River House.

The Chestertown Room is an exceptional interior, carefully composed, with richly carved details. The room reflects late Georgian style architecture and includes Adamesque and exotic motifs popularized in pattern books such as William Pain's *The Practical Builder*, published in London in 1774, and later editions.

A wainscot wrapping the entire room transforms into a pedestal beneath the window architraves. Full-height panels above the wainscot and dramatic window surrounds lend height to the room. Two doors are given attention with broken pediments in the overdoors, echoing the mantel. Throughout the room, Chinese fretwork, rope moldings, delicate dentils, and beads and reels balance the sobriety of the fully paneled walls.

The Chestertown Room is a sophisticated room full of graceful details. Immediately elegant and comfortable, it demonstrates the power of good design.

The Chestertown Room mixes a range or ornamental motifs, all elegantly complementing each other.

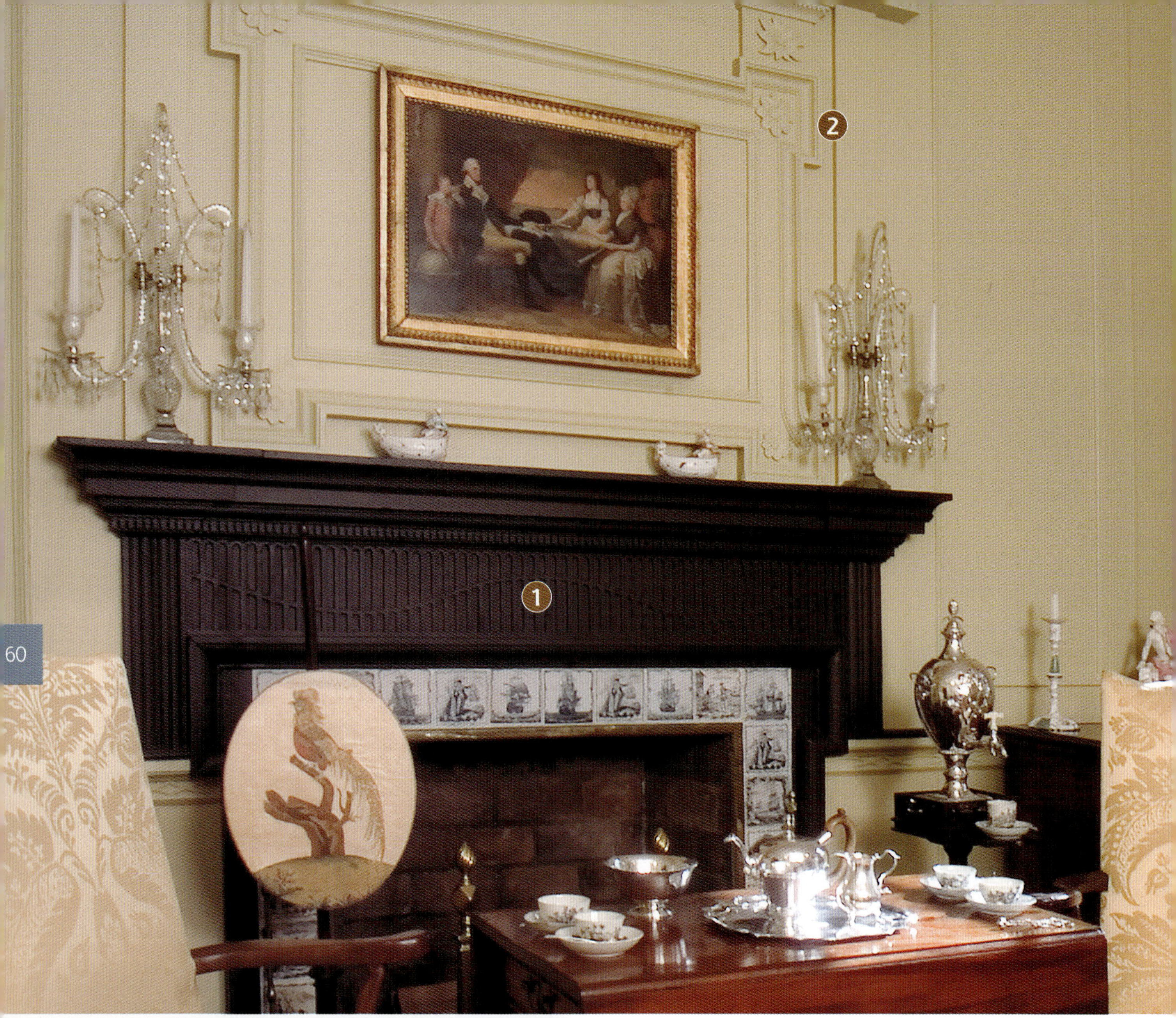

Mantel

A tall fluted frieze and overlaid serpentine pattern (1) articulate the mantelpiece. Above, a crossetted frame (2) adorned with flowers and a broken pediment (previous page) form the overmantel. The inspiration for the mantel likely comes from William Pain's pattern book, *The Practical Builder*, published in London in 1774. The room's mantel and room composition are also similar to Plate 23 in Volume II of Abraham Swan's *Designs in Architecture*, published in London in 1757.

Cornice

The cornice is composed of recognizable molding forms ornamented with Classical motifs. A small cavetto (3) forms the crown as in the Doric Order. A bead-and-reel (4) above a cavetto separate it from the corona below. The corona's face is elaborated with a sort of tongue-and-dart pattern and small drilled holes (5). Beneath, a bedmold is formed of an ovolo (6), a row of dentils (7), and a cavetto (8). These dentils employ the small drill hole and swag at the interdentil, sometimes referred to as an "i" dentil for the shape made by the thin space between the dentils and the dot drilled above.

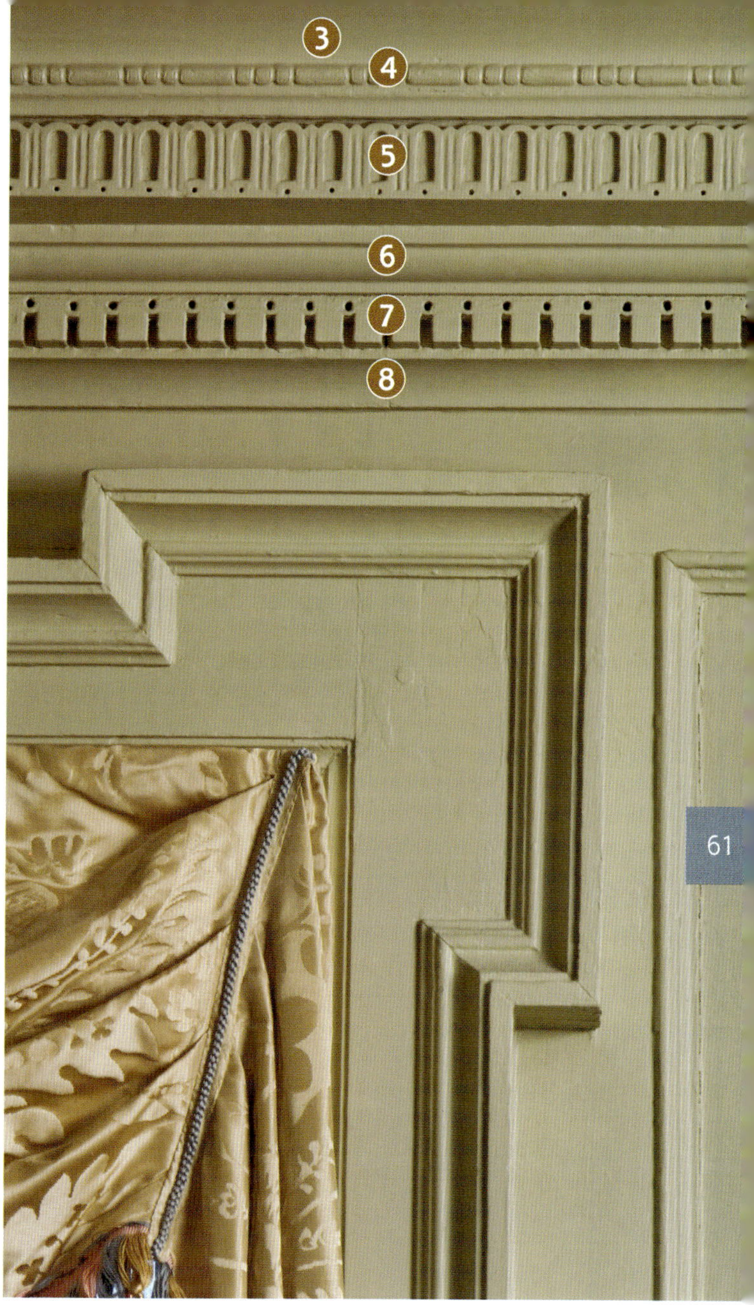

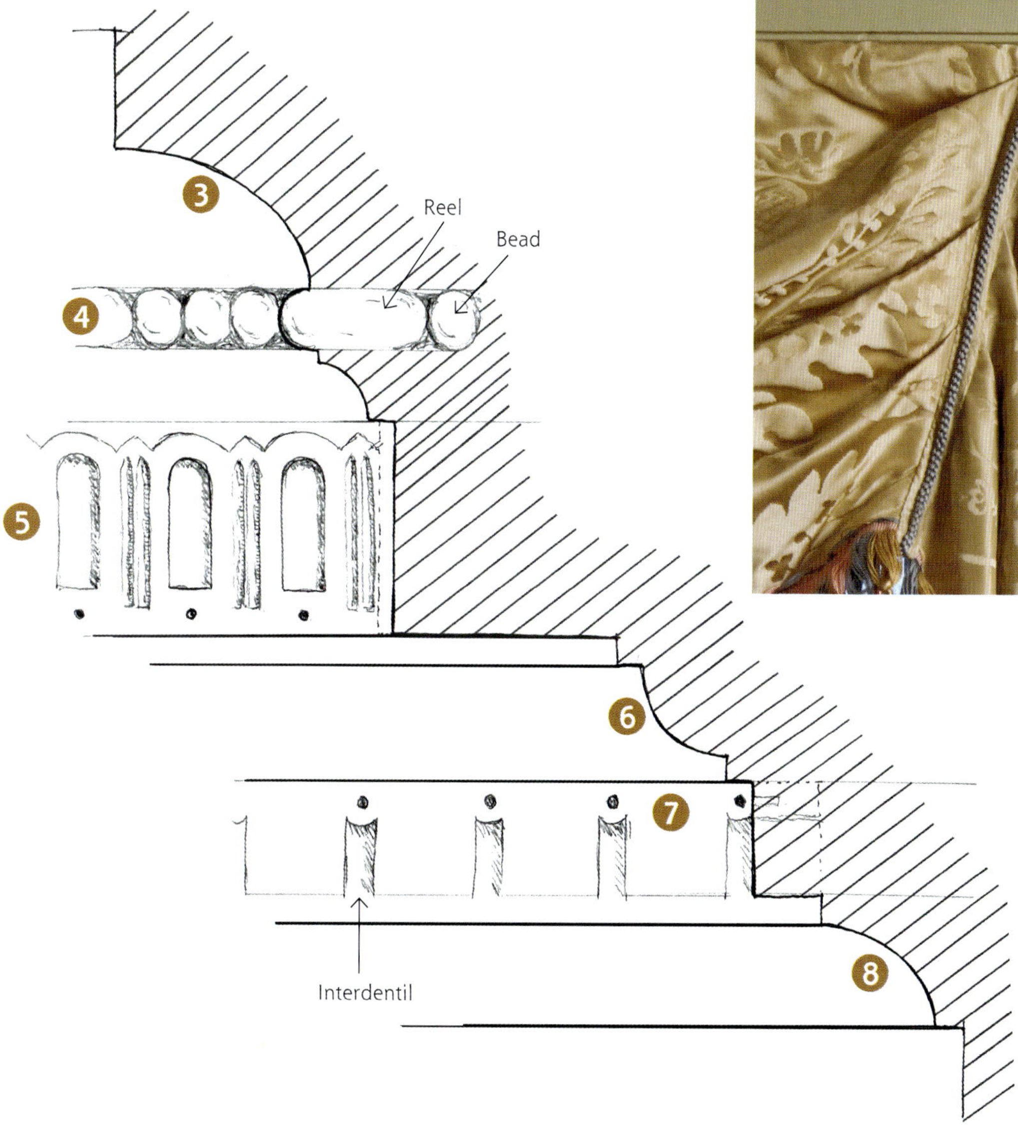

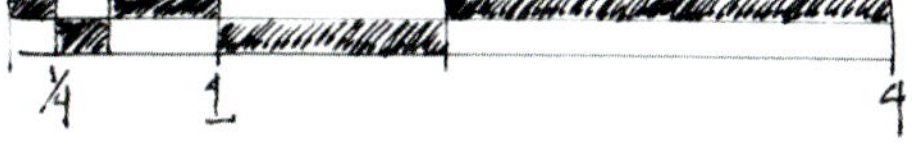

Architraves

Set against the fully paneled walls, a refined architrave highlights the door and window openings. Concurrent with the room's cornice, the architrave's outermost molding is a cavetto (1) and is separated from the first fascia by a bead and small cyma reversa (2). Another cavetto (3) defines the separation of the two fascias. The overdoor is composed of a broken pediment corresponding to both the overmantel and the exact profiles and articulation of the room cornice, though in the overdoors and overmantel it is scaled down appropriately. The window architraves gracefully curve outward to rest on the chair rail (4, next page), as do the door architraves as they join their plinths. This curve modifies the bottom corners of a crossetted frame and lends a baroque aspect to the room.

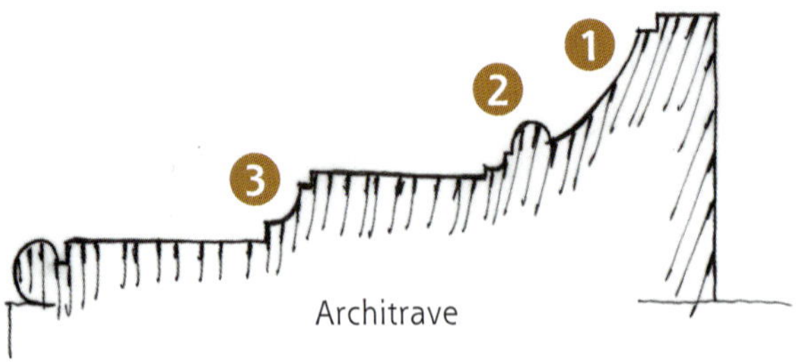

Architrave

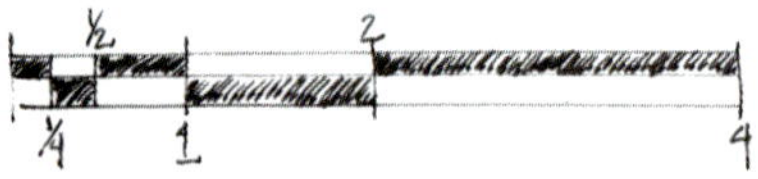

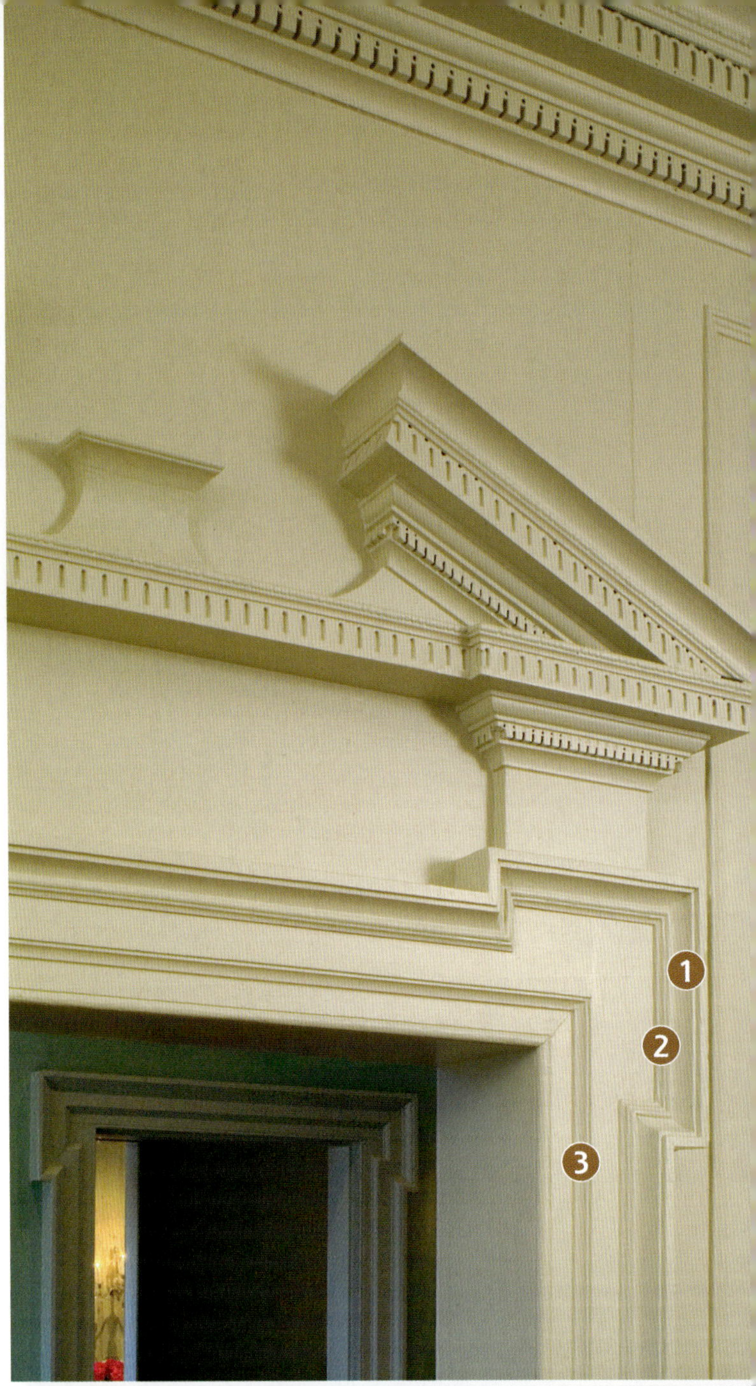

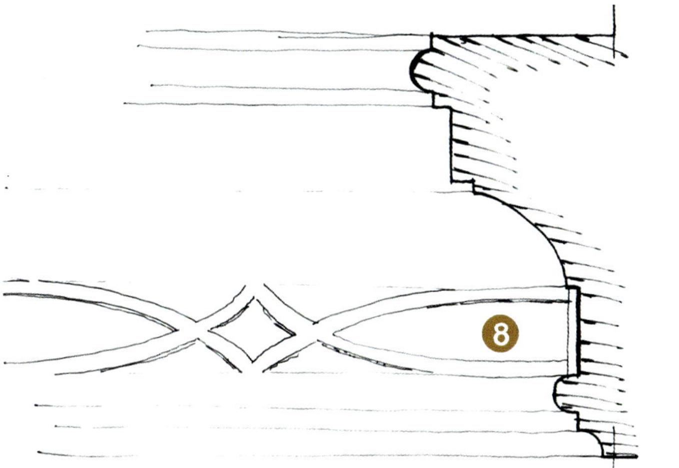

Panel Mold

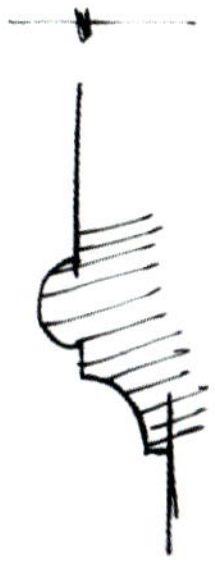

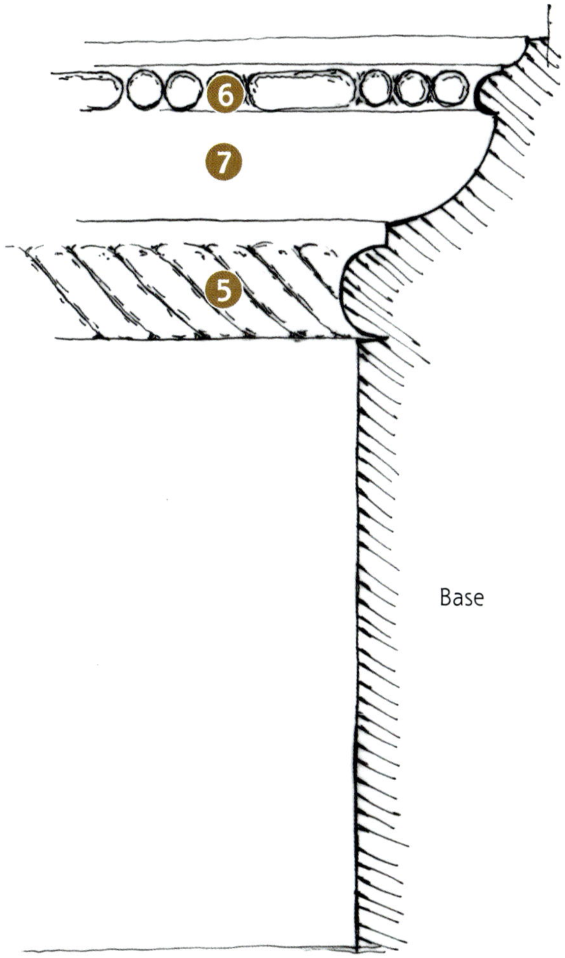

Base

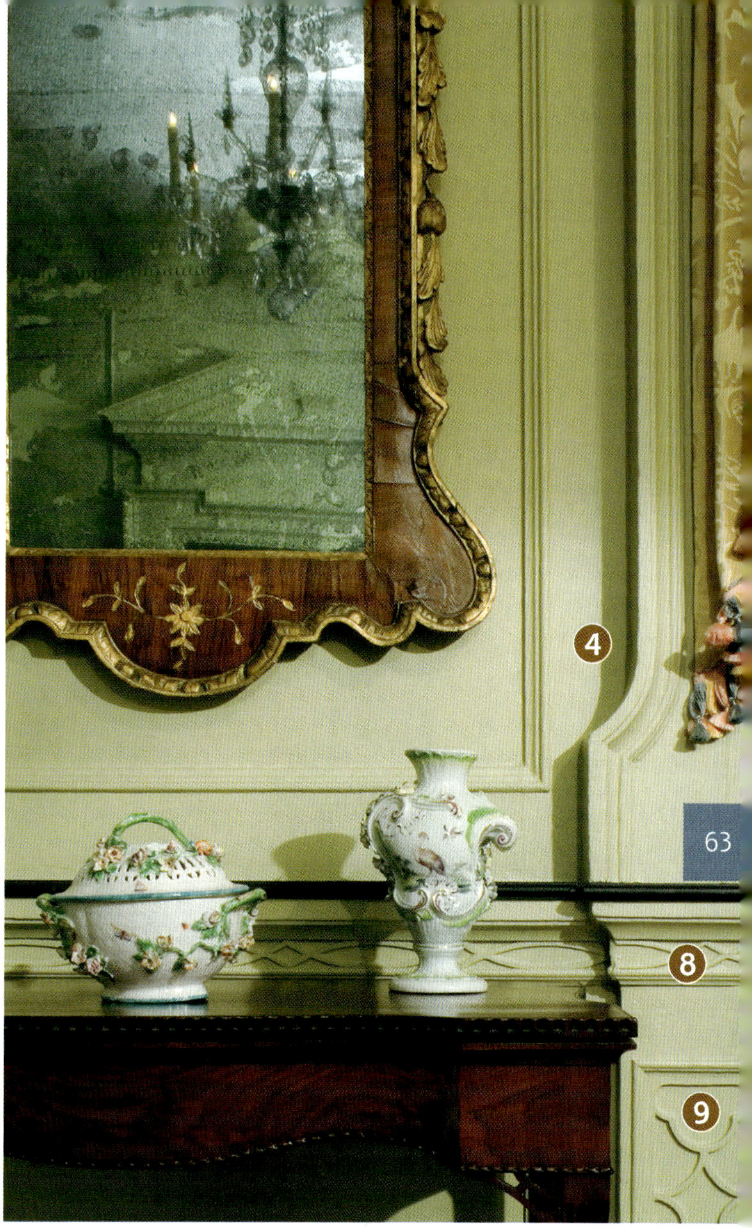

Wainscot

The base molding is carved with a rope detail on the torus (5) and a bead and reel (6) at the astragal. Again, ornamentation such as the bead-and-reel, as well as the use of the cavetto (7) in the base cap, ties this into the rest of the room's design through repetition of forms. The surbase includes a fretwork design (8) with diamonds and elongated ovals under the cap. And similar Chinese-inspired fretwork (9) adorns the panels of the pedestals supporting the window architraves, lending an exotic, sophisticated character to the room.

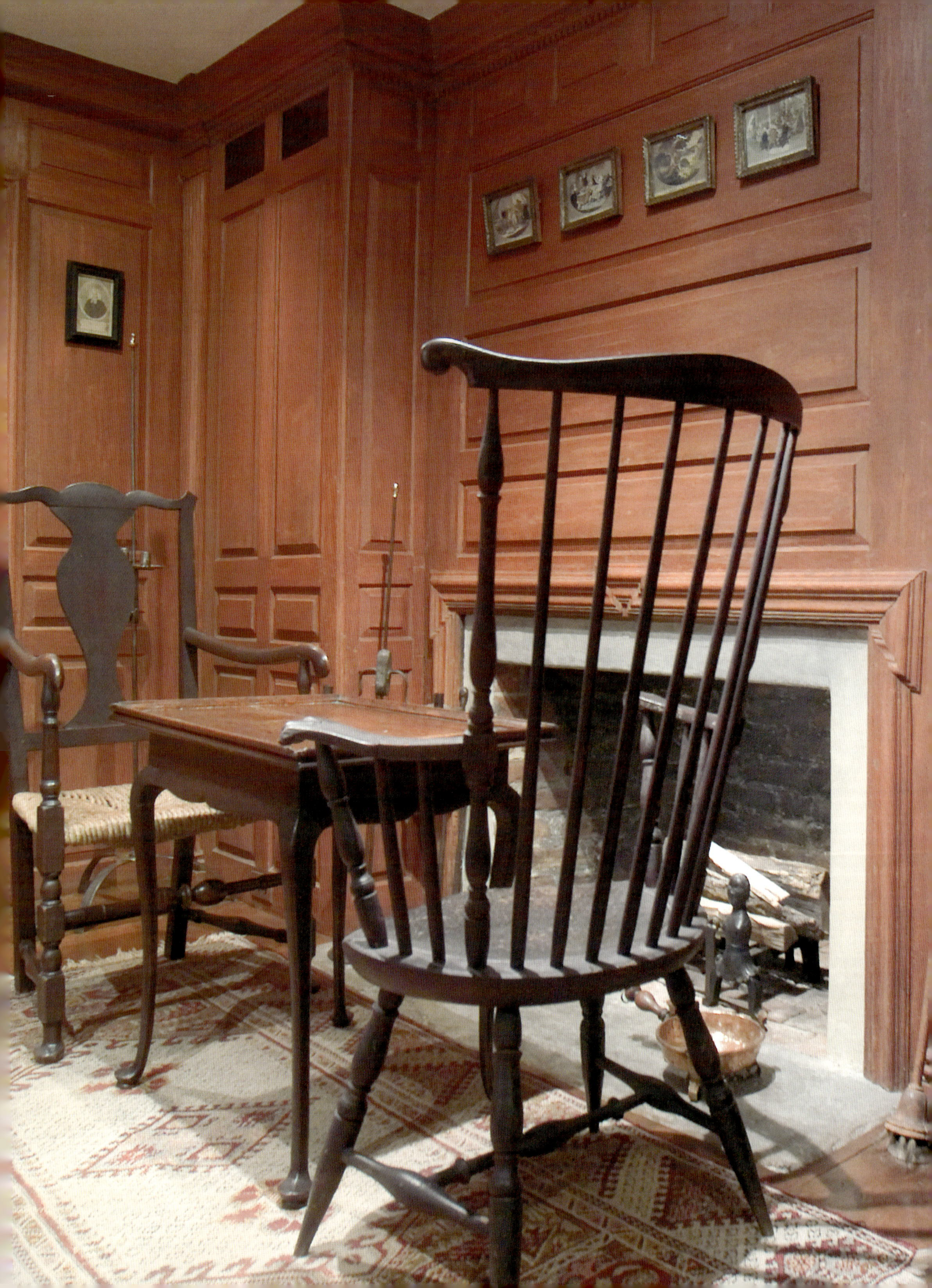

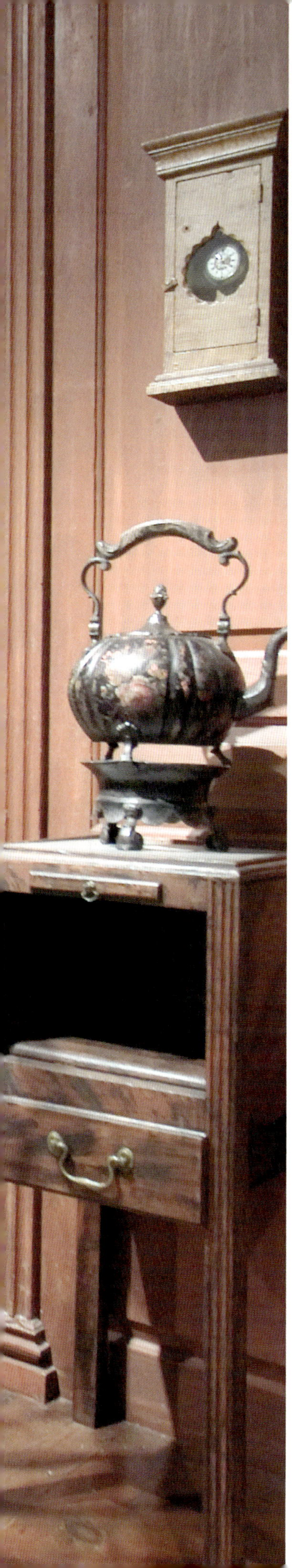

Dunlap Room

Bedford, New Hampshire, 1777

7' 4" high by 15' 4" wide by 10' 11" long

The woodwork in the Dunlap Room, named in honor of the Dunlap family of craftsmen and furniture makers, comes from a tavern-keeper's house in the small, rural New England town of Bedford, New Hampshire. The house was built for Thomas Chandler, who ran an inn on the road between the larger towns of Nashua and Concord. The inn became the first house of entertainment between the two larger cities. Bedford is also just fifty-two miles north of Boston on the Merrimack River. As a stopping spot for travelers among these three large cities, Chandler's Inn prospered.

Thomas Chandler hired John Dunlap to panel the parlor of his house. With five brothers, it is difficult to know which Dunlap family members did the work, though it may have been John and two brothers who worked for him as journeyman carpenters.

The design of the room, with its fully paneled walls and the lack of a mantelshelf on the fireplace, reflects earlier Georgian interiors. It is not uncommon for rural architecture of early America to reflect stylistic trends earlier than the date of construction.

Though its composition is not highly refined and its execution a little naive, the Dunlap Room's small scale and low eight-foot-high ceiling create an intimate space well suited to cold northern winters and useful as a model for a sitting room or keeping room today.

Low ceilings, fully panled walls, and informal composition create a relaxed, inviting setting in the Dunlap Room.

Cornice

One fluted pilaster (1) is on either side of the fireplace; the pilaster capitals (2) and the room cornice (3) are the same, with the cornice breaking forward over the pilasters. Though not canonic in composition, the cornice employs simple classical moldings to good effect. The cymatium (4) rests on a cyma reversa (5), beneath which a fascia (6) and ovolo (7) are found.

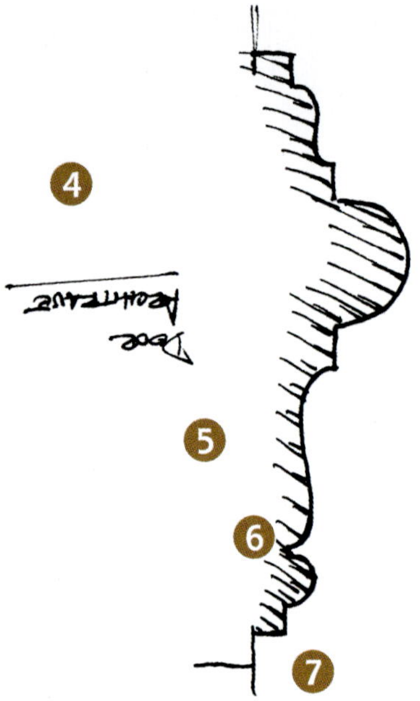

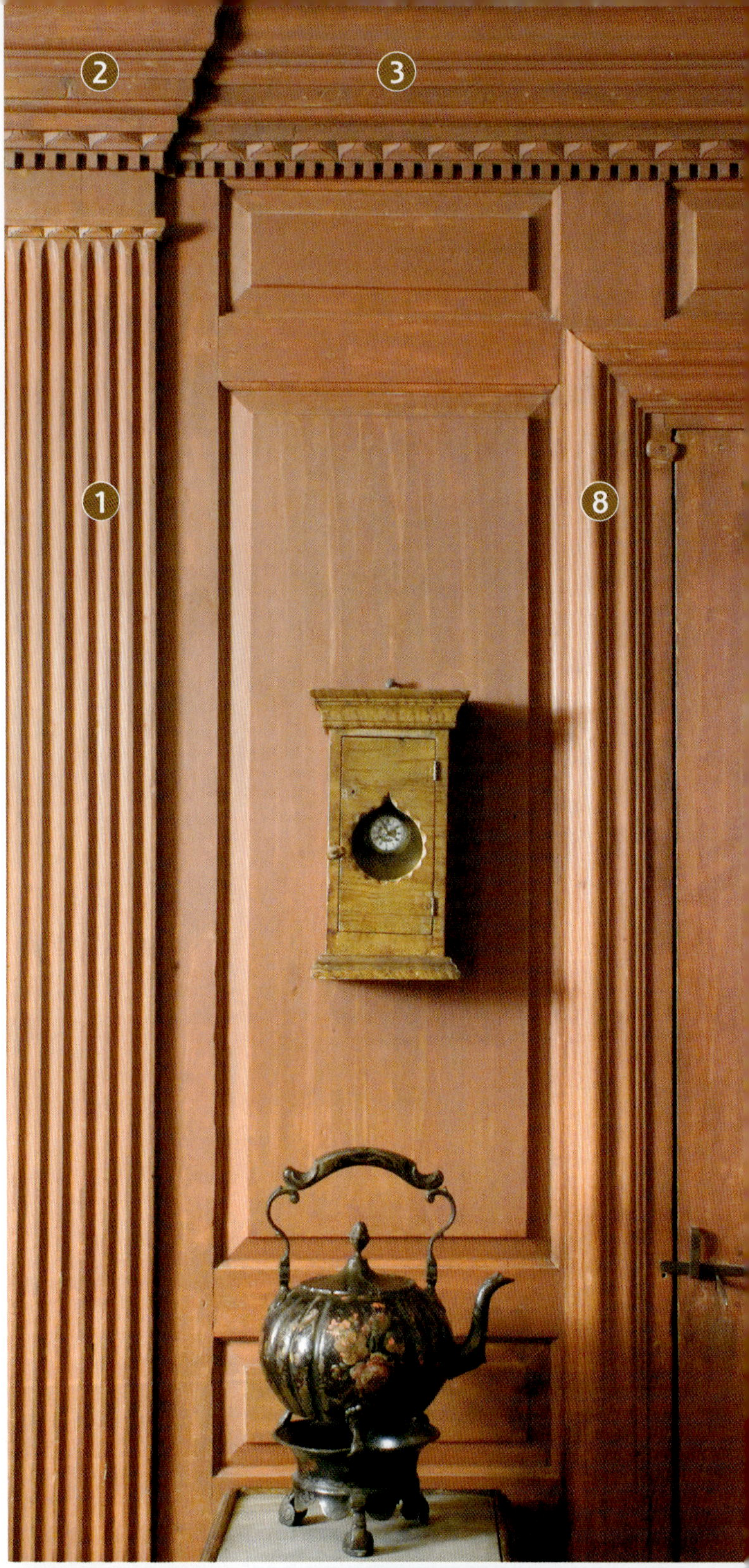

Architraves

The door and window architraves are related to the fireplace surround. All use alternating curves, separated by beads and fillets to create a bolection-like molding around the openings in the room (8). This differs from the other common Georgian architrave with a bead, two fascias, and a large backband.

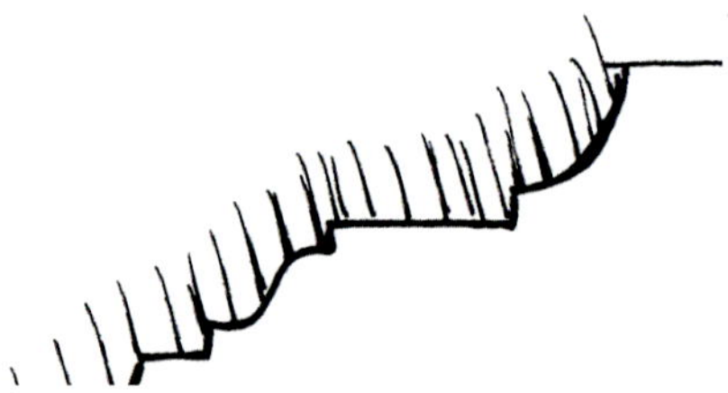

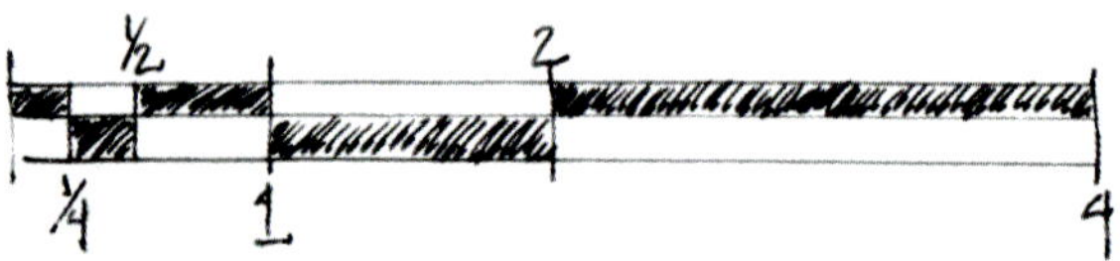

Wainscot

A small base, raised panels, and chair rail form the wainscot. Notice how the profile of the surbase, or chair rail (9), is related to the design of the door and window architraves with its alternating curves and fillets.

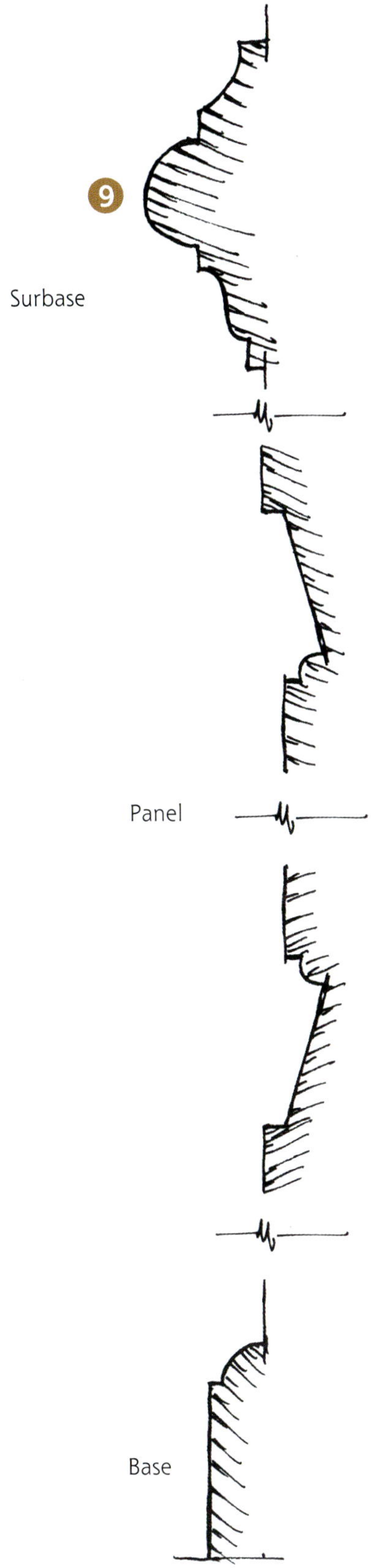

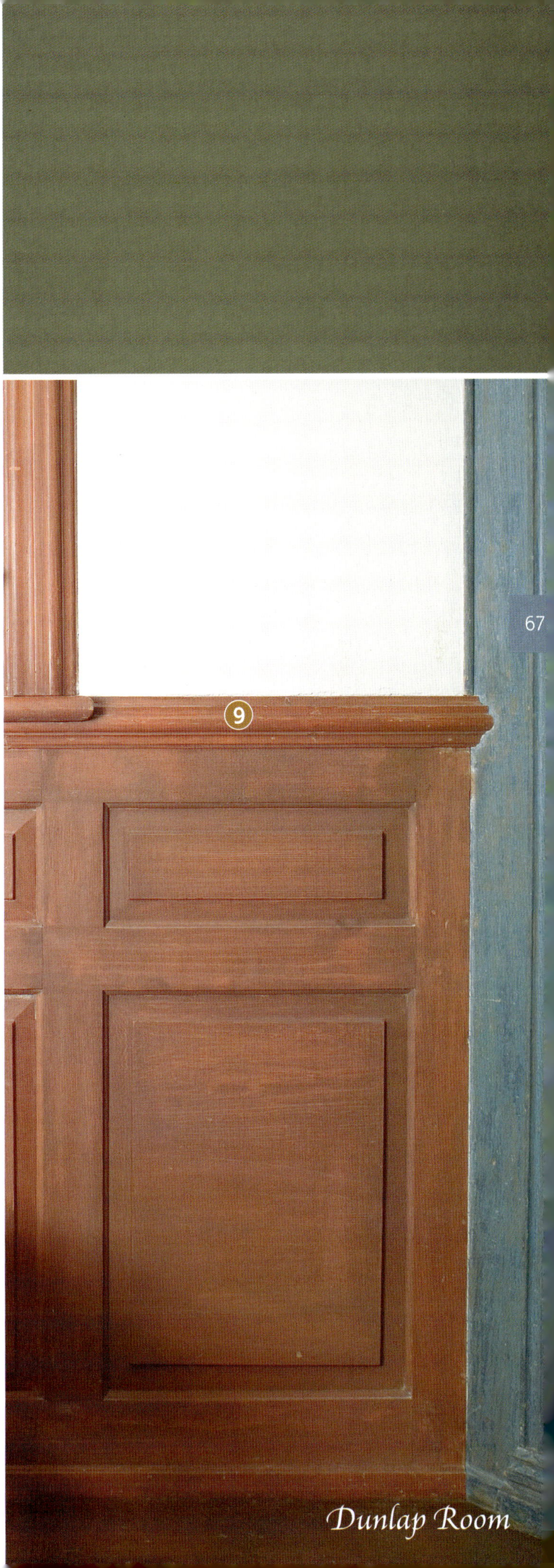

Dunlap Room

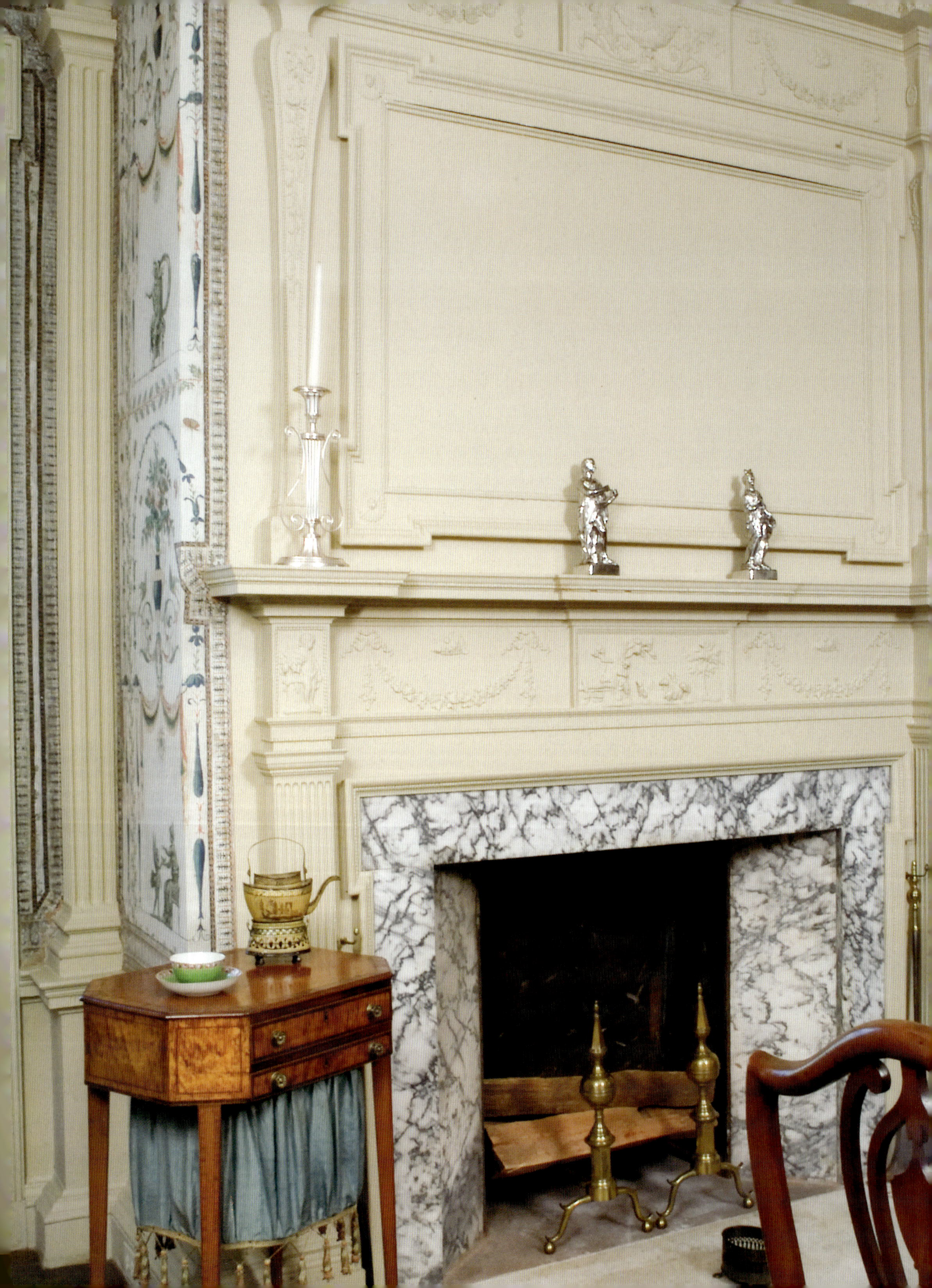

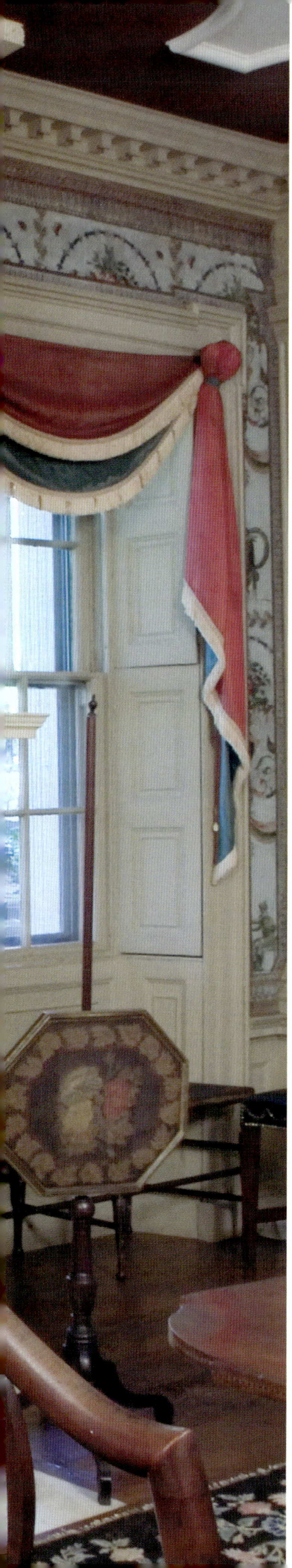

Federal Parlor

Phelps-Hatheway House, Suffield, Connecticut, 1794-1795

10'2" high by 18'6" wide by 20'3" long

Oliver Phelps apprenticed as a merchant, but through land speculation, he became America's largest landowner as well as a judge, bank owner, and congressman before dying in debtor's prison in 1809.

A tour de force of a Federal-style interior, each corner of Phelps' exquisite Federal Parlor reveals a complete order with pedestal, fluted pilaster, and full entablature including architrave and frieze. This fully revealed order shows how the order proportions the dado and cornice, which are the only two parts of the order to continue around the entire room. The pilaster, architrave, and frieze may be understood to be within the wall even when not visible.

The door surrounds have an overdoor with applied composition swags in the frieze. The cornices of the overdoors are consistent with the room cornice above, including the gouged carving in the corona.

Asher Benjamin, an architect and author of important builder's books, is known to have worked on the house as a young man, possibly as an apprentice under the builder, Thomas Hayden. Records show Phelps paid Benjamin for Ionic capitals.

Oliver Phelps was a visionary who bought the Hatheway house in 1788; he created the elegant Federal Parlor when he remodeled the house several years later.

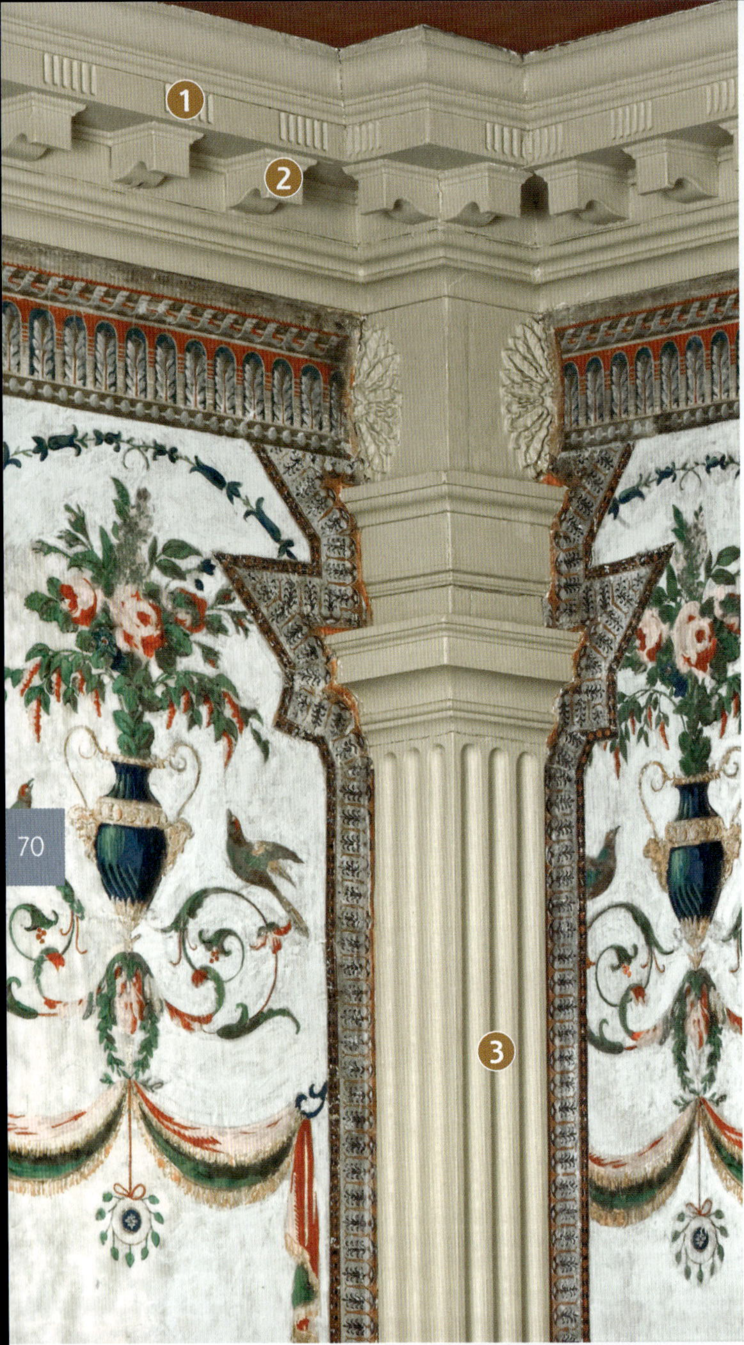

Cornice

The cornice moldings are small in scale, giving a delicate sensibility to the room. The gouging in the corona (1), which visually lightens that otherwise flat plane, enhances the delicate sensibility. Modillions (2) support the corona, an Ionic feature not usually found in the Doric Order, such as the modified Doric Order pilasters (3) used here. The pilasters sit on a pedestal (4) forming the dado, which continues around the room. Each corner pilaster has four flutes and an attic base.

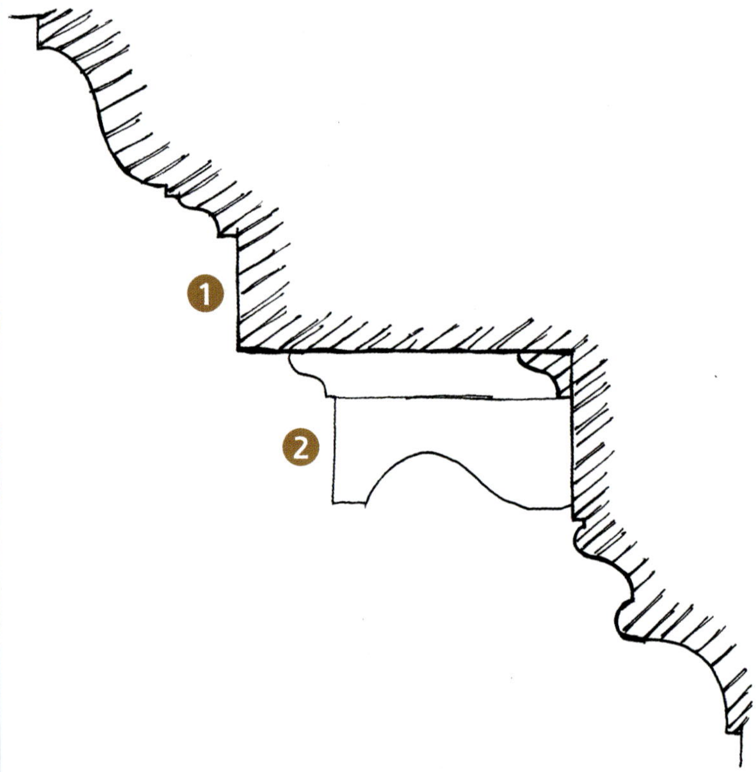

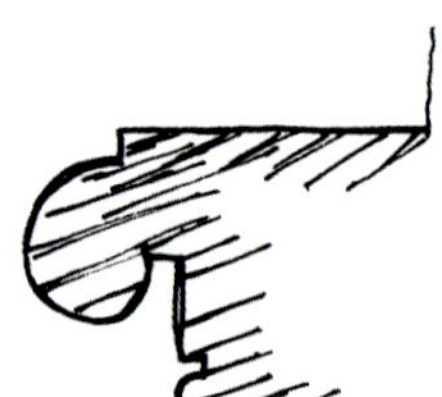

Architrave

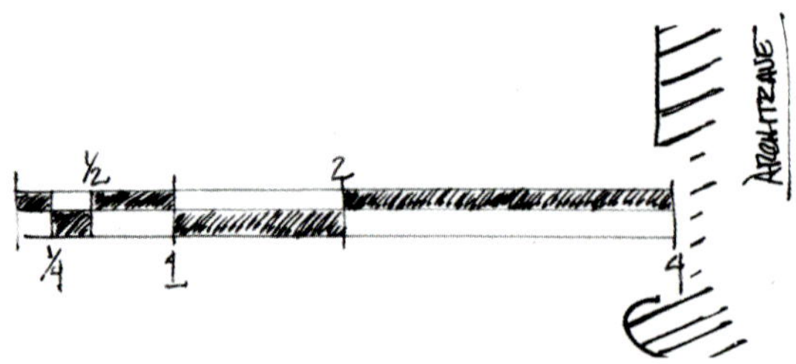

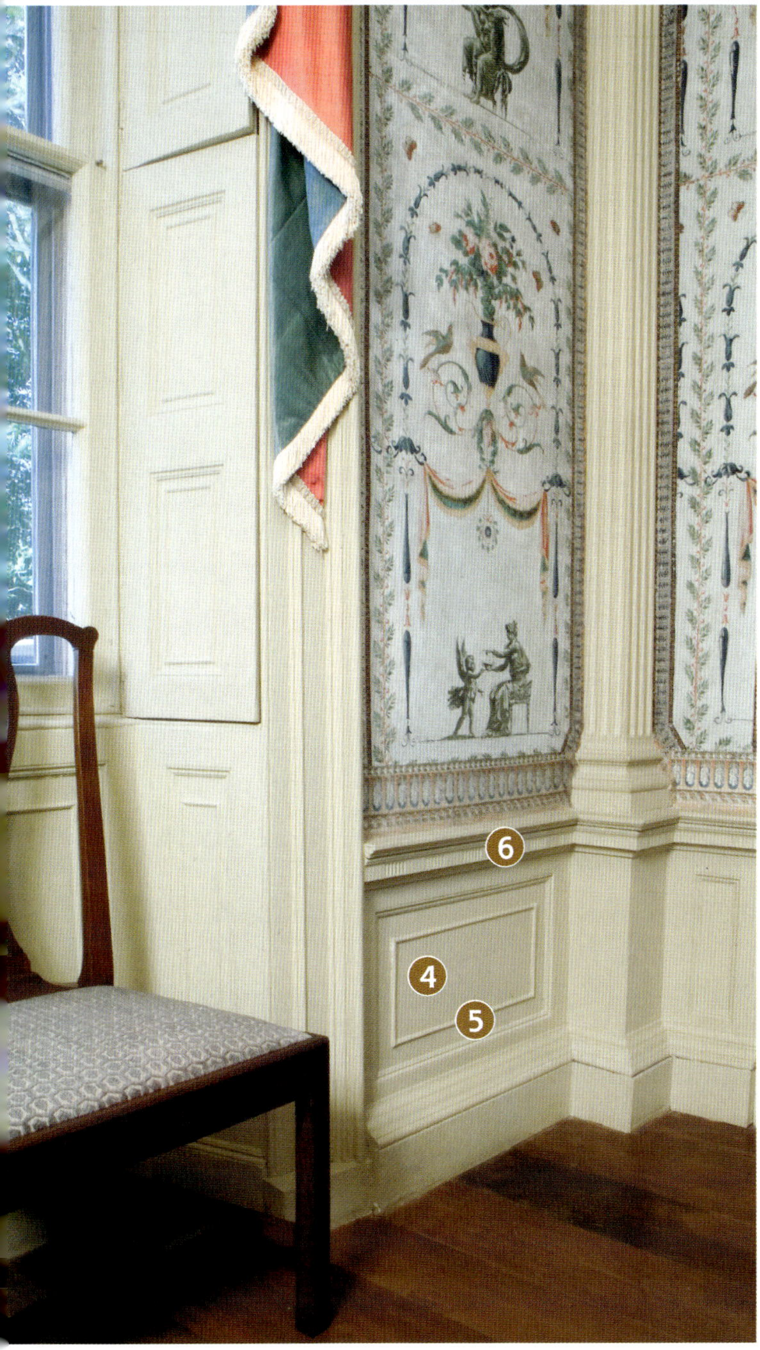

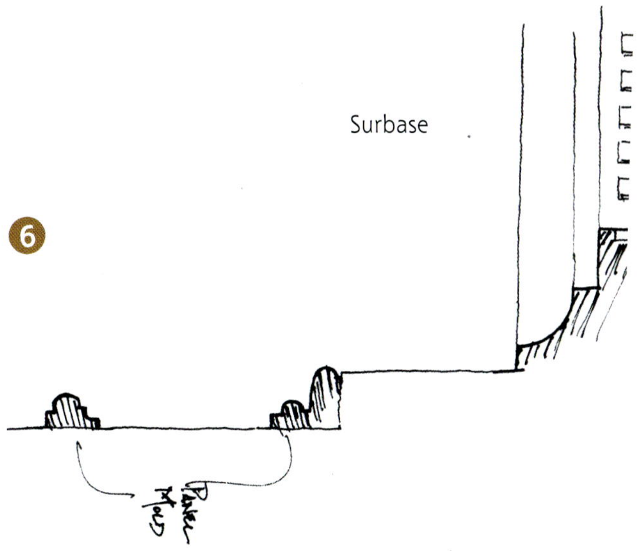

5
4
Panel Mold
5

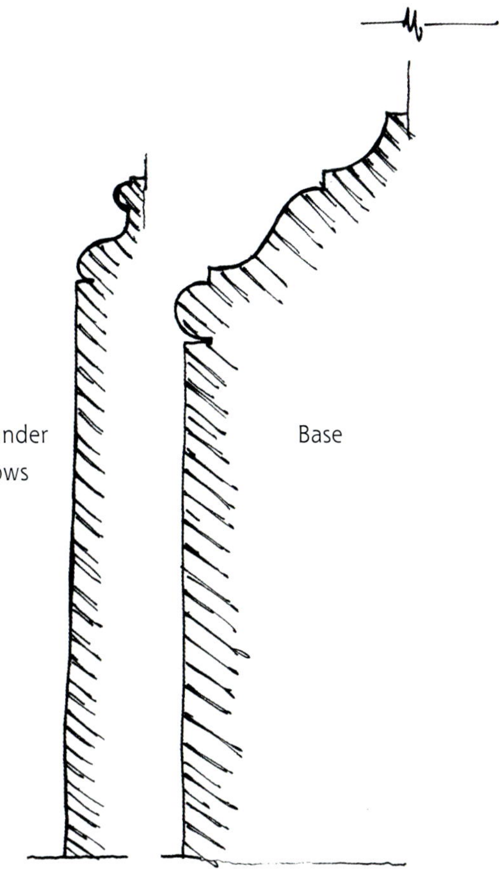

Wainscot & Base

The dado is made up of flat panels (4) and applied panel molds (5), common to the Federal style. The surbase (6) mimics the cornice with six vertical gouges in the fascias. The main base molding in the room is bold for the Federal style. Under the windows, the base is more compressed.

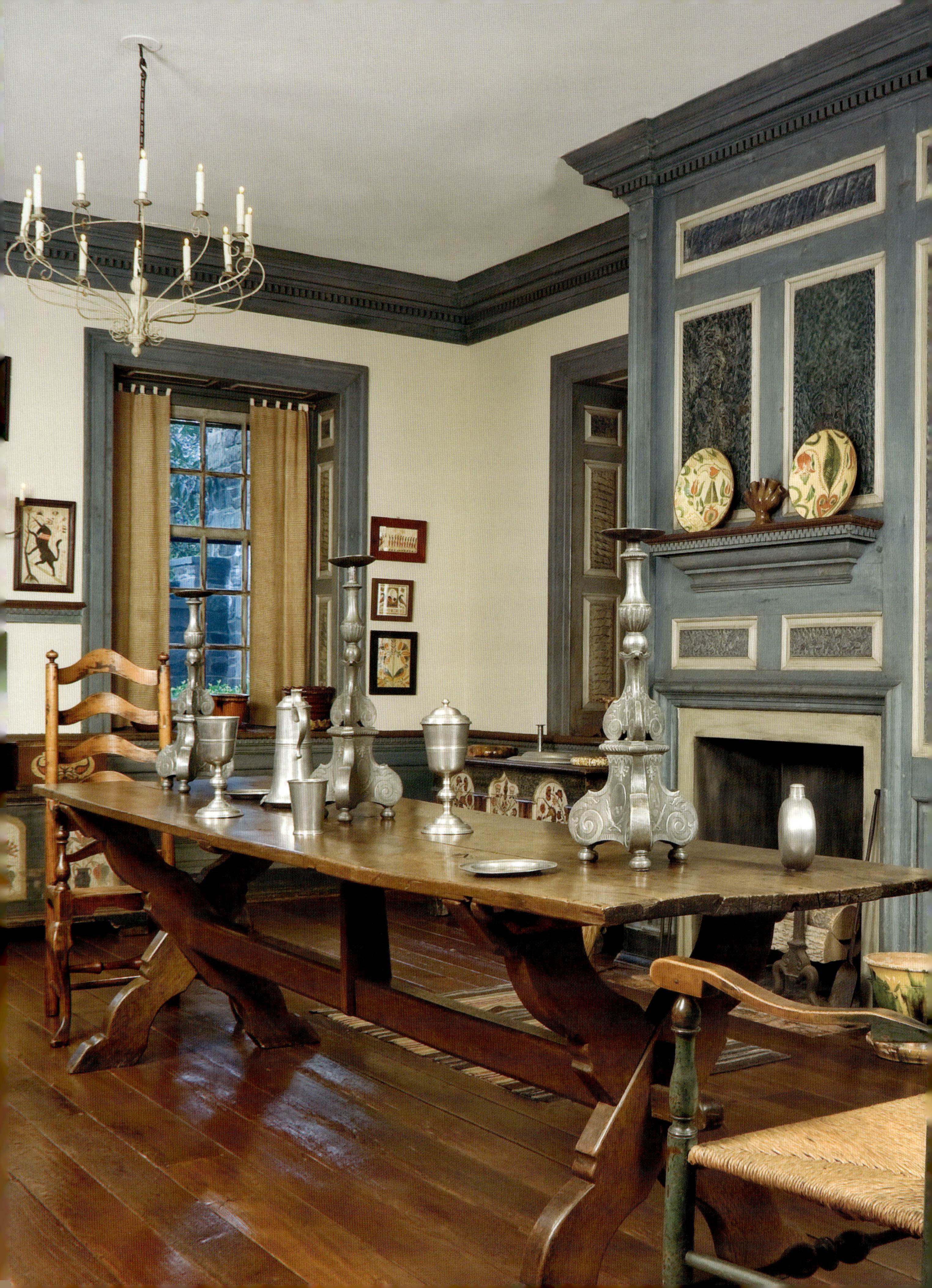

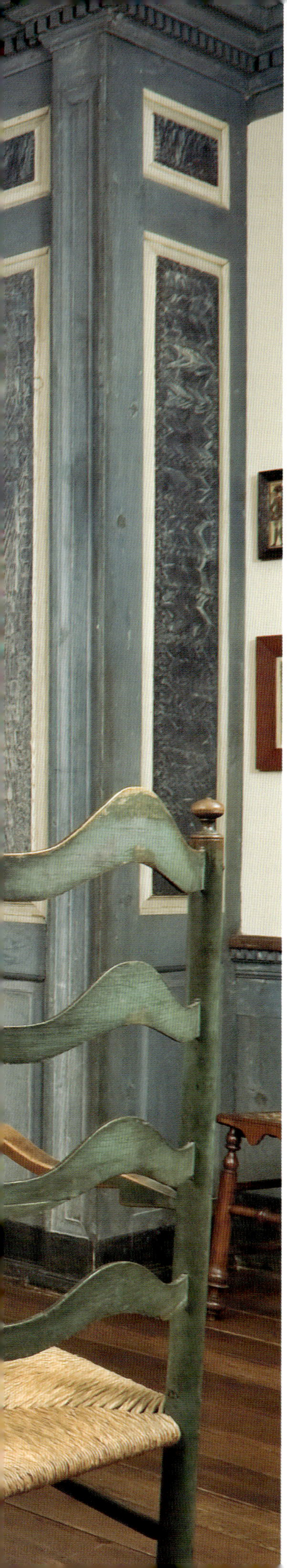

Fraktur Room

Hottenstein House, Kutztown, Pennsylvania, 1783

9'11" high by 17'8" wide by 26'8" long

The Fraktur Room at Winterthur is a refined example of a late-eighteenth-century rural Pennsylvania German interior. From a house built for David and Catharine Hottenstein in 1783 near Kutztown, Berks County, the Fraktur Room is named for the decorative manuscripts displayed on the walls. Fraktur is a traditional Pennsylvania German folk art and includes birth and baptismal certificates, writing exercises, and other documents that commemorate important events such as births, baptisms, and marriages.

The house was most likely built by local craftsmen and displays regional influences. The Fraktur Room comes from the second floor of the home. The fireplace is off-center, which allowed the first-floor fireplace flue to run up beside it. This asymmetrical composition is typical of second-floor rooms with fireplaces.

The scale of the Fraktur Room is generous, lending a sense of spaciousness to the room.

Cornice

The canonically composed cornice has dentils with a vee-shaped swag at the interdentil (1). The recess in the soffit (2) shows the room's architectural refinement.

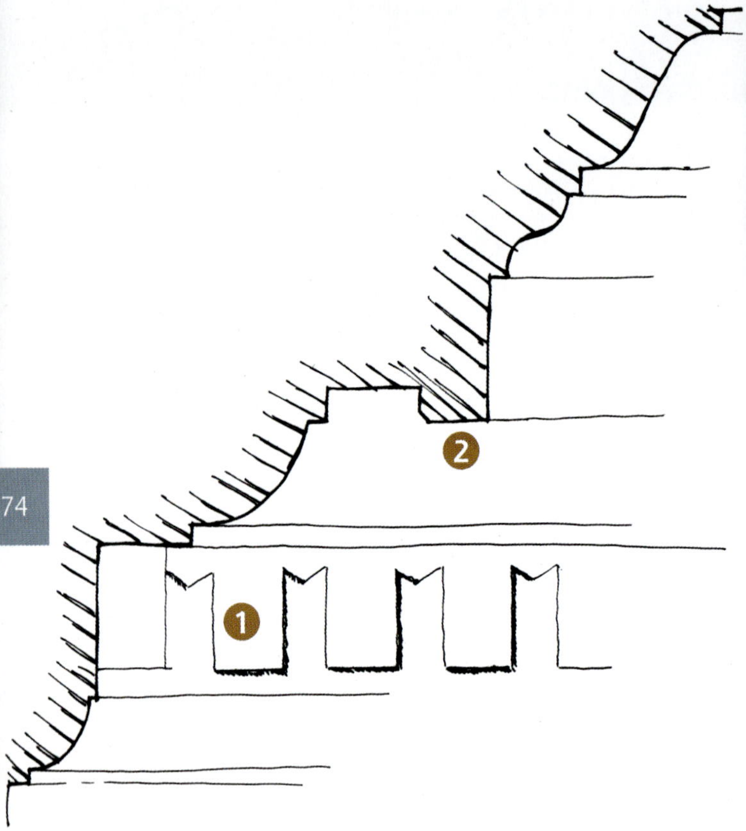

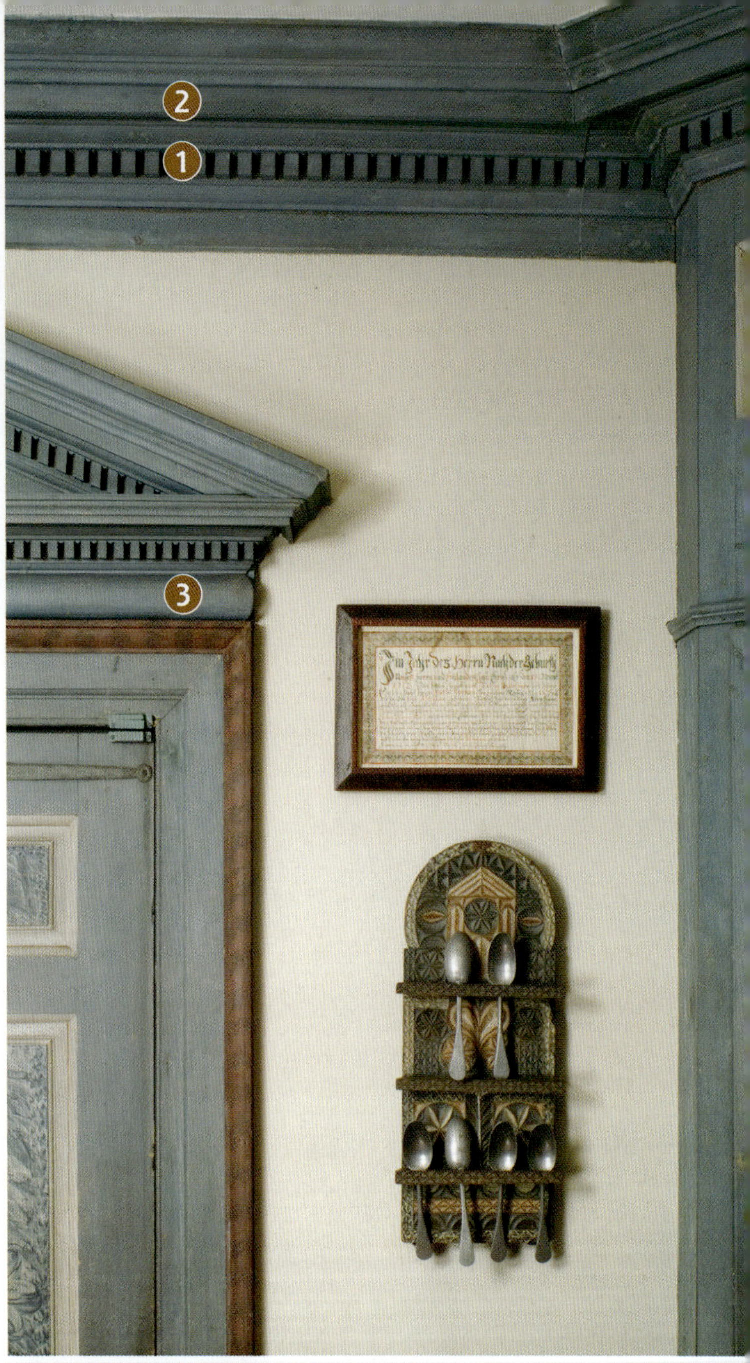

Architraves

The door and window architraves are Georgian in character with bold moldings based on a circular profile. Opposite the fireplace, a door is given importance with an overdoor expressed with a pulvinated frieze (3) and pediment in the same Ionic Order as the room. The windows utilize the same architrave as the doors, and a built-in cupboard occupies a corner of the room.

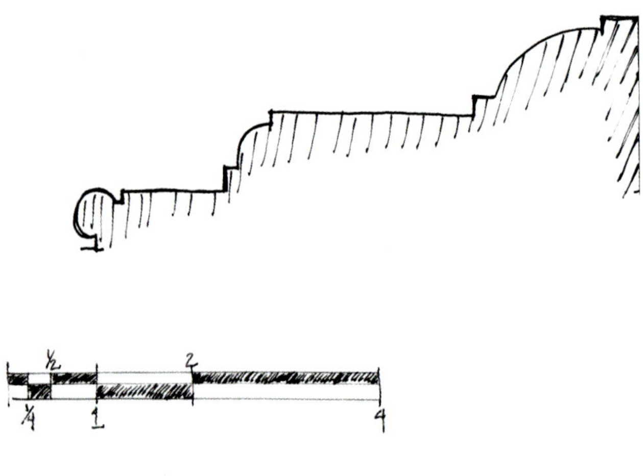

Wainscot

A seven-inch-tall painted black zone on the lower part of the wainscot represents the base (4). A small shoe molding (5) between the wall and floor is a large ovolo, about two inches in size, including its fillets. The wainscot is subdivided by long horizontal panels and capped with a light brown molding that stands out from the original blue paint on the rest of the woodwork. This brown cap to the surbase is repeated in the backband of the door architrave. The surbase also has an interesting dentil detail. Alternating gouges form the fretwork dentils (6).

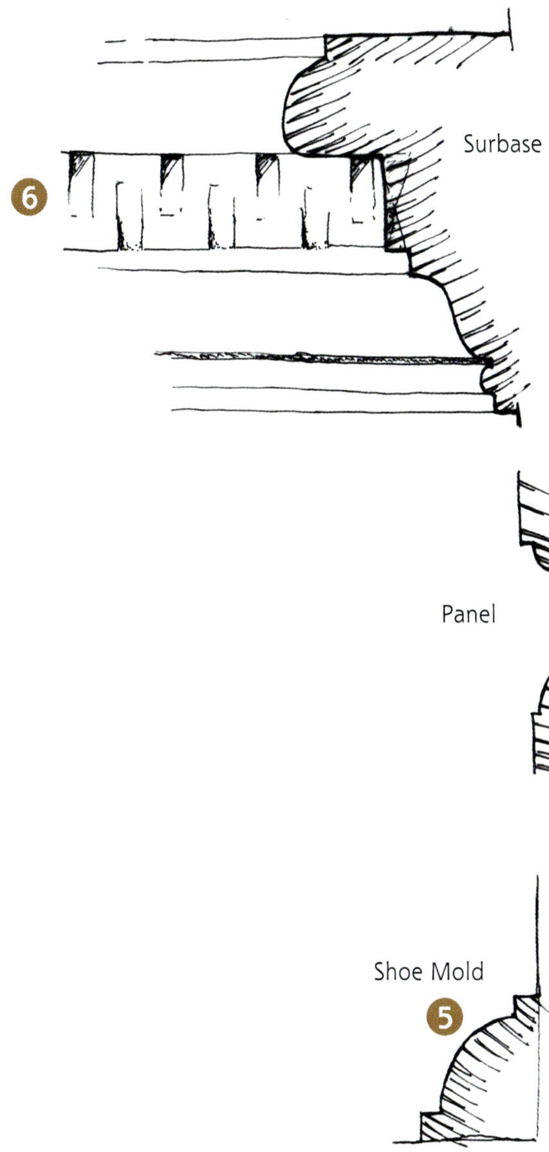

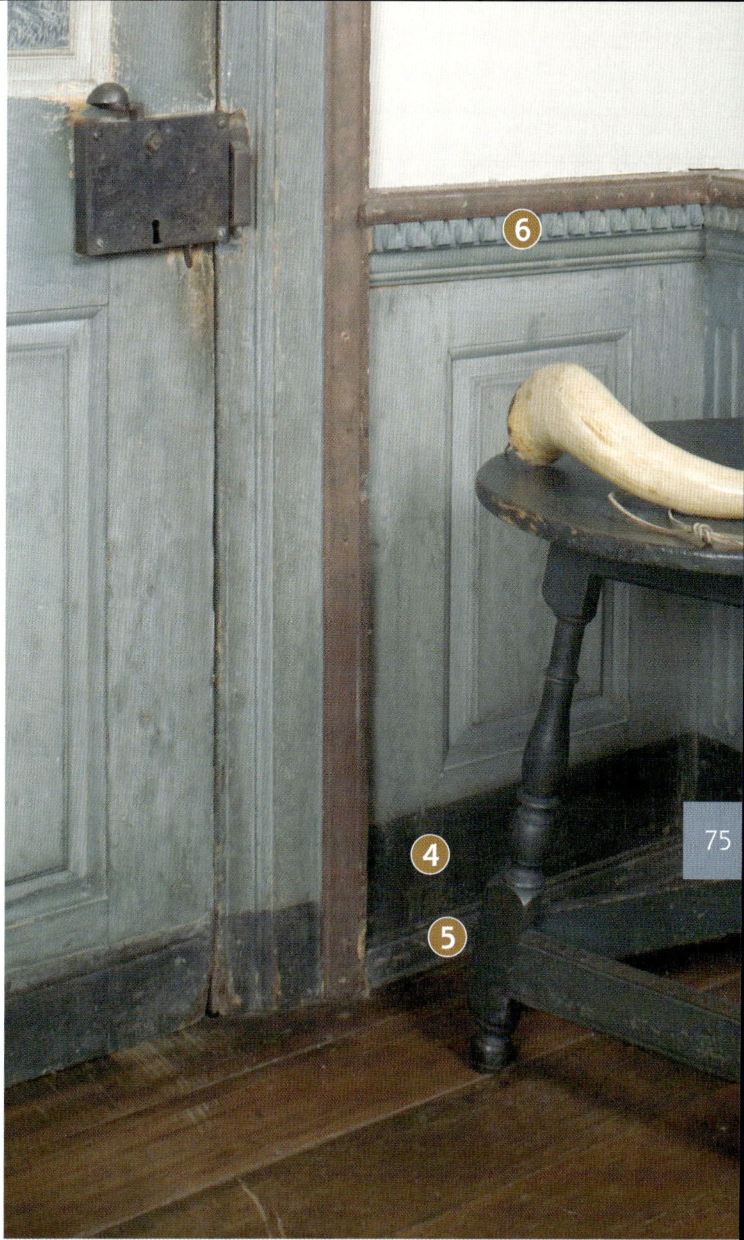

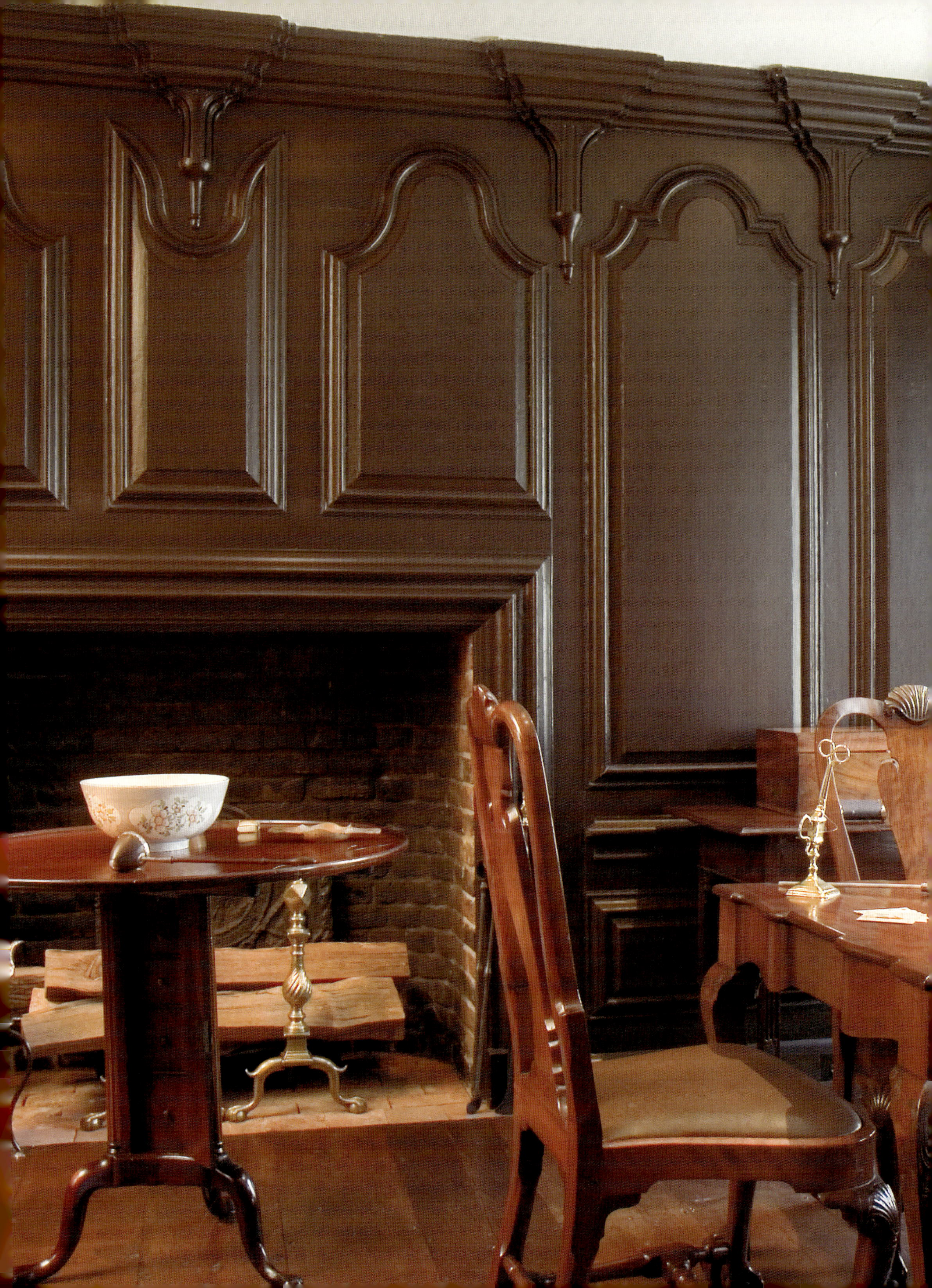

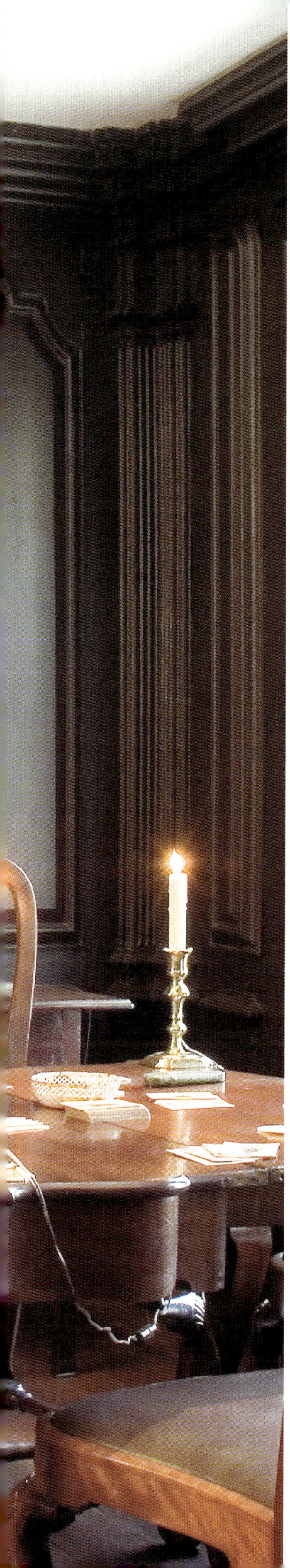

Gidley Room

Newport, Rhode Island, circa 1740

7'10" high by 11' wide by 13'5" long

The Gidley Room is one of Winterthur's finest architectural acquisitions. In 1960, when Winterthur's curator, John Sweeney, and director, Charles Montgomery, recommended the Gidley paneling to Mr. du Pont, they advised, "We believe this woodwork ranks as the most important domestic paneling of its period." Its installation provided Winterthur with one of the greatest examples of early eighteenth-century American domestic architecture in existence.

The original home was built in 1724 for John Gidley, an influential merchant. In 1742 he was appointed Judge of the Admiralty and expanded his home soon after. It is unclear whether the paneling at Winterthur dates from the earlier home or the later addition.

The designer may have been the renowned Richard Munday, although it is possible the Gidley Room was designed after Munday's death in 1739 and it was simply influenced by his Newport work. Munday's known buildings share distinctive similarities with the Gidley Room, including the alternating curved panel configurations, the projections in the cornice over pendant drops, and the doubled corner pilasters resting on pedestals. For example, Munday's Colony House, Rhode Island's original statehouse, has similar cornice breaks and drops in the Senate Chamber.

The Gidley Room is an extraordinary example of the baroque aspects of early American Georgian architectural design. It is creative in its composition and fluid movement.

The Gidley Room's lively style reflects Newport's early architectural heritage.

Cornice

The cornice breaks (1) and pendant drops (2) are not typical of canonic classical architecture, nor are they seen in later Palladian-influenced work; rather they reflect the baroque work of architects like Sir Christopher Wren. The cornice profile itself is formed of alternating coves and beads, adding to the sensual quality of the room.

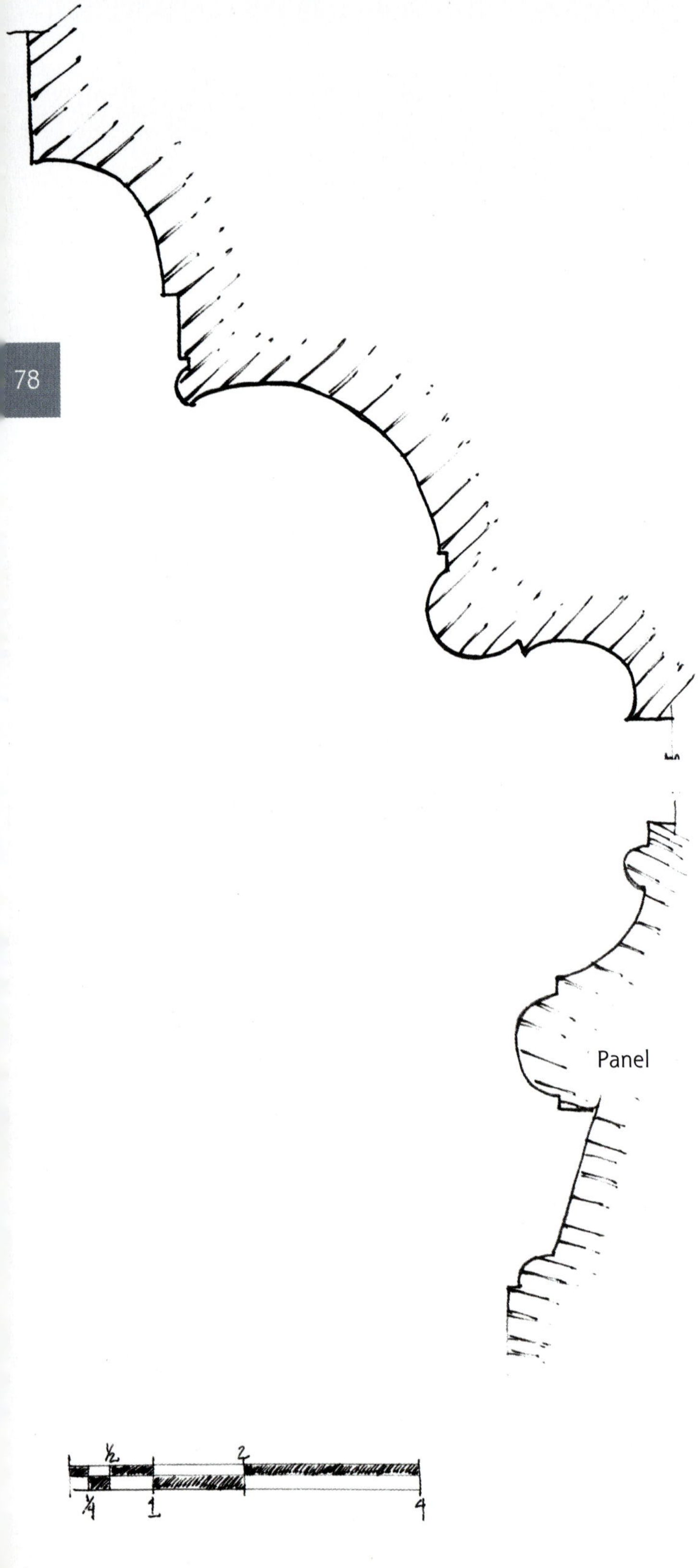

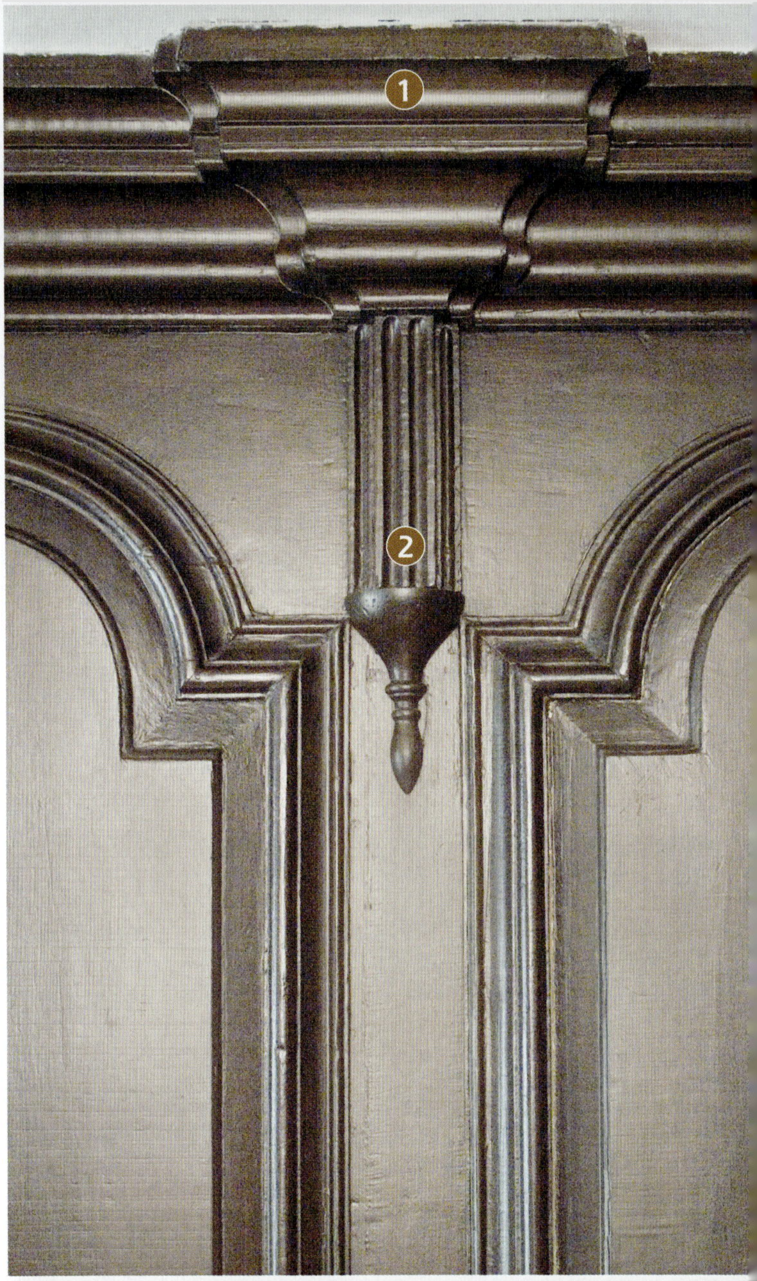

Panels & Chair Rail

The bolection panels, with six different variations of arched tops, also reflect baroque influences. The alternating curves and varying arched tops animate the room with movement. This specialized detail would have required more time and greater skill than a rectangular panel.

The panels and their bolection moldings rise above the surface of the stiles and rails, further adding to the sculptural quality of the room. The base has a strong cove molding (3), contrasting with the large half-round molding (4) forming the architrave.

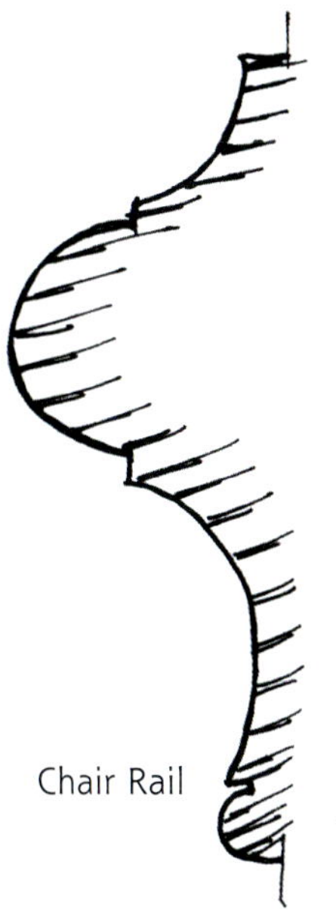

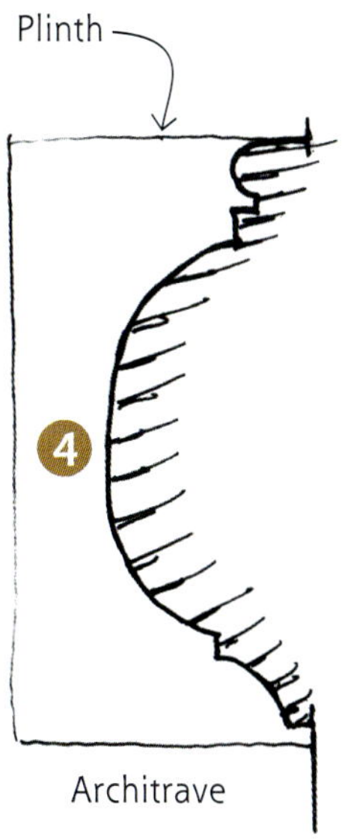

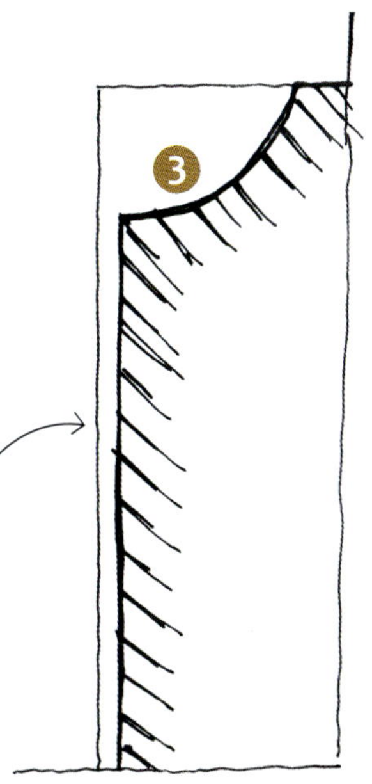

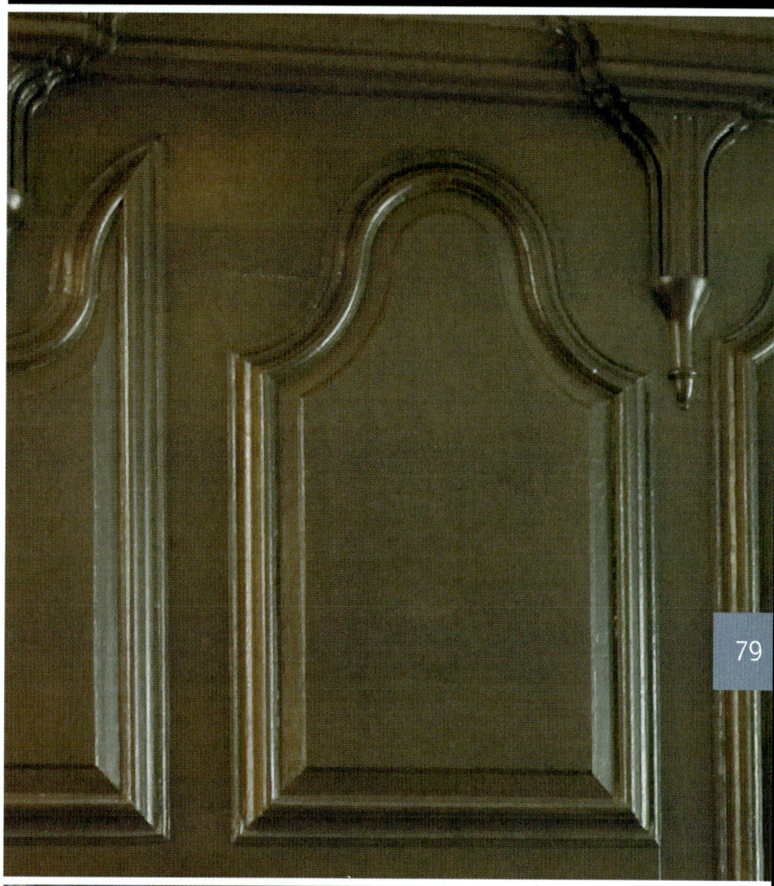

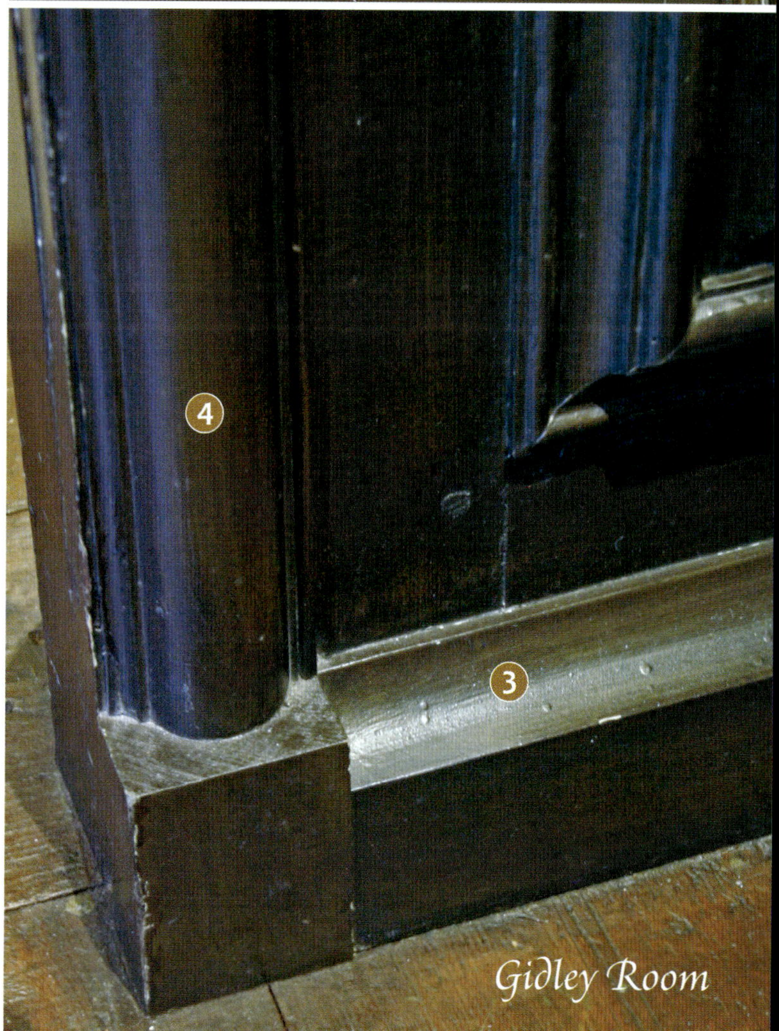

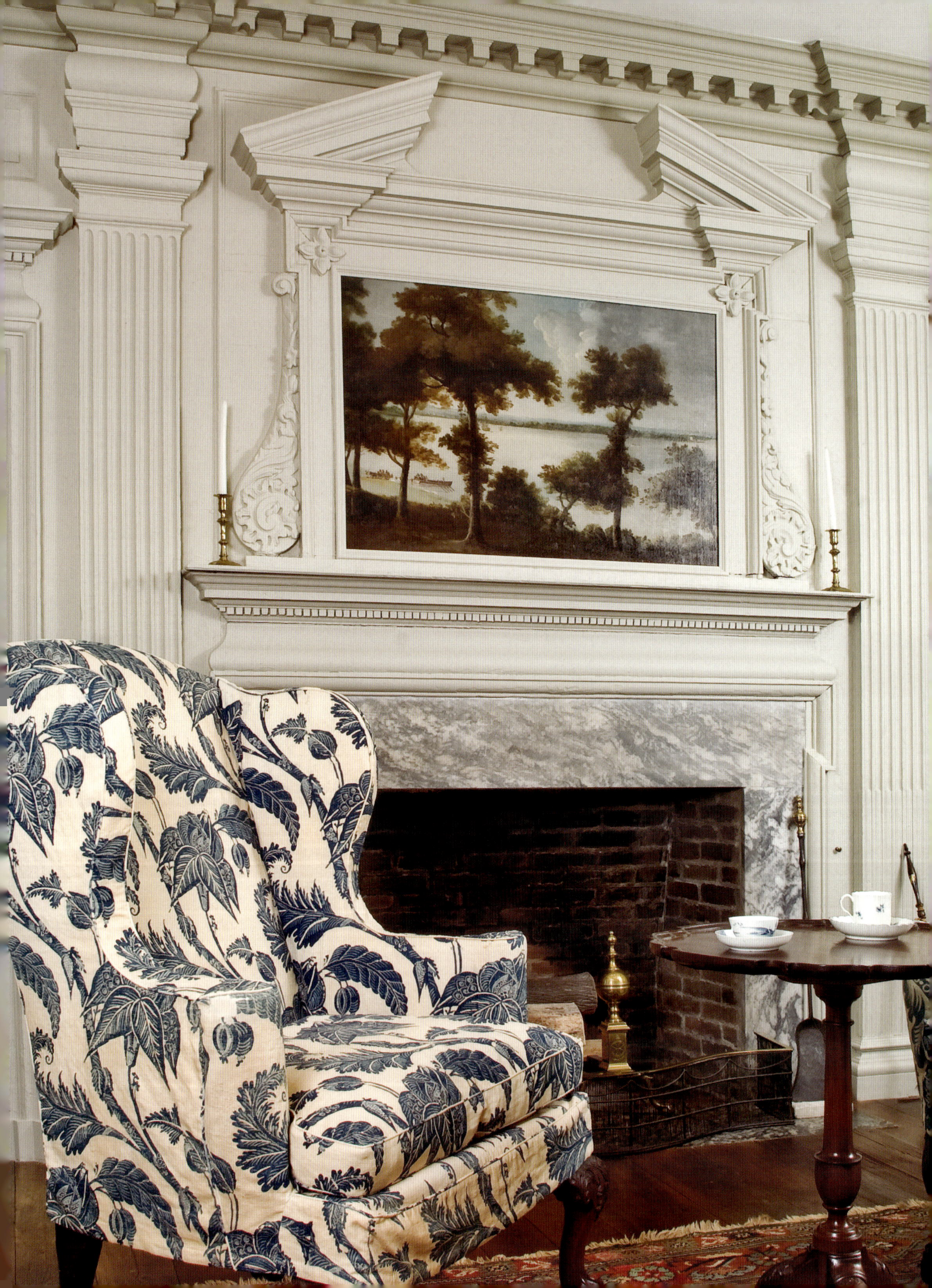

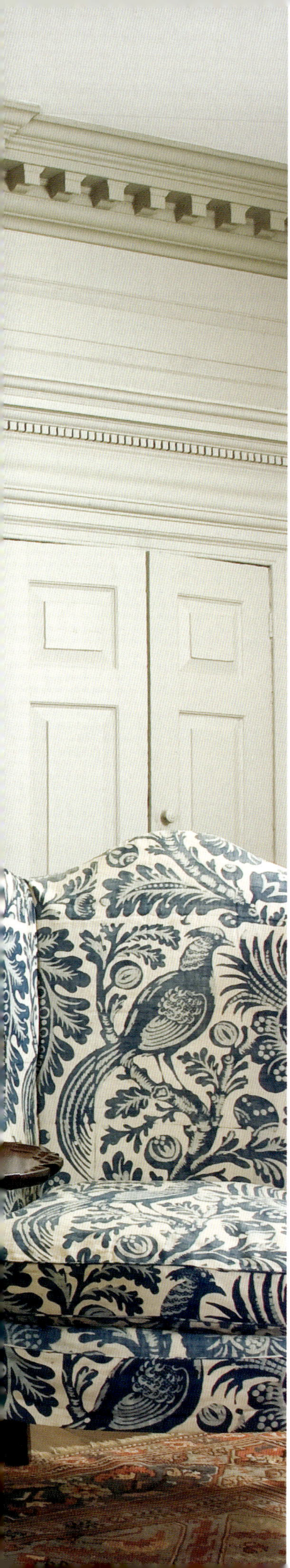

Hampton Room

Hampton Court, Elizabeth, New Jersey, 1761

9'9" high by 19'2" wide by 16'8" long

The Hampton Room, on Winterthur's seventh floor, was used as a guest room for du Pont friends who visited from all over. The superb woodwork comes from the parlor of Dr. William Barnett, a New Jersey surgeon.

The room's focus is the fireplace wall with cupboards behind paneled doors flanking a handsome mantel and overmantel. H. F. du Pont added the left cupboard in 1966 to balance the design. Its design bears similarities to Plate LXXXV in Batty Langley's *The City and Country Builder's and Workman's Treasury of Designs* (page 16), and Plate LXXVI of the same book. The use of pattern books as models for designs was common in mid-eighteenth-century America, and Batty Langley's *Treasury*, first published in London in 1740, was very popular. Certain elements, such as the entablature, for example, are direct models from architectural treatises to which craftsmen were known to have access.

The Hampton Room's Doric pilasters frame the fireplace, possibly inspired by a Batty Langley design.

Fireplace Wall

The symmetrical composition of the fireplace wall has fluted Doric pilasters supporting a full Ionic entablature, which closely follows Palladio's Ionic Order. The pilasters are stop-fluted, meaning the bottom third of the flutes are filled with a convex molding. The full entablature (architrave, frieze, and cornice) only appears above the pilasters, while the cornice and its supporting modillions (1) continue around the entire room.

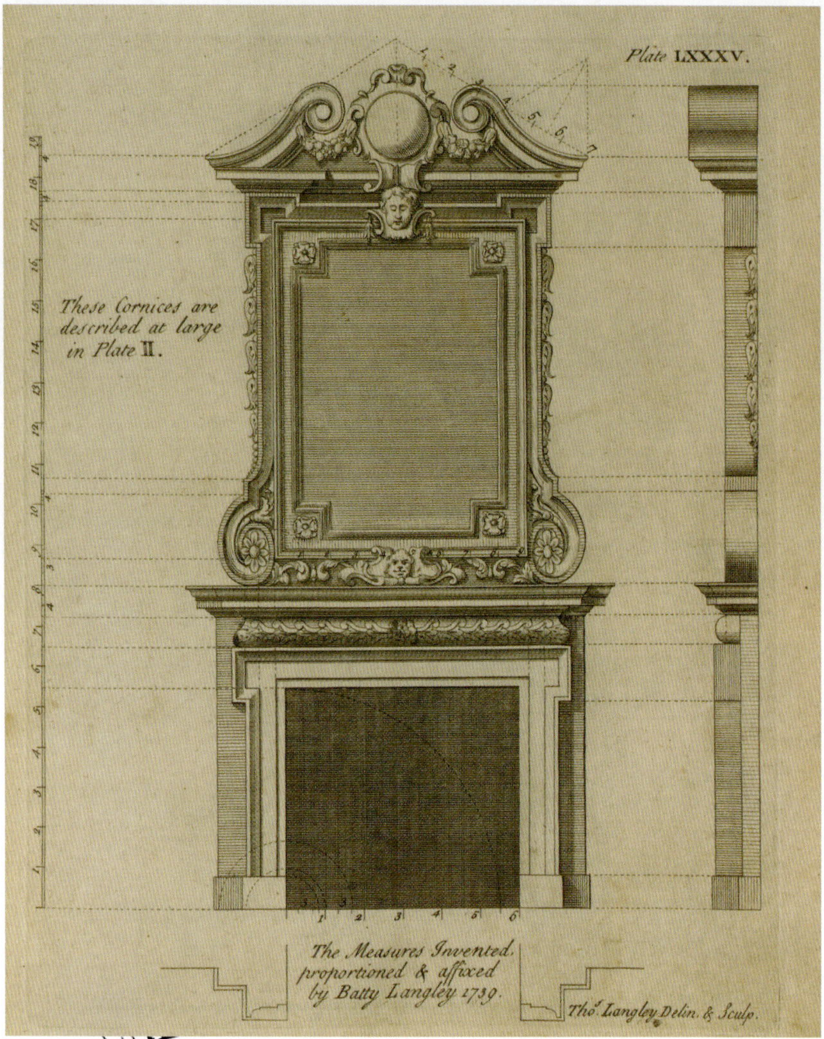

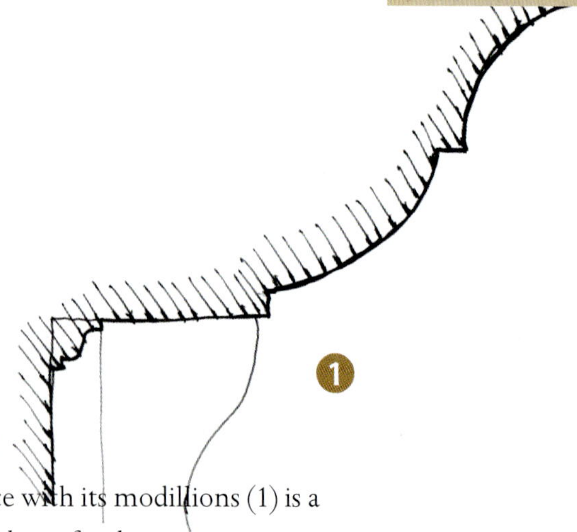

Cornice

The Ionic cornice with its modillions (1) is a refined detail without further ornamentation of the moldings. The modillions give the cornice visual support and depth.

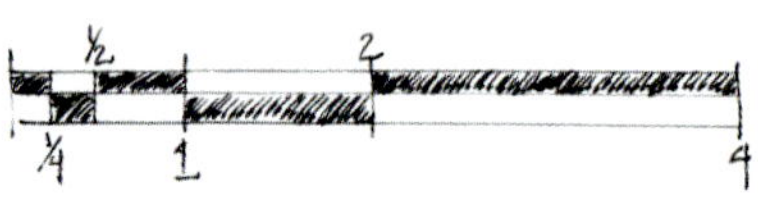

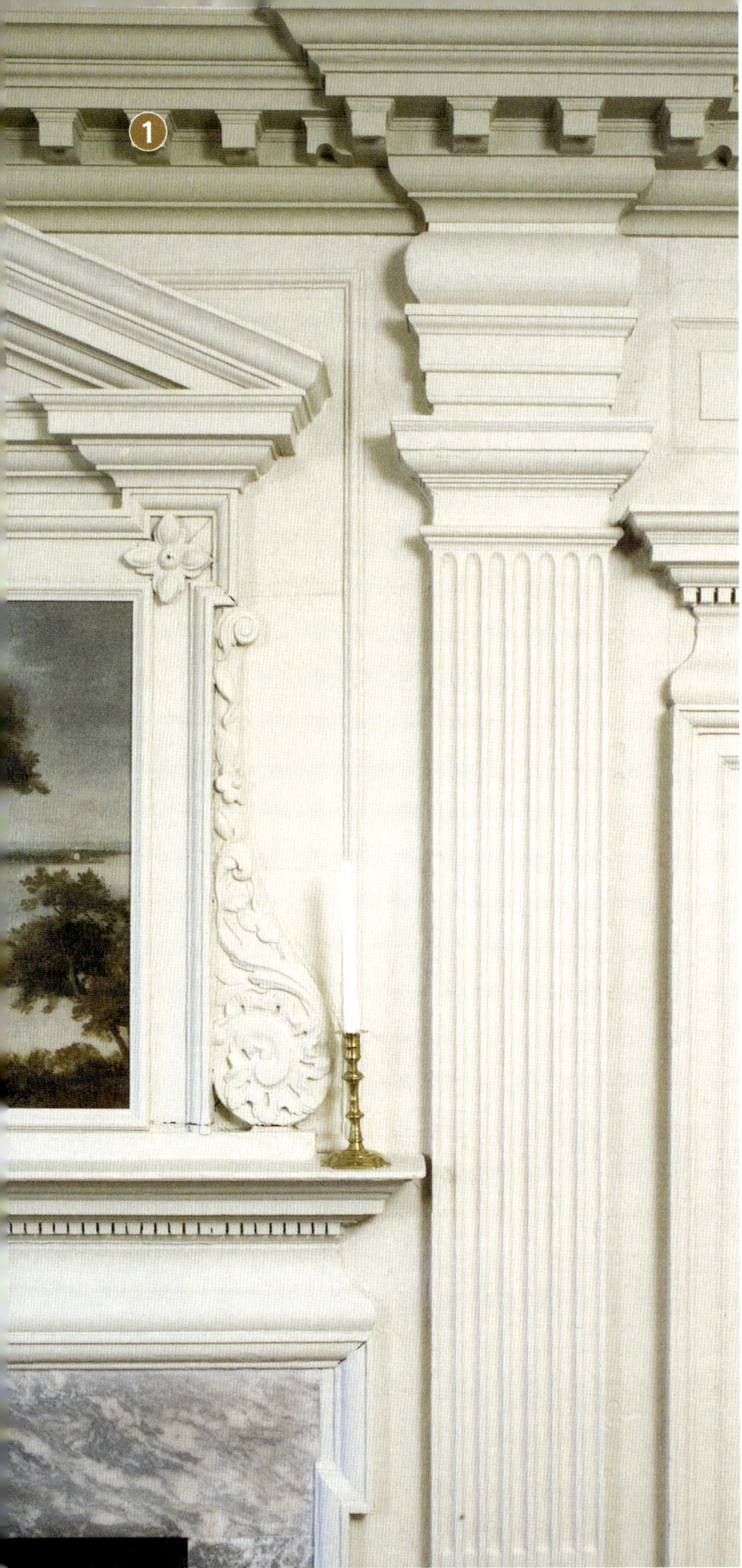

Architraves

The door architrave is robust, projecting two inches from the wall. Plinth blocks resolve the meeting of the door architrave with the base plinth and cap, which project one inch.

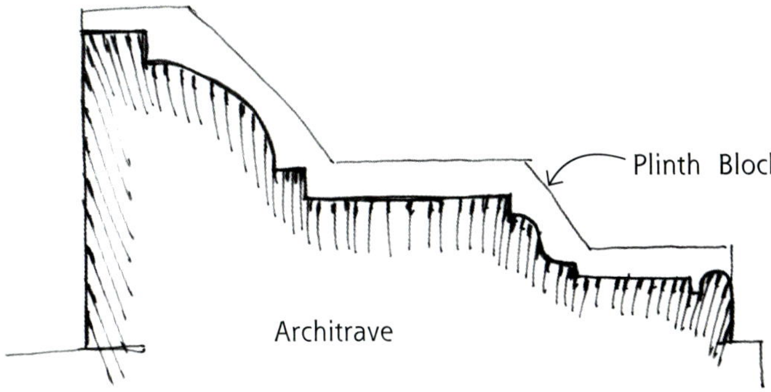

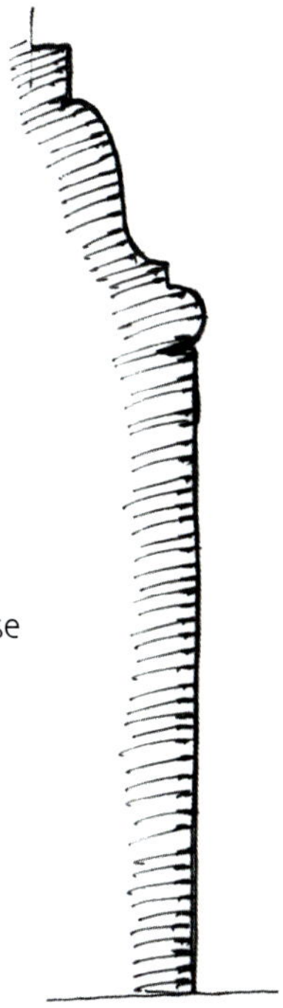

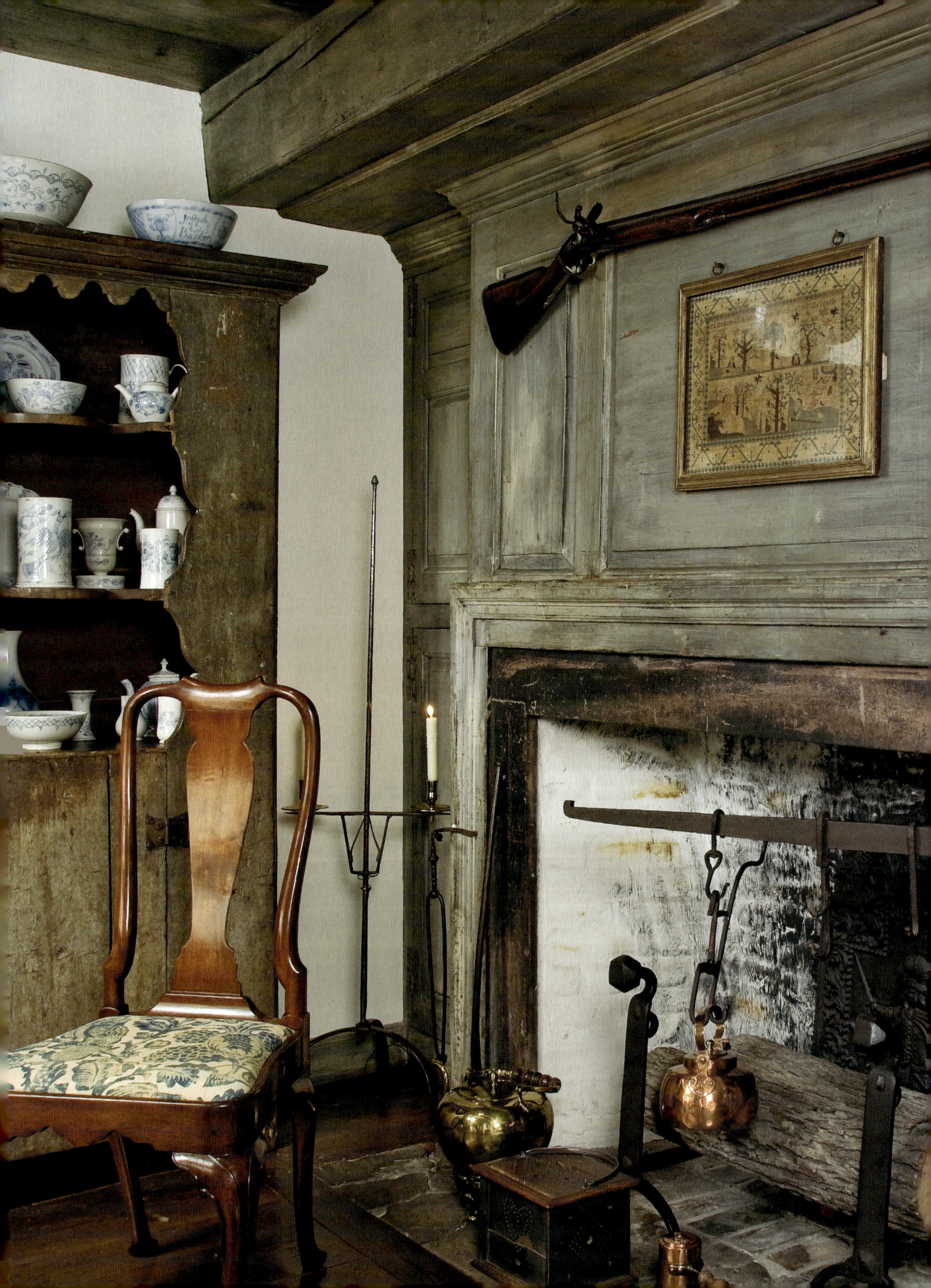
Joseph
Barker

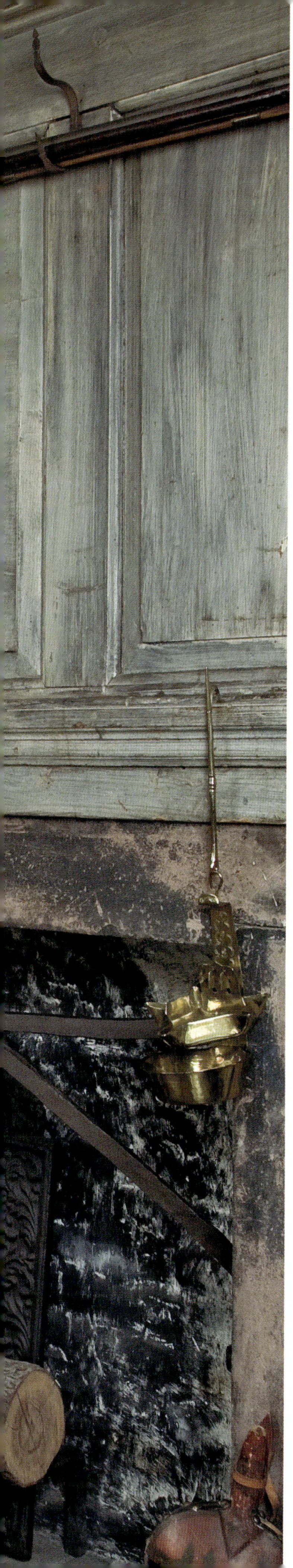

Hardenbergh Parlor

Hudson Valley, New York, 1762

7'8" high by 16'9" wide by 10'8" long

The majority of colonial-era Americans lived in simple homes reflecting local cultures and building traditions. The Hardenbergh Parlor represents just such a modest house.

Though of moderate means, the Hardenberghs had a historically prominent name in the Dutch-settled Hudson Valley because a great deal of land had been granted to the family by Queen Anne in 1708. Johannes Hardenbergh, who built this home, was the fifth generation to live in the valley.

As is typical in both houses in the north and those of Dutch colonists, the ceilings are low and the structural beams are exposed. Lower ceilings helped to keep a room warm during cold northern winters. And it was common in simpler houses of the seventeenth and eighteenth centuries to leave ceiling beams exposed, ornamented only with small beads. The simplicity and restraint seen in this parlor are typical of the Hudson Valley, for although the Dutch controlled the area for only a short while (1609-1644) their sober influence lived on well into the eighteenth century.

The Dutch-inspired Hardenbergh Parlor embodies the lifestyle of a rural, middle-class family in the mid-1700s.

Fireplace Wall

The main woodwork appears on the fireplace wall, while the remaining walls are stuccoed and painted white, as is typical in the Dutch tradition. Three panels, a large center panel and two narrower ones flanking it for balance, sit above a simple architrave molding that surrounds the wide firebox. Two levels of cupboards, hidden behind paneled doors on either side of the fireplace, provide ample storage.

Architraves and Base

The door architrave (shown at right) has a simple backband, not nearly as deep as typical Georgian architraves, but it is still composed of classical profiles and proportions with its two fascias (3), bead (4), and backband (5). Below is a sketch of another architrave in the room. Both illustrate the restraint inherent in the Dutch colonial architrave of the region.

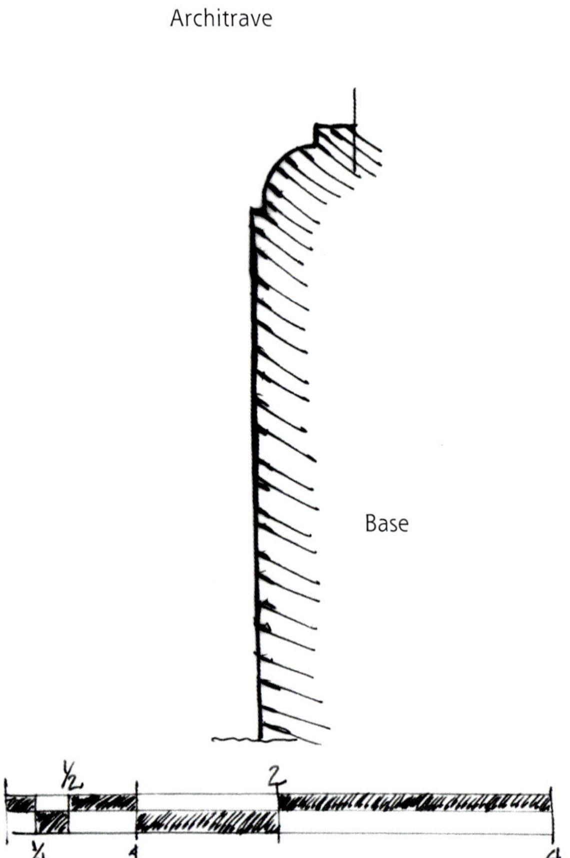

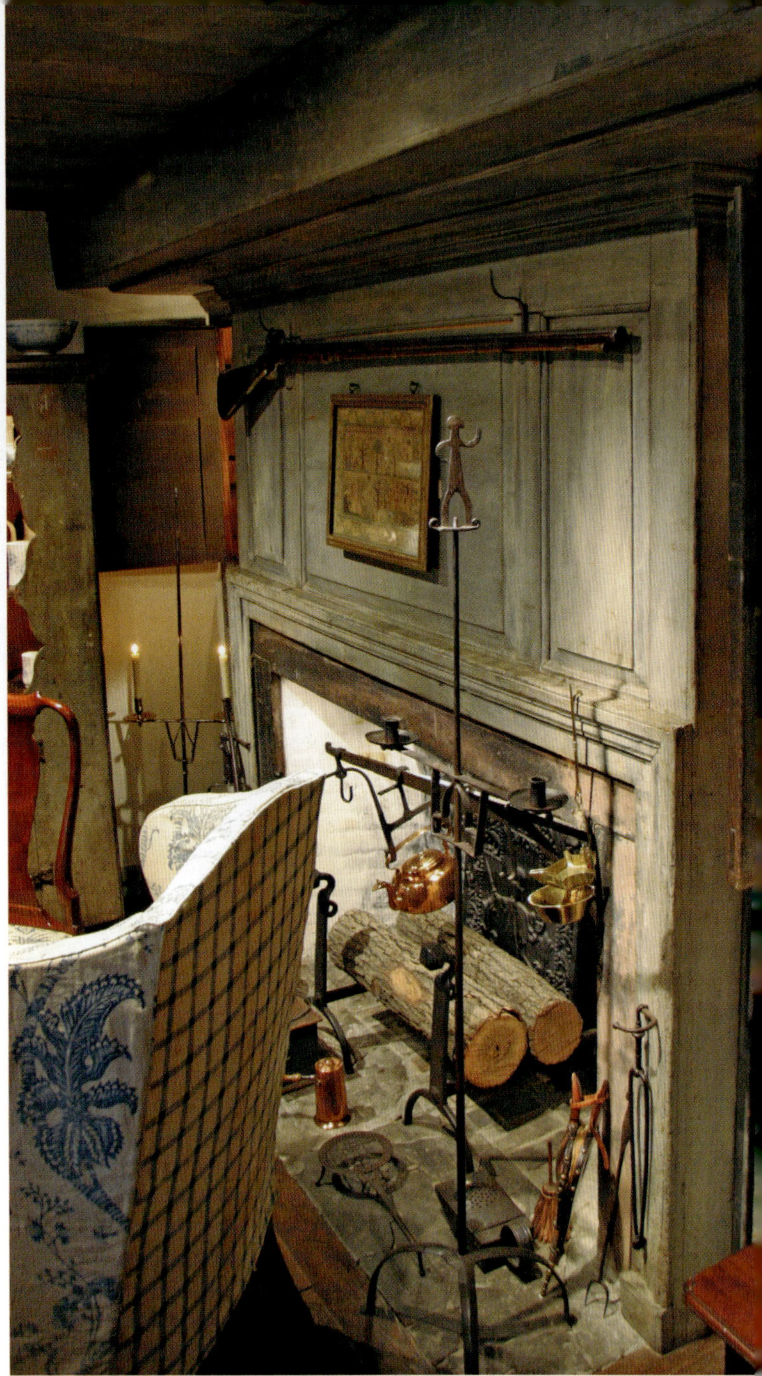

This view shows the beam adjacent to the fireplace wall, directly above the cornice. Note the bead ornamenting the corner of the beam.

Cornice

A simple cornice hides the joints along the fireplace wall and under the planked ceiling. It appears to be a single piece of wood. Unlike high-style rooms, no moldings compose the room in a formal way. However, the cornice has the classical elements of a cymatium (1) supported on a cyma reversa bedmold (2).

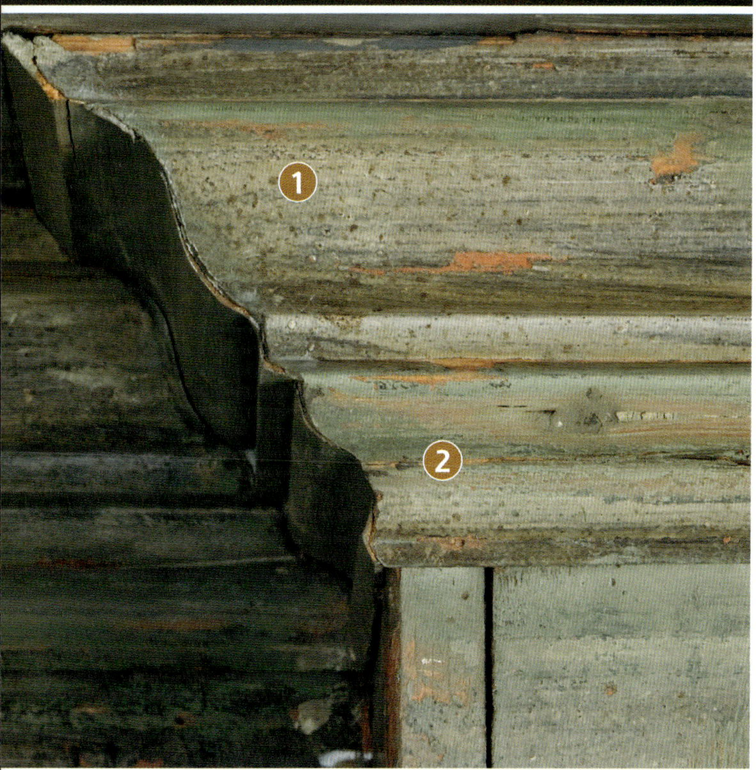

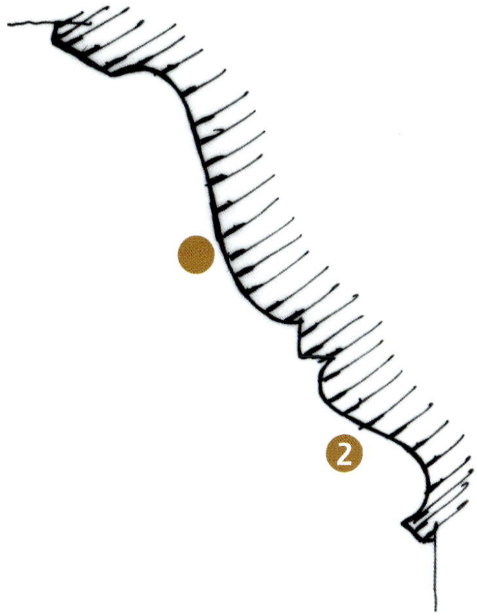

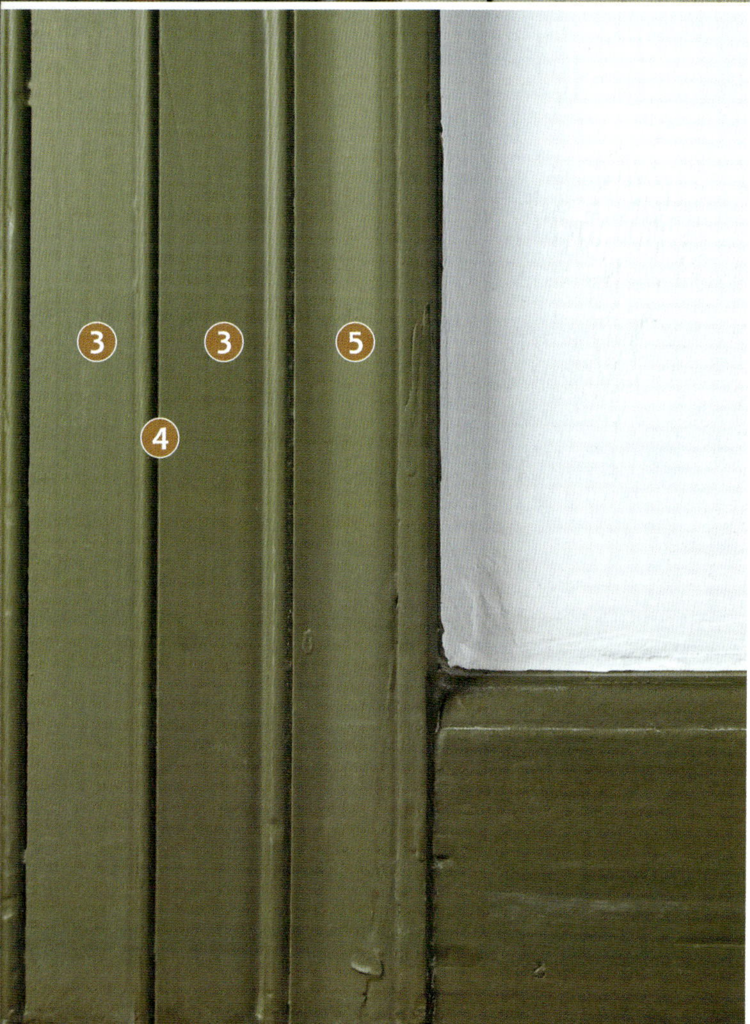

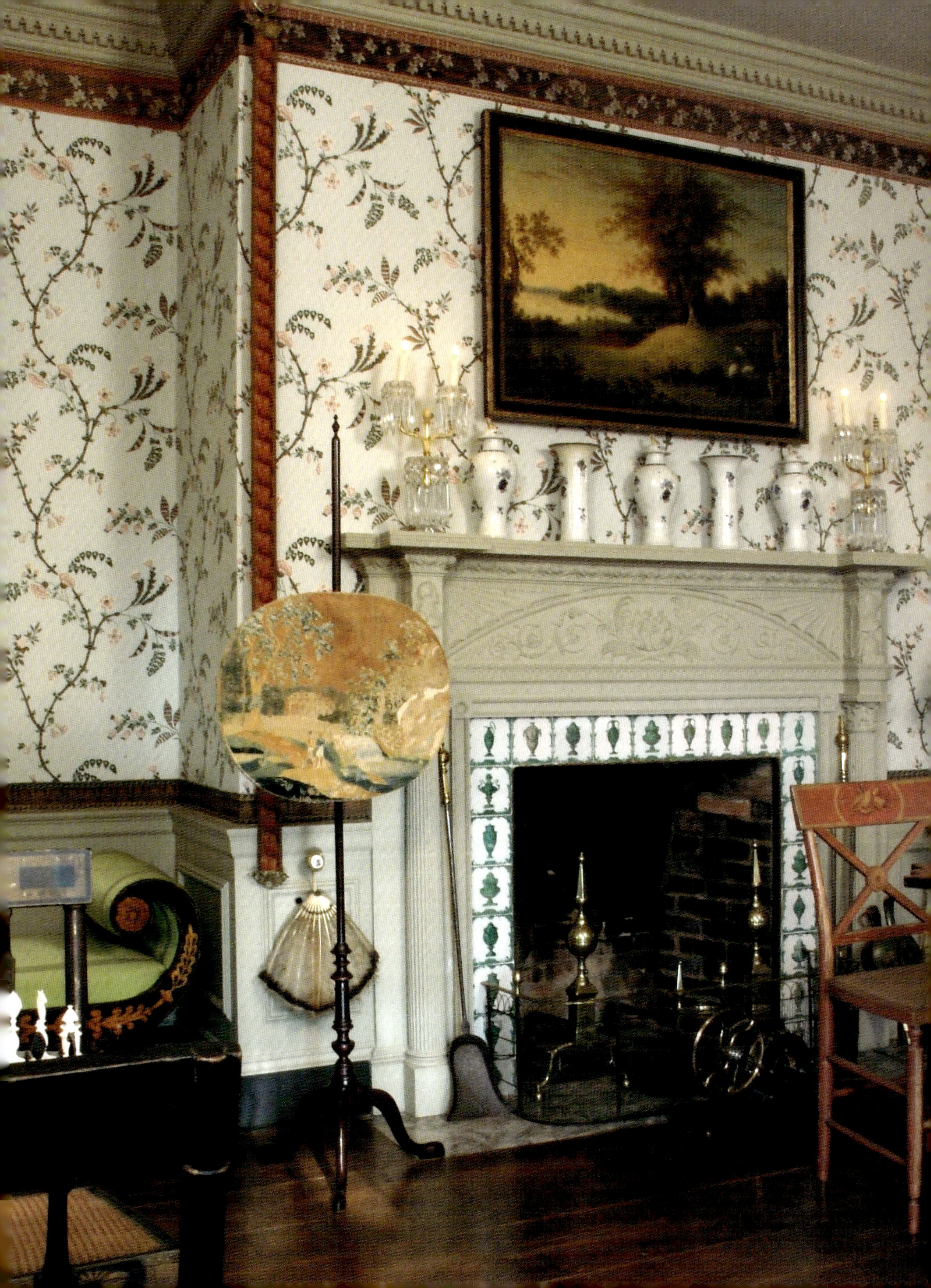

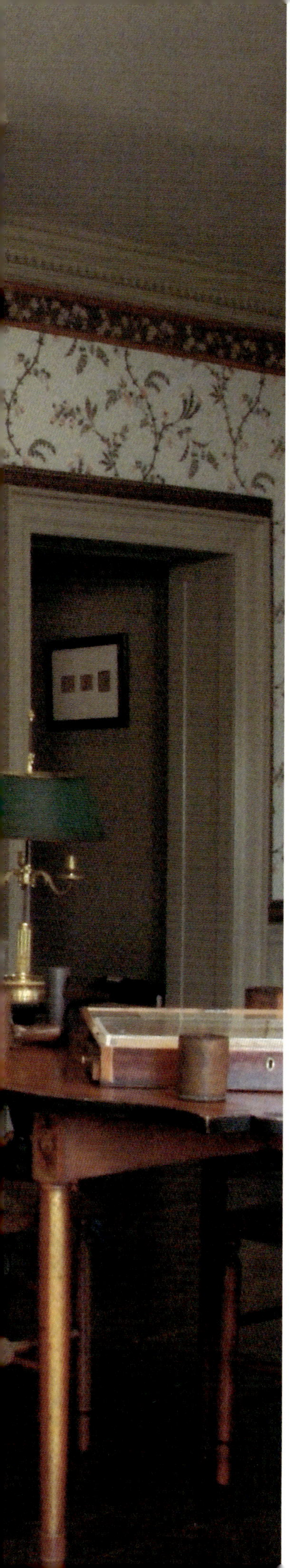

Imlay Room

Allentown, New Jersey, 1790

9'4" high by 16'4" wide by 22'4" long

John Imlay retired to his birthplace in Allentown, New Jersey, following a successful career in the Philadelphia shipping business. He then built himself the home from which this room comes. Because of the high level of detailing throughout, it is believed Imlay hired craftsmen from Philadelphia to build the house.

Mr. Imlay's fine home included eleven mantels, some of which employ applied composition, or compo, decorative moldings attributed to Robert Wellford, the well-known composition manufacturer active in Philadelphia at the turn of the century.

The Imlay Room at Winterthur is characteristic of the Federal style with its broad expanse of wall above a flat-paneled dado, its delicate proportions, the shape of its molding profiles, and its use of classical ornamental motifs. For example, the fan-like decoration in the mantel frieze spandrels, and the *rinceau*, or scrolling vines and leaves, in the mantel frieze arch, are both common motifs in Roman classical architecture.

A finely composed mantel, with applied composition decoration, is the focal point of the room.

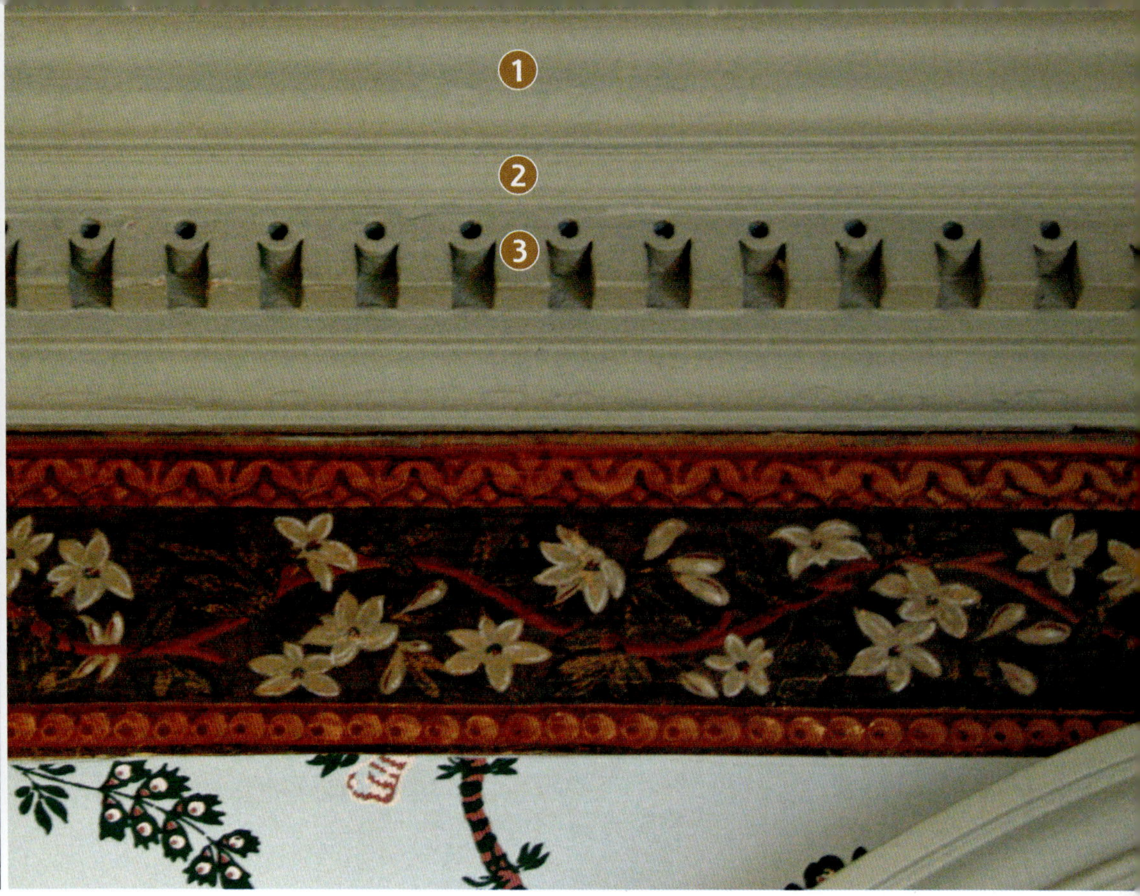

Cornice

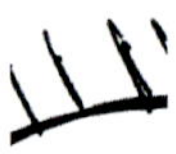

The cornice molding is interestingly adapted from a standard cornice. A cymatium (1) and cyma reversa (2) surmount a dentil course (3) rather than the usual projection of the corona. The dentils are delicately rendered with a swag and drilled hole at the space between each dentil. This feature creates a lacy shadow effect and gives the cornice a light and airy feel, common to Federal-style interiors.

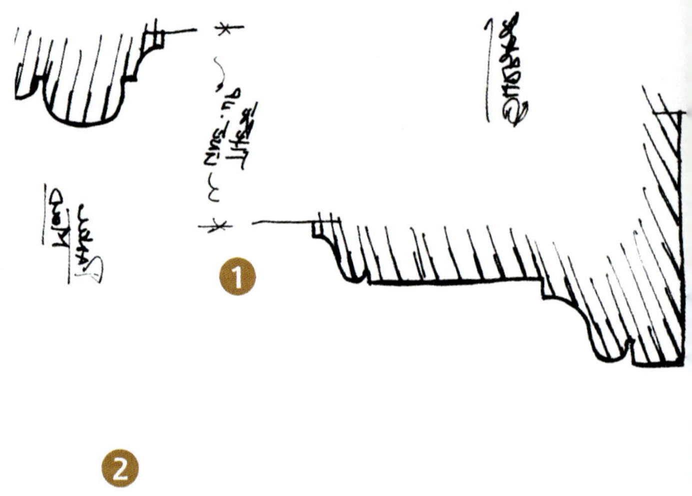

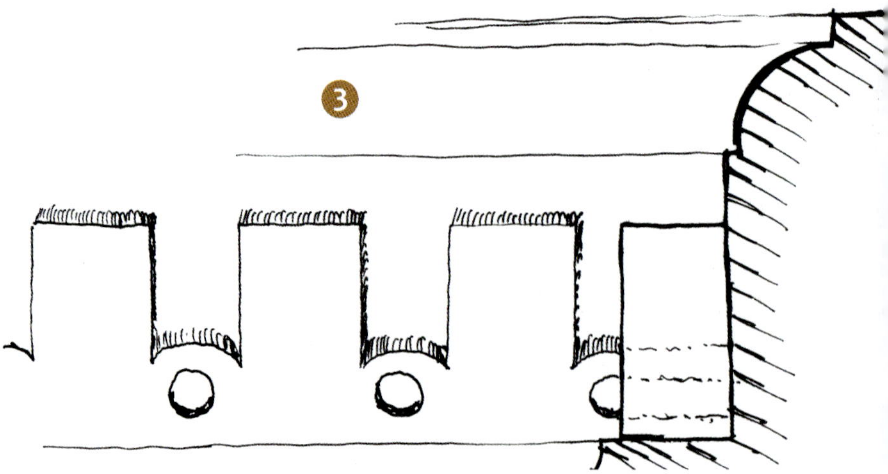

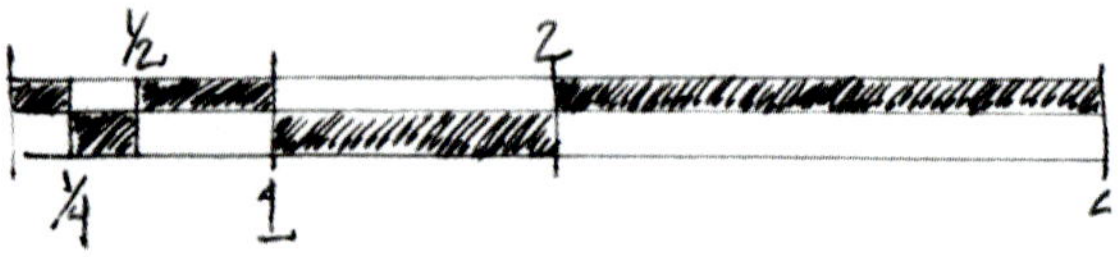

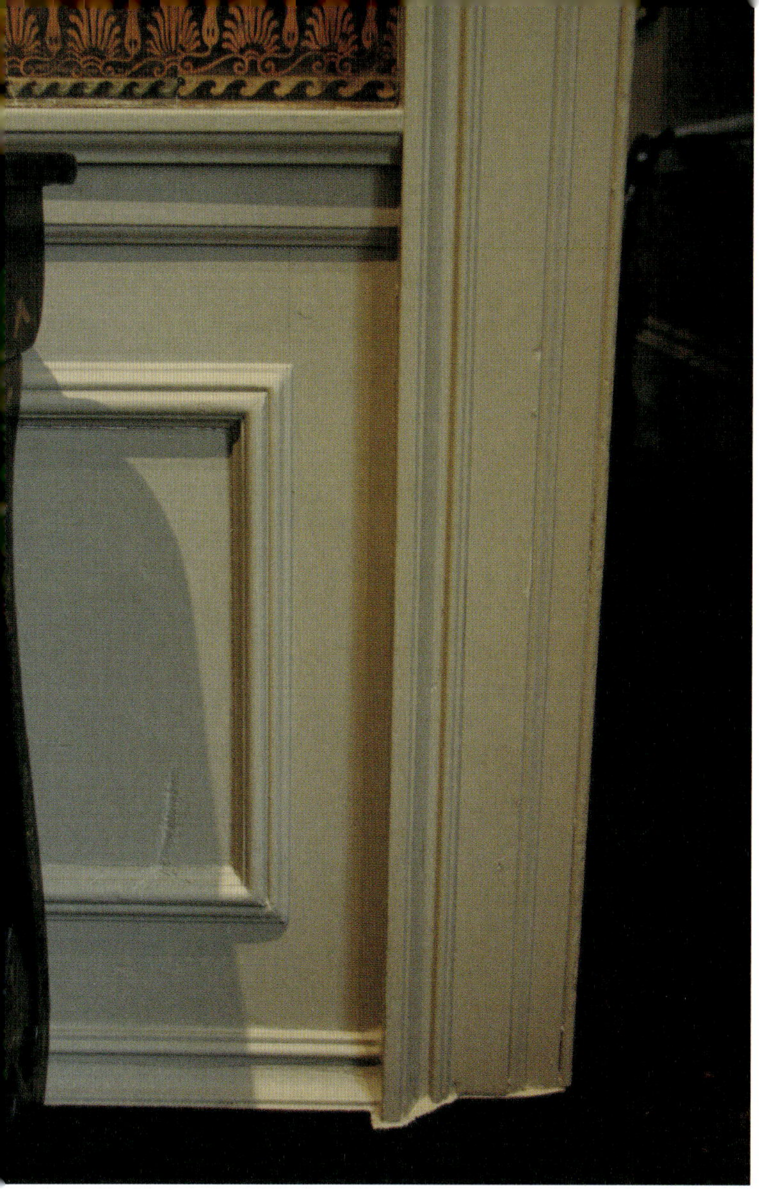

Wainscot

The tall height of the base is accentuated by a cap formed of a truncated scotia, or cove-shaped, molding (4) sweeping upward to a small bead (5). It supports a flat-paneled wainscot with applied moldings forming the panels. A simple surbase finishes the wainscot and projects two inches.

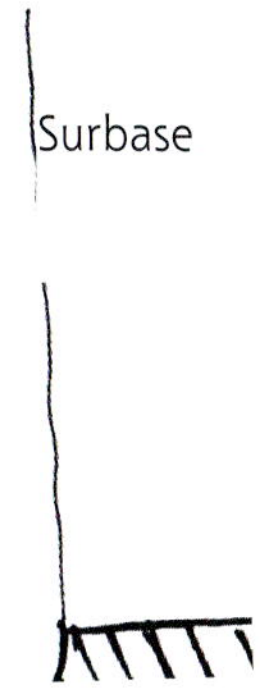

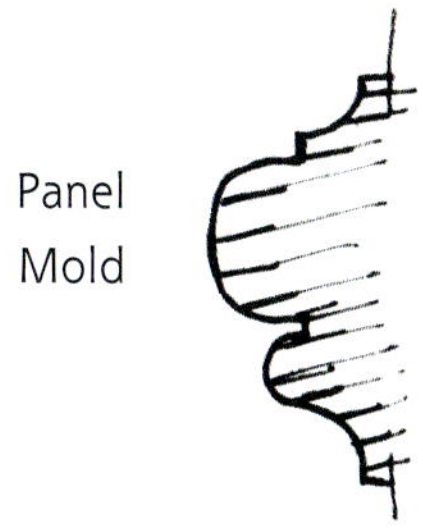

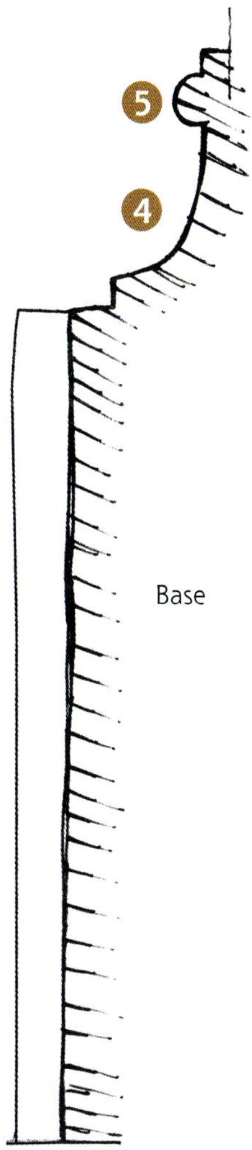

Architraves

The door architraves are quite deep, with a deep cove (6) sweeping inward to bead (7) and cyma reversa (8) separating the fascias (9). A plinth following the shape of the door architrave catches both the architrave and the base molding. The door to the hall is arched, with an attractive keystone at the peak of the arch.

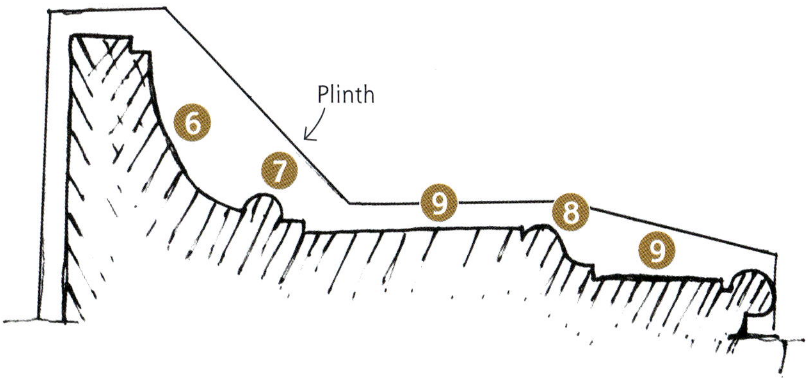

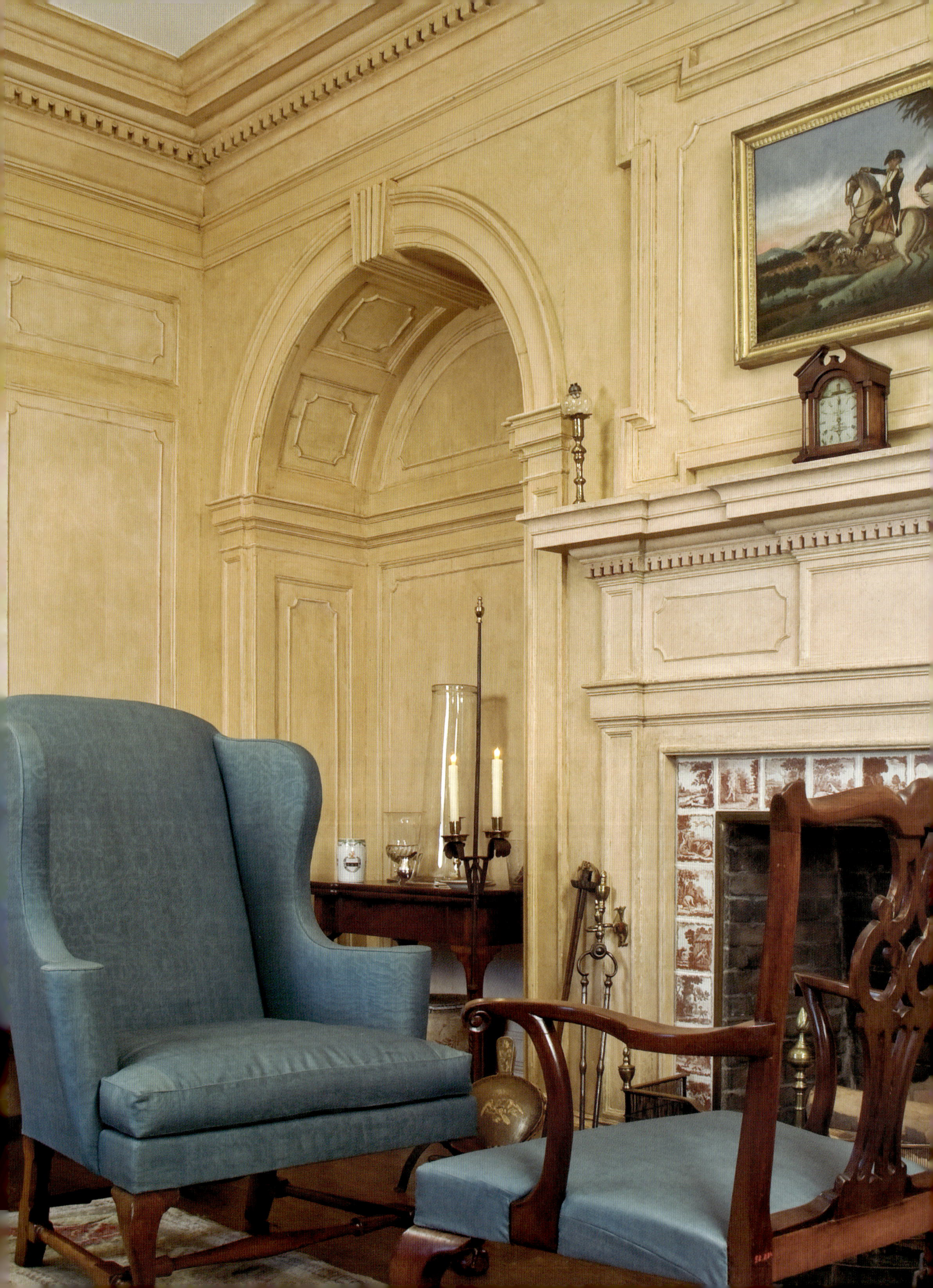

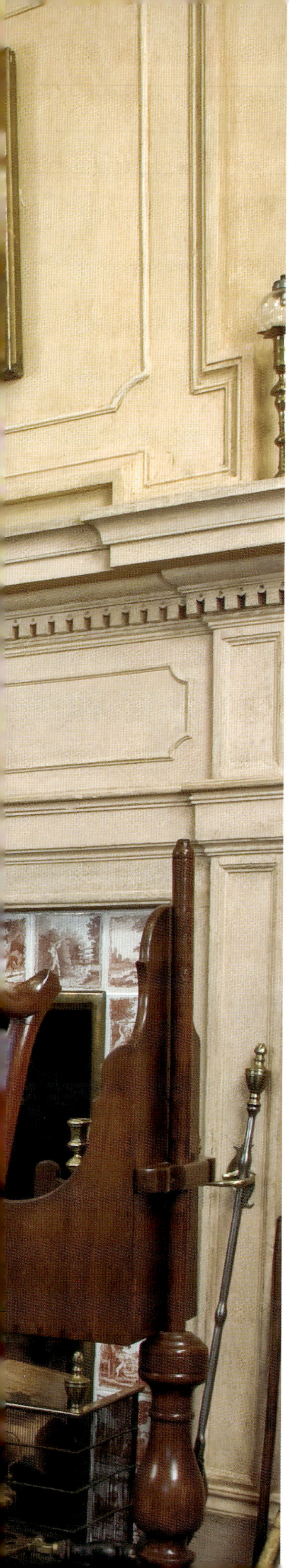

Lancaster Room

Belle Isle Plantation, Litwalton, Lancaster County, Virginia, 1802

10'11" high by 14'9" wide by 18'11" long

The Lancaster Room is from Belle Isle, a spectacular plantation on the Rappahannock River near the Chesapeake Bay. Also from Belle Isle is the Walnut Room (page 170). Originally built as part of an early 1800s addition to Belle Isle plantation, the Lancaster Room, just down a short hall from the Cecil Bedroom, was used at Winterthur as Mr. du Pont's office. Much of Winterthur's business was managed in this room.

The Lancaster Room mixes Georgian elements with a few Federal touches. Its fully paneled walls and heavy cornice are characteristically Georgian. The thin applied panel moldings, with concave corners, are reminiscent of panel variations shown in publications known to be available in America, such as Abraham Swan's *A Collection of Designs in Architecture*. The composition of the fireplace surround, with its center panel and tall frieze, and the profiles of the moldings, are more Federal in character.

The delightful, pink-paneled Lancaster Room is entirely wrapped with a full entablature.

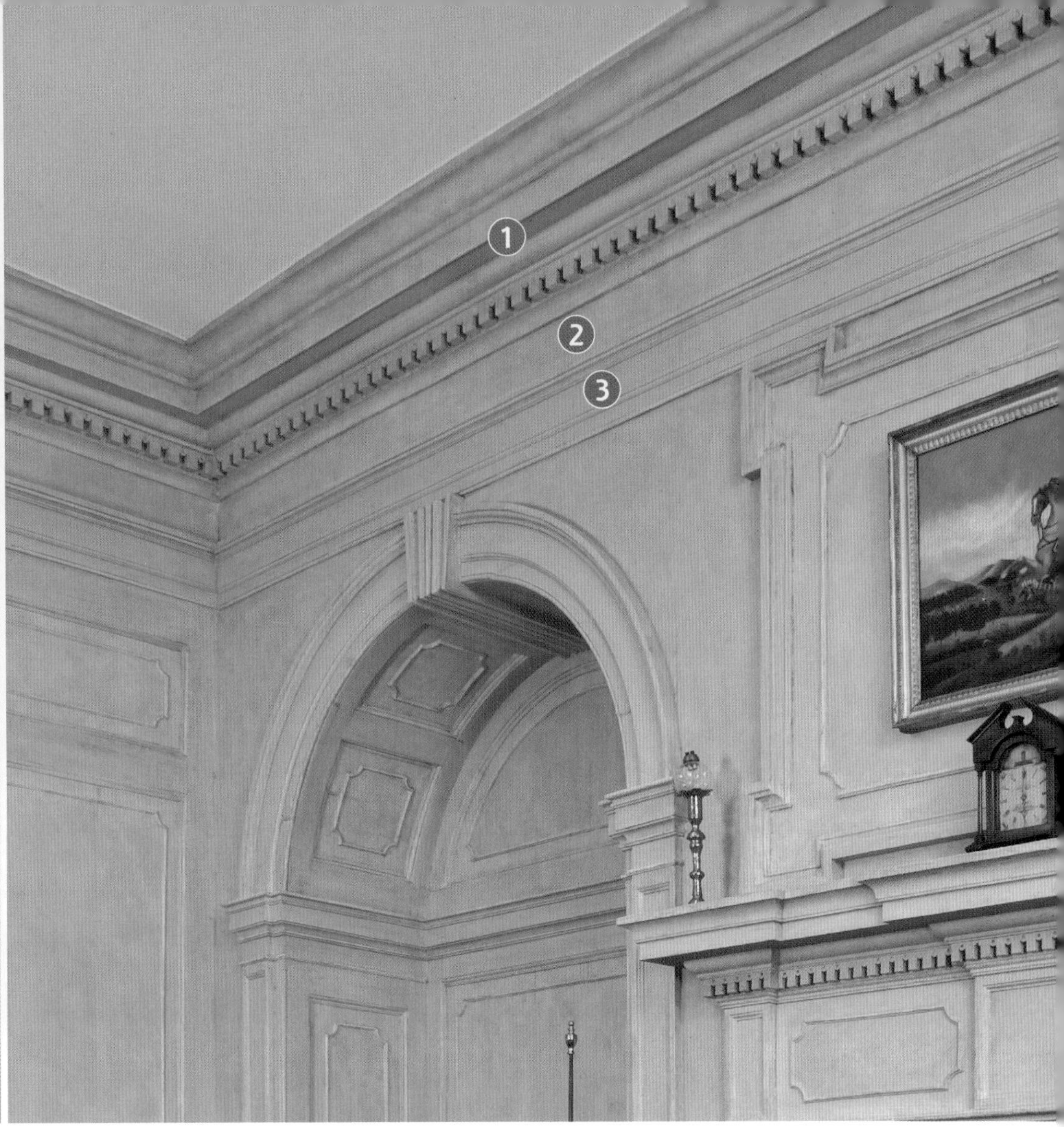

Cornice

The Lancaster Room has a full entablature composed of a cornice (1), frieze (2), and architrave (3) wrapping the room. It is not common to express the full entablature in interior conditions as it can appear too heavy, but here in the Lancaster Room, it meshes well with the paneled and arched elements beneath it. The cornice has its recognizable elements of cymatium (4), corona (5), ovolo (6), and dentil (7). Here the dentils, with a swag and drilled hole at the interdentil are similar to those in the Imlay Room (page 88).

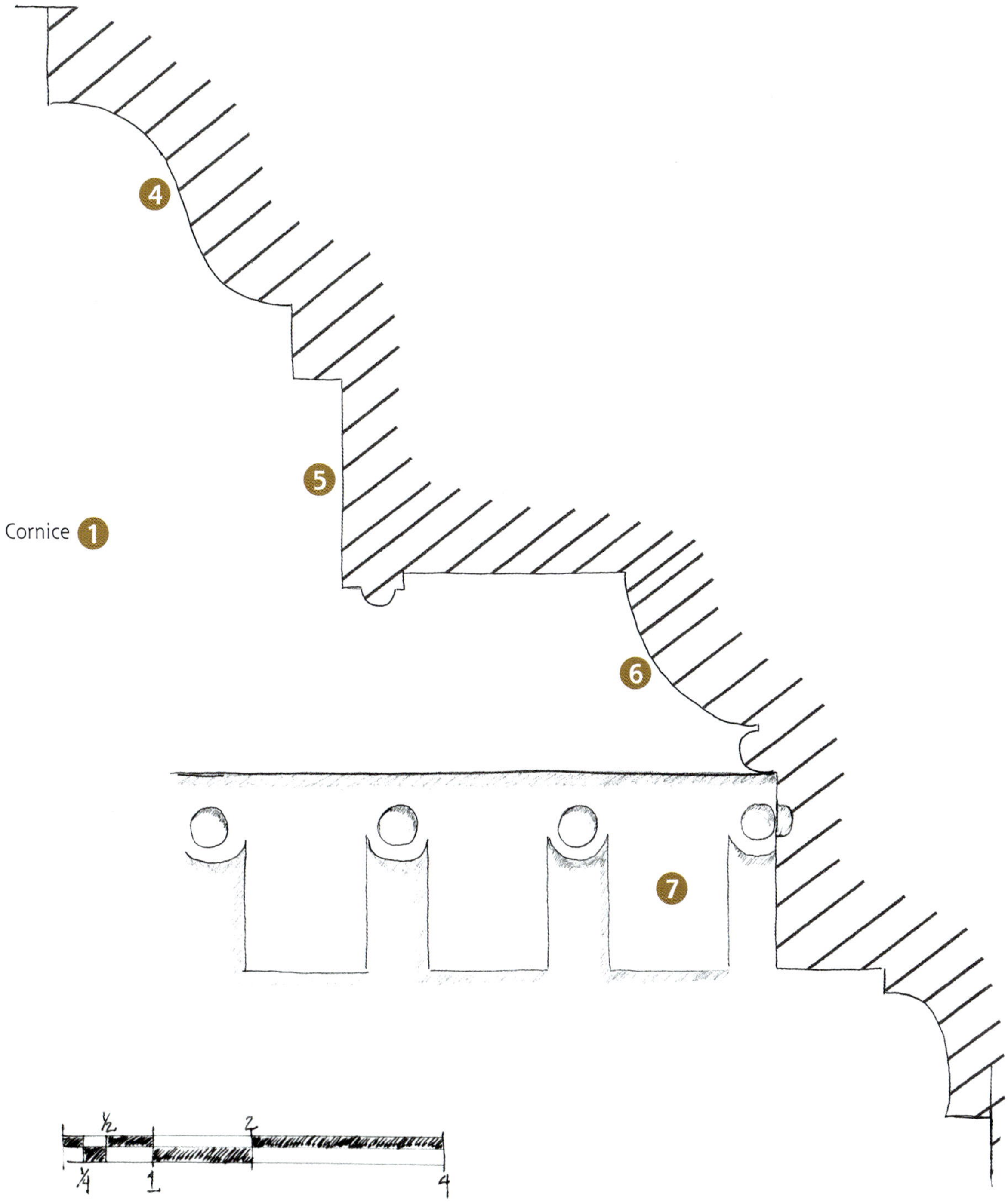

Cornice 1
4
5
6
7
1/2
2
1/4
1
4

Wainscot & Architrave

Robust base and architrave moldings complete the room. Small beads and elliptical, rather than circular, shapes form the moldings, both common elements in later Georgian- and Federal-style architecture.

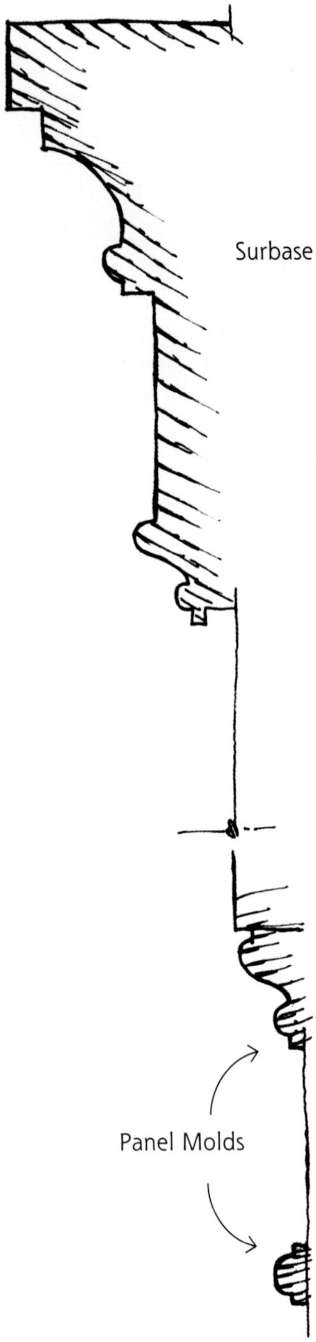

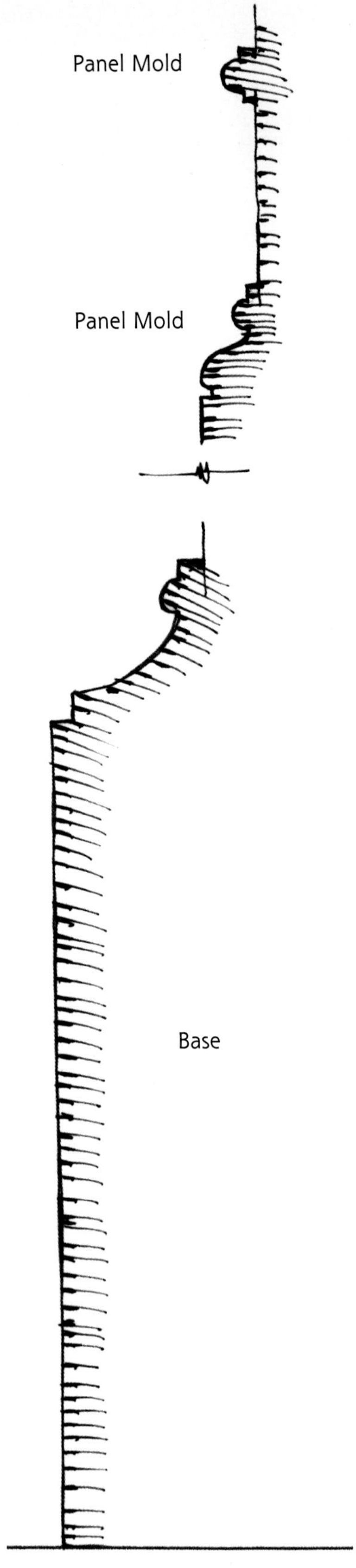

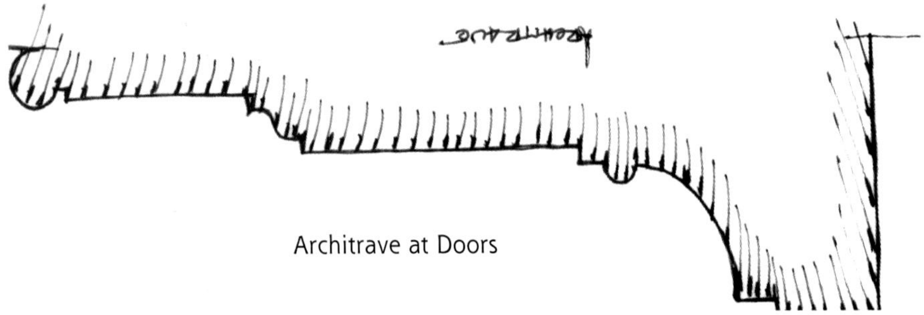

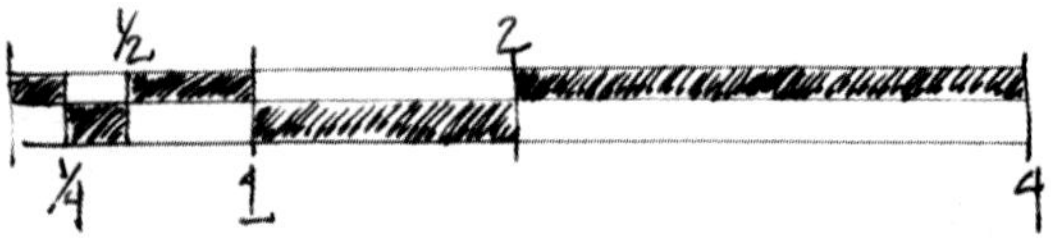

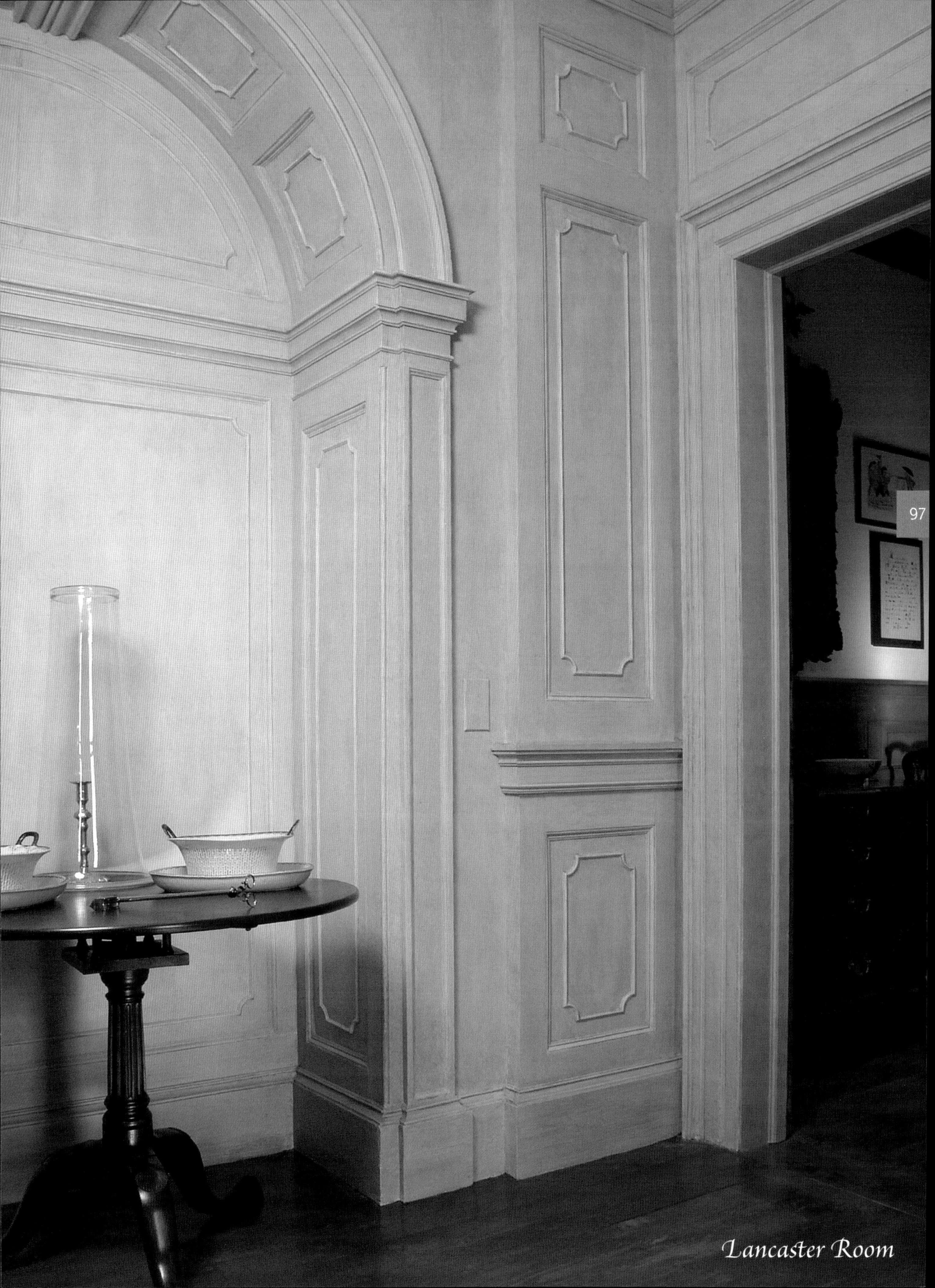

Lancaster Room

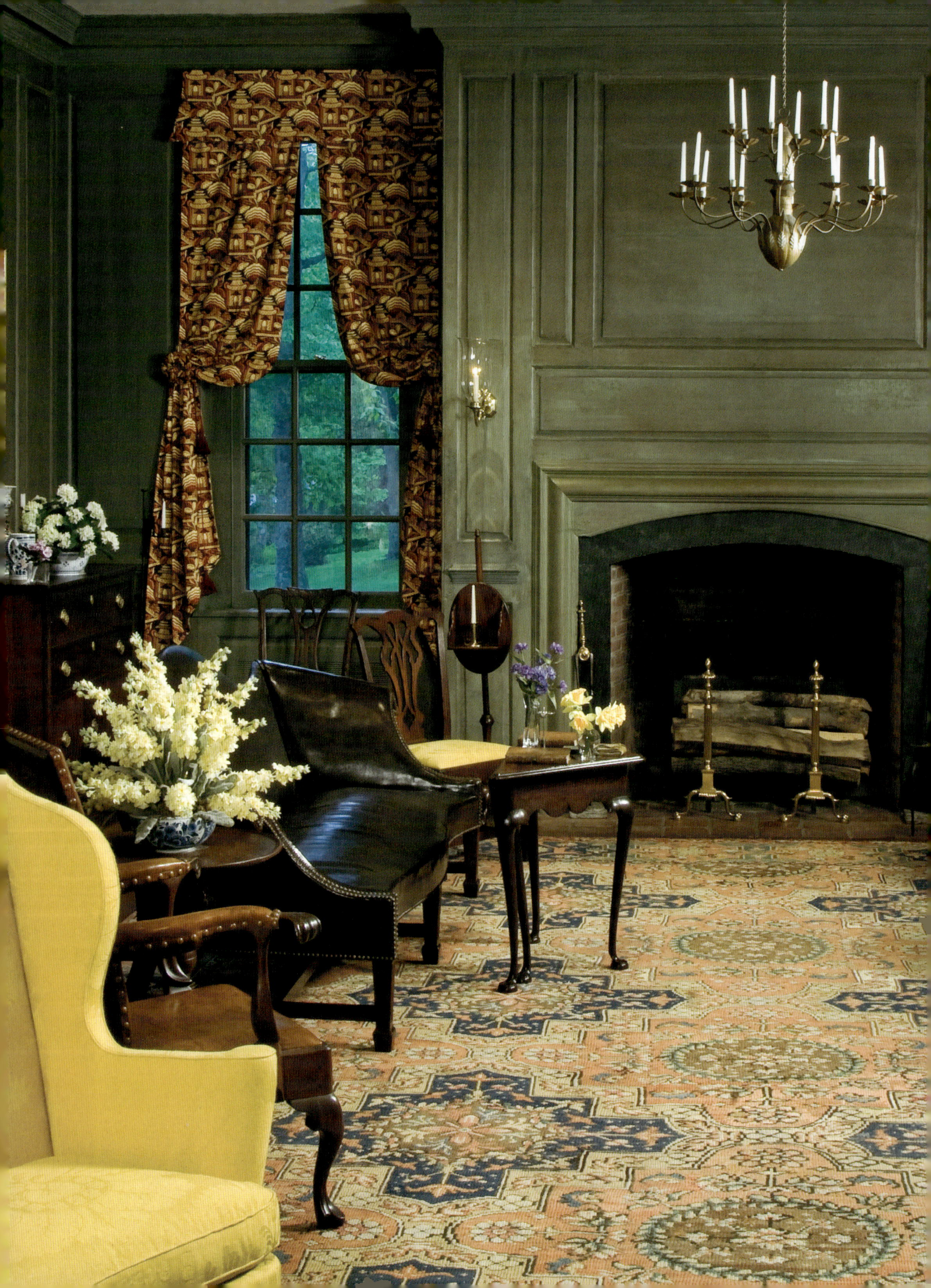

Marlboro Room

Patuxent Manor, Lower Marlboro, Maryland, 1744-1747

11'11" high by 19'1" wide by 22'6" long

The Marlboro Room's woodwork came from the Patuxent Manor, or Grahame House, near the Patuxent River in Calvert County, Maryland. Charles Grahame, the owner, was well established in the area, with ties to both aristocracy and wealth.

It is thought the Tidewater manor was built in 1744, as it is the date inscribed on the original iron fireback. The woodwork from two rooms was combined to become the Marlboro Room, a large room of graceful proportions. The entire room is fully paneled and divided into a dado, or pedestal level, and an upper register of panels at the wall above the dado. A simple cornice finishes the room. This composition of cornice, paneled walls, and dado is the simplest expression of the classical language with only the necessary parts present to hint at the invisible order of the room. It is common to a room of this period in America, unlike rooms with fully expressed Orders.

The Marlboro Room served as the Winterthur sitting room during the du Pont's residence.

Panels

The paneled walls lend a dignified air to the room with a tall upper panel creating the perception of height. A chair rail and lower panels in the dado visually support the upper panels and divide the room vertically. This is a classical method of establishing the scale of a room and proportioning the separate regions of the wall plane.

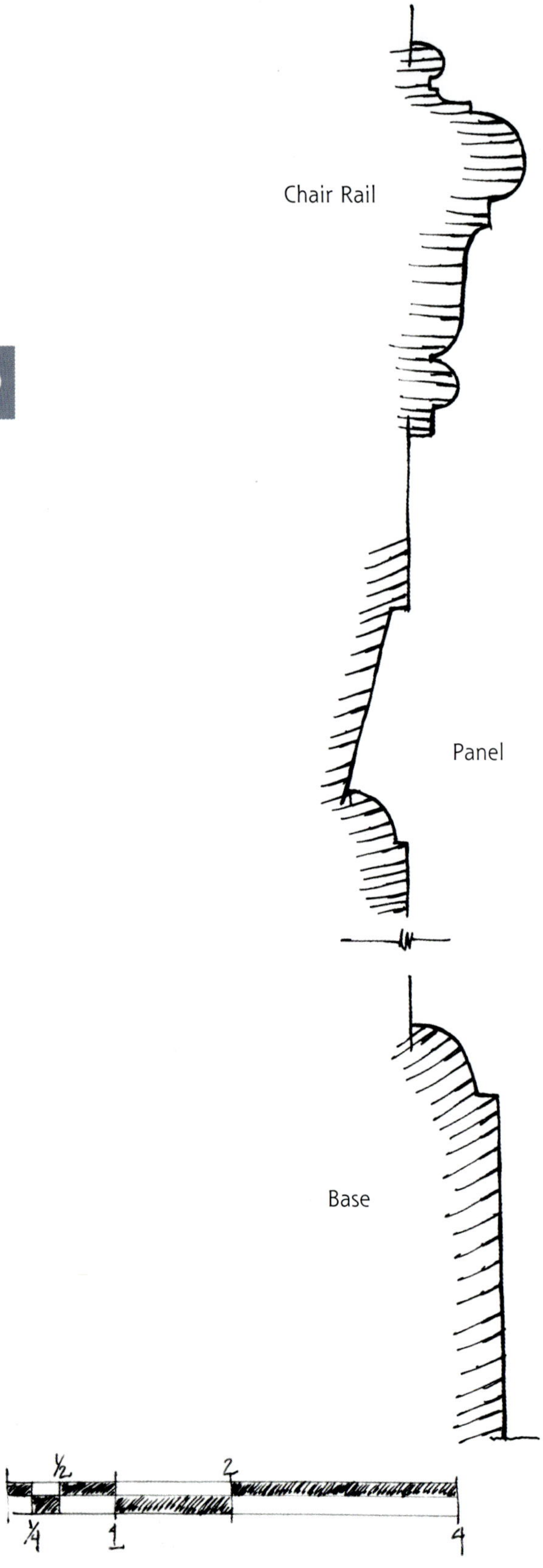

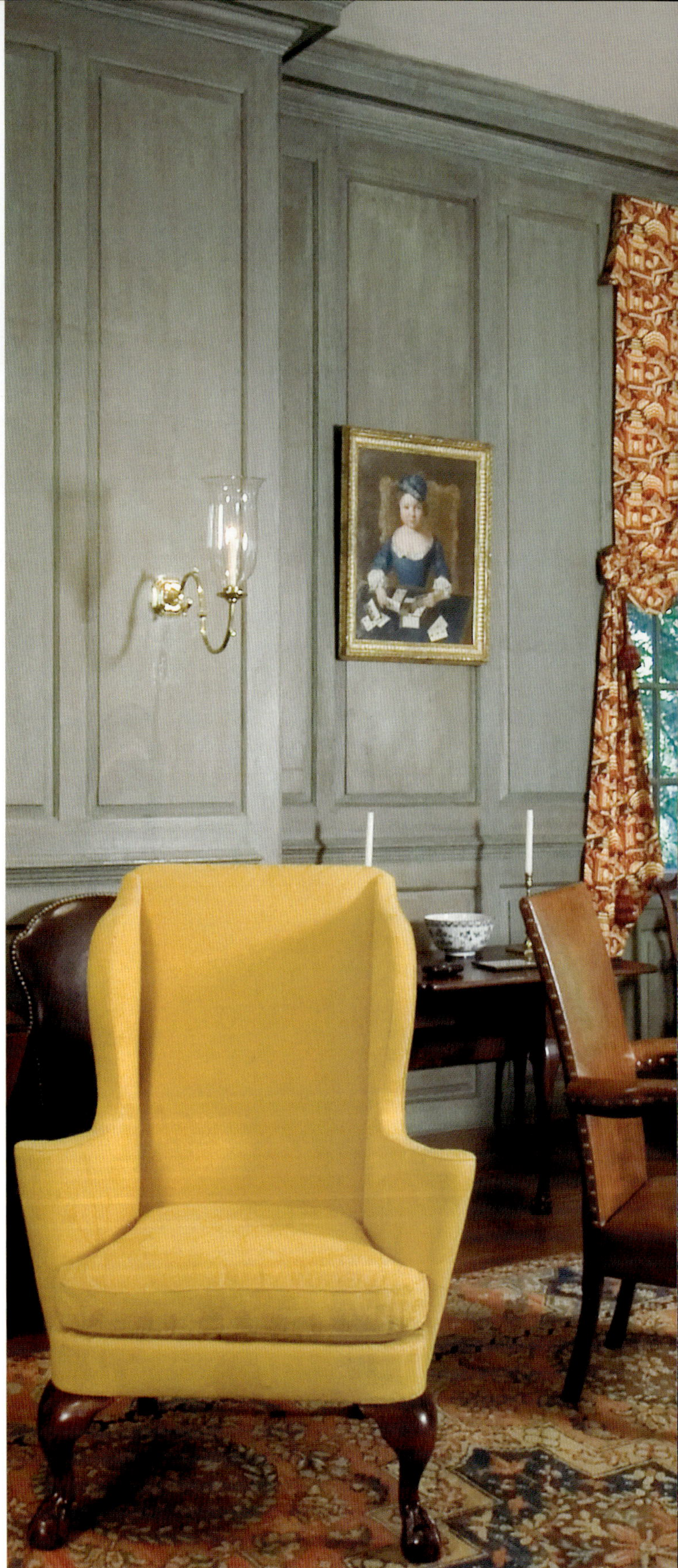

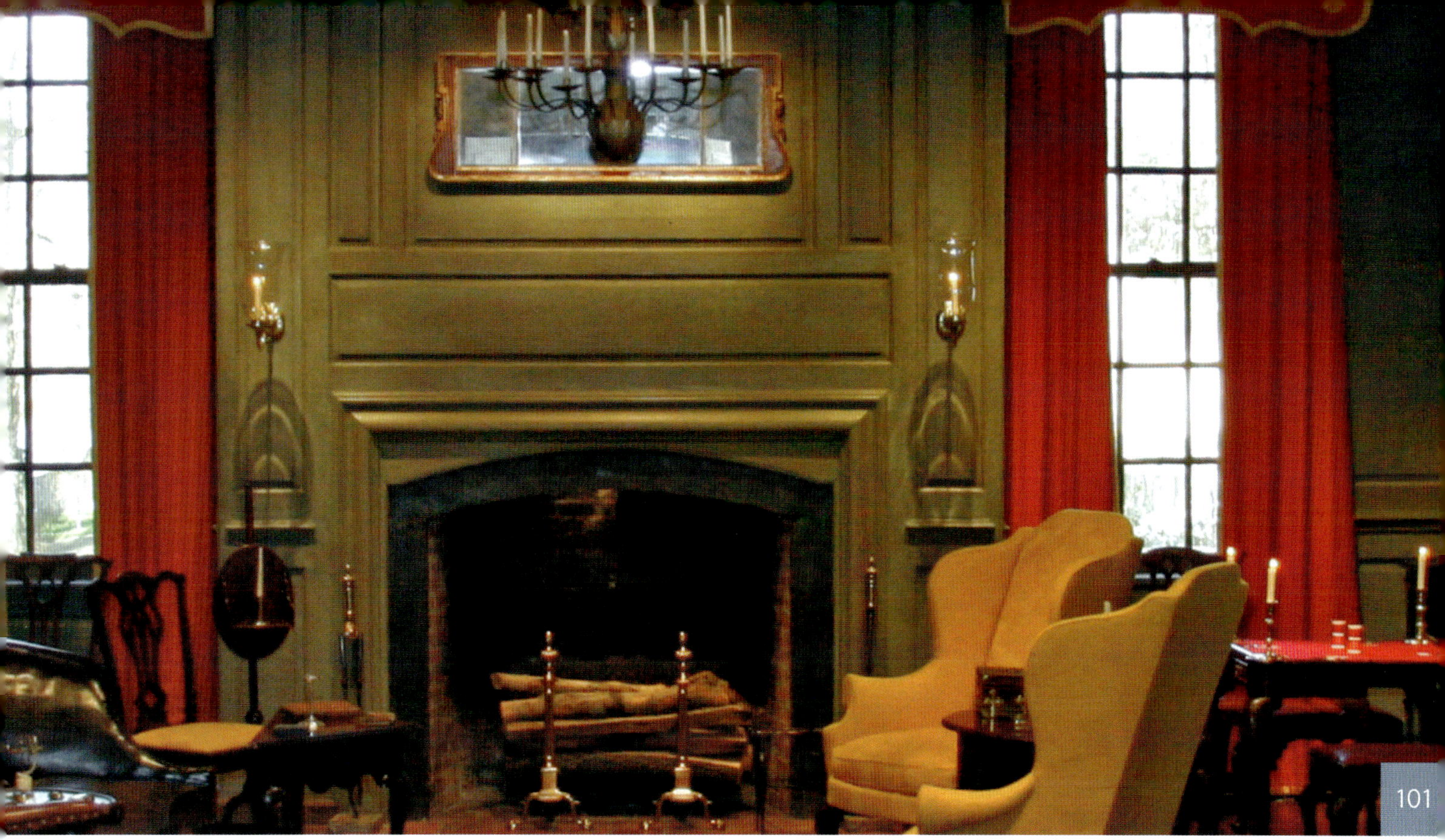

Fireplace Wall

The firebox is arched and wrapped in a square frame articulated by a bolection molding. On either side of the fireplace, tall thin panels above the chair rail can be read as columnar-like elements resting on the pedestal-like area of the dado.

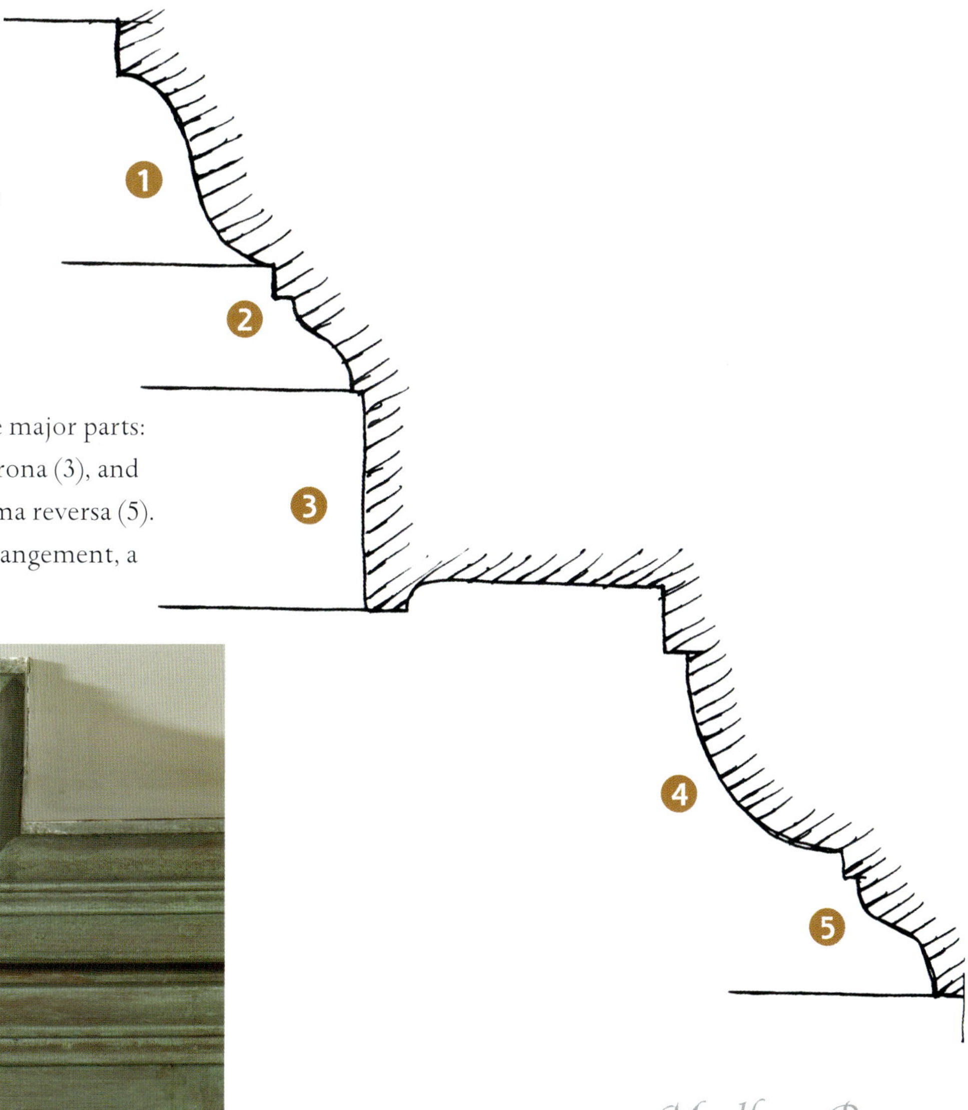

Cornice

The cornice is simple and formed of three major parts: a cymatium (1) with its bedmold (2), a corona (3), and a bedmold formed of an ovolo (4) and cyma reversa (5). Georgian cornices commonly use this arrangement, a simplified Ionic cornice profile.

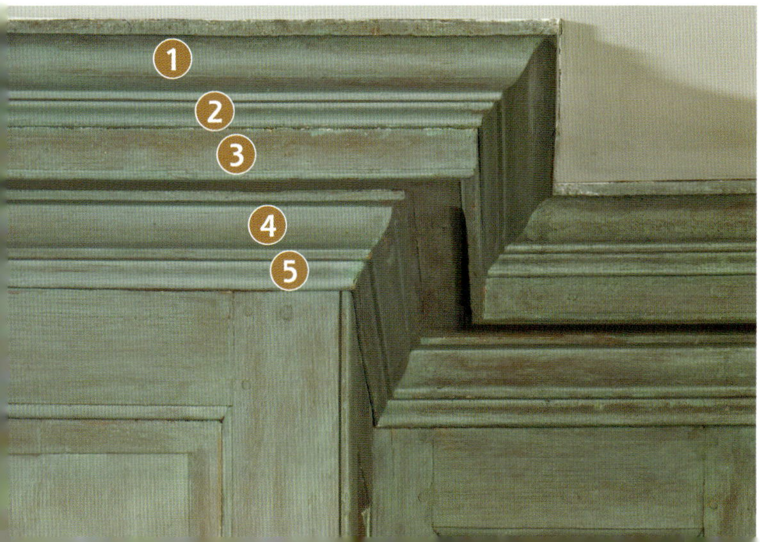

Marlboro Room

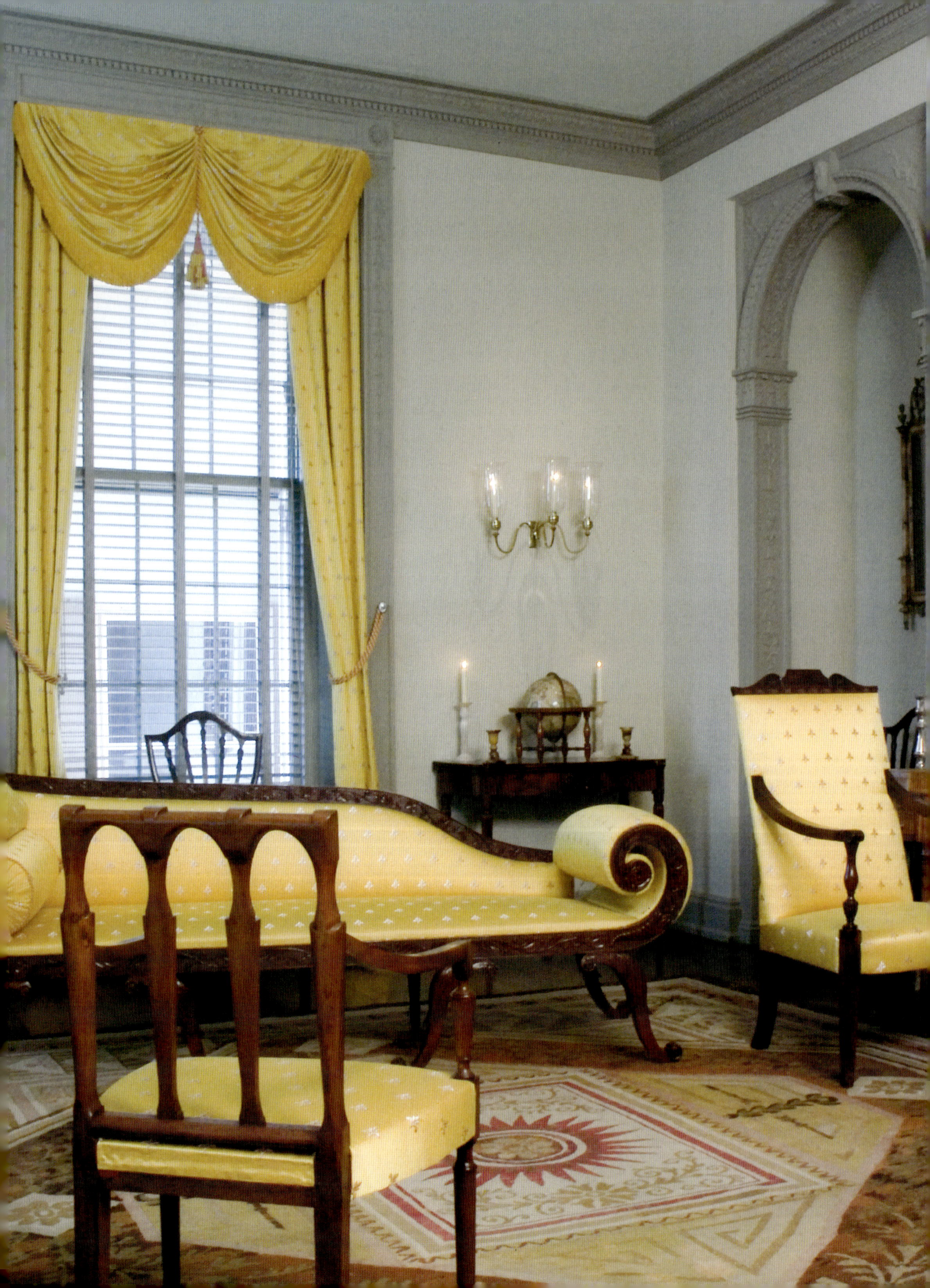

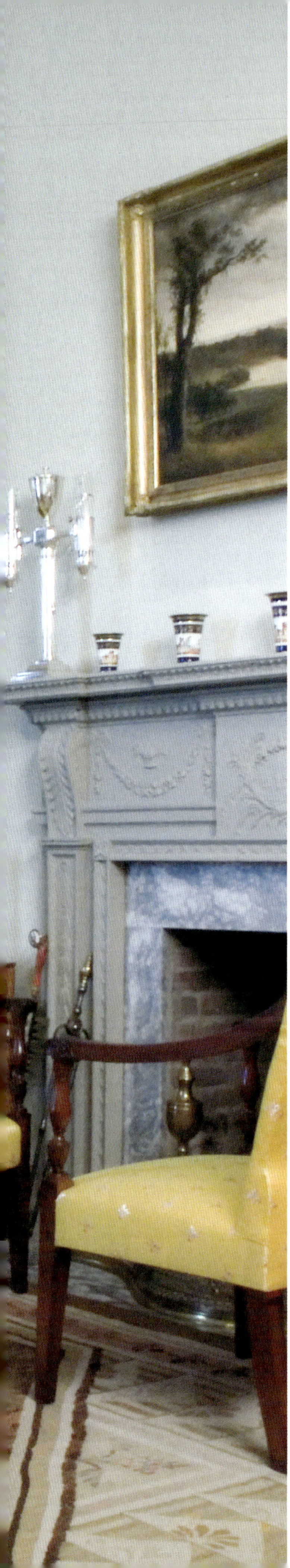

McIntire Bedroom

Philadelphia, Pennsylvania, 1810

11'4" high by 14'4" wide by 28'2" long

The McIntire Bedroom is named after Samuel McIntire, a talented wood carver from Salem, Massachusetts, who is thought to have carved the bed in the room. The room also has ties to another famous craftsman, Robert Wellford, who built the Breen House and lived in it a short time. Ironically, Wellford, a Philadelphia craftsman, was known for his composition ornament, or compo, which is a less-expensive means of attaining the look of carved wood or plaster.

The house was built early in Wellford's career and was an opportunity to display his composition decorations and his skills to his patrons. Wellford's work is well represented at Winterthur in this and other rooms.

The McIntire Bedroom is a quintessentially Federal-style room, with smooth plain walls rising without a dado or panels, delicately proportioned moldings with a generous layer of applied decoration, and a mantelpiece with a tall frieze and center panel, also decorated with classical motifs.

The McIntire Bedroom is decorated with fine composition ornament.

Cornice

In comparison to the height of the room, the cornice isn't large. It consists of an acanthus-ornamented cymatium (1) with a row of dentils below (2) supported by a bedmold (3) with an applied water leaf motif. The overall cornice, without an extended corona, only projects six and one-quarter inches and is a mere eight inches tall. The base molding rises up about seven inches and is topped with a double-beaded cap (see base molding, facing page).

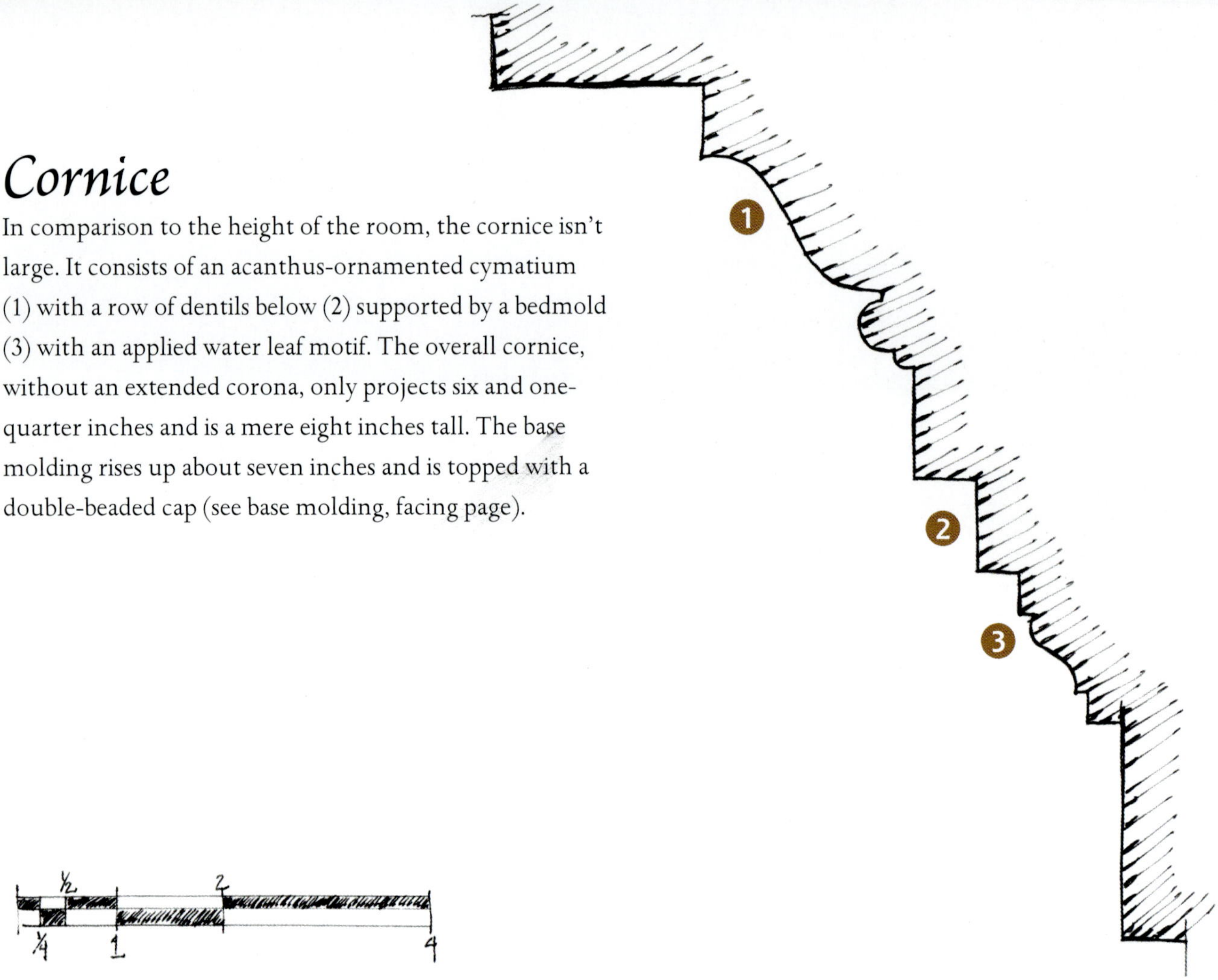

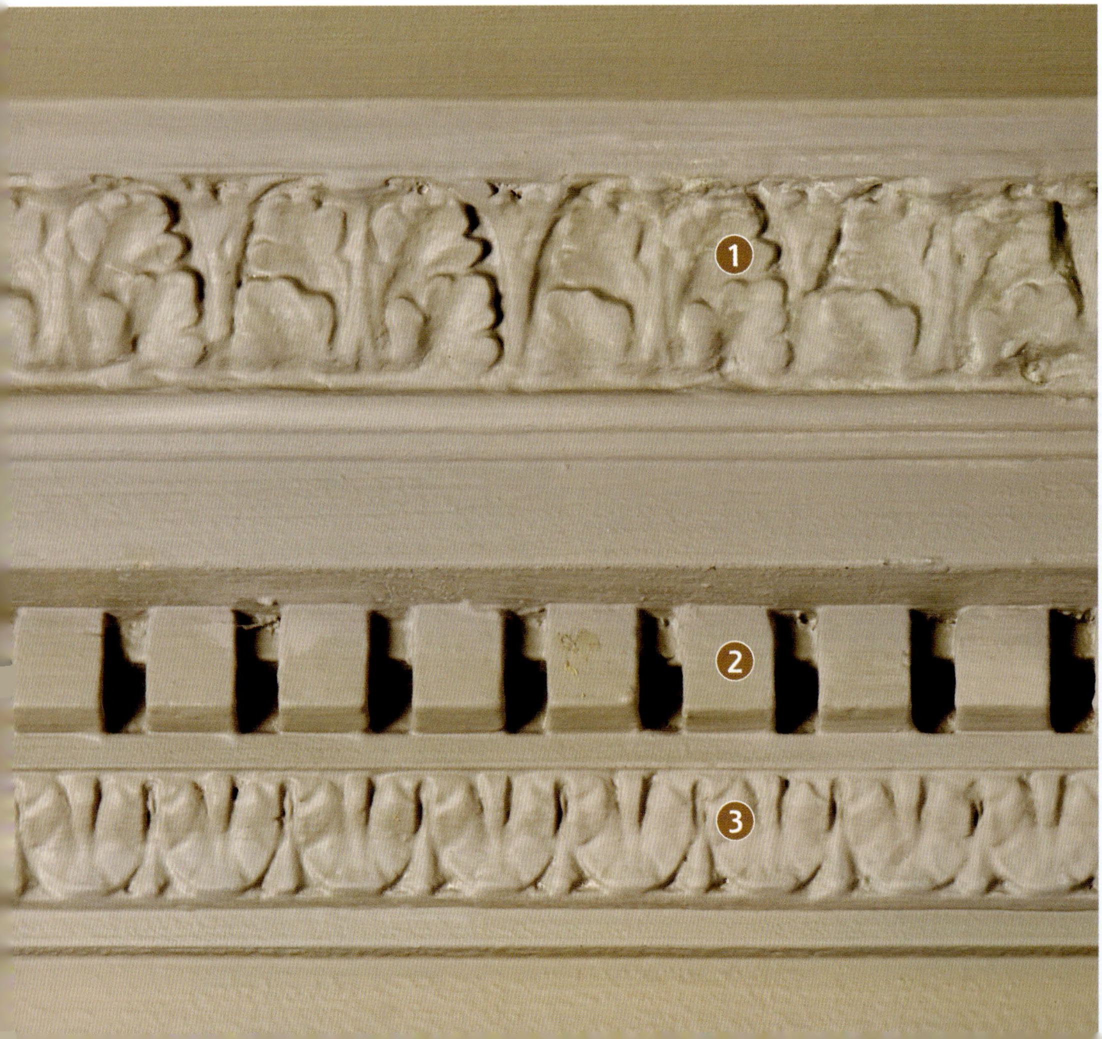

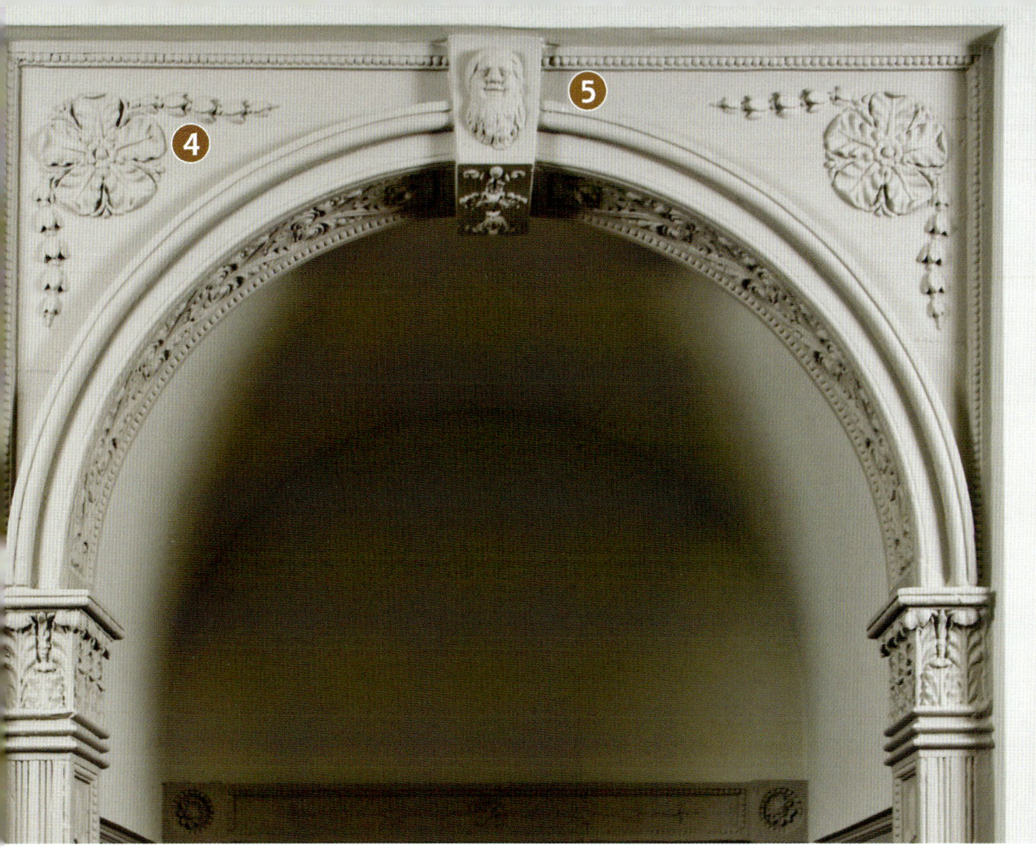

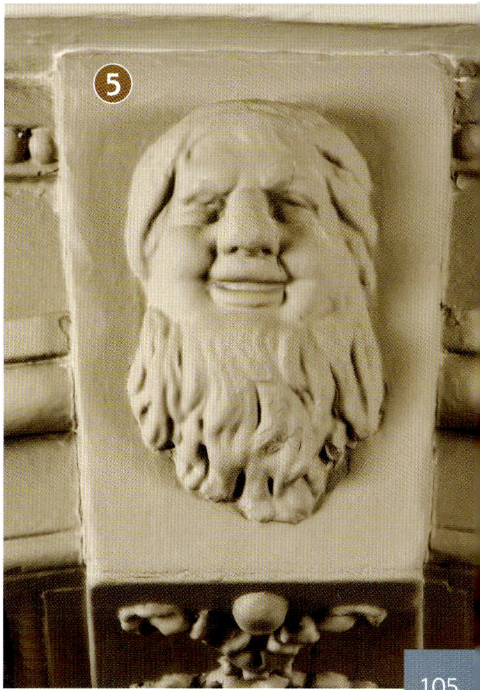

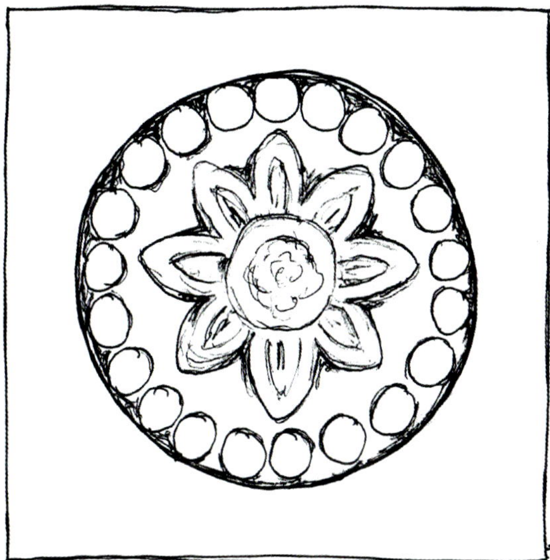

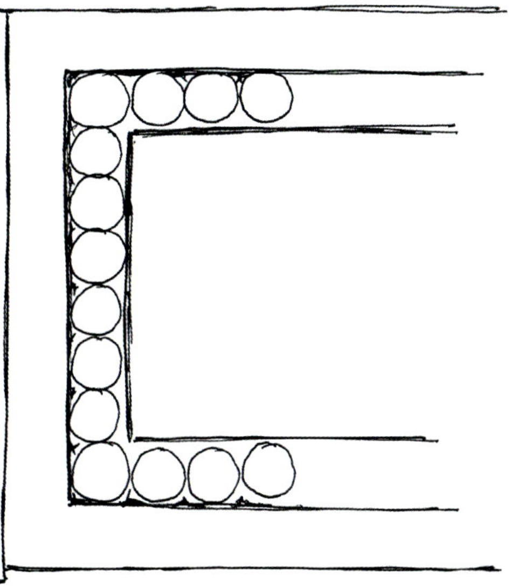

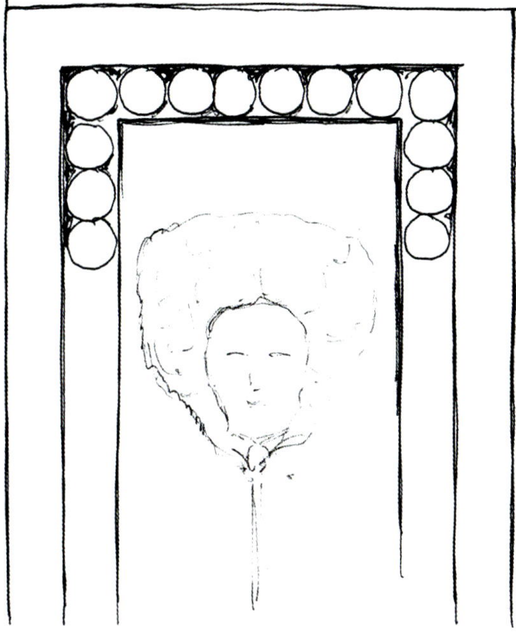

Architraves

Aside from the mantelpiece, the most interesting decorative elements occur around the doors and windows. Two great arches flank the fireplace; the spandrels (4) and pilasters are decorated with composition, and a whimsical face graces the keystone (5). The door and window architraves are decorated with a beaded panel mold and a garland of flowers in the panel field. A flower element punctuates the corner blocks where the vertical and horizontal architraves meet (left).

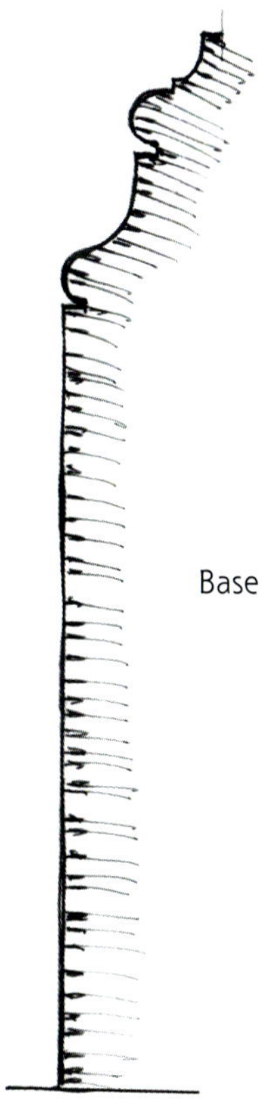

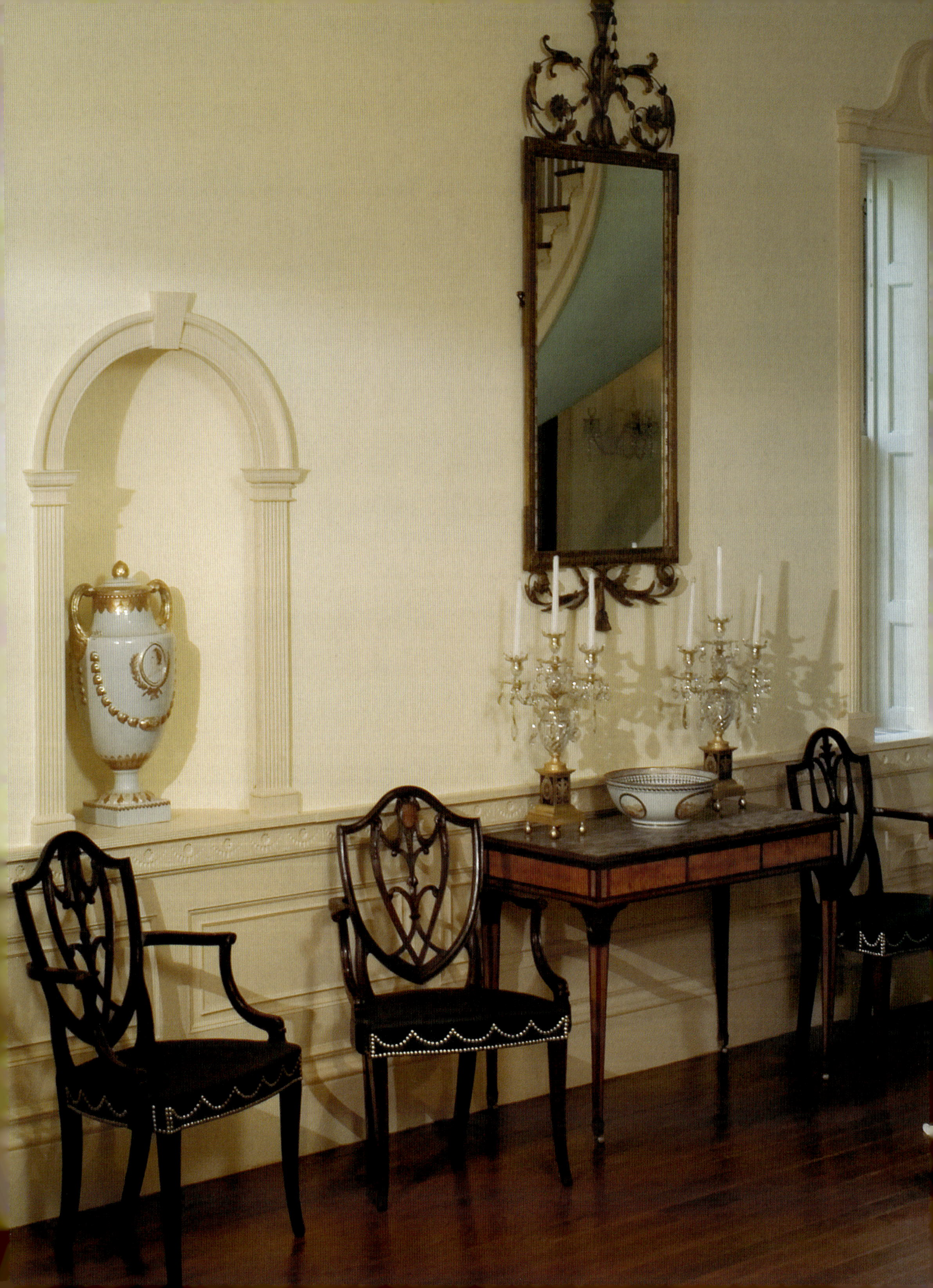

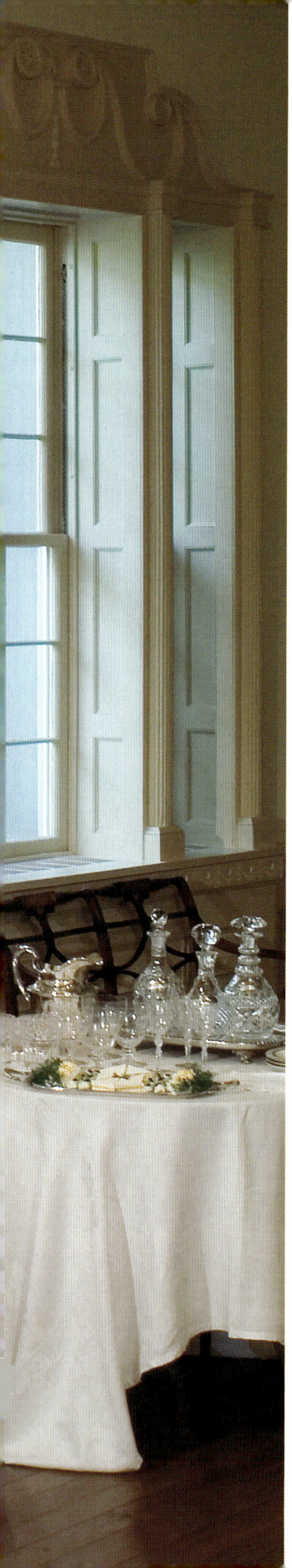

Montmorenci

Shocco Springs, North Carolina, circa 1822

General William Williams, a colorful character and wealthy plantation owner, built Montmorenci in Shocco Springs, North Carolina. The region's mountains and natural springs attracted people from port cities, who sought to escape from the summer's coastal heat and malaria. As such, Shocco Springs had a lively social life in the summers, and General Williams' house, set amid more than 6,000 acres of wheat and tobacco fields, became a hub of social activity.

The most striking feature from Montmorenci, its freestanding staircase, was originally round in plan and rose only one floor in height. At Winterthur, it was rebuilt to be elliptical in plan and rising up a full two floors. Though modified from the original, these rooms from Montmorenci, created using Federal-era millwork, were done with flair and knowledge of the Federal style.

Montmorenci's main stair hall captures Federal-style elegance with its graceful ornamentation.

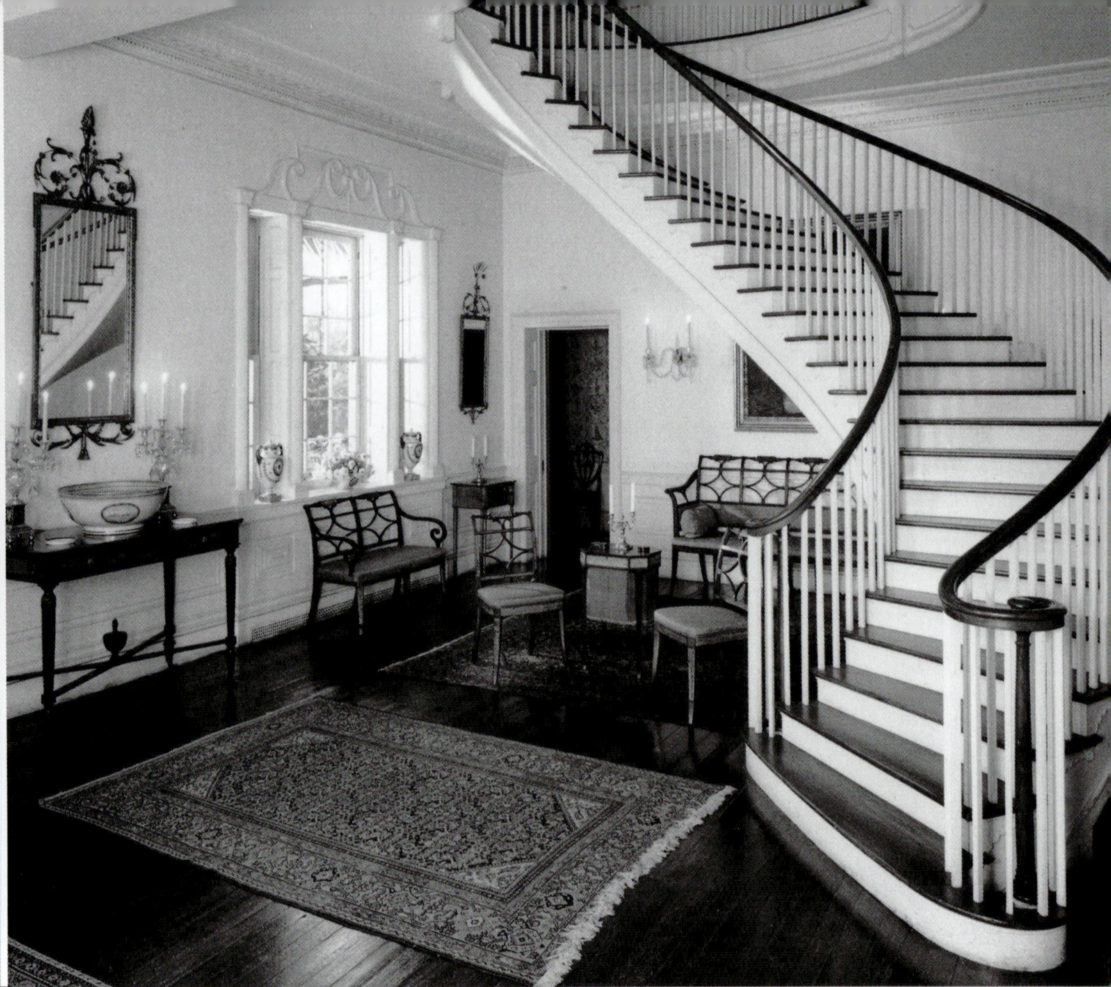

The remarkable staircase spans from the fifth to the seventh floors at Winterthur.

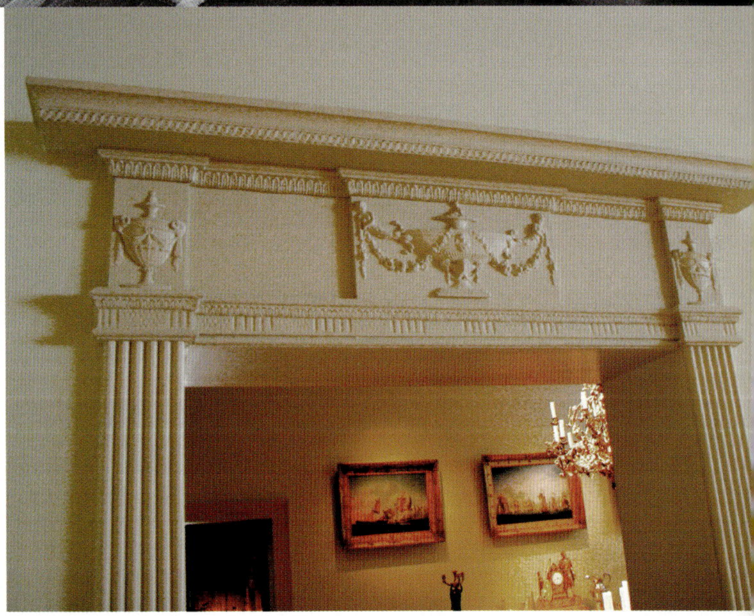

The glorious staircase and house appealed to Mr. du Pont, who bought the interior woodwork and exterior façade before the house was destroyed. Because of its detailing, some believe it was built by Thomas Bragg, a prominent area builder, or James Burgess, his carpenter.

Composition moldings resembling those made by Robert Wellford of Philadelphia grace the interiors. It is known that General Williams traveled to Philadelphia, where Wellford was based, and to Petersburg, North Carolina, where Williams sold his tobacco and Wellford had an agent selling his composition work.

Three of Montmorenci's rooms, the Stair Hall, Empire Hall, and Library Cross Hall, are included here for study.

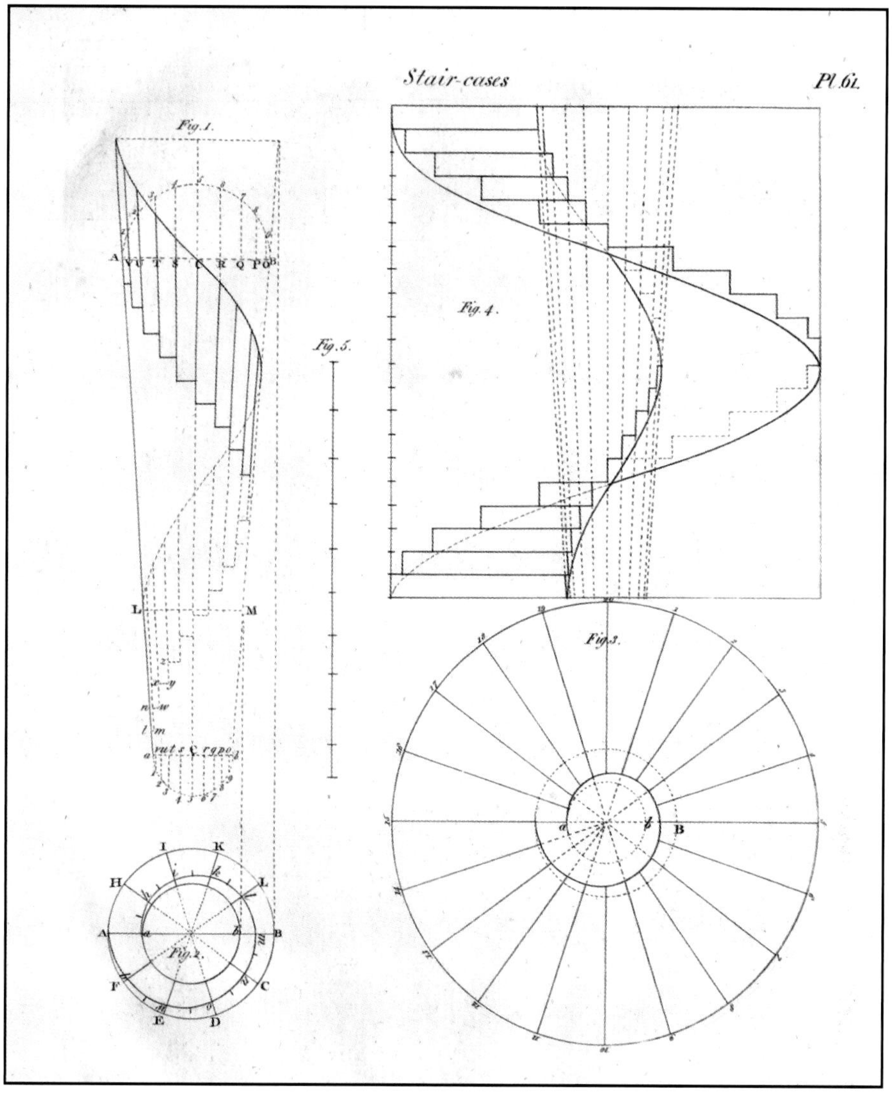

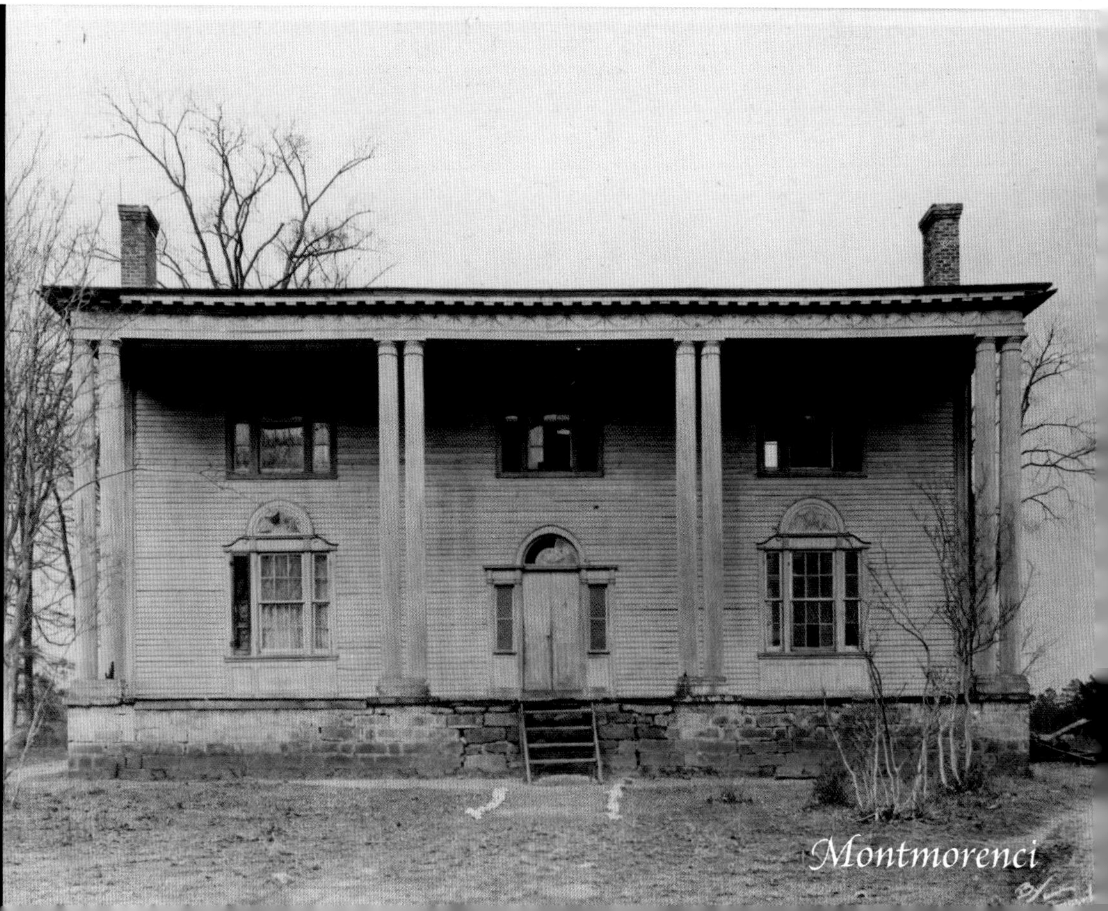

Montmorenci's front porch, with its tall, paired columns, shaded the front elevation of the house from the warm southern sun. High ceilings allowed warm air to rise upward and tall windows aligned for optimal air flow. A three-bay house, Montmorenci's arched front door and sidelights were flanked with three-part windows on both floors.

Photo courtesy Denmark Photo.

Montmorenci Stair Hall

12'6" high by 19'6" wide by 33'5" long

The Stair Hall is the most prominent and striking room from Montmorenci. Spanning two floors in its installation at Winterthur, the hall is most stunning at the base of the stairs looking up at the beautiful, sweeping rise (previous page). Pale walls contrast with dark painted doors, and delicate ornament animates surfaces in the room.

Cornice

The room's cornice is ornamented plaster projecting ten inches along the ceiling yet it is only seven-and-a-half-inches tall. The proportional arrangement is common in Federal-style cornices; earlier Georgian cornices often had a projection equal to their height. In Montmorenci, the soffit of the five-inch-wide corona is detailed with a diamond pattern (1).

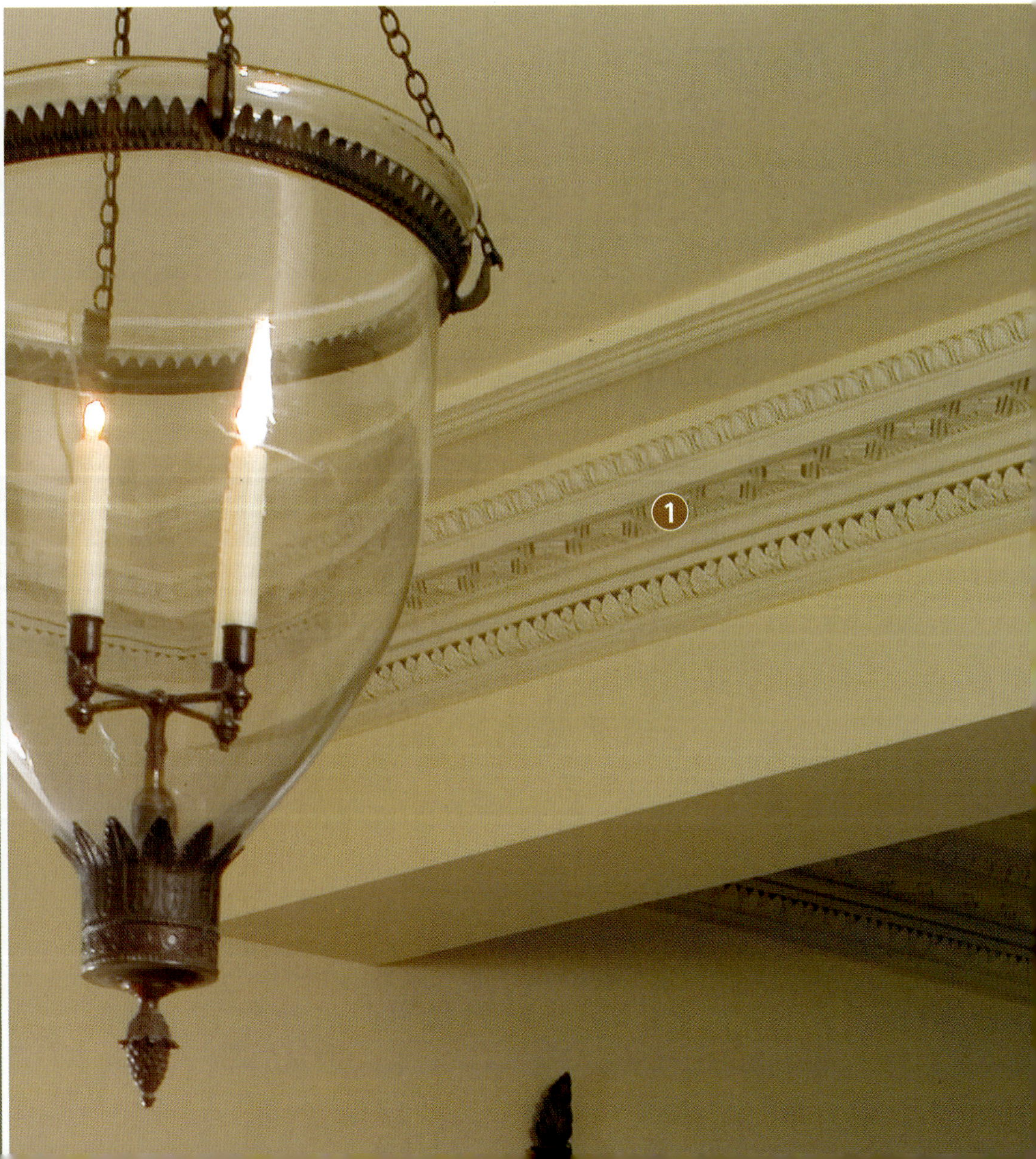

Wainscot

The Stair Hall has a fine wood wainscot that rises up about thirty-five inches. The surbase has a lyrical swag and floral medallion pattern (2) gouged into its surface, the shadows of which give a soft textural effect around the room.

The panels are flat, as is common in the Federal period, and inside the panel is a small applied molding, further lightening the effect. The base is tall, nearly twelve inches in height, with a large base cap (3).

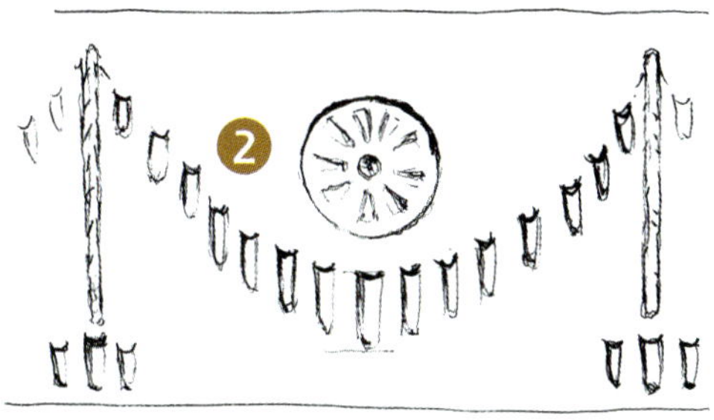

Surbase

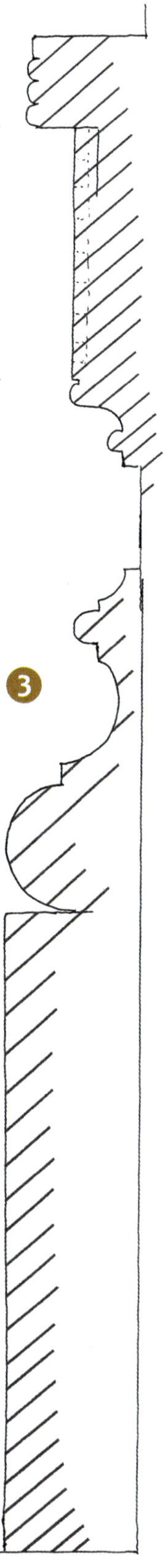

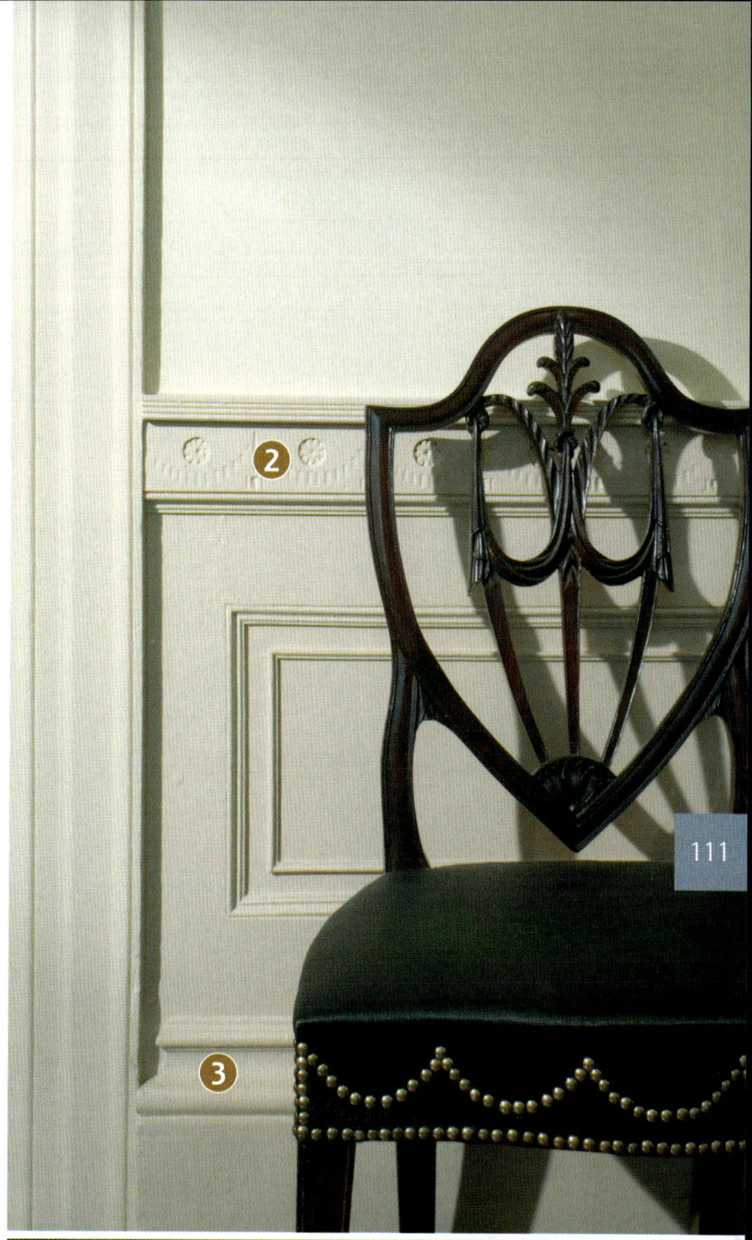

Architraves

Of particular note are the door and window surrounds, the most prominent of which are the most decorated. For example, the wainscot panels (below) under the windows are designed differently than the wainscot panels throughout the rest of the room. Layered, built-up panels frame a center panel with reed-like ornaments that contrast with the flat panels in the wainscot around the room. The overdoor friezes (facing page) have applied ornament in common Federal motifs like wheat sheaves, flowers, swags, and patriotic themes. In particular, the door leading into the Marlboro Room (created from a fireplace surround) depicts the Battle of Lake Erie (right), a victorious naval battle in the War of 1812, and a popular motif at the time.

The architraves around less-important doors are simple, neither carved nor ornamented. These different levels of elaboration establish hierarchy among different areas of the room.

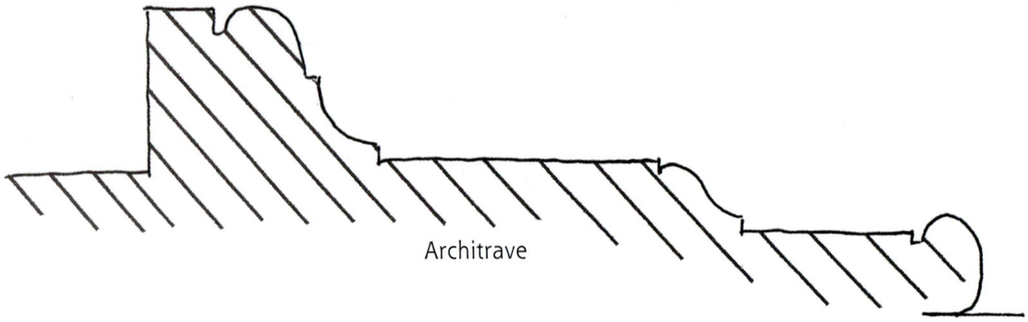
Architrave

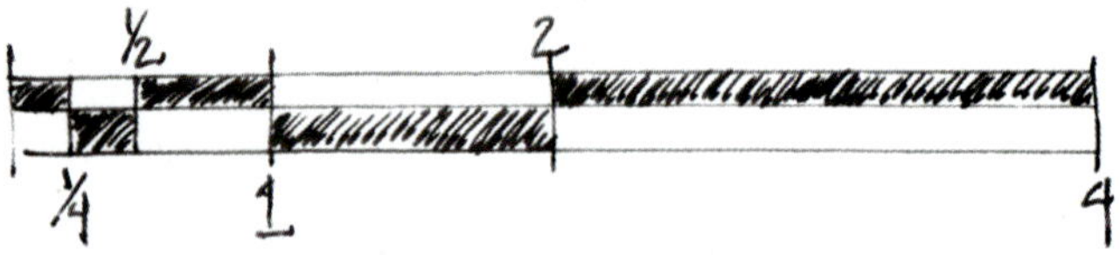

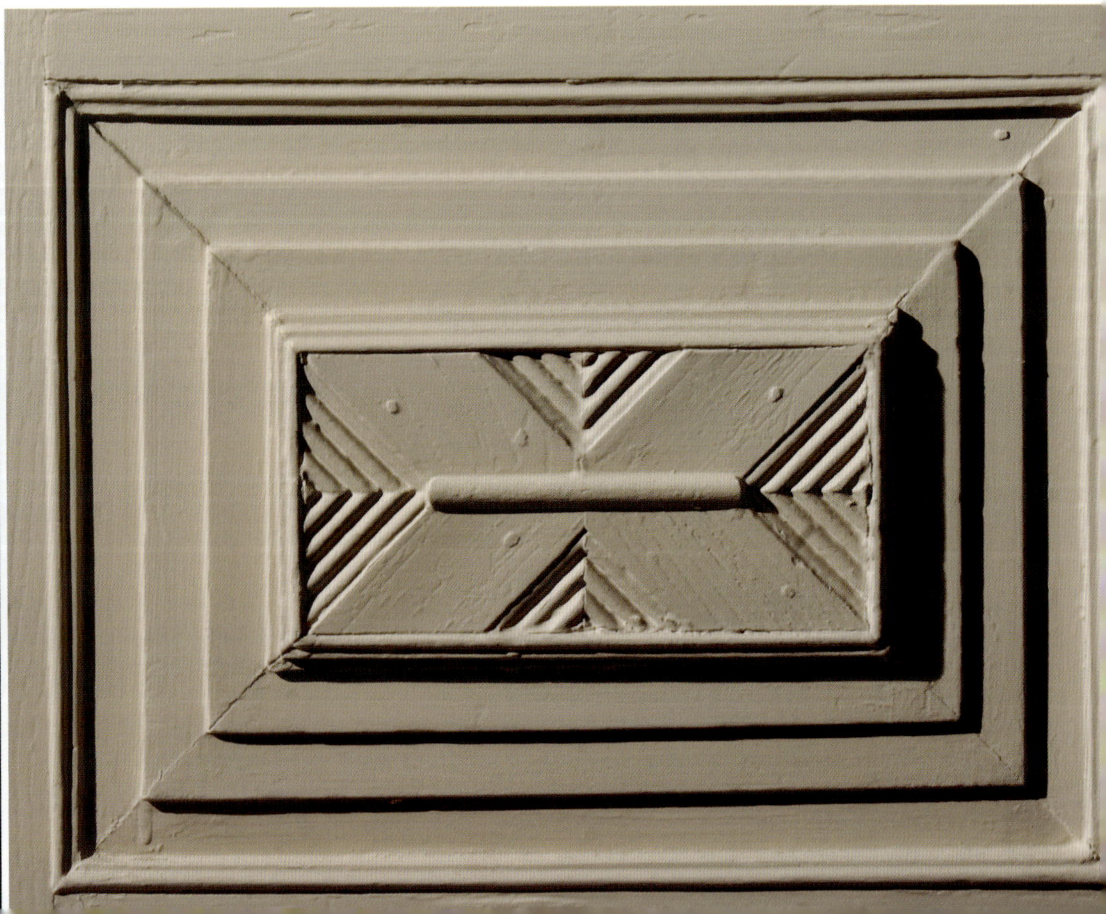

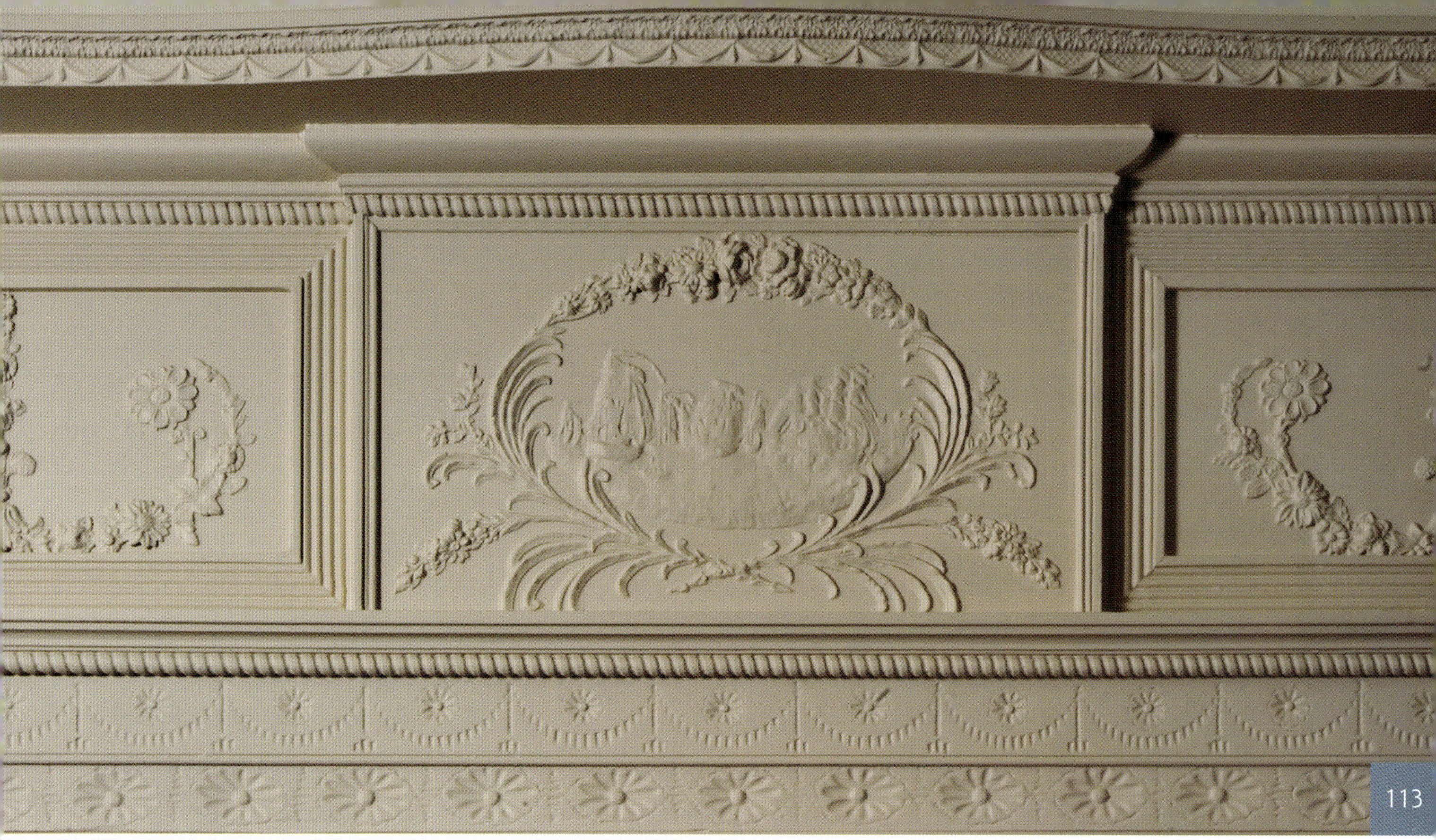

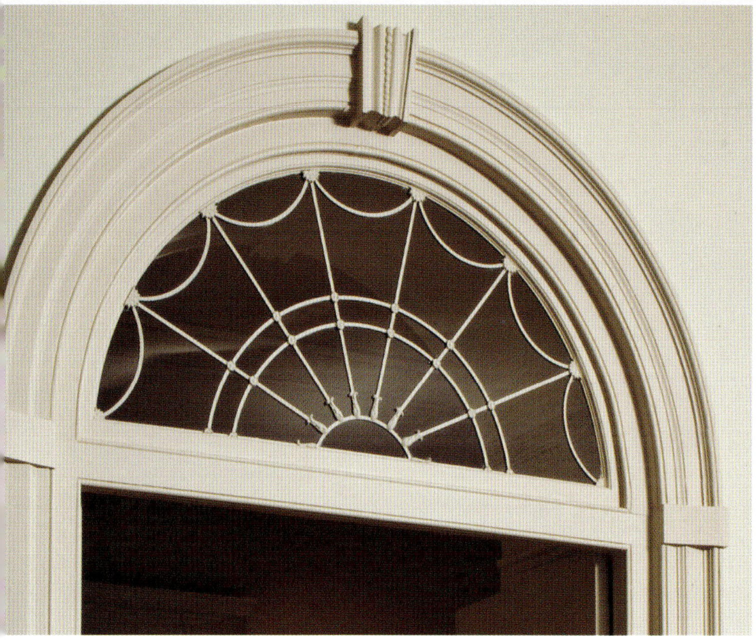

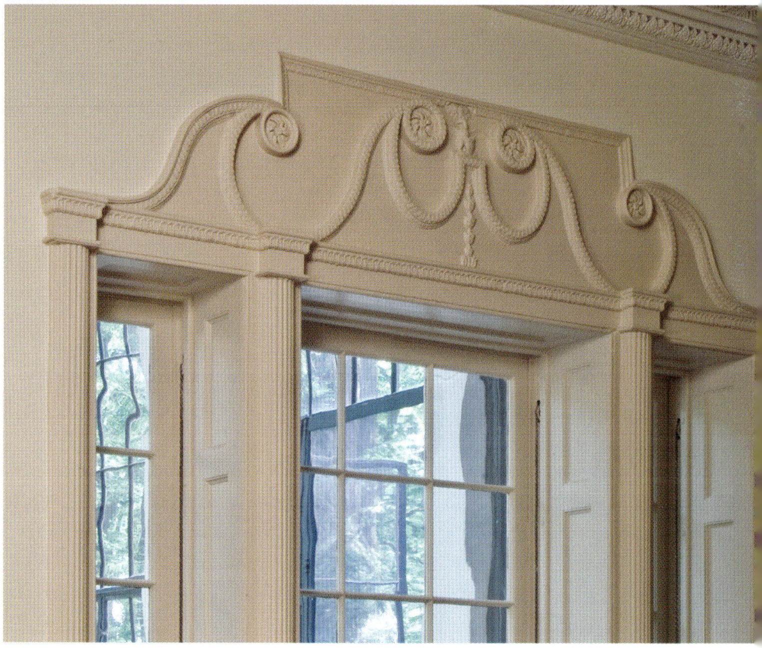

Library Cross Hall

11′ 6″ high by 8′ wide by 32′ long

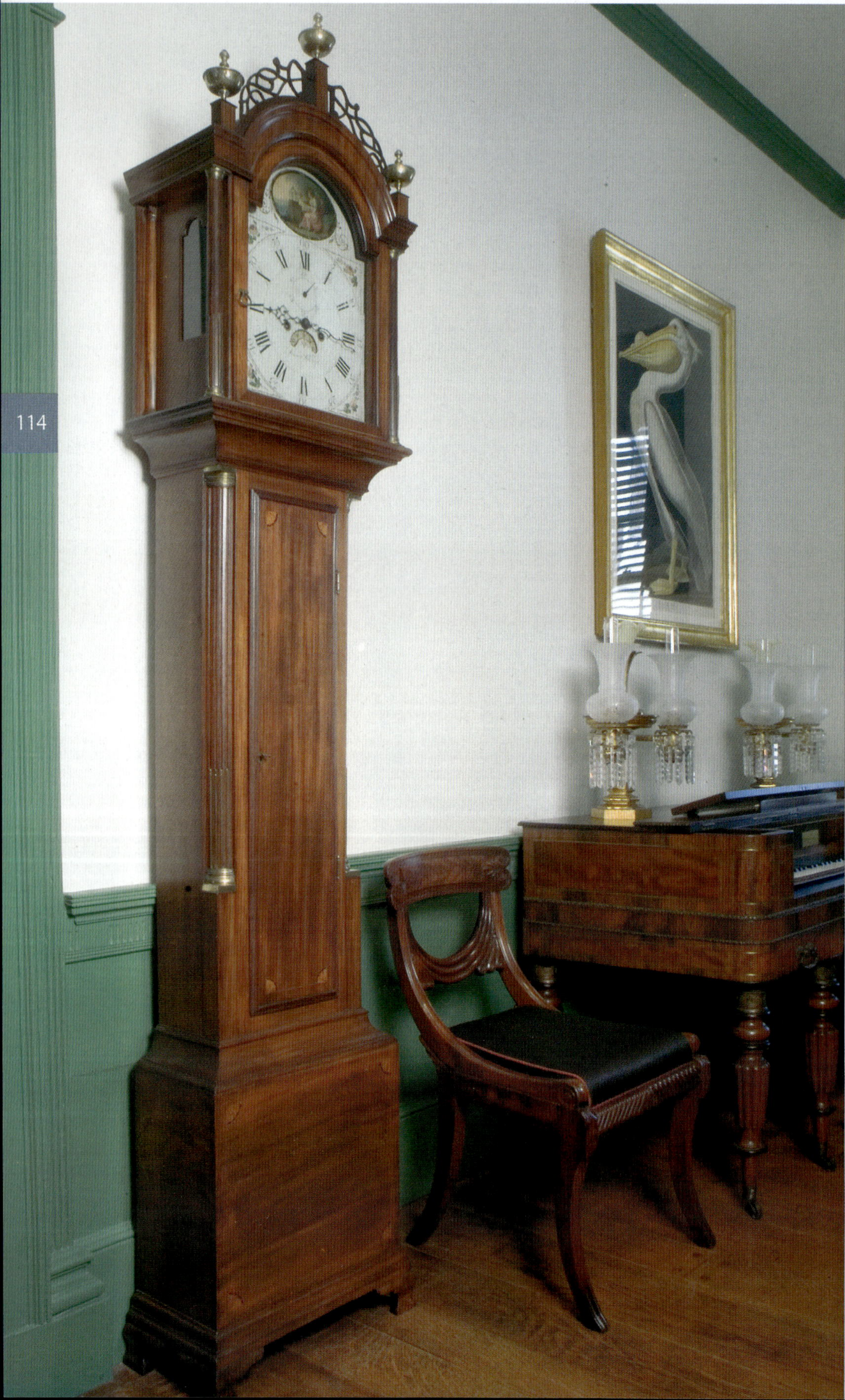

The wide, T-shaped Library Cross Hall connects several rooms at Winterthur.

Cornice

Federal-style moldings, such as this cornice (right), are less canonic than Georgian ones. Here, for example, the cornice elements of cymatium (1), corona (2), and bedmold (3) are formed from uncommon shapes. The carved modillion-like blocks (4) create a rhythm of punctuation around the room.

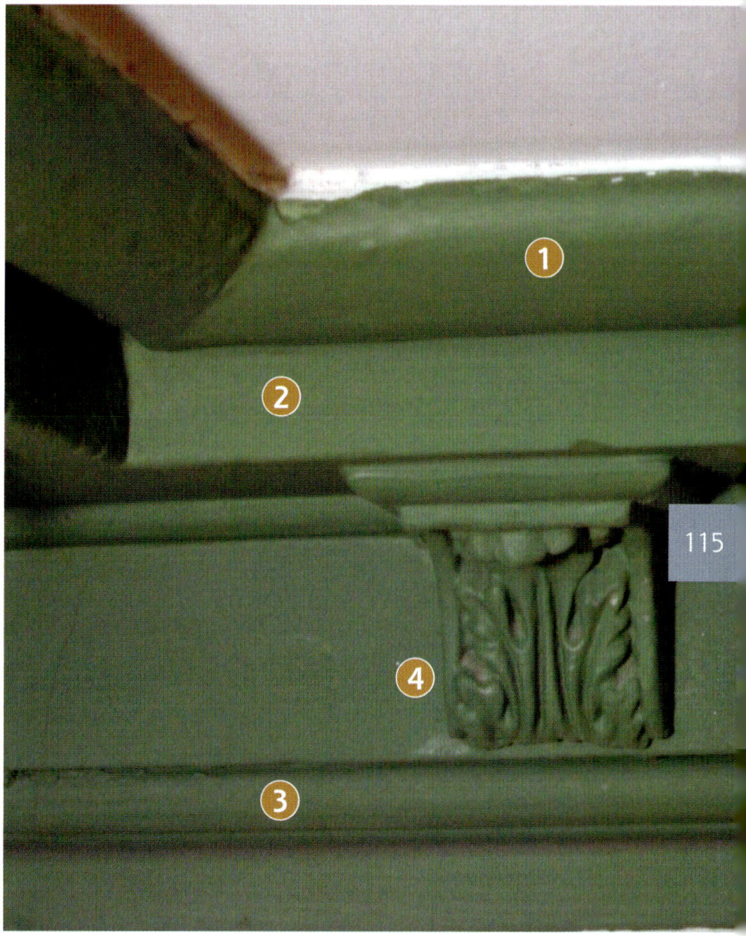

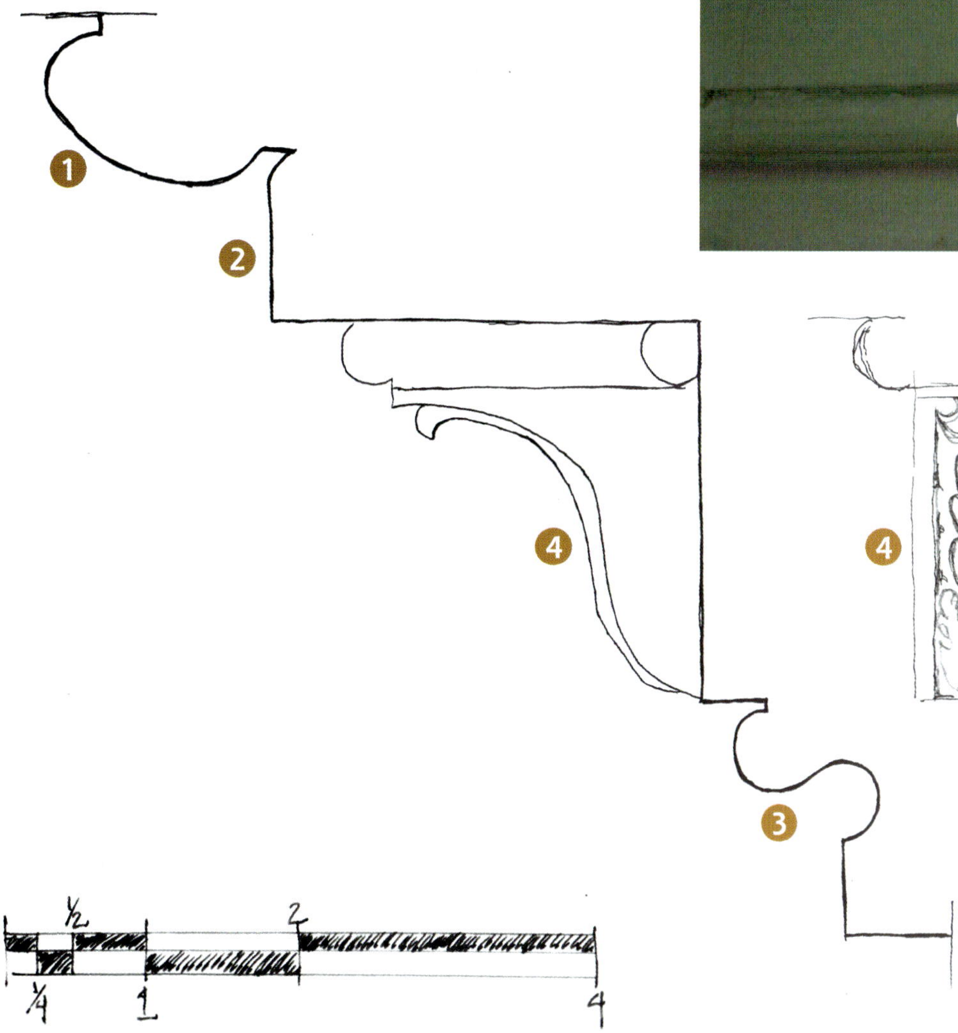

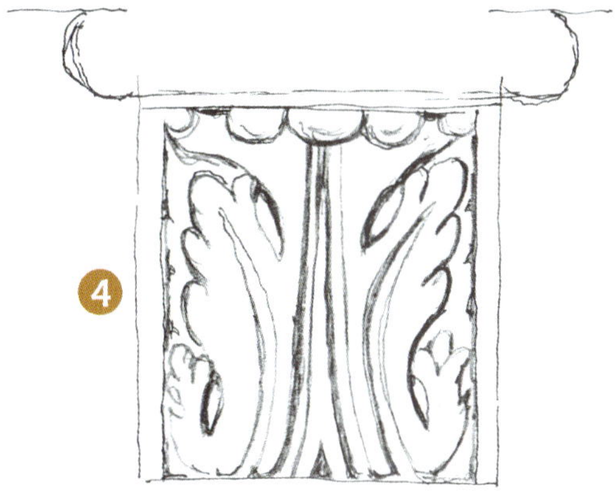

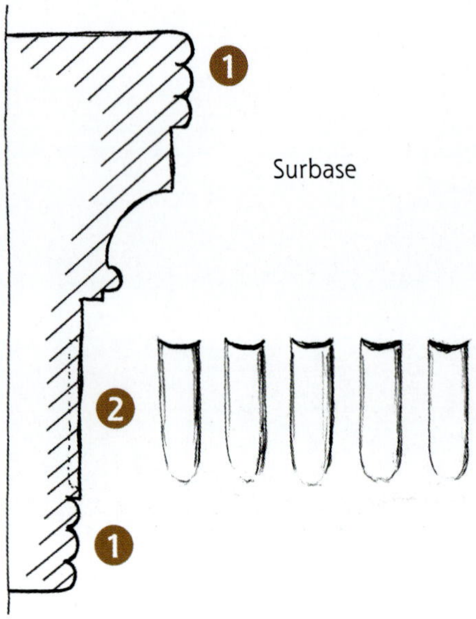

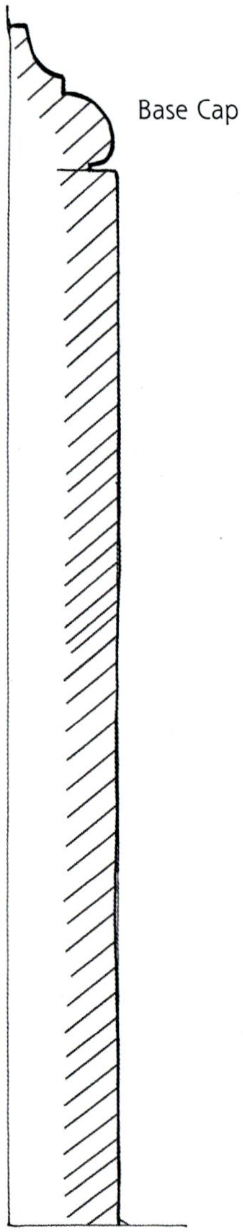

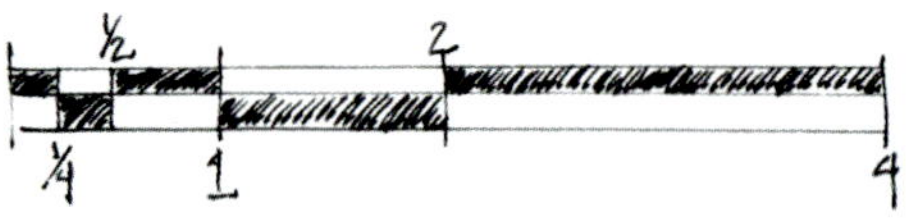

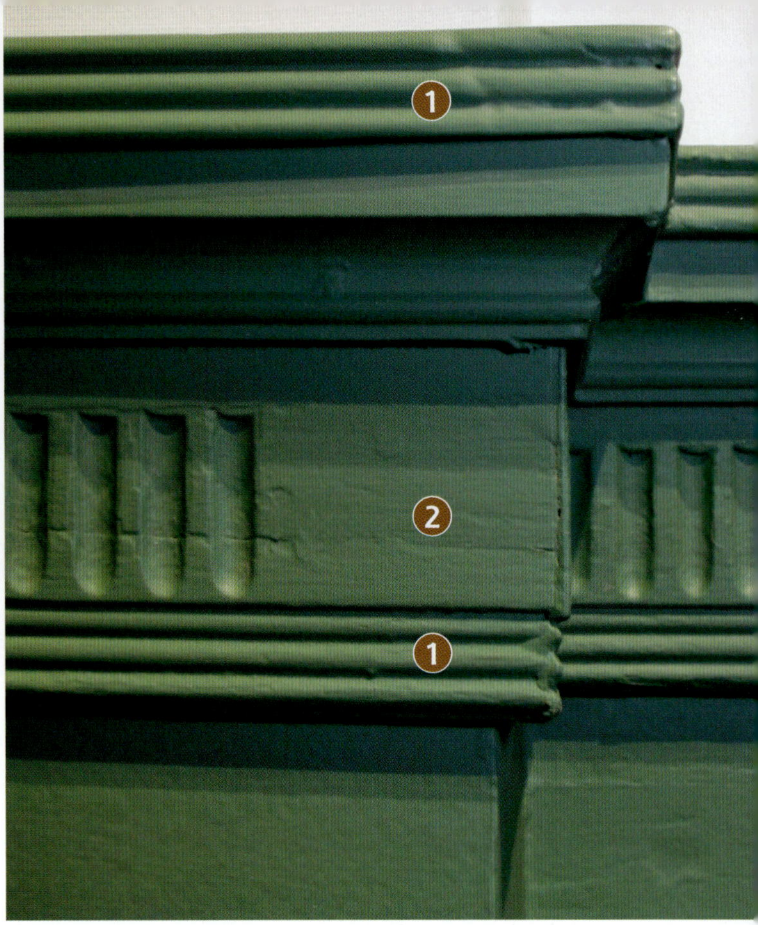

Wainscot

The Cross Hall's wainscot rises up thirty-two inches. Plain and unpaneled, it is capped with an interesting surbase with the top and bottom fillets reeded (1), and a pattern of five short vertical gouges repeated along the fascia (2). The wainscot is grounded with a nine-inch-tall thin base with a simple base cap.

Architraves

The door architraves are simple two-part compositions with some uncommon configurations, such as the cyma recta (3) separating the two fascias (4). They rest on a ten-inch-tall plinth (5), which also projects out to catch the base molding. The main doors are surrounded with reeded half pilasters (6) set outside the architrave and a panel and reeded frieze in the overdoor (7).

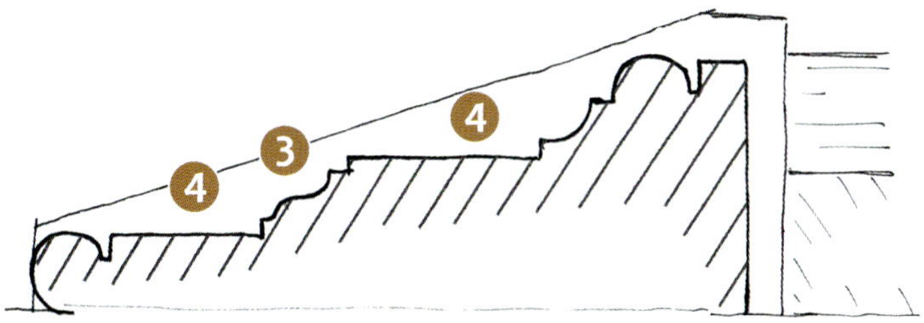

Architrave

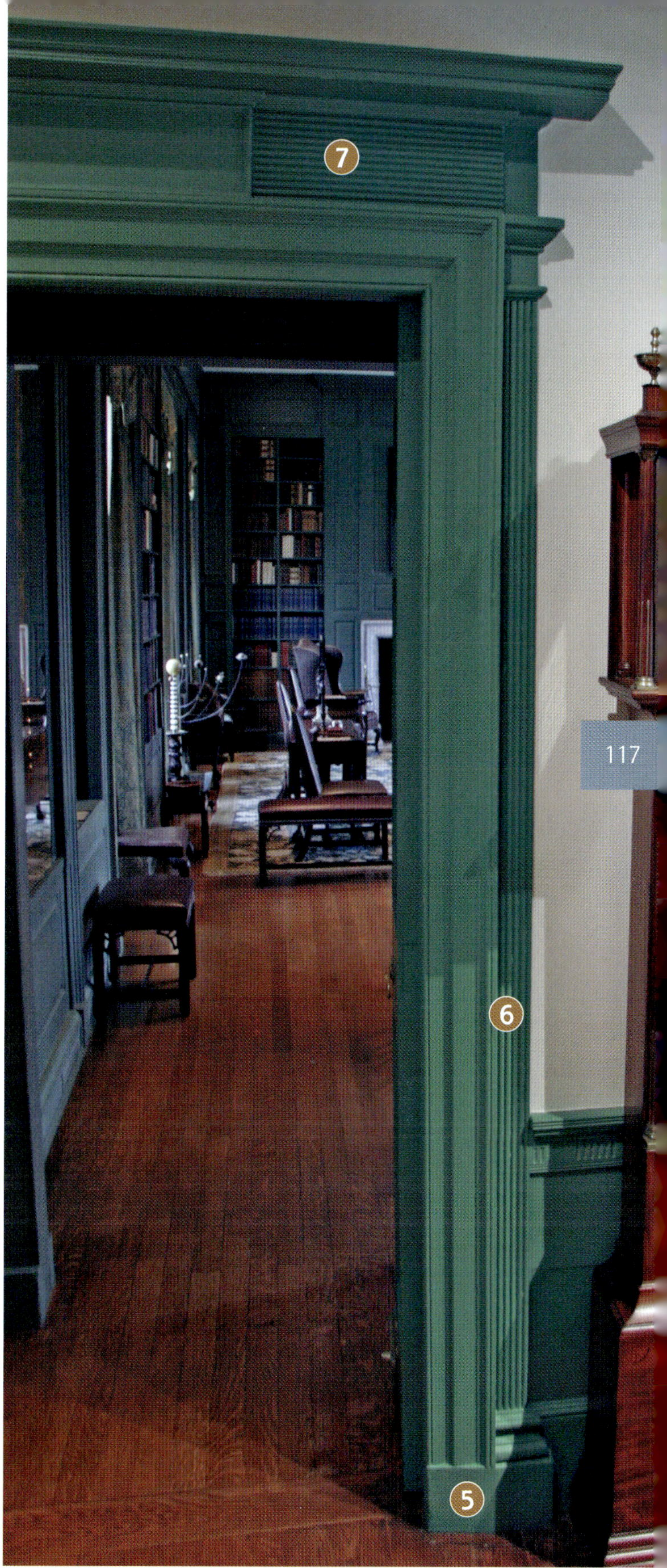

Empire Hall

11'3" high by 16'7" wide by 20'2" long

Opening off the top floor of the two-story Montmorenci Stair Hall, the Empire Hall is named for the style of furniture in the room. While different from the Stair Hall, the Empire Hall's ornamentation continues the graceful beauty established in the Stair Hall below.

Cornice

This cornice has the common elements of cymatium (1), corona (2), soffit (3), and bedmold (4). But, its curved profiles are formed of elliptical sections, and thin beads rather than fillets further soften its effect.

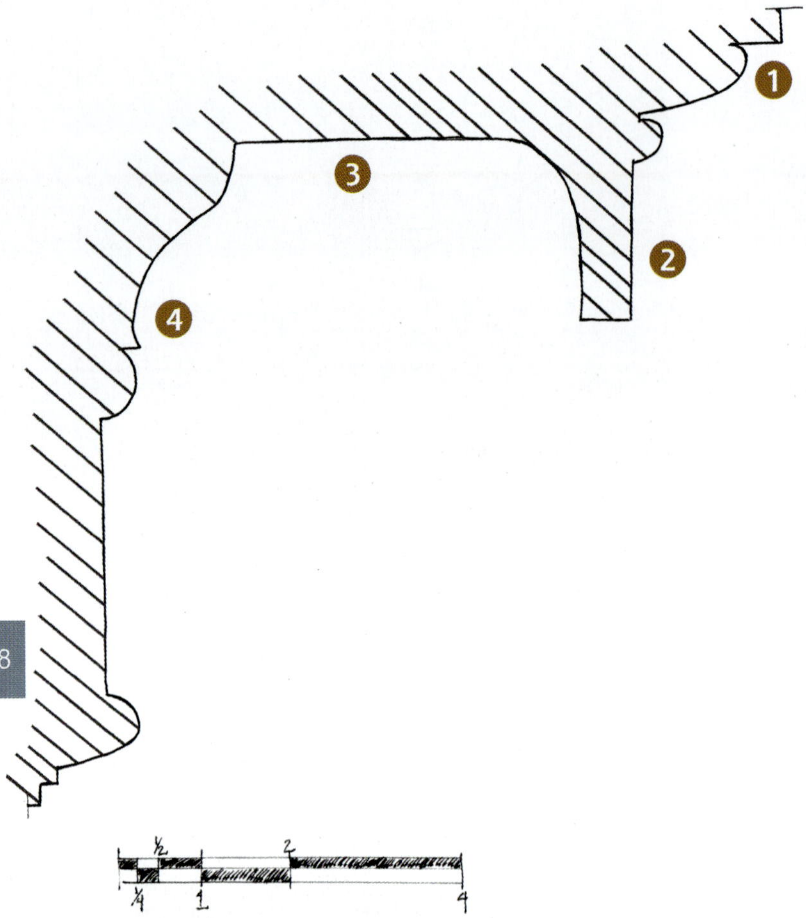

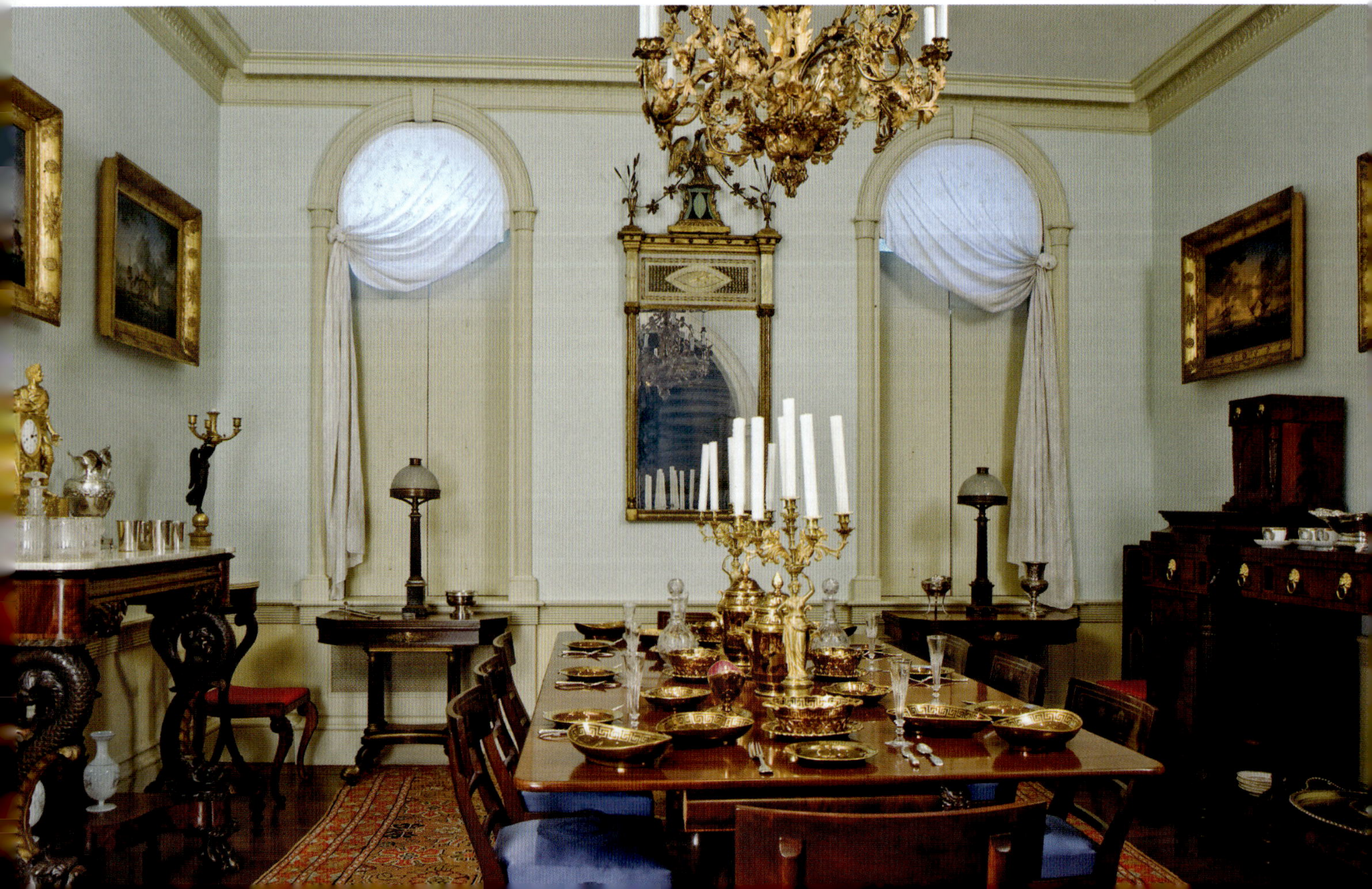

Wainscot & Architraves

The Empire Hall's doors are flanked with reeded pilasters (5). Reeding the surface in this manner creates a more delicate, attenuated pilaster. That sensibility is continued along the surbase, where it is also reeded (6), and the door's pilaster base becomes the base molding of the room (7), visually connecting the two.

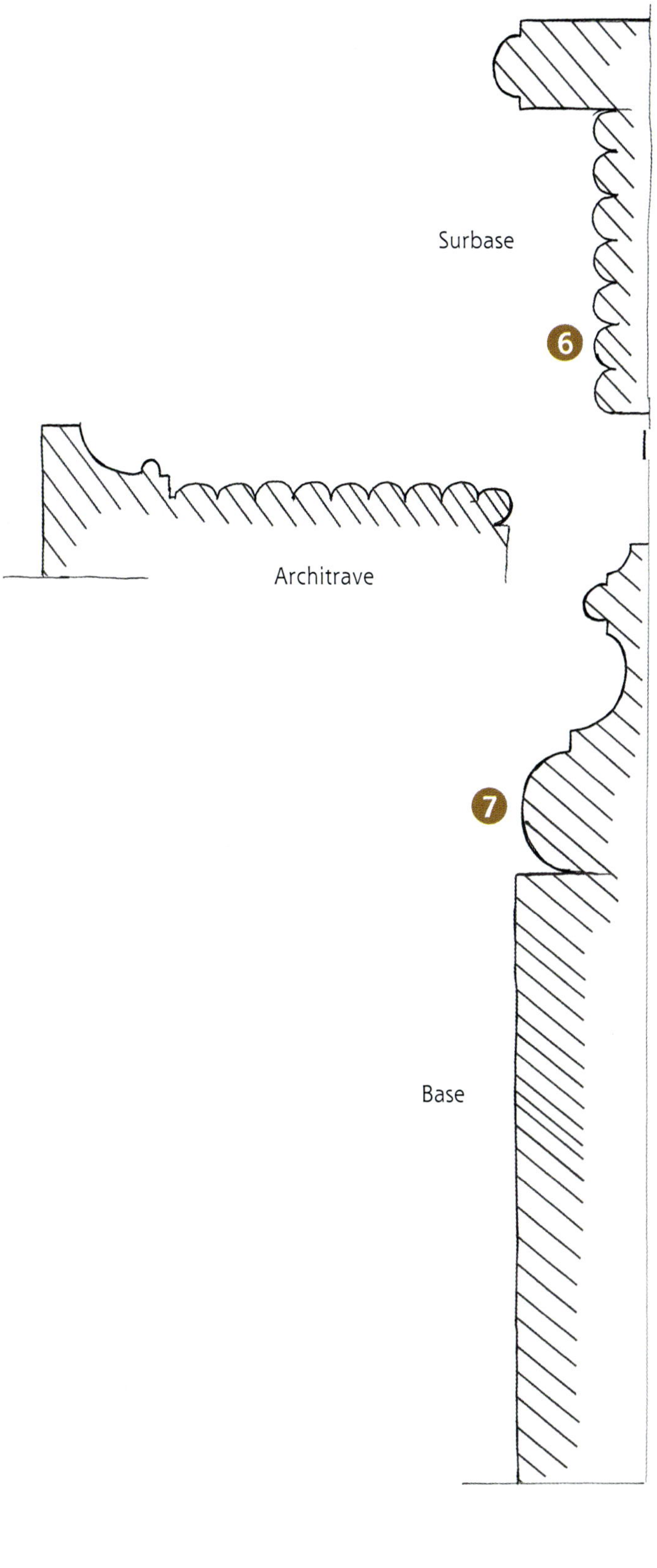

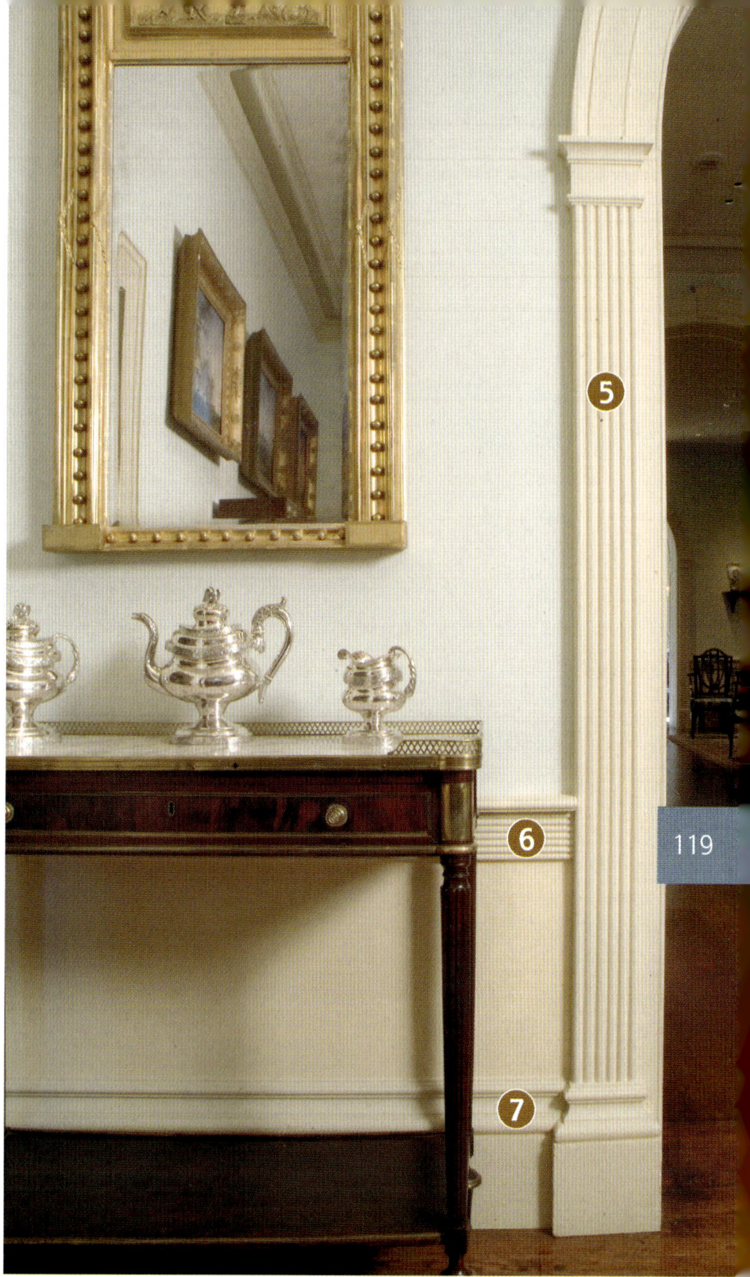

Montmorenci

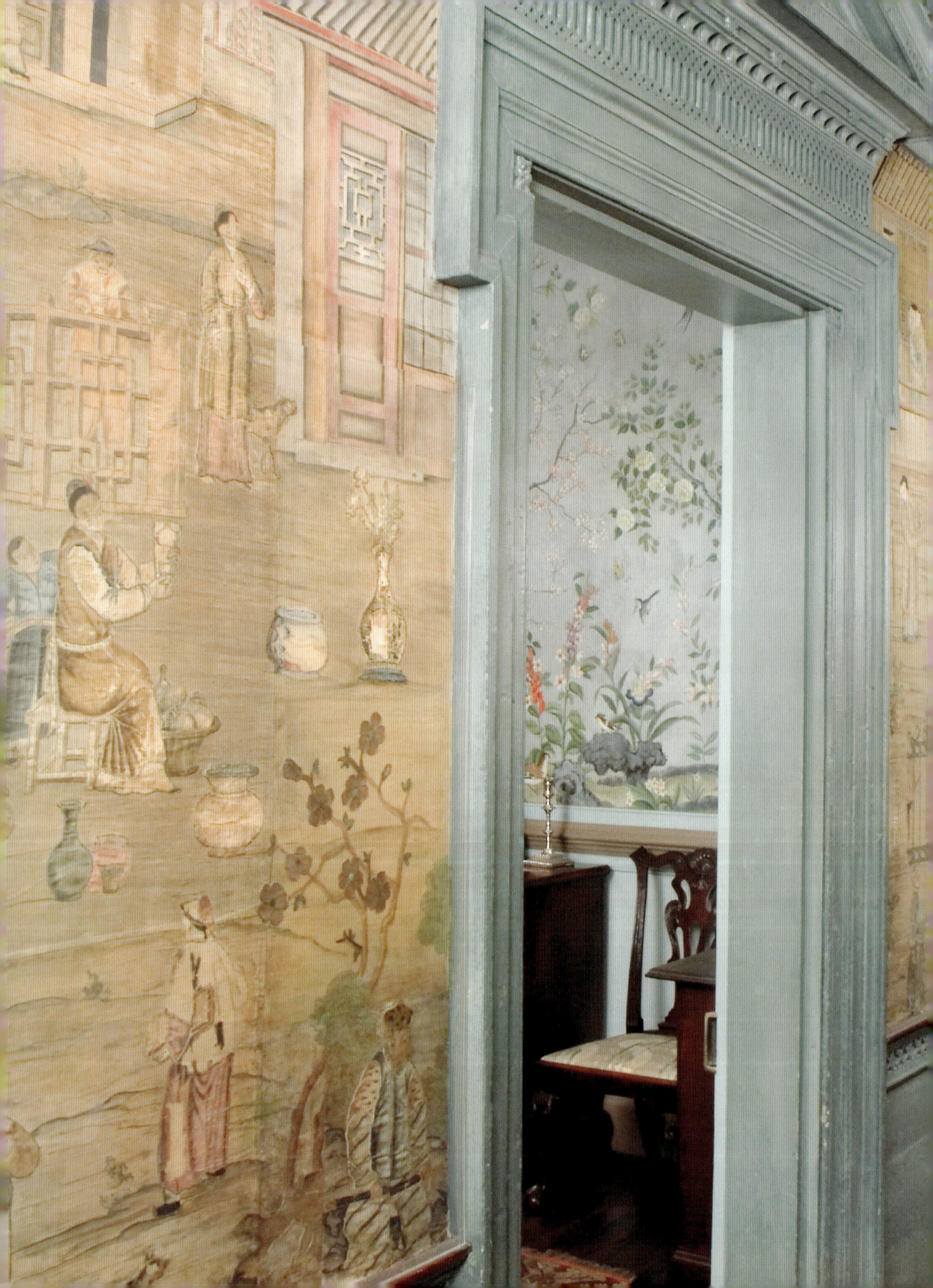

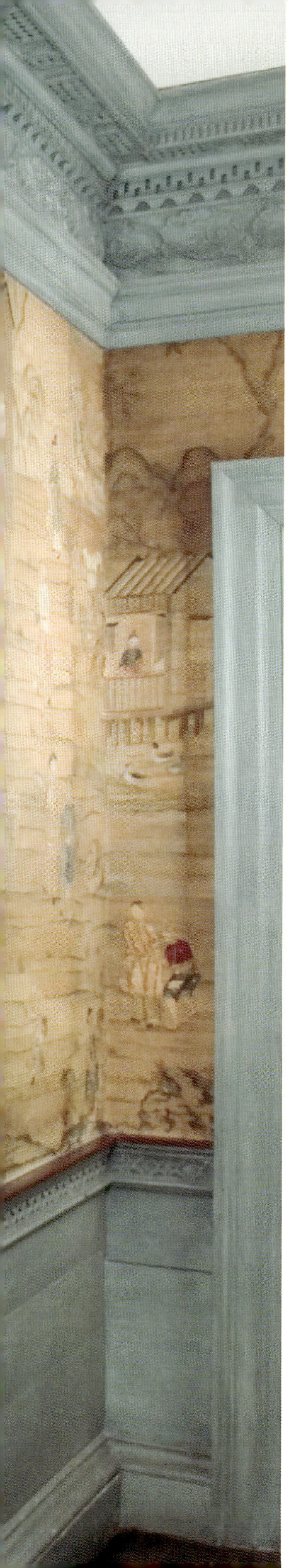

Philadelphia Hall

Solomon Engels House, Philadelphia, Pennsylvania, 1761

10'2" high by 6' wide by 15'11" long

The Philadelphia Hall highlights a stylistic trend for exotic elements found in some Georgian architecture. Chinese-inspired motifs in Western architecture and the decorative arts appeared when trade between the East and West increased and a general interest formed for exotic and revival styles. Both Chinese and Gothic motifs appeared in pattern books, furniture, decorative arts, and architecture.

Gunston Hall in Virginia, for example, has a Gothic-influenced porch with ogee, or pointed, arches, as well as Chinese-inspired interior ornament in its Chinese Parlor. Books like Sir William Chambers' *Designs of Chinese Buildings* (1757) helped popularize this trend. The Philadelphia Hall's woodwork reflects this taste for chinoiserie.

The woodwork in the hall comes from the Solomon Engels house on Pine Street in Philadelphia. Though the room is small, it is rich in detail and evocative of its time.

Imagery and patterns meant to evoke an imagined China, or chinoiserie, are used to charming effect in Philadelphia Hall.

Cornice

The room contains a full entablature with carved cornice, decorated frieze, and two-part architrave. The corona is articulated with vertical gouges (1), below which a non-canonic pattern of mutules alternates between mutules with six and eighteen guttae (2). The fretwork dentils (3) and cove molding below, carved into small ogee arches (4) begin to evoke Chinese- and Gothic-inspired patterns. The frieze (5), by contrast, is filled with a common classical *rinceau*, or horizontal scrolled pattern of vines, leaves, and flowers. Taken all together, elaborate patterns and various textures are created.

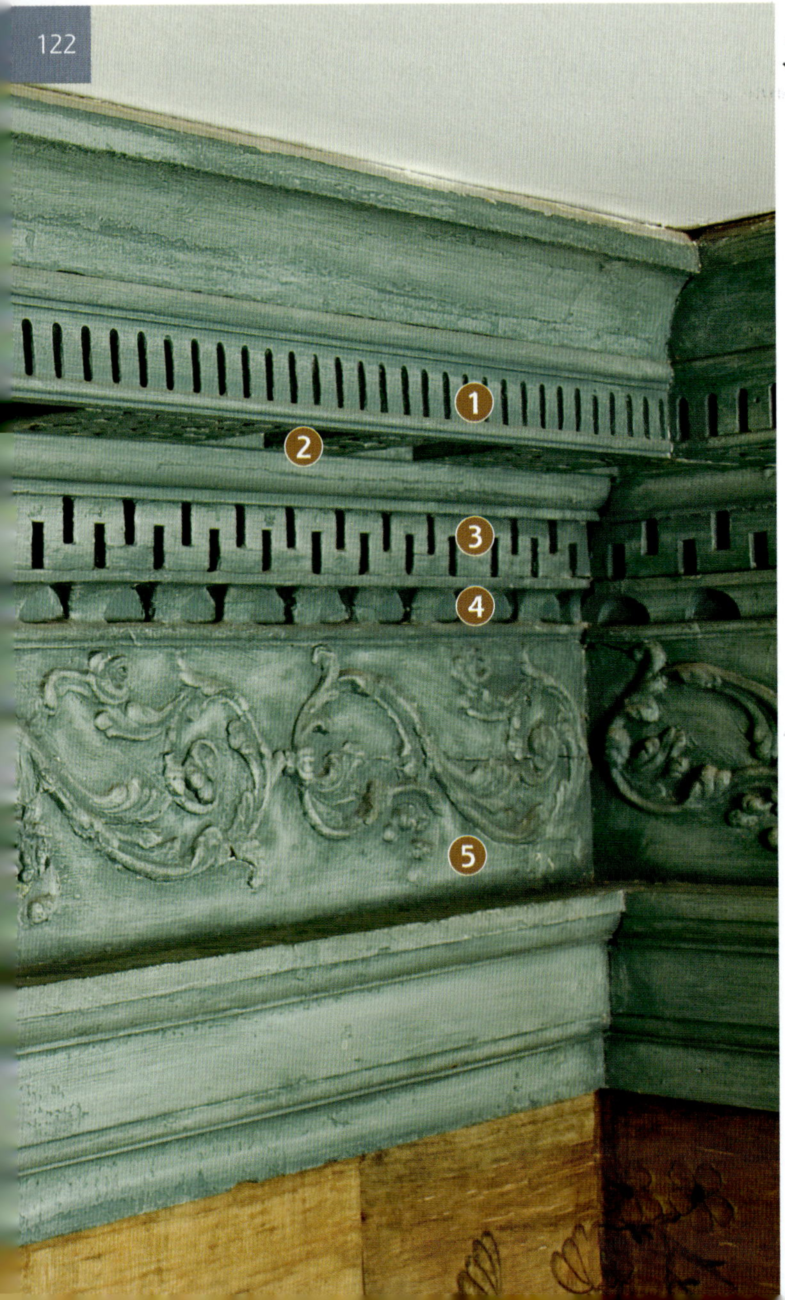

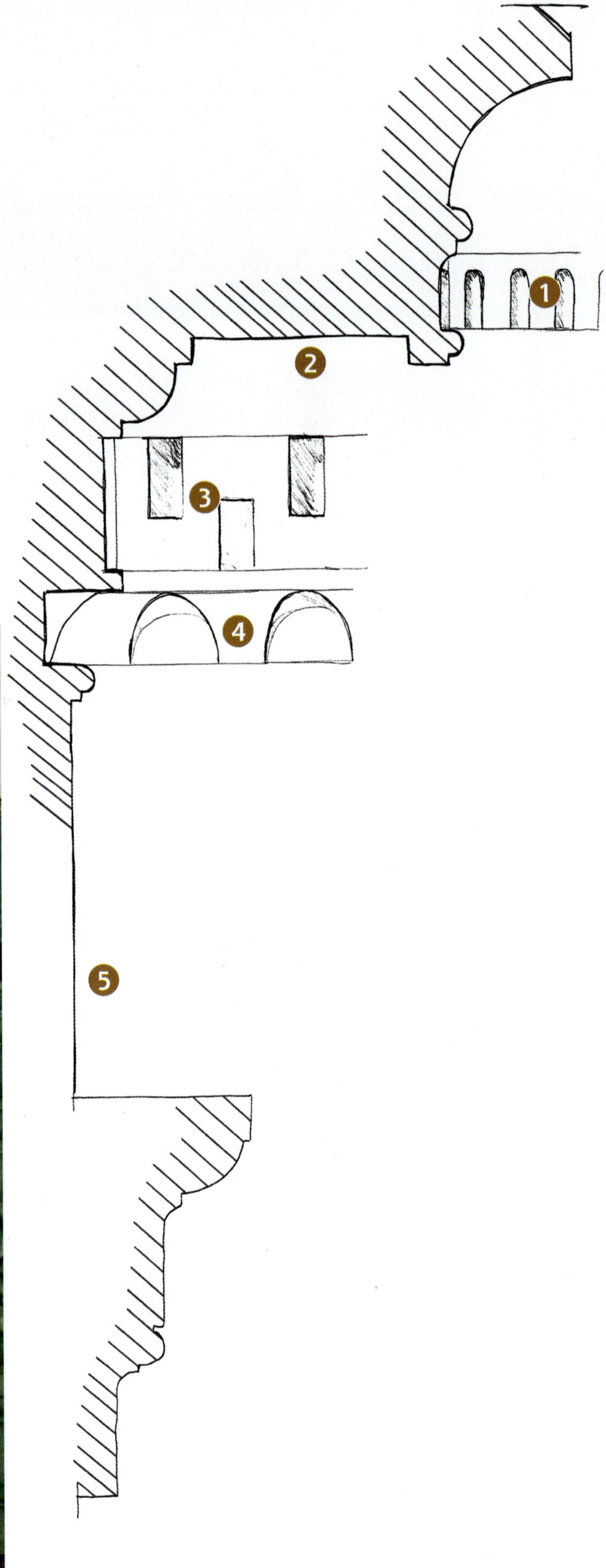

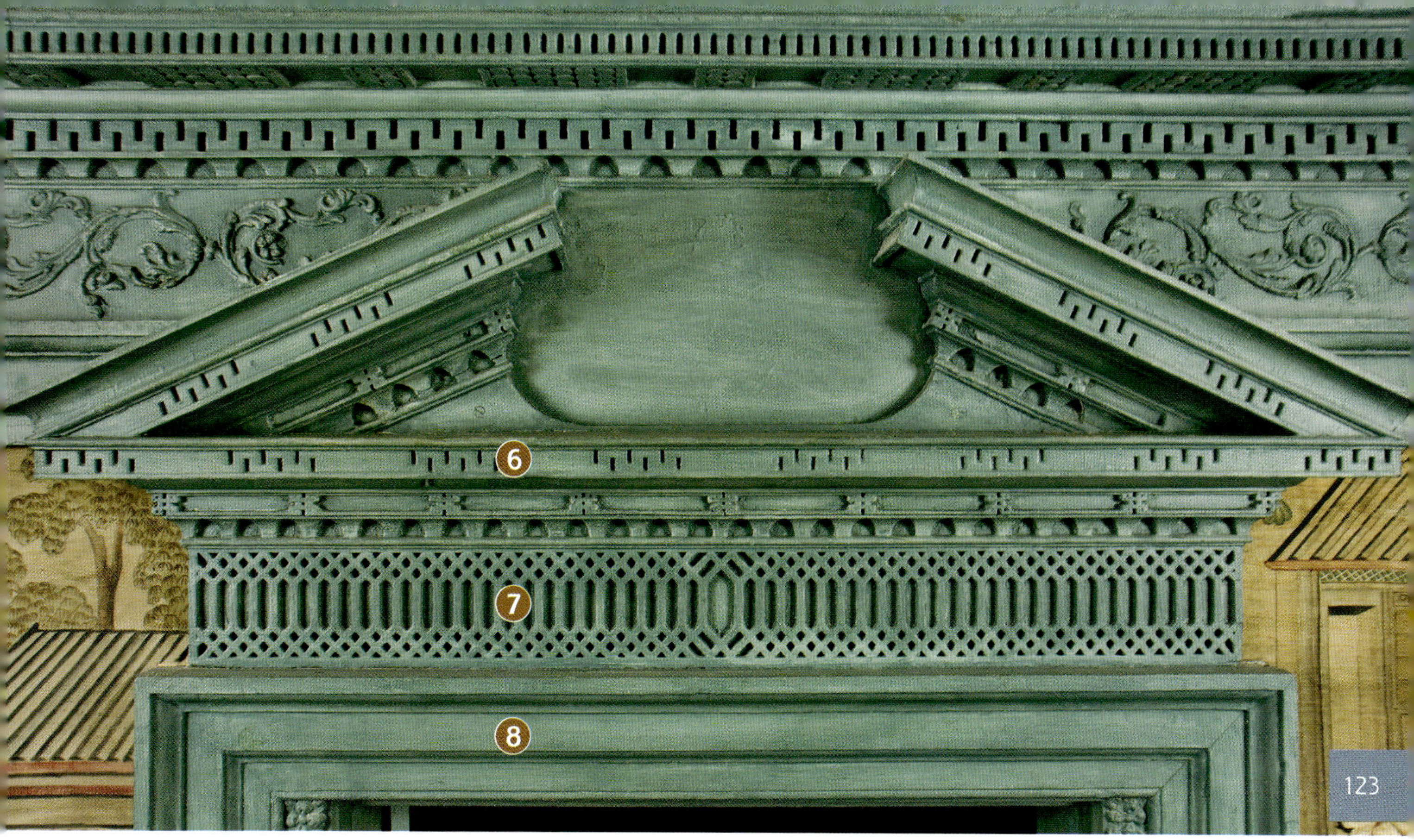

Architraves

The door on the long wall has an elaborate overdoor with a broken pediment and intricate frieze. In the corona, a memory of the fretwork dentils is applied (6). The frieze is overlaid with a woven pattern (7), above which Gothicized dentils hover. The unornamented architrave (8) is almost six inches wide and projects two-and-one-half inches off the wall. It has crossetted corners adorned with small classical flowers, which can be seen in the photo on the previous spread. Classical-, Chinese-, and Gothic-inspired motifs all appear here, again creating elaborate textures.

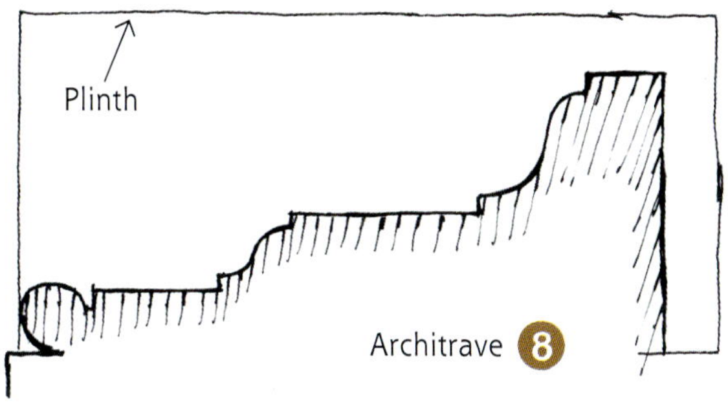

Wainscot

The wainscot wraps the room; there is no paneling. The surbase is decorated with a Chinese-inspired pattern reminiscent of the patterns in wooden screens found in the wallpaper above (page 120). It has a stained wooden cap (1). The large base is seven inches tall and projects two inches from the wall (2).

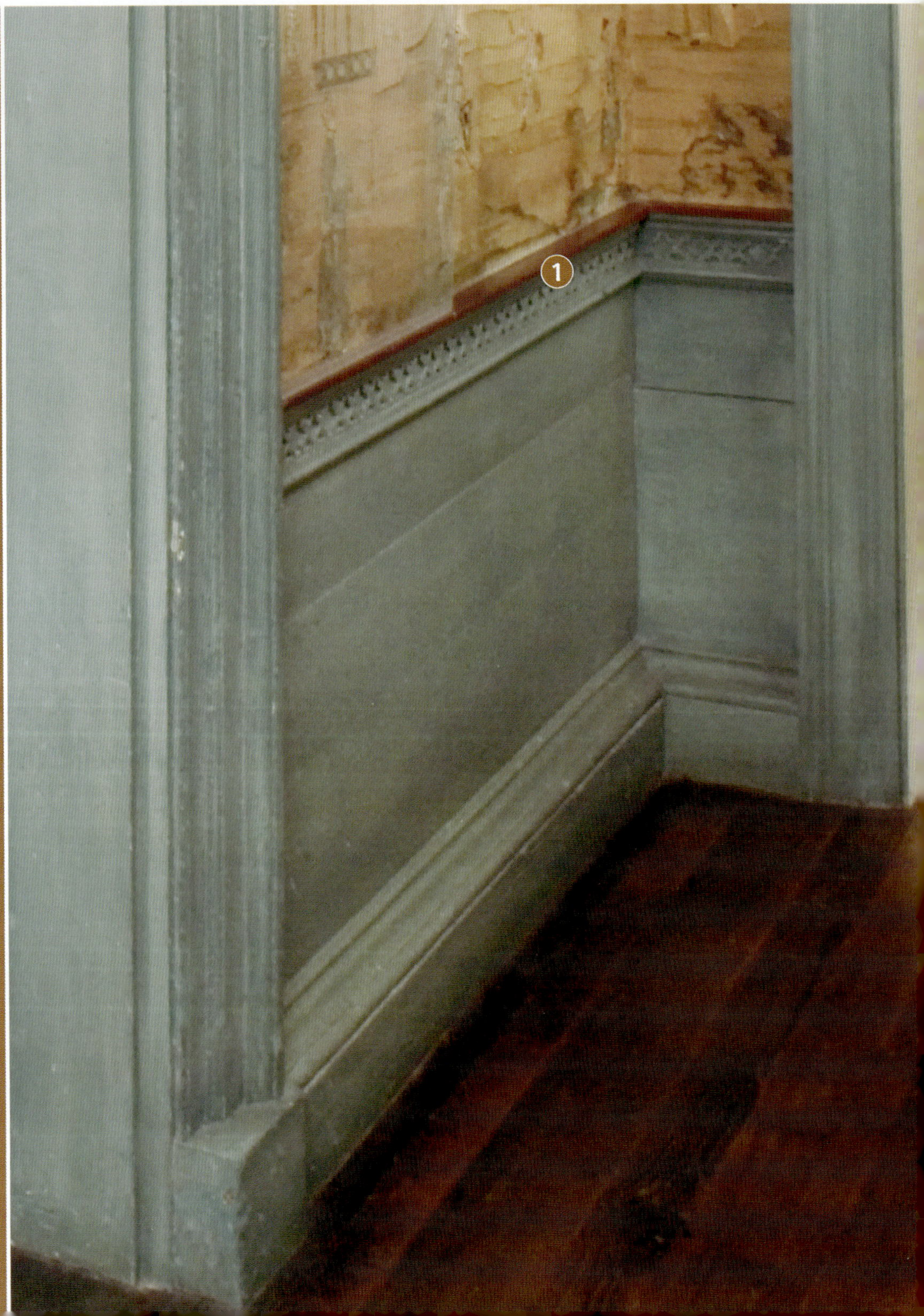

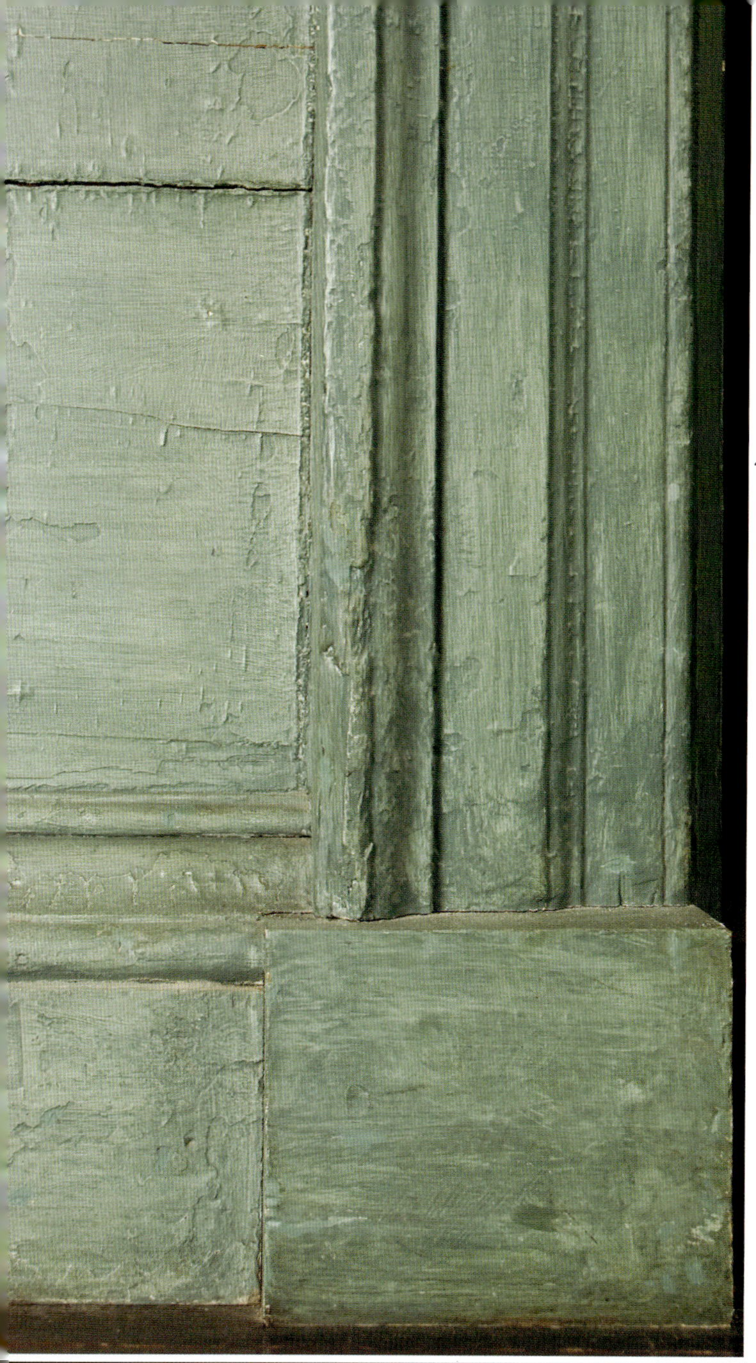

The door architrave sits upon a plain plinth block that cuts into the base molding.

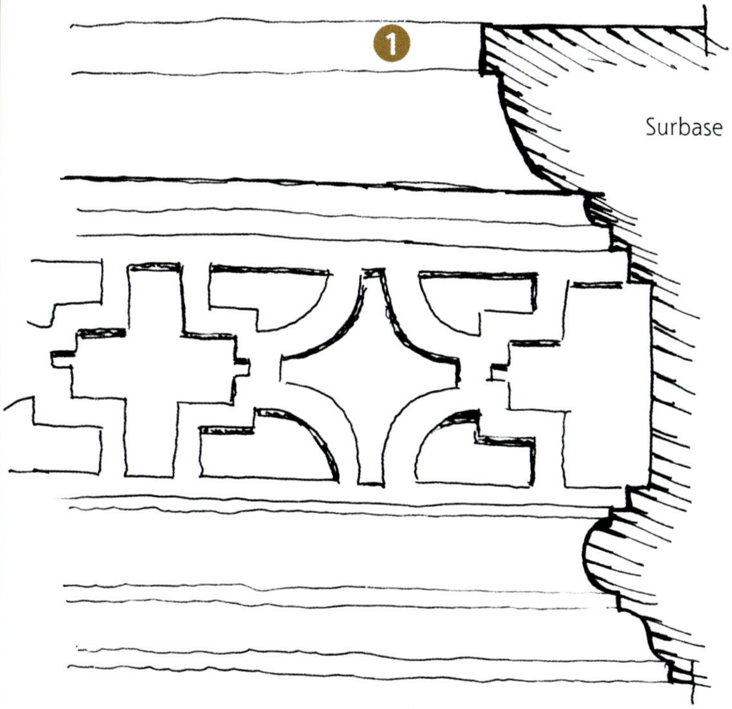

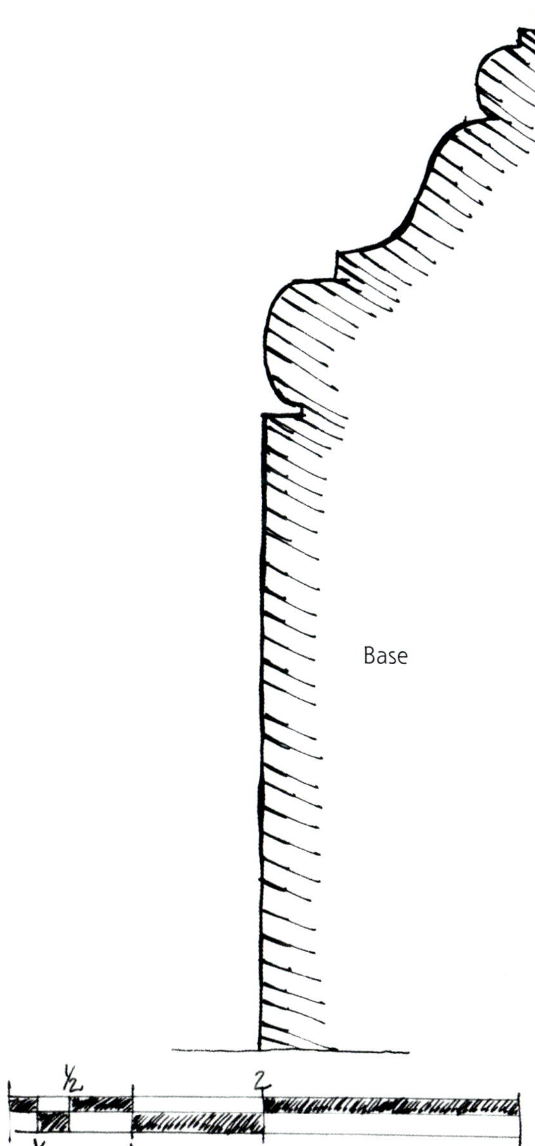

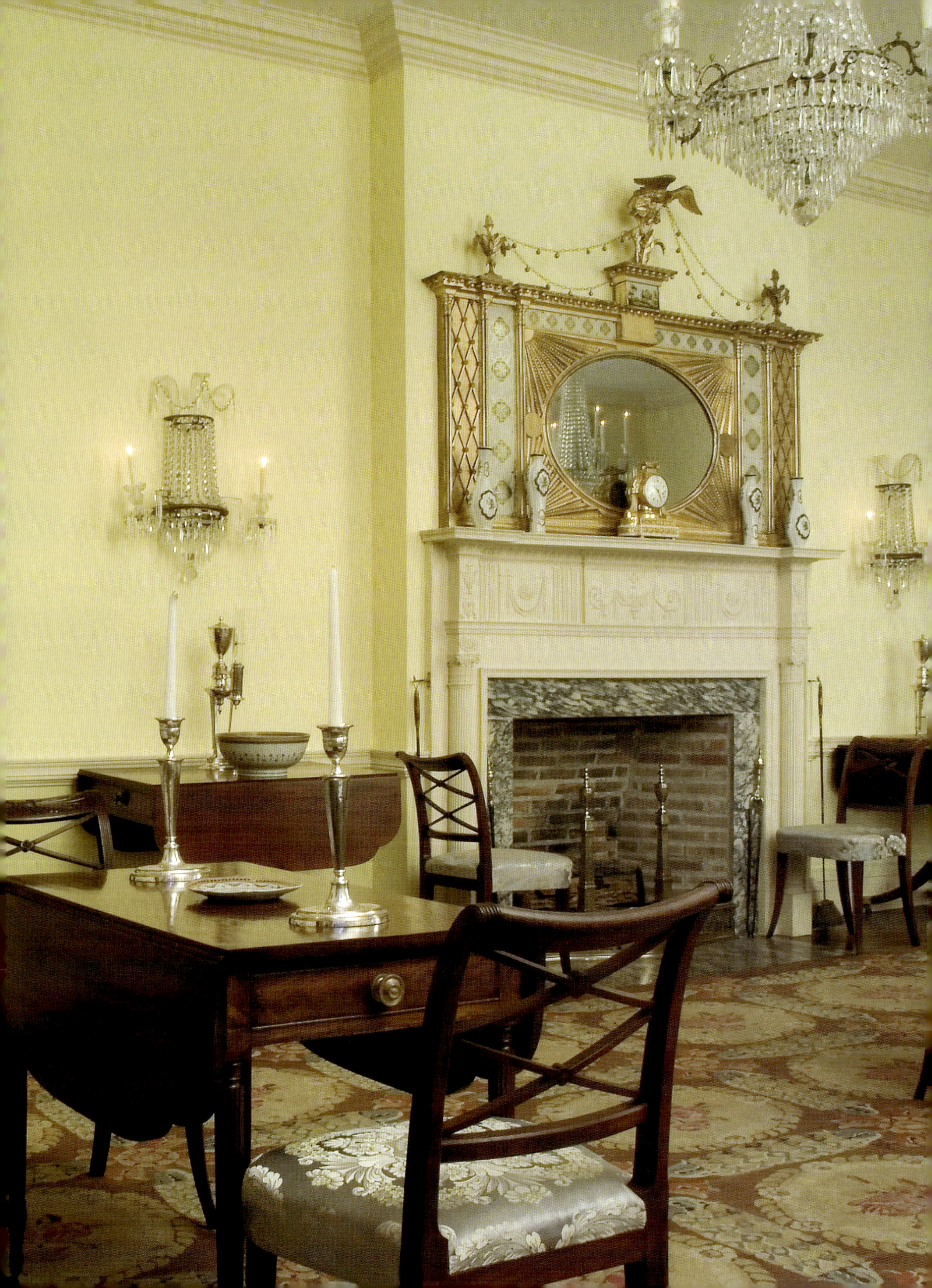

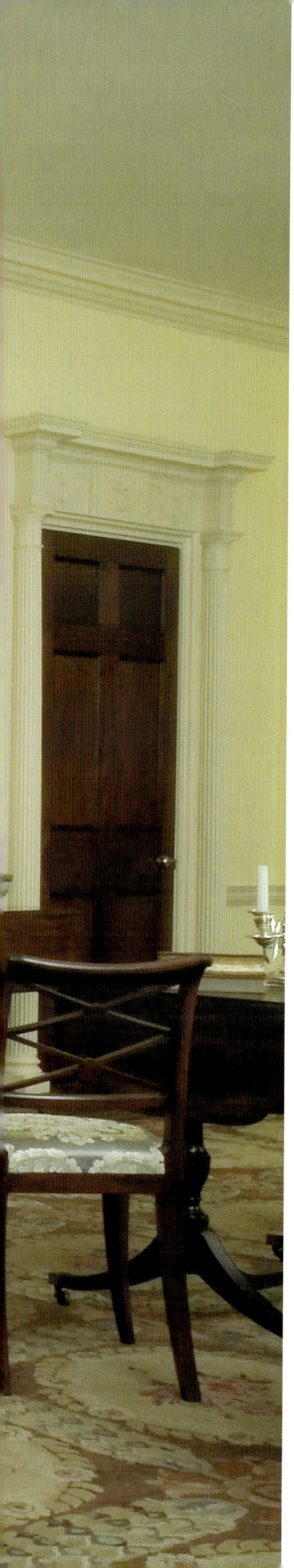

Phyfe Room

Moses Rogers House, New York, New York, 1806

11'4" high by 17'8" wide by 32'4" long

The Phyfe Room at Winterthur comes from the Moses Rogers home. His Federal period house at No. 7 State Street in New York City was begun in 1794 by James Watson and added to by Rogers in 1806, according to the Historic American Buildings Survey. Rogers was an influential New York businessperson, one of the early trade and mercantile subscribers in the city. The coffee house he joined near Wall Street was partly responsible for the later formation of the financial districts in that part of Manhattan.

This room captures the sophistication and style of New York at this time. Indeed, State Street was lined with fashionable Federal-style houses, and the room's individual elements are instructive in characteristics of the Federal style. The Phyfe Room at Winterthur is a large room, with plain expanses of walls balancing elements such as the mantel and door surrounds that are ornamented with classical motifs. Simple, lightly scaled moldings skim the remaining transition points of the room at the cornice, chair rail, and base.

The Phyfe Room is named after Duncan Phyfe, an influential New York furniture maker who made a number of the important pieces of furniture showcased in the room.

Cornice

The cornice moldings are unornamented, but the curvilinear shapes composing it, particularly the echinus-like bedmold at the bottom (1) and the cymatium at the top (2) with its quirked return, create a rhythm of curves and shadows that line the top of the room. It projects out and down about six inches.

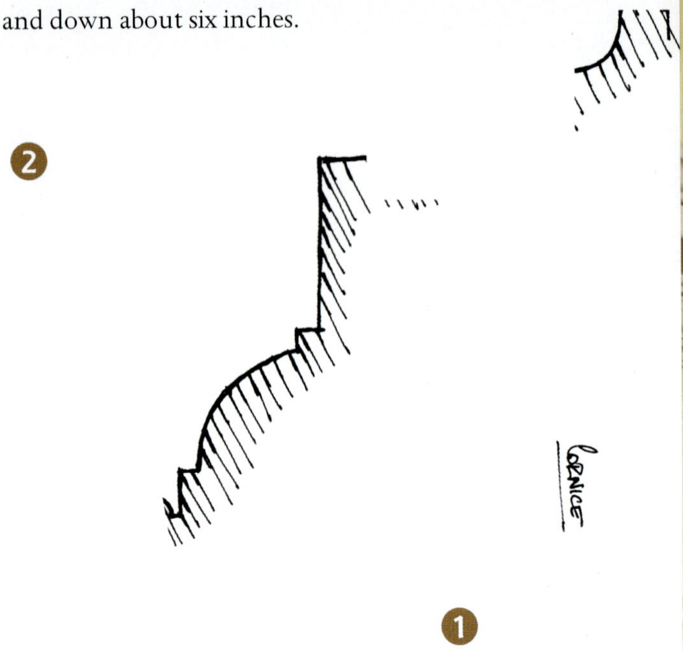

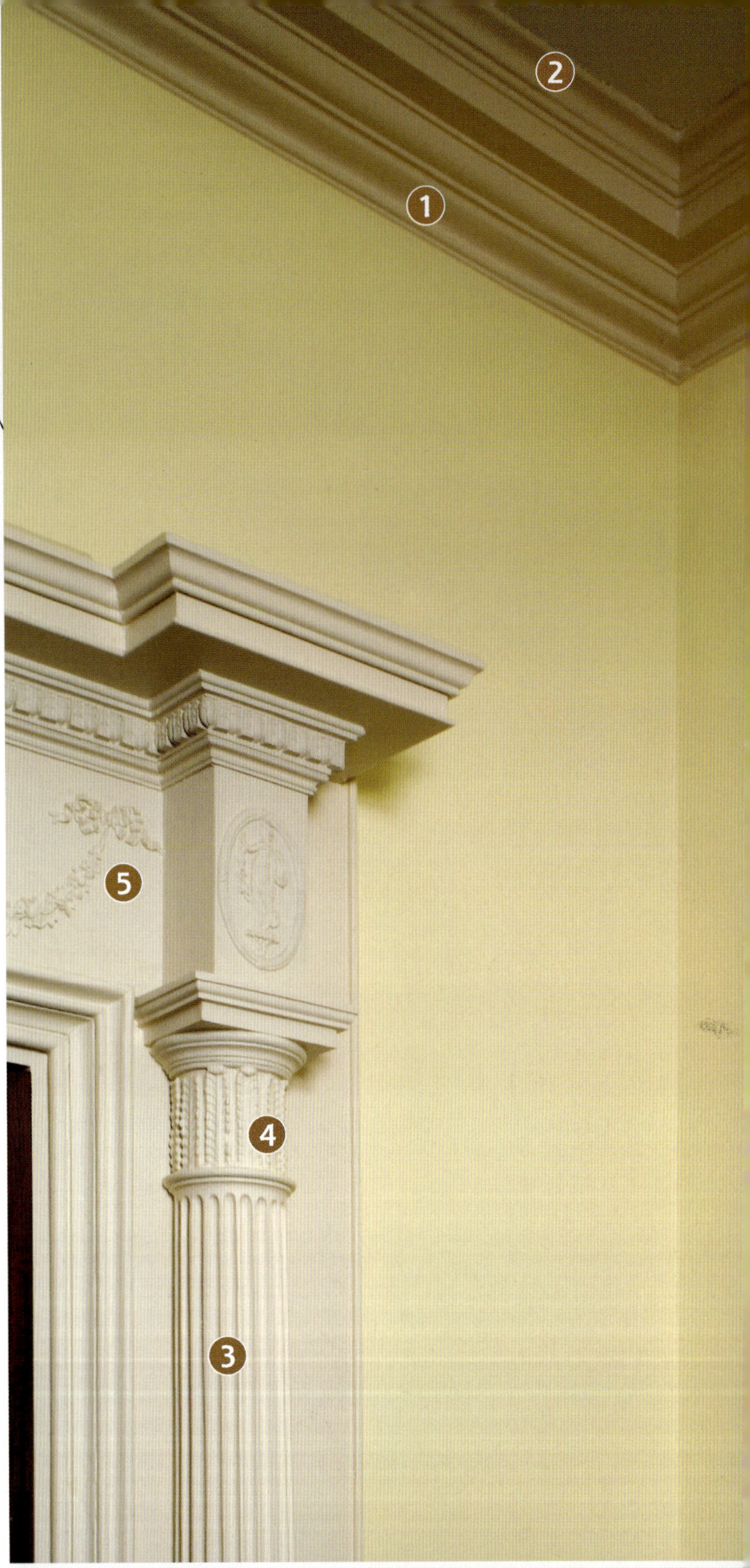

Architraves

High-style Federal elements are seen in the doorways on either side of the mantel. These door surrounds are formed of engaged fluted columns (3) with their necking ornamented with elongated acanthus leaves (4). The frieze above displays applied Federal-style decoration common in the finest homes of this era: swags of flowers and medallions with classical figures (5). Such elaboration plays well against the plain wall surface.

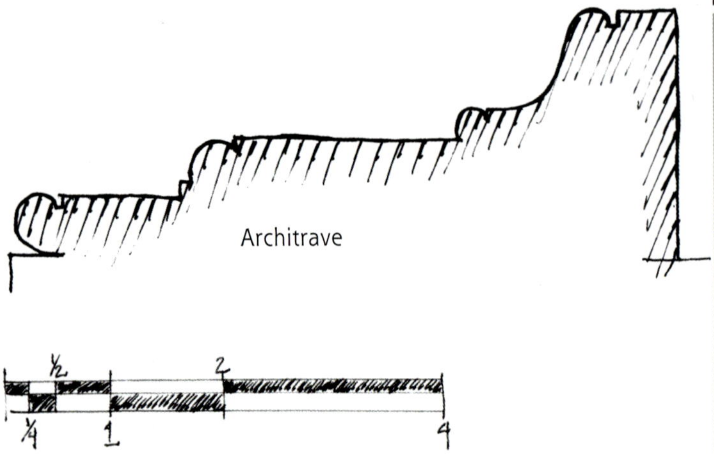

Wainscot

The Phyfe Room has no panels in its wainscot. Instead, a chair rail at just more than thirty-two inches tall projects one-and-three-eighths inches from the wall (6). The base rises to a height of eight-and-one-half inches, and its plinth is segmented into three planes at the bottom. Its base cap, projecting one-and-one-half inches (7), has molding shapes related to those in the rest of the room, repeating the alternating light and shadow lines found in the cornice.

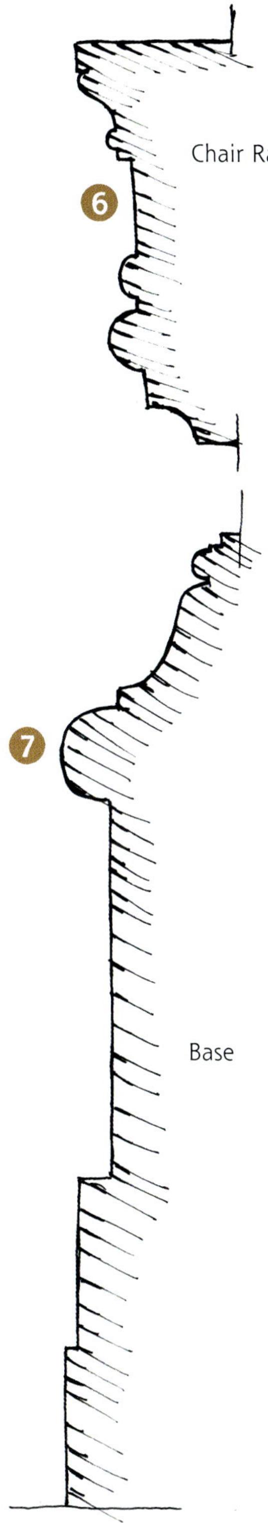

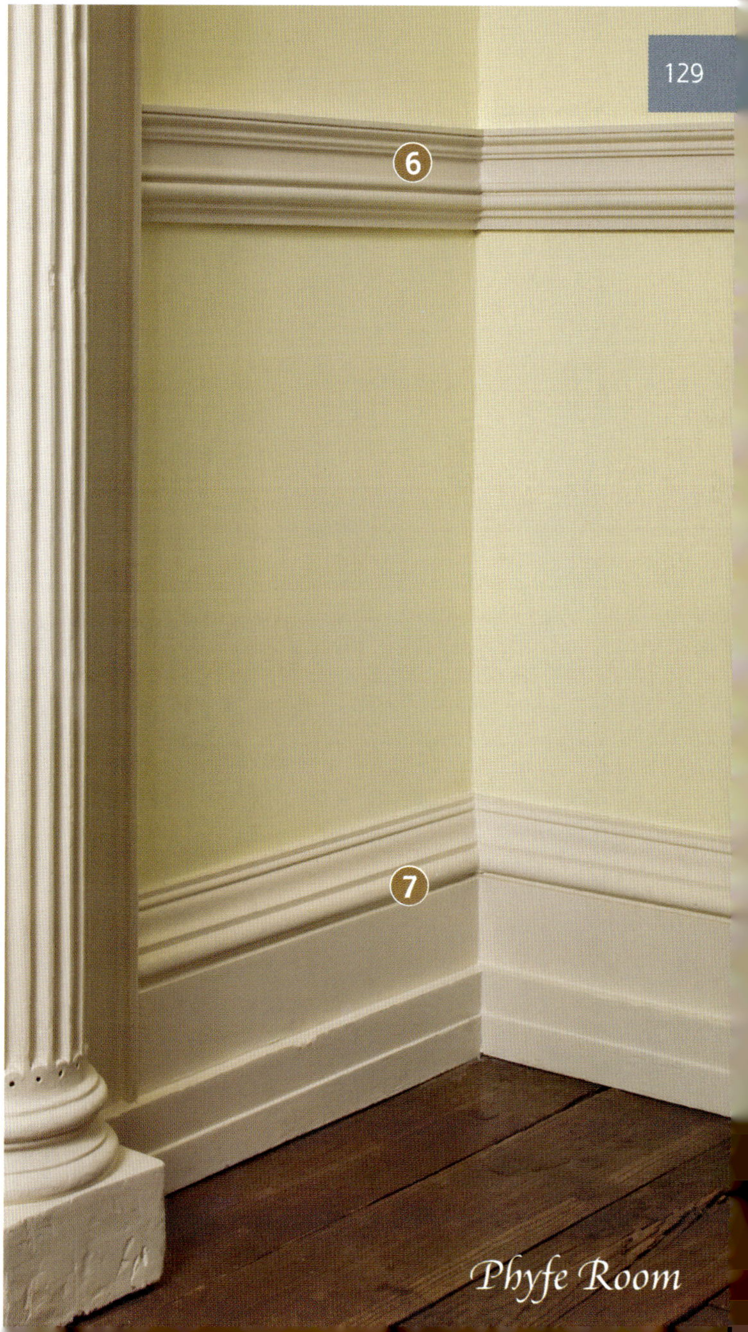

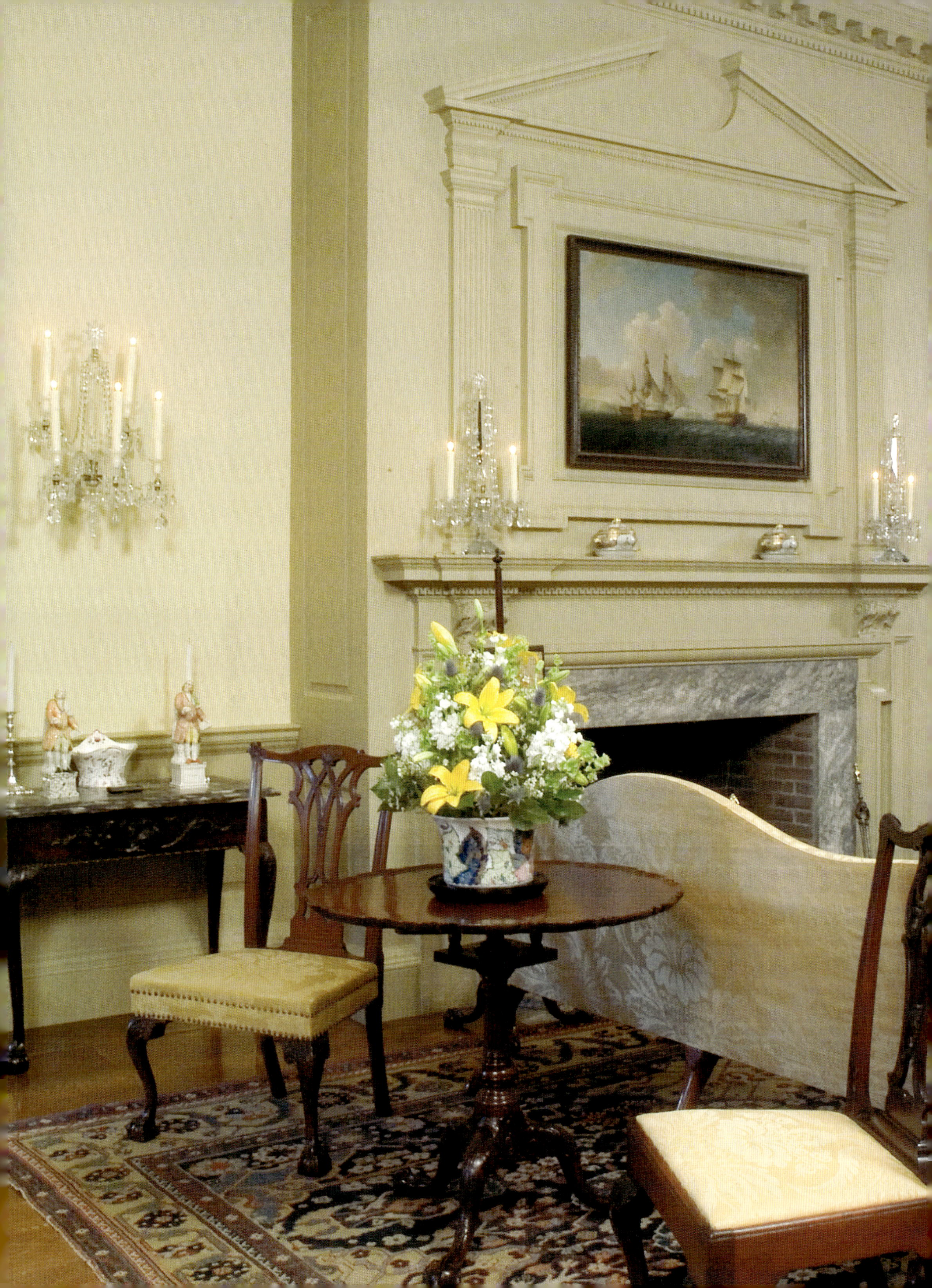

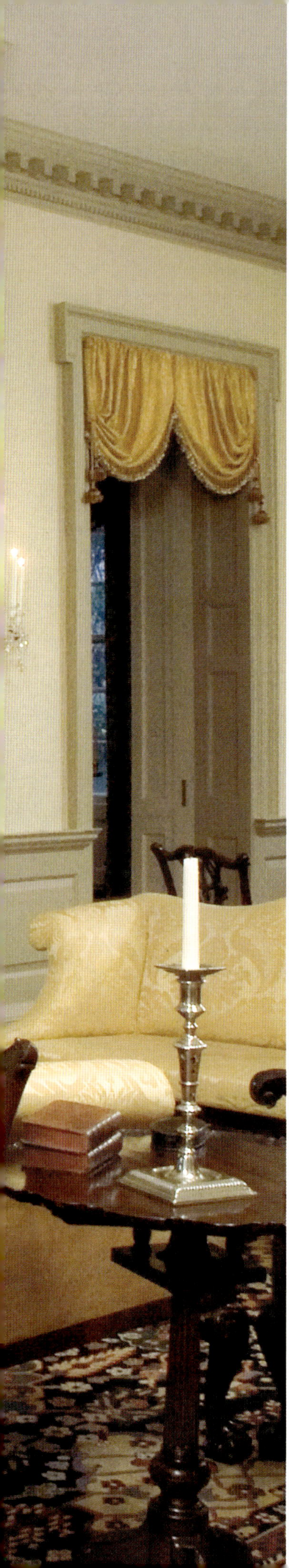

Port Royal

Frankford (Philadelphia), Pennsylvania, circa 1762

Edward Stiles already owned homes in Philadelphia and his native Port Royal, Bermuda, when he bought land six miles outside the city for a country estate befitting his stature as a prosperous gentleman merchant.

Named after Mr. Stile's birthplace, Port Royal bears striking similarities to Mount Pleasant, a famous home built nearby a few years earlier. Both houses are near-textbook examples of late Georgian style American houses influenced by English Palladianism. The attributed or possible master builder at Port Royal, Gunning Bedford, was a good friend of Mount Pleasant's builder, known as Nevel. How closely Nevel and Bedford collaborated on Port Royal is not clear, although Nevel "charged Bedford for measuring Edward Stiles home in Frankford," according to Nevel's daybook. In those days, having construction "measured" by a fellow master builder was one method of calculating costs.

The five Port Royal rooms at Winterthur are the Entrance Hall, Parlor, the upstairs Dining Room Cross Hall, and two bedrooms. The two hallways are treated hierarchically with the Entrance Hall in the Doric Order and the upstairs Dining Room Cross Hall in the Ionic Order. The public hallway spaces and the Parlor are the most highly detailed.

The Port Royal rooms are some of the tallest at Winterthur: the downstairs rooms measure over twelve feet tall, and the upstairs rooms are over eleven feet. Within these heights, the rooms are proportioned and articulated in accordance with Palladian and English Palladian precedents.

The elegant Port Royal Parlor features a robust central fireplace with an elaborate mantel and overmantel.

Port Royal Entrance Hall

The Entrance Hall is in the Doric Order, with a nearly complete entablature. It lacks only bucrania (garlanded ox skulls) or other bas-relief ornament in the metopes (2) between its triglyphs (1). The entablature and pilasters reflect Palladio's Roman Doric Order, which was represented in numerous English pattern books. Matching arched front and rear entrances grace the Entrance Hall. The magnificent front door is the focus of the original house's symmetrical five-bay façade. The central bay projects from the house with a second-floor Palladian window lighting the upper Dining Room Cross Hall and a pediment above. The rear entrance opens into the garden.

Entablature

The Doric entablature is twenty-seven inches tall. As seen in the photo, a full entablature with two-part architrave, frieze replete with triglyphs (1) but blank metopes (2), and mutules (3) above create a robust, canonic composition appropriately scaled to the height and length of the room.

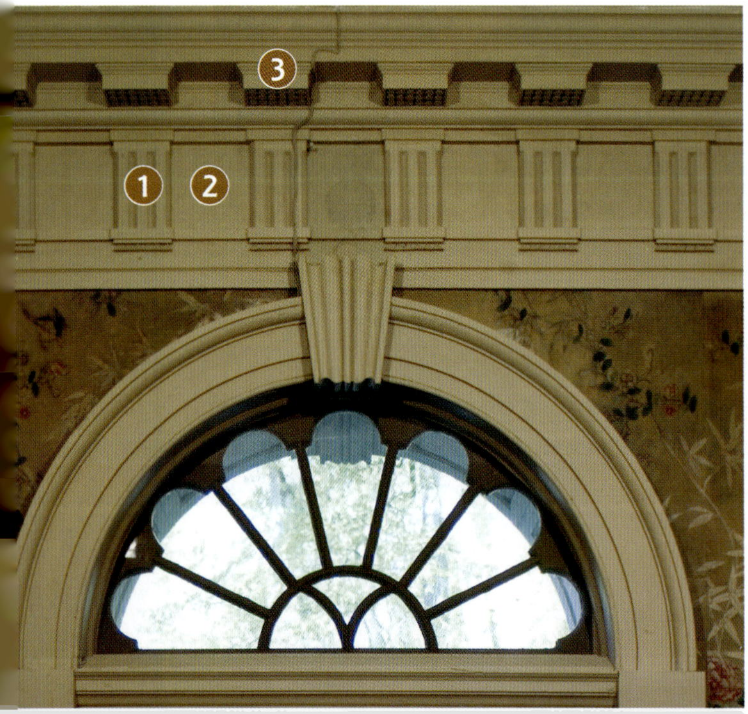

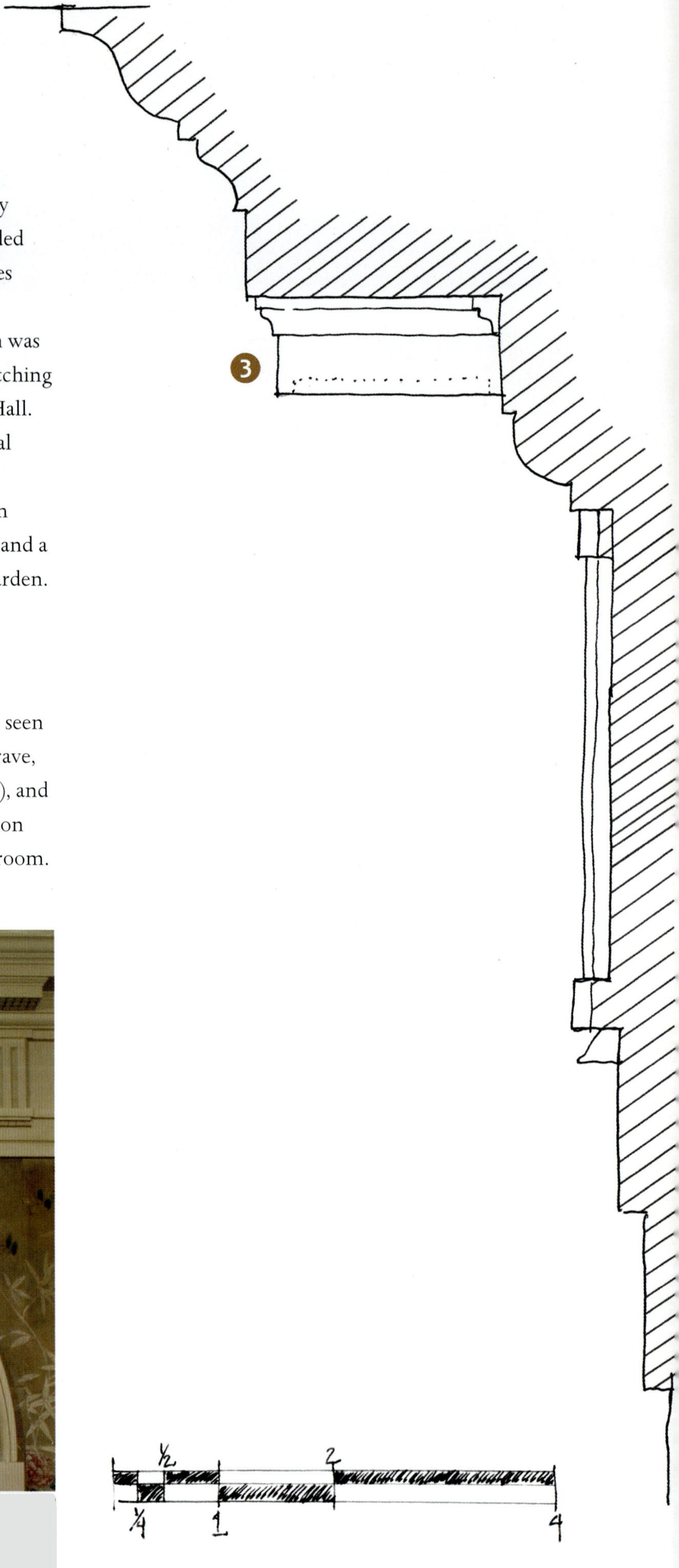

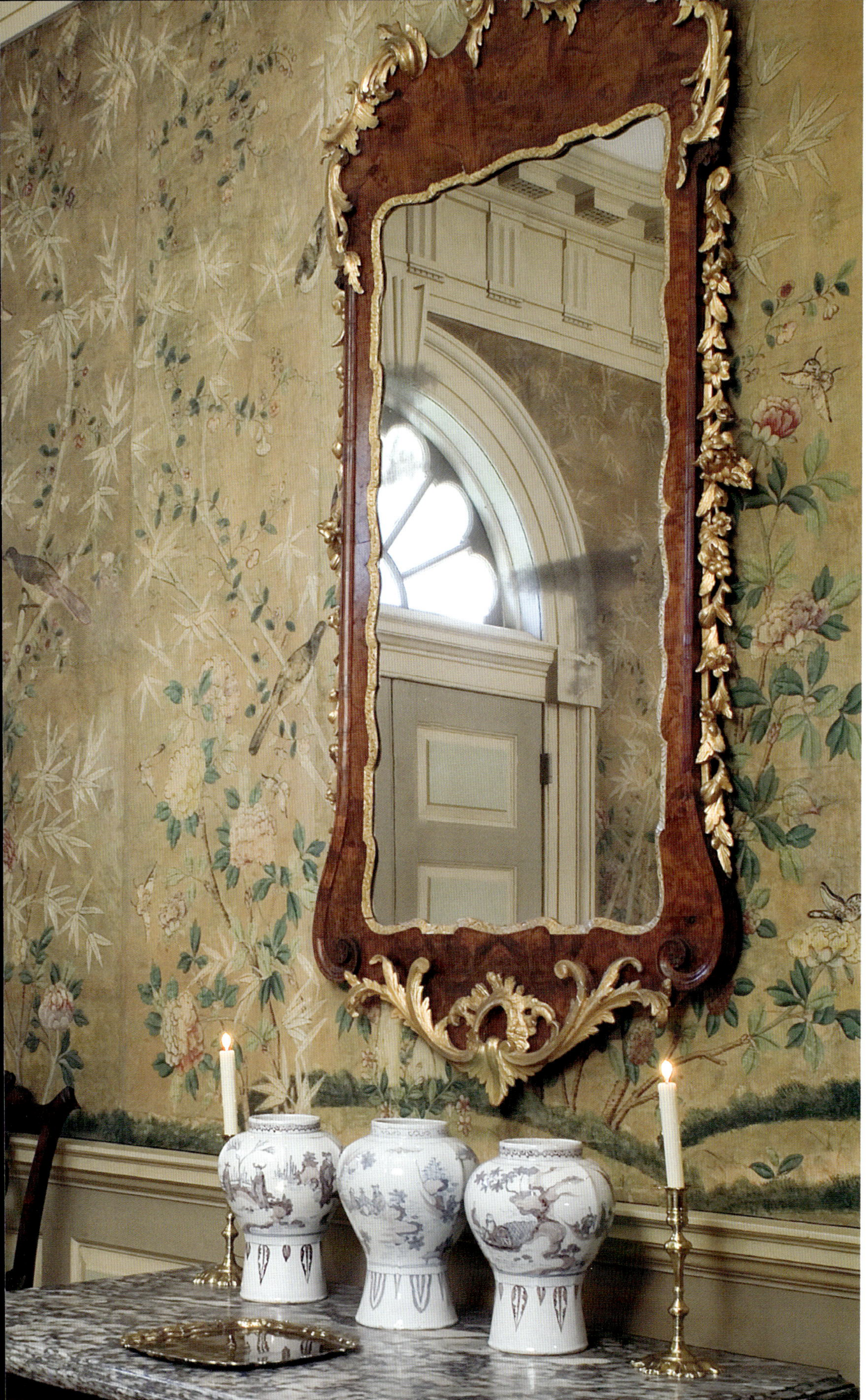

Like so many rooms in the house, Mr. du Pont added hand-painted Chinese wallpaper and Philadelphia Chippendale furniture to the Port Royal Entrance Hall, which serves also as Winterthur's front entrance.

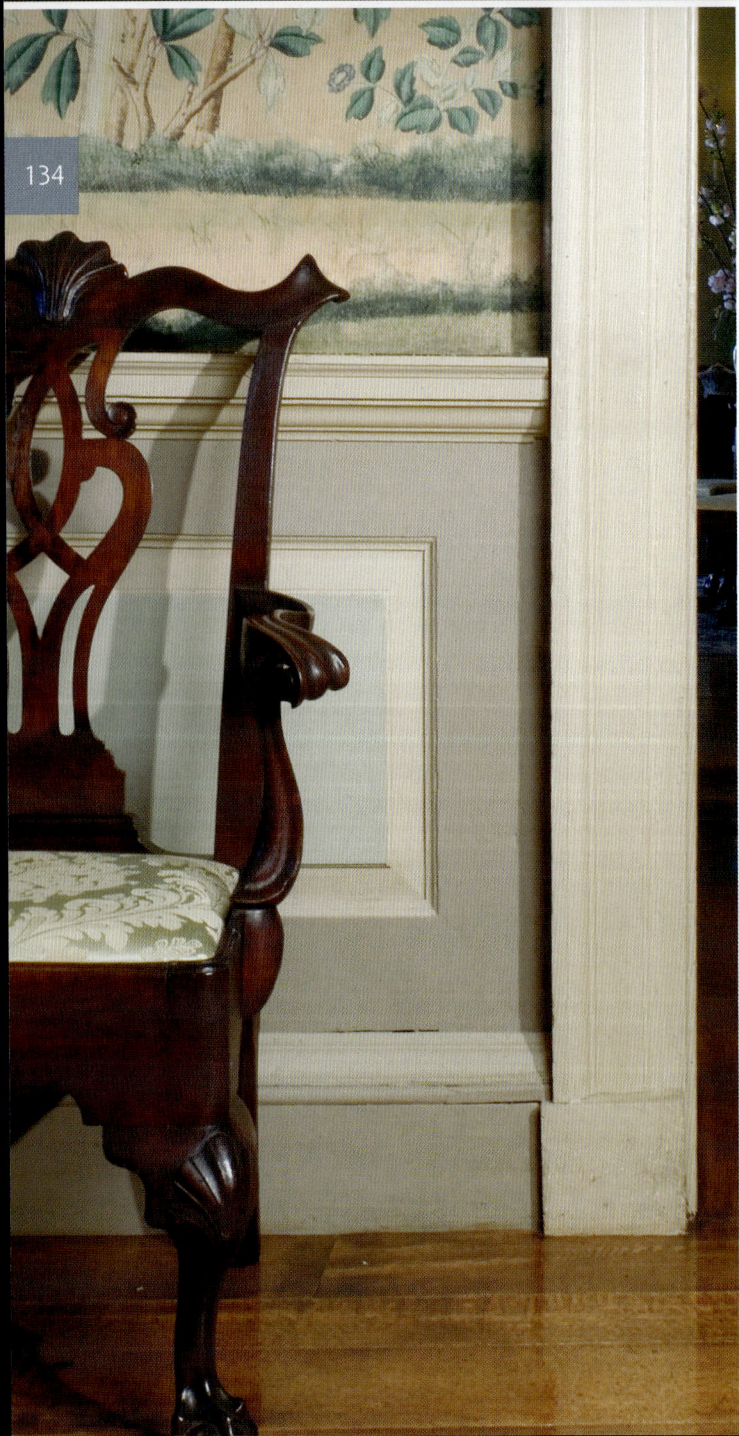

Architraves

The Port Royal Entrance Hall's carefully scaled design, which Mr. du Pont expanded, is carried through the other moldings in the room. The large front door is framed by a seven-inch-wide architrave that projects three inches from the wall surface. Architraves for the doors leading to the parlor and halls are the same profile but are scaled down to six inches wide and two-and-one-half inches deep, appropriately sized for these door openings.

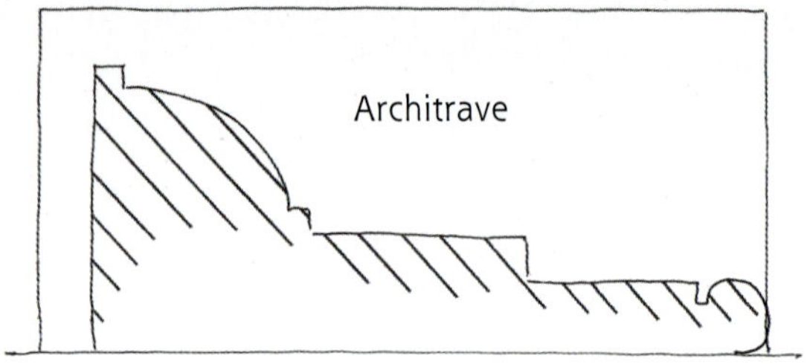

Wainscot

The entrance's handsome paneled wainscot is three feet high. The eight-and-one-half-inch base is over two-and-one-half-inches thick. The surbase echoes the room's cornice. The surbase is bold in profile, well balanced with the rest of the room.

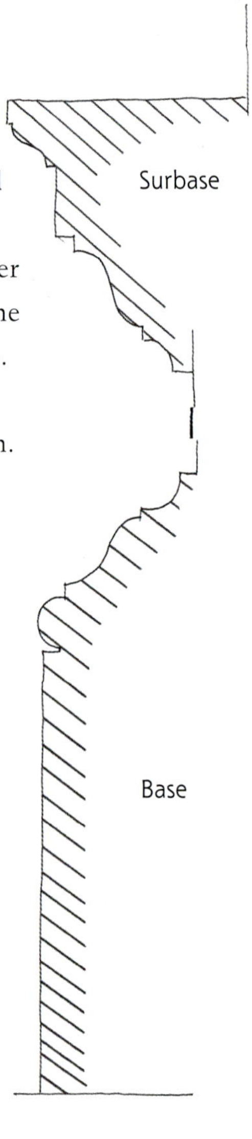

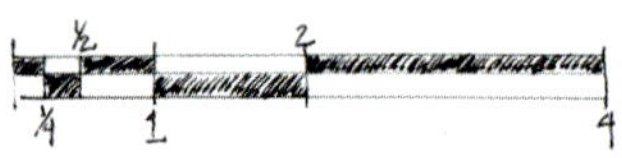

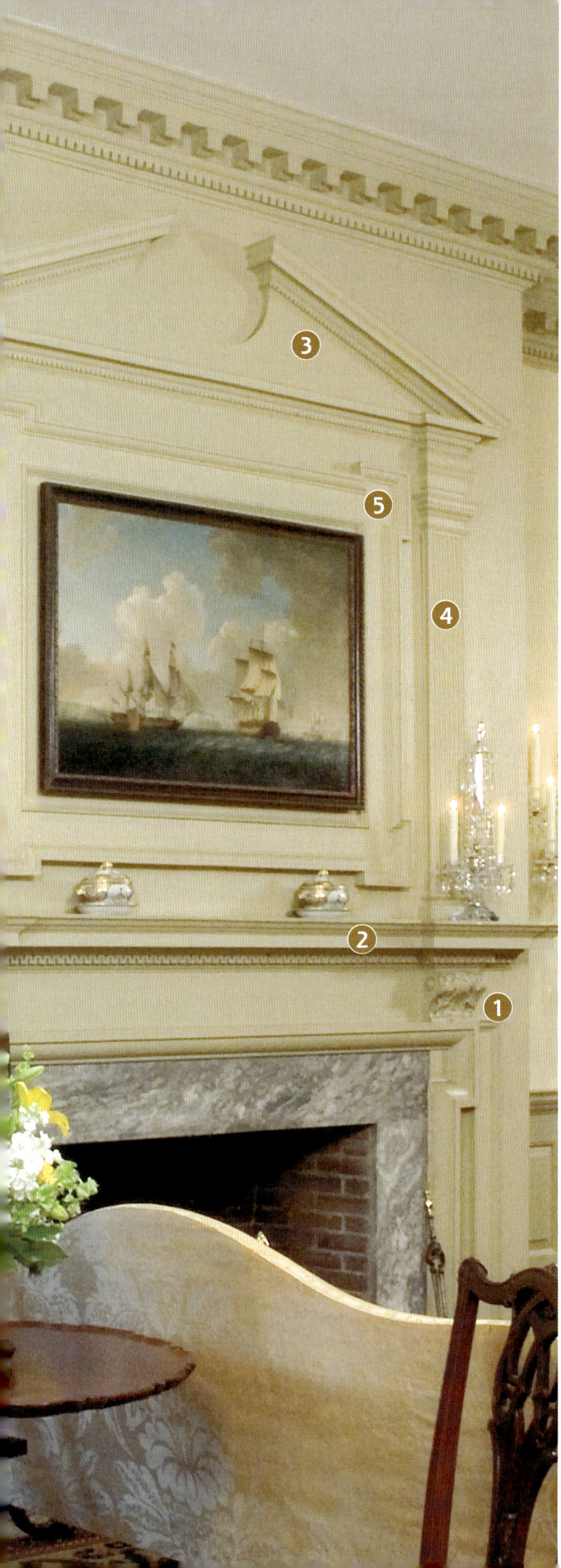

Port Royal Parlor

12'4" high by 46'8" wide by 23' long

Mantel

The parlor is symmetrically composed about a central fireplace. Ornate corbels (1) that rest on a simple architrave support the mantelshelf (2). Fretwork dentils form a delicate bedmold beneath the mantelshelf. The overmantel has a broken pediment (3) supported by fluted pilasters (4) resting on the mantelshelf. The overmantel surrounds a center panel with double-crossetted corners (5).

Cornice

The parlor uses only a cornice, which is more common in interior spaces than the Entrance Hall's full entablature. Apparently taking cues from Scamozzi's Ionic Order, this cornice uses a modillion block (1), a dentil course (2), and a cyma reversa bedmold (3) below the dentils. The dentils are the "i" type with a circular drill hole and swag in the interdentil.

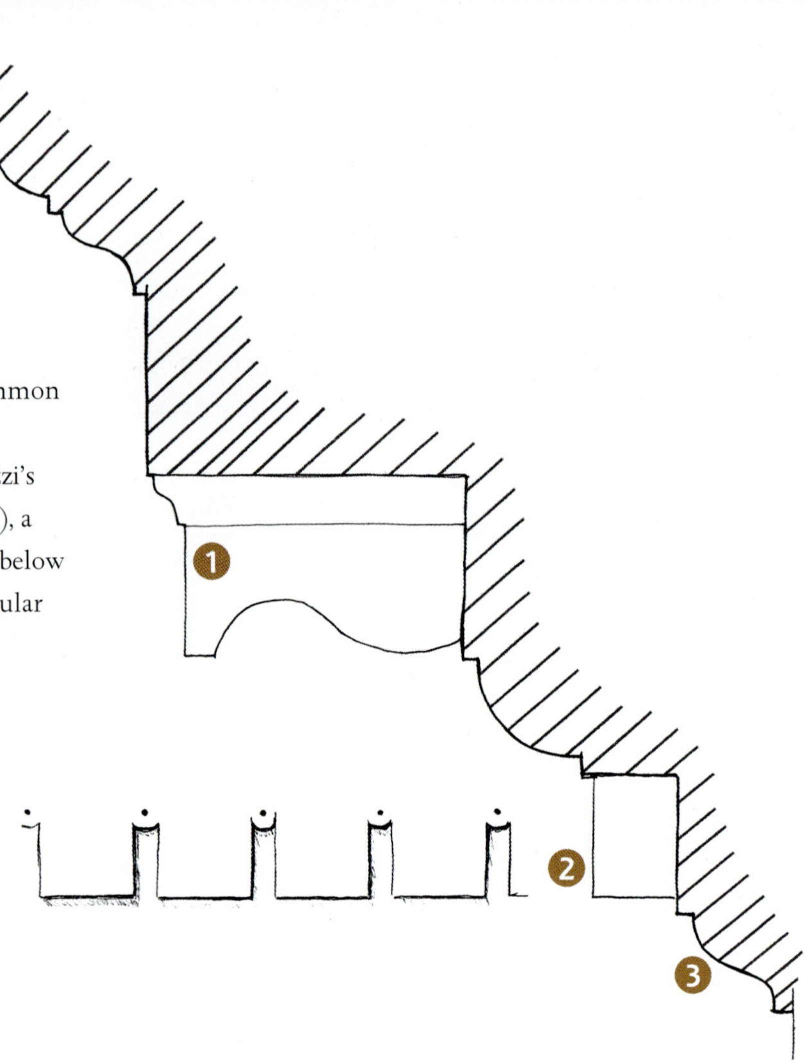

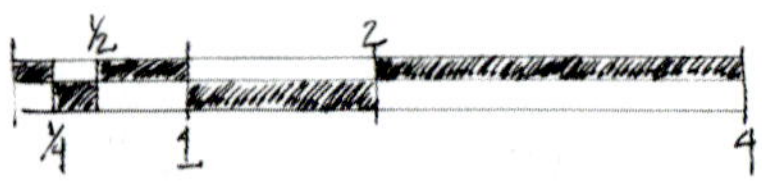

The modillions are two-and-one-eighth-inches wide with a four-and-one-half-inch separation.

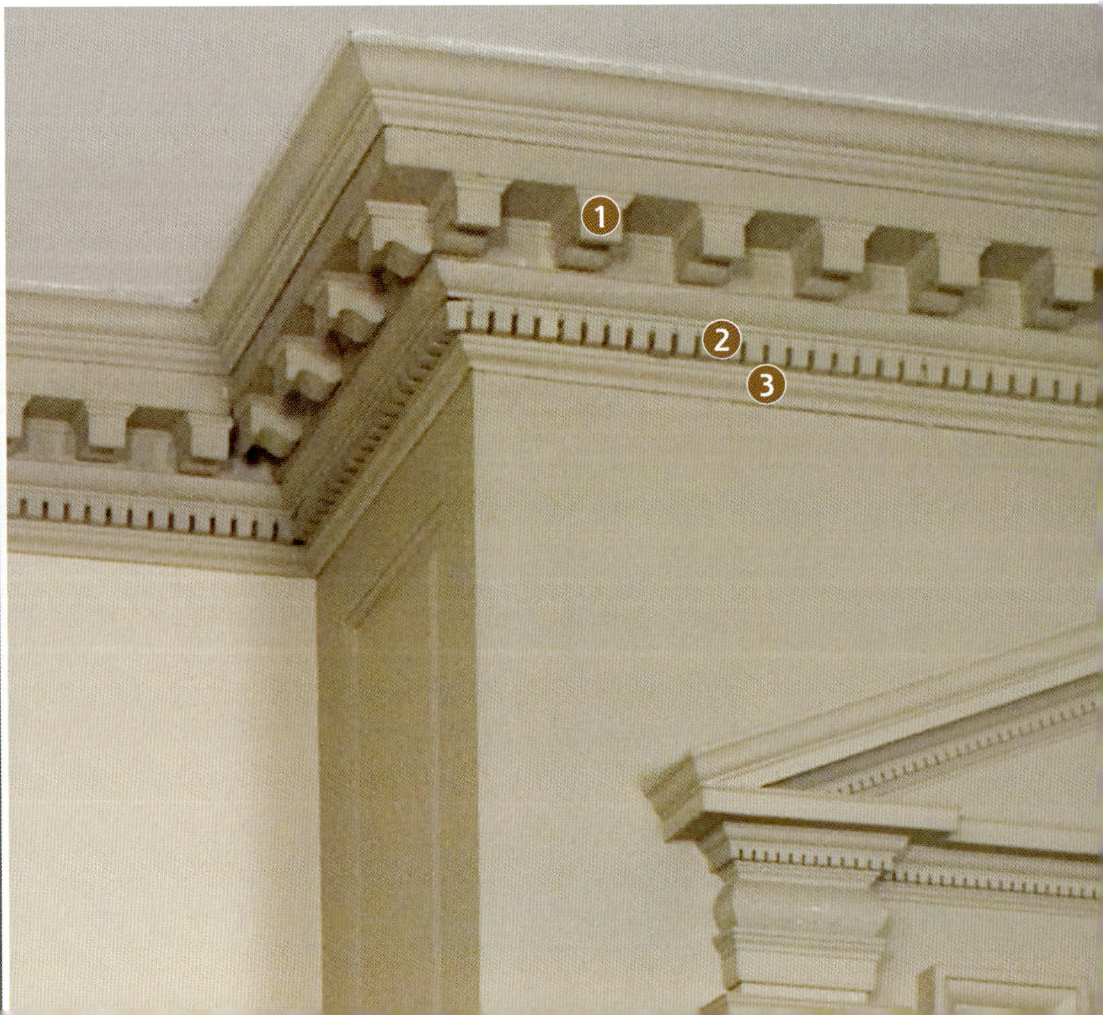

Wainscot

A raised-panel wainscot wraps the room at three feet with a one-and-three-fourths-inch deep base, visually anchoring the room. The surbase (1) is composed of alternating curves including a cyma reversa (2), a cyma recta (3), and a cavetto (4) below, creating thin shadow lines around the room that accentuate the composition. This is echoed in the composition of the base cap molding (5).

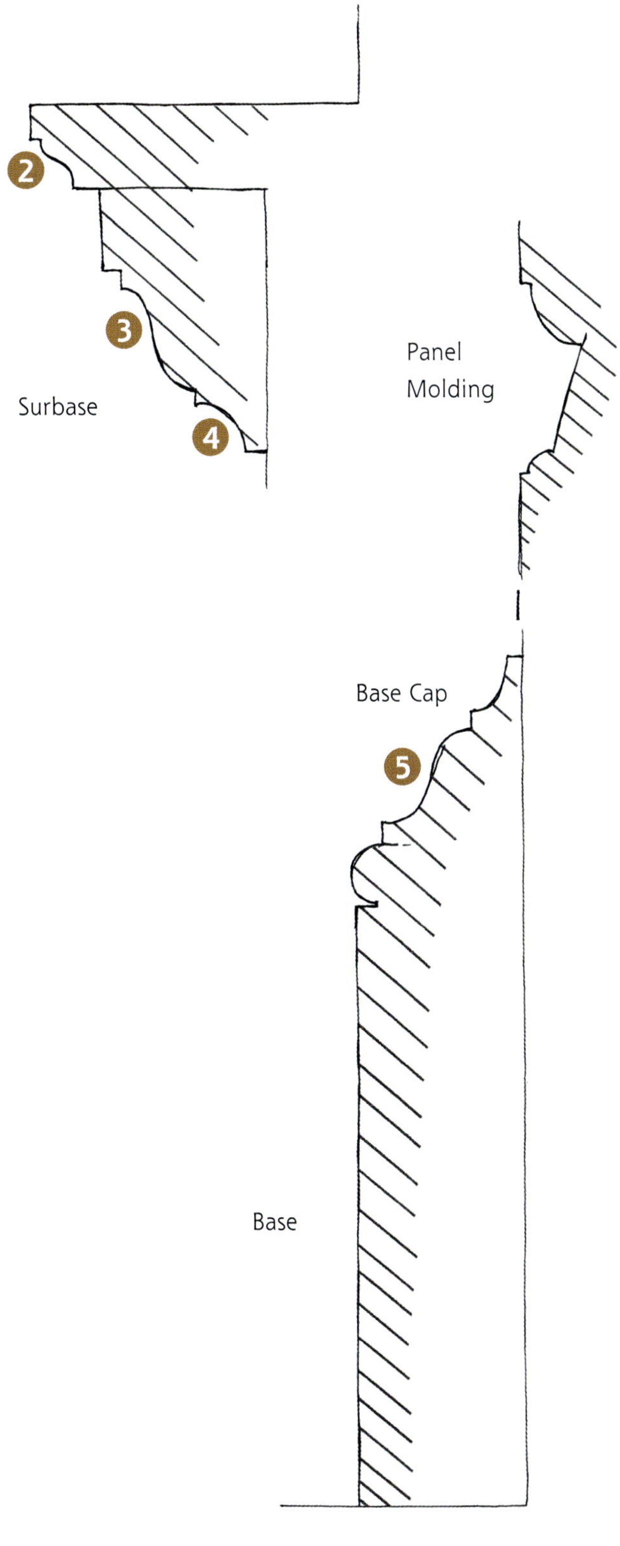

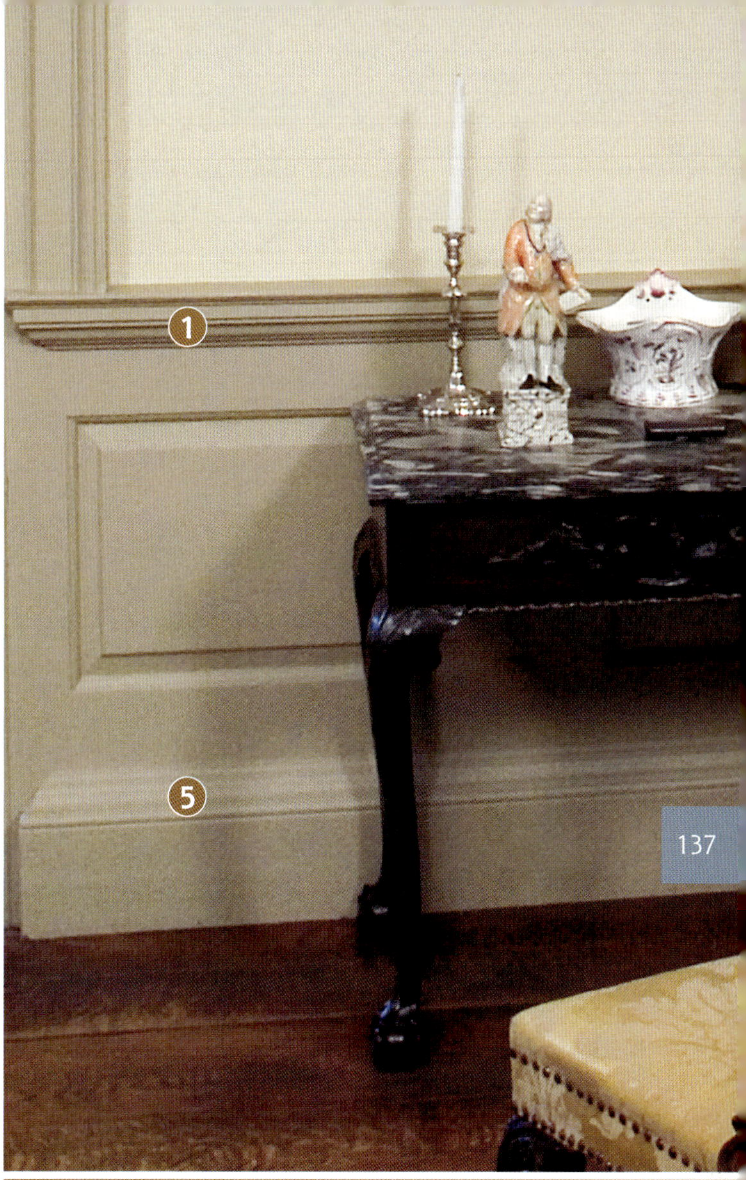

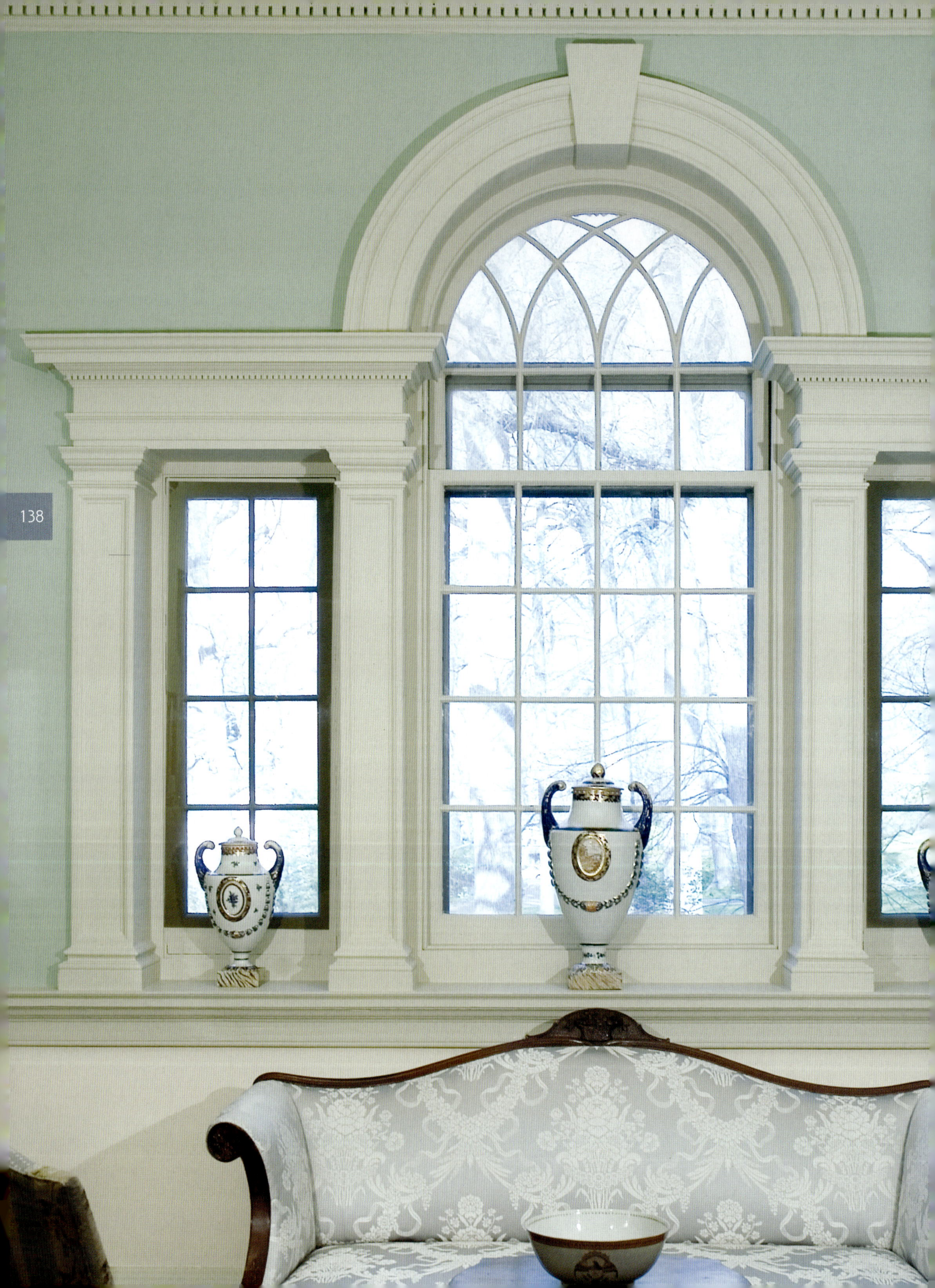

Dining Room Cross Hall

Directly above the Entrance Hall, the dazzling Dining Room Cross Hall is in the Ionic Order and highlighted by matching Palladian, or Serlian, windows at either end. The Palladian window, formed by a central arched opening and two smaller flanking rectangular openings, was first described by the Renaissance architect Sebastiano Serlio and then used frequently by Andrea Palladio in his work. For many it is a symbol of grace and beauty; in the Cross Hall these windows give the room exceptional elegance.

Cornice

A full entablature with an Ionic pulvinated frieze (1) appears over the door pilasters (2), and the denticulated cornice (3) above continues around the room, fully integrating the composition of the door surround with the room.

Door Surround

A graceful pilastered entrance in the Ionic Order is featured on the long wall. These fluted pilasters use Scamozzi's Ionic capital (5) derived from the Temple of Saturn, with corner volutes springing from the egg-and-dart ornamented echinus rather than connecting at the center.

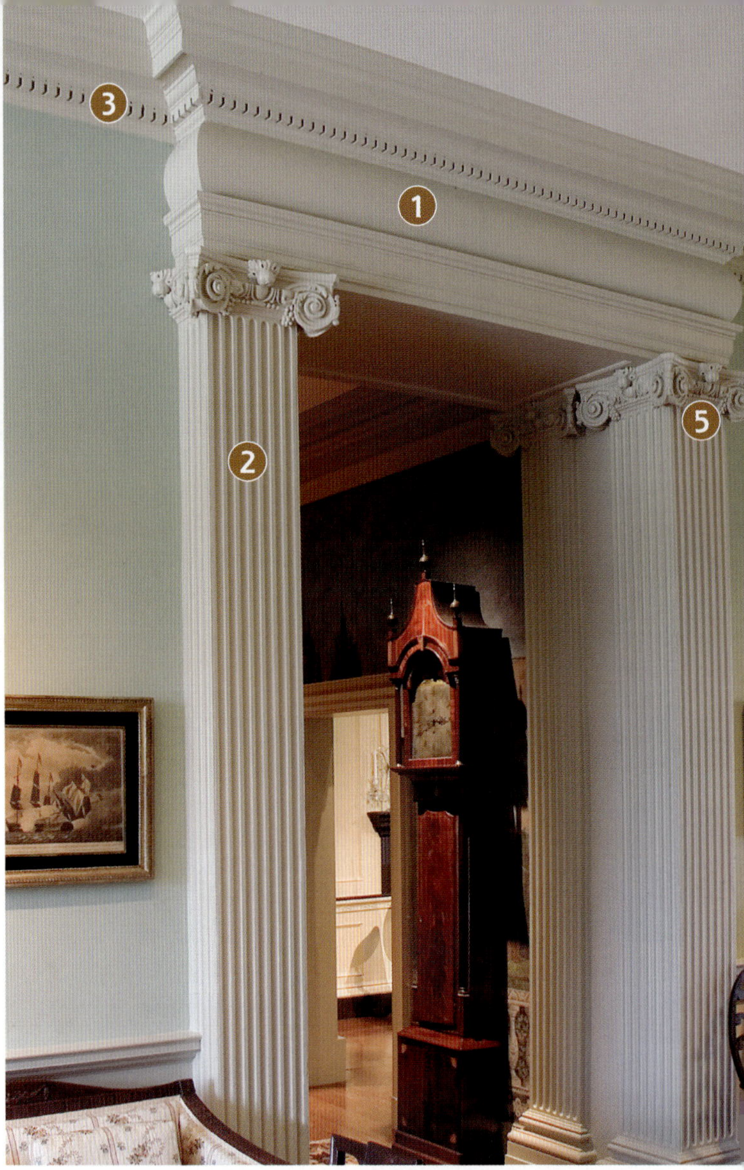

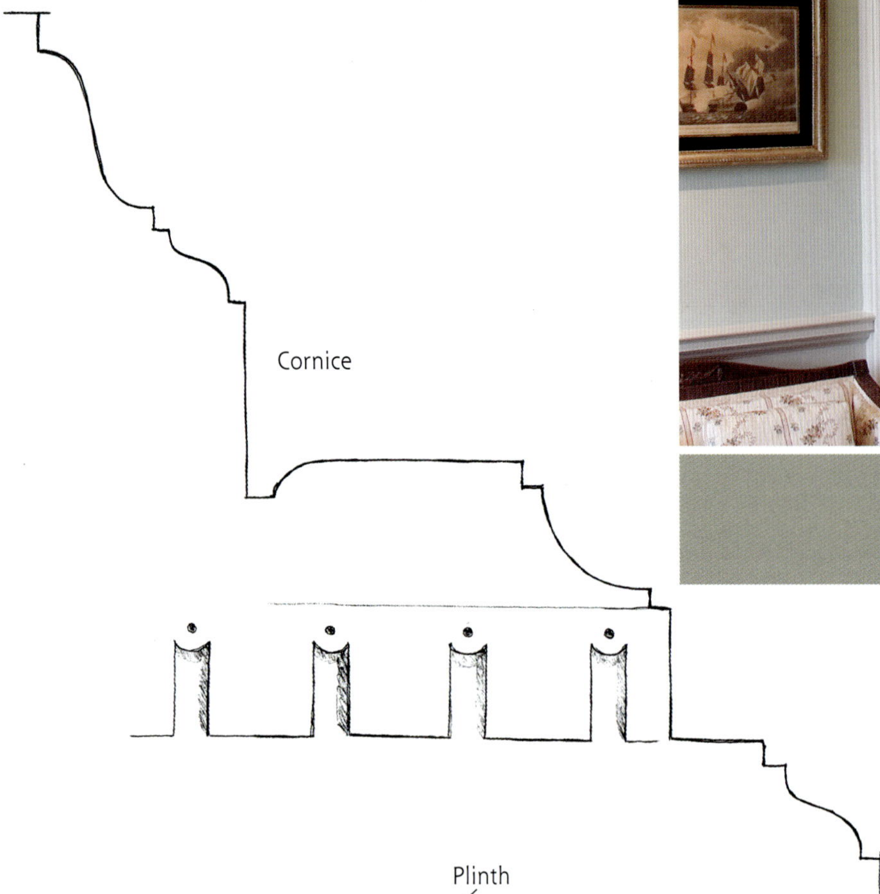

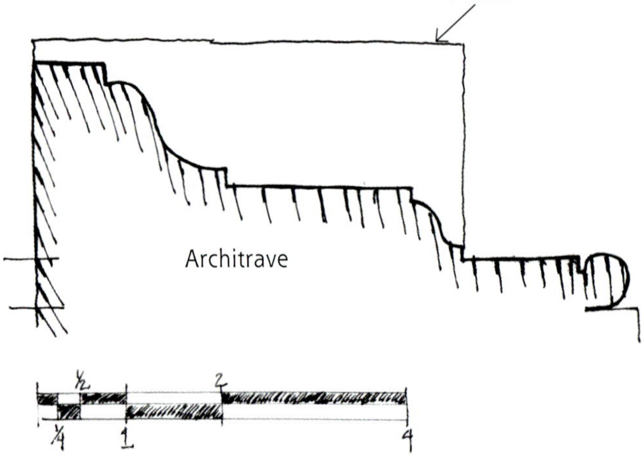

Wainscot

The wainscot is not paneled, but the base and surbase carry around the room to maintain the scale.

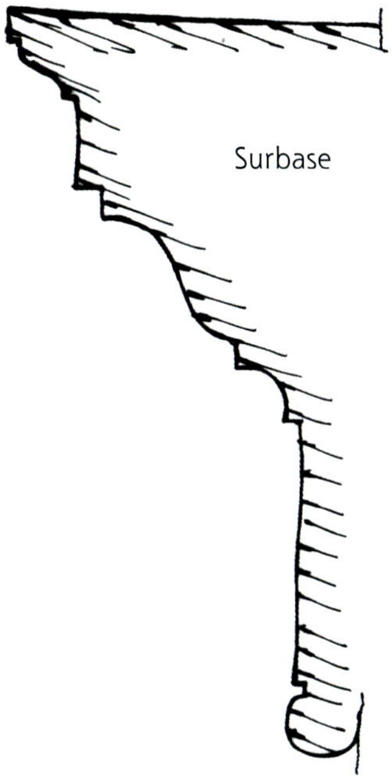

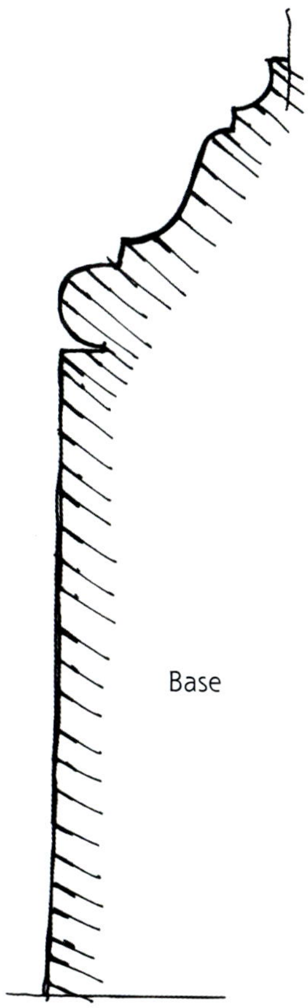

Port Royal

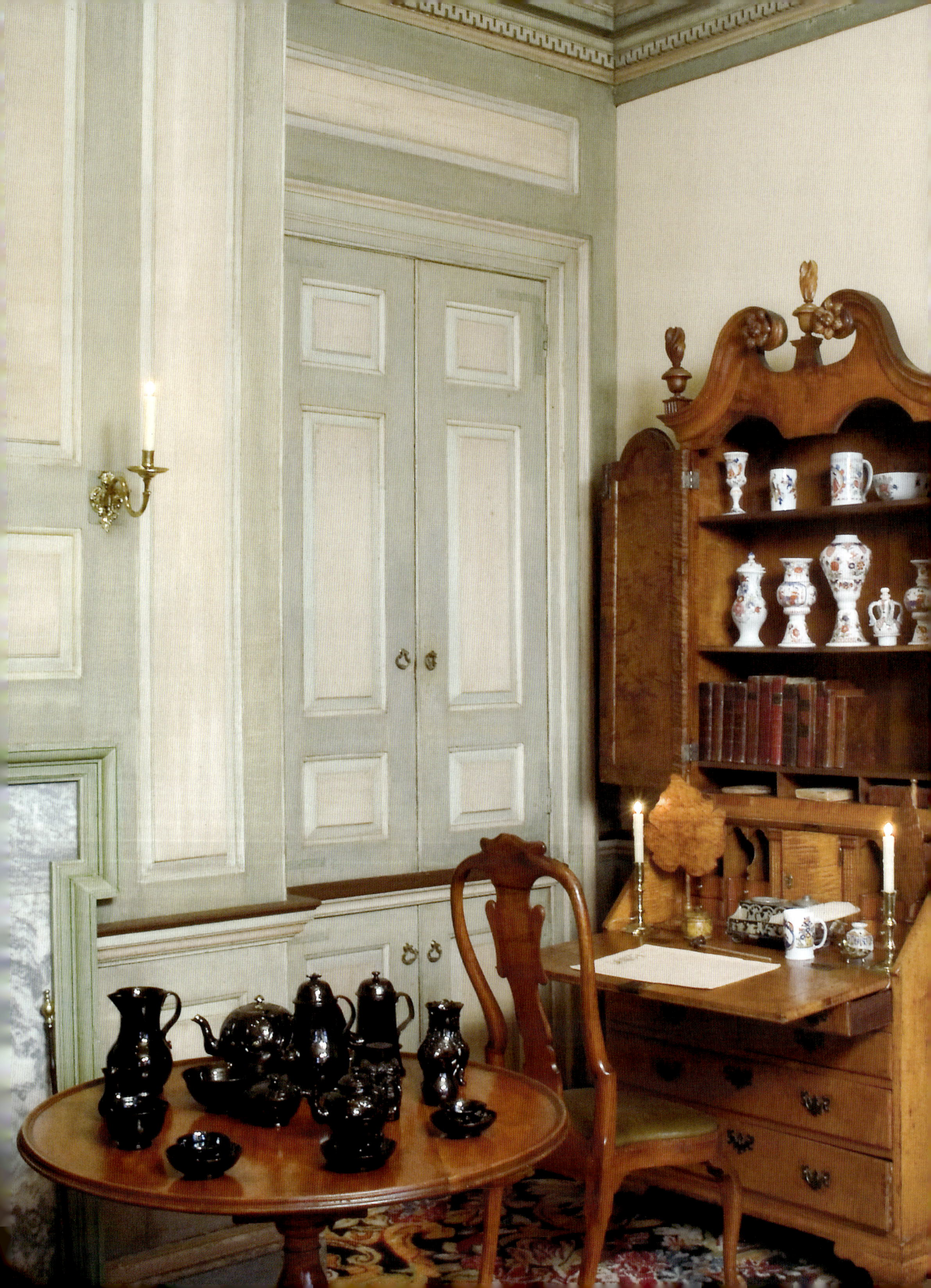

Maple Bedroom

The two Port Royal bedrooms were created from the original dining room of the house. The Maple Bedroom, shown here, is the more ornate of the two rooms. Its fireplace projects into the room and is balanced by doors on both sides. The cornice has fretwork dentils (1) common in Georgian architecture and is similar to those from the Baths of Diocletian's Roman Doric Order illustrated in Chambray's *Parallel*.

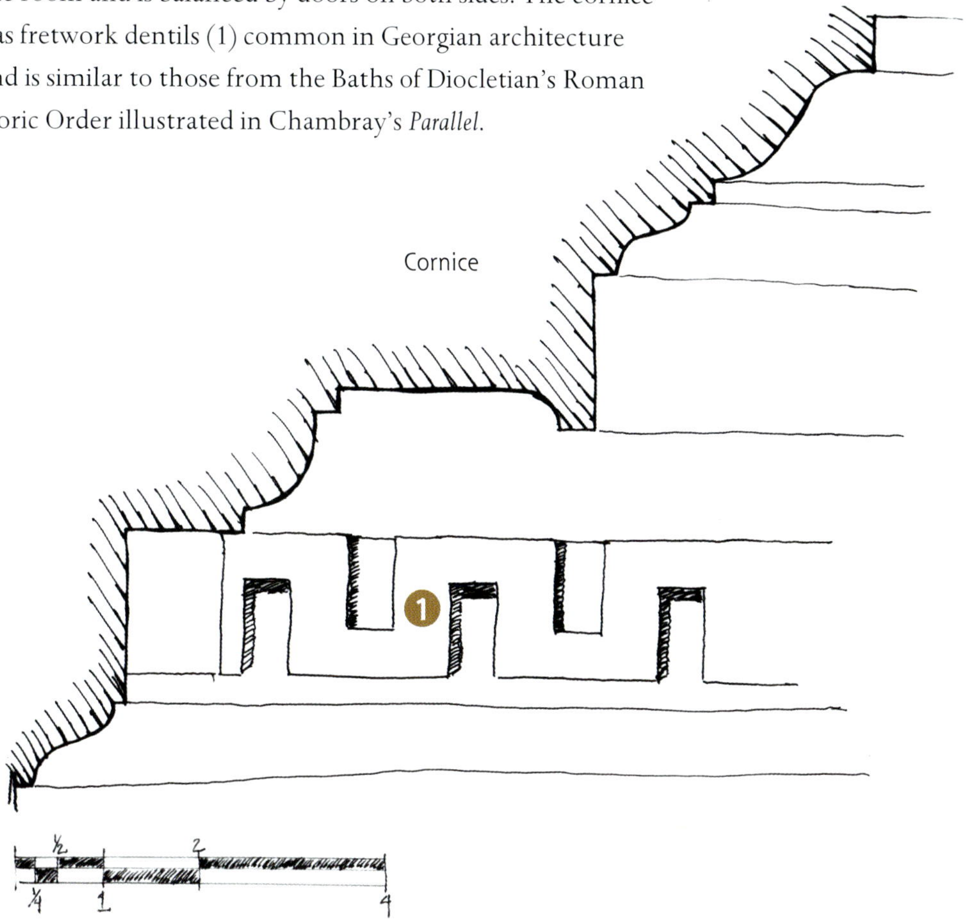

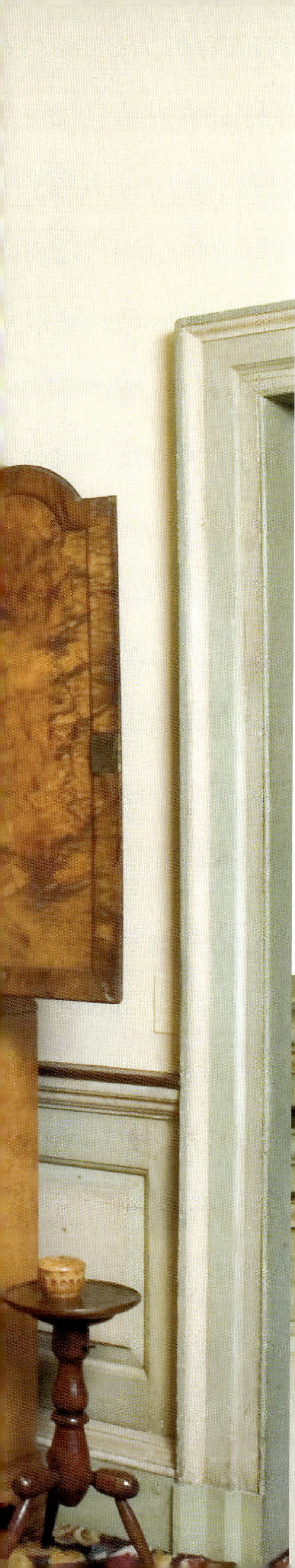

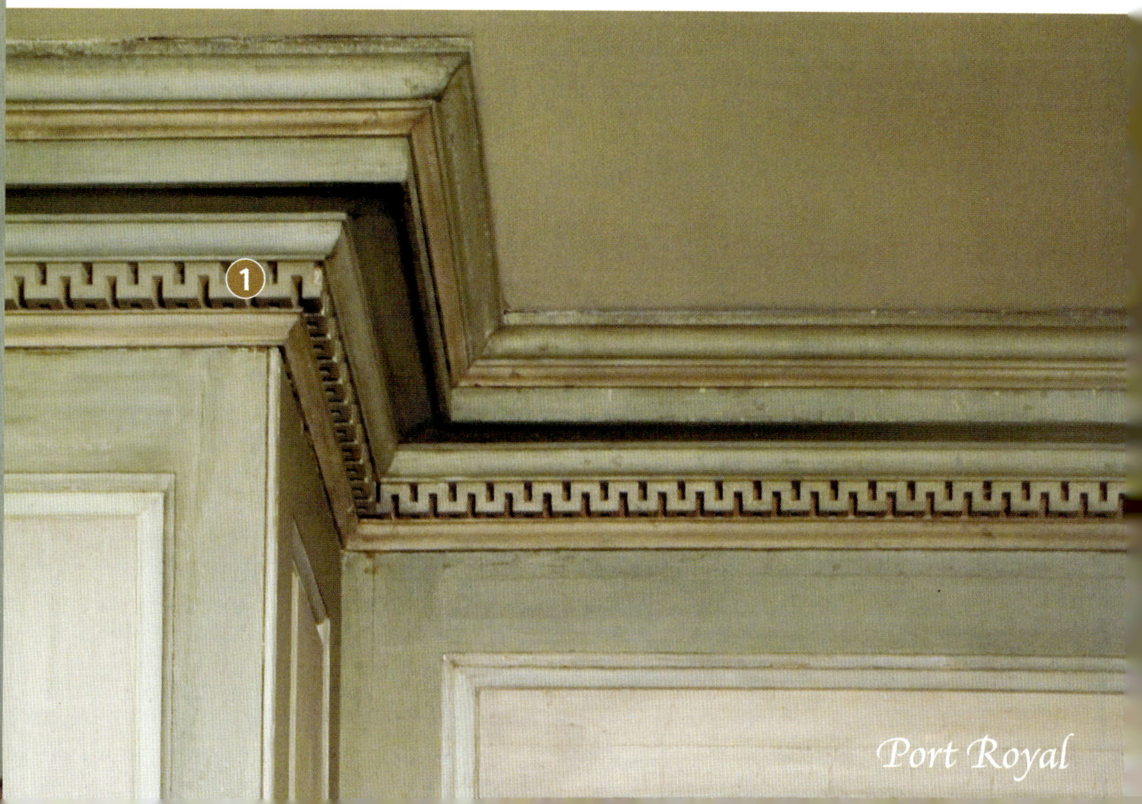

Maple Bedroom

Wainscot and Architraves

Simple raised panels on the fireplace wall harmonize with the paneling of the wainscot and nearby doors. Typical bold Georgian style moldings form the surbase, panel molds, and base. The two-part architrave with its deep backband is equally robust.

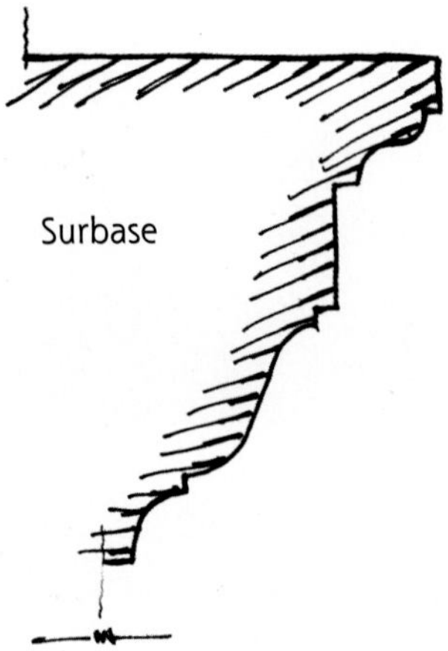

Surbase

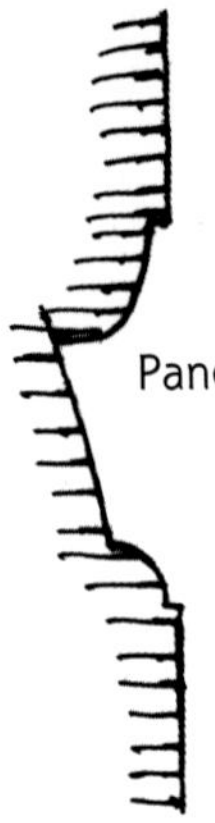

Panel

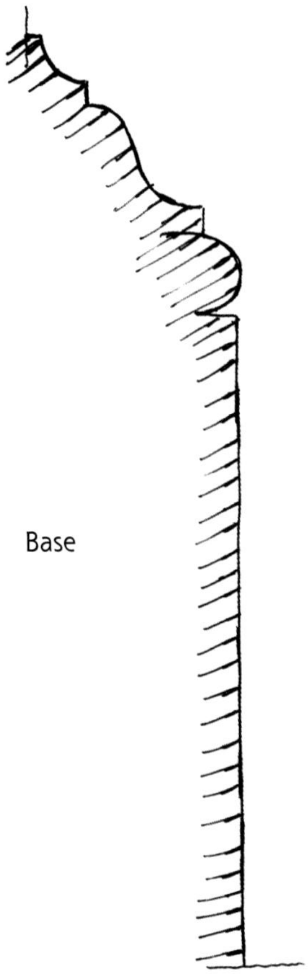

Base

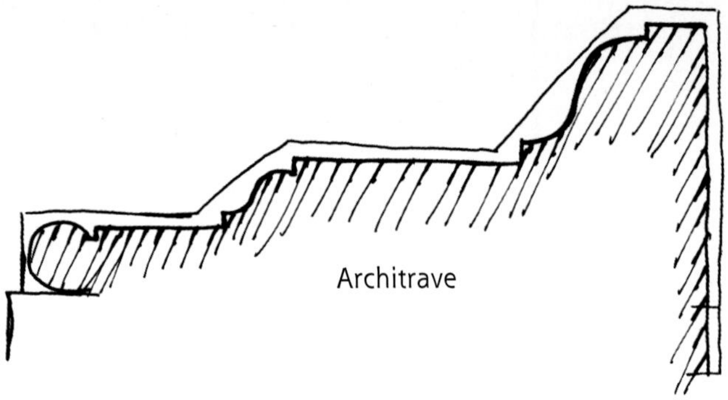

Architrave

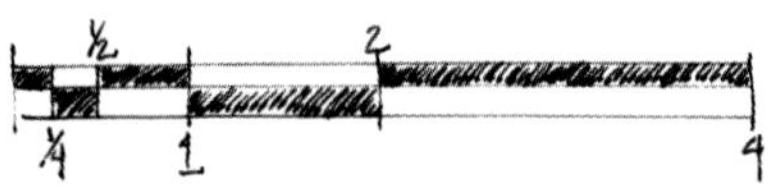

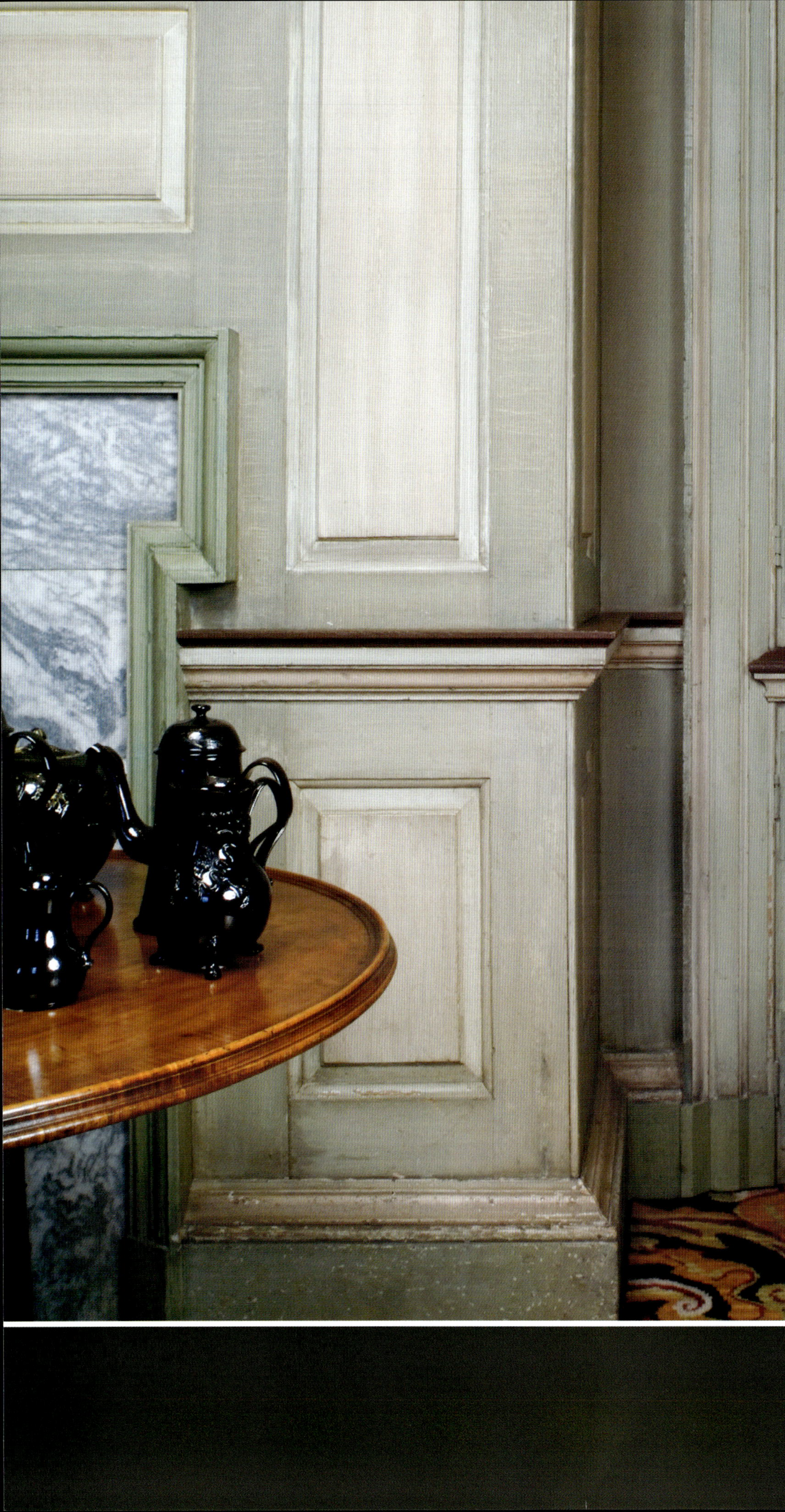

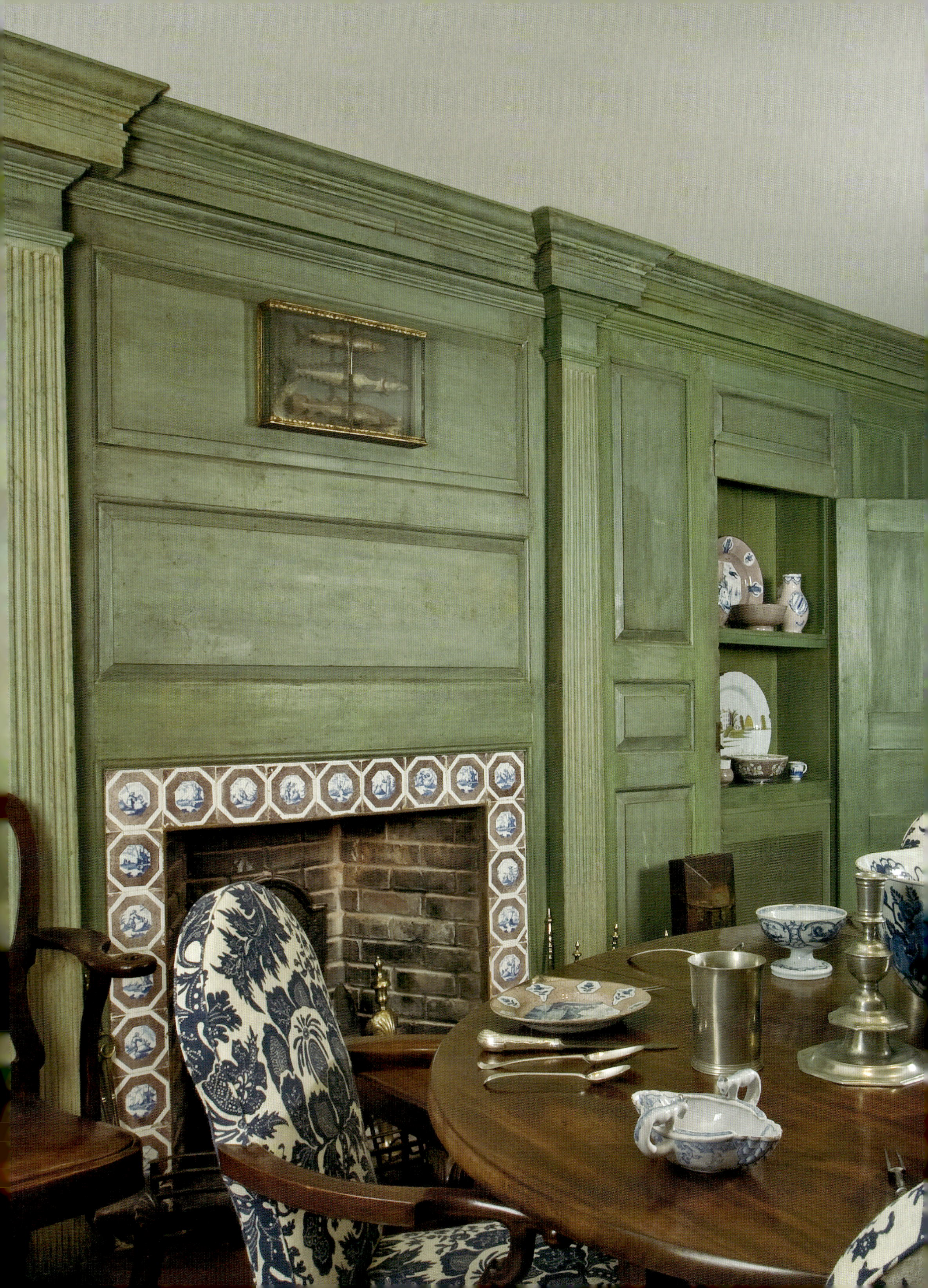

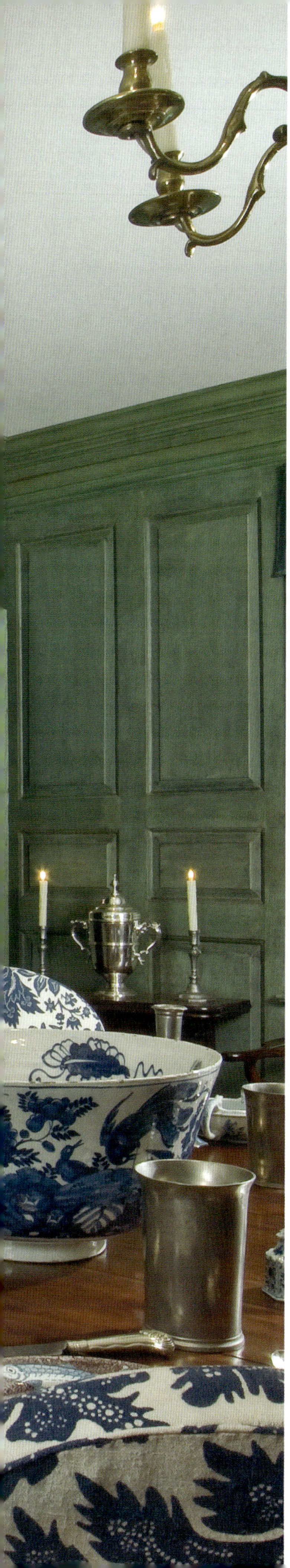

Queen Anne Dining Room

William Wescott Scott House, East Derry, New Hampshire, circa 1760

7'9" high by 14'9" wide by 18'10" long

The Queen Anne Dining Room came from the William Wescott Scott house in East Derry, New Hampshire. A refined composition of three levels of panels spans the walls from floor to ceiling, hinting at dado, chair rail, and wall zones. Fluted pilasters frame the firebox and integrate into the wall composition. The pilasters have a small astragal above the flutes. A necking above the astragal is the same dimension as the upper rail of the panels, above which the cornice projects out at each pilaster, emphasizing them as compositional elements in the room.

The ceiling is low, less than eight feet in height, though not uncommonly low in northern houses of this period. There is no architrave set on the wall surface at the windows and doors; rather, the paneled jamb simply projects and overlaps the wall plane, forming a thin molding around the windows. The Queen Anne Dining Room is a fine example of how to adapt the full classical language, such as that seen in the Hampton Room (page 80), to the simpler character of this room.

Mr. du Pont bought the Queen Anne woodwork from a Connecticut antiques dealer.

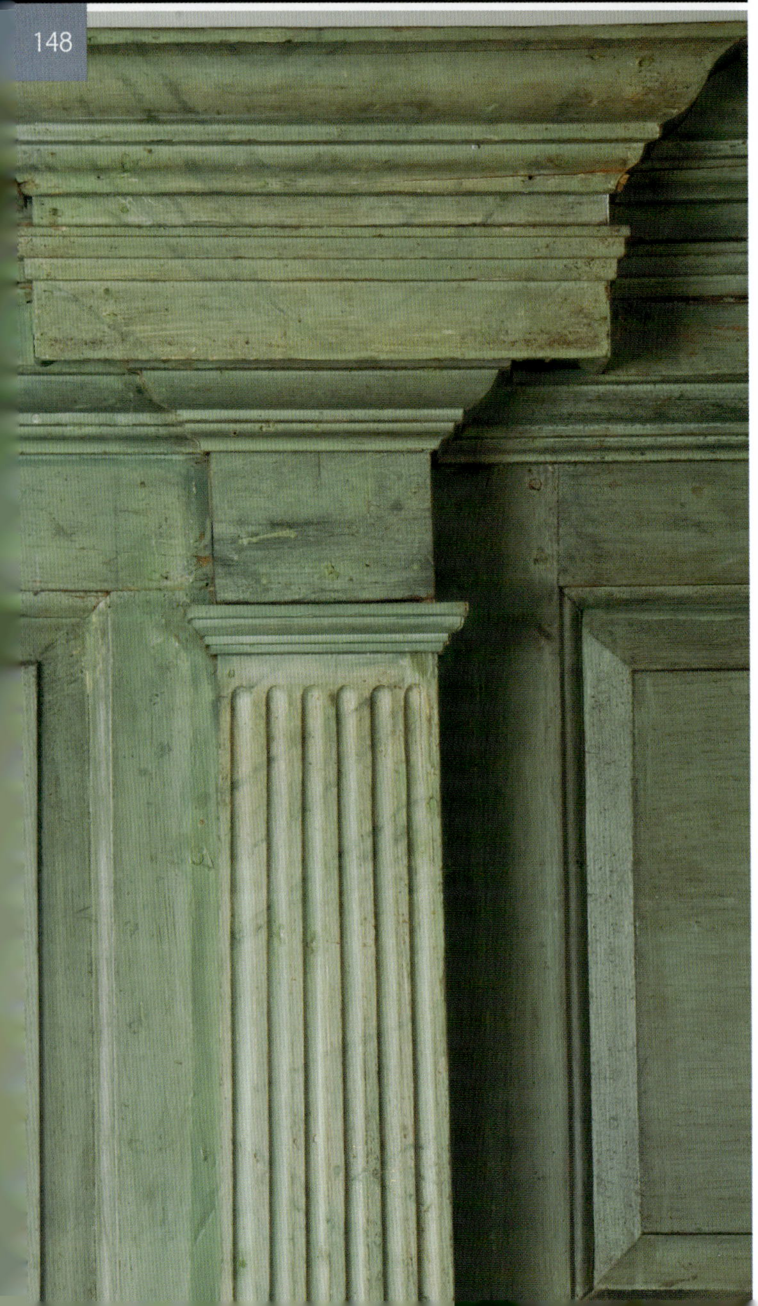

Cornice

The cornice is largely scaled for the height of the room. It projects six inches and is eight inches tall.

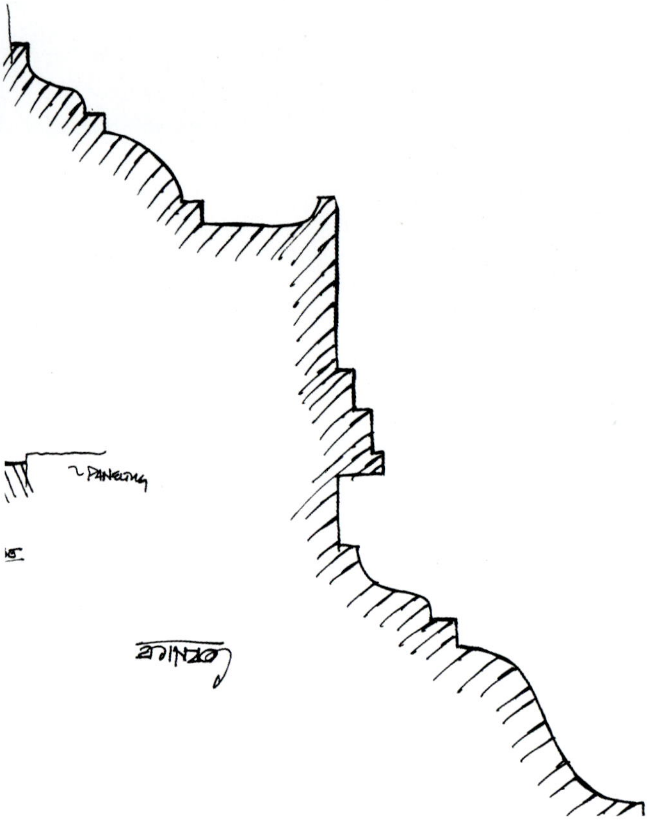

Panels & Base

In this room, panels establish the scale. These fully paneled walls are laid out so the middle panel (facing page) creates a chair rail-like zone between an upper wall and lower pedestal. A simple, thin base transitions from the raised panels of the wall to the floor.

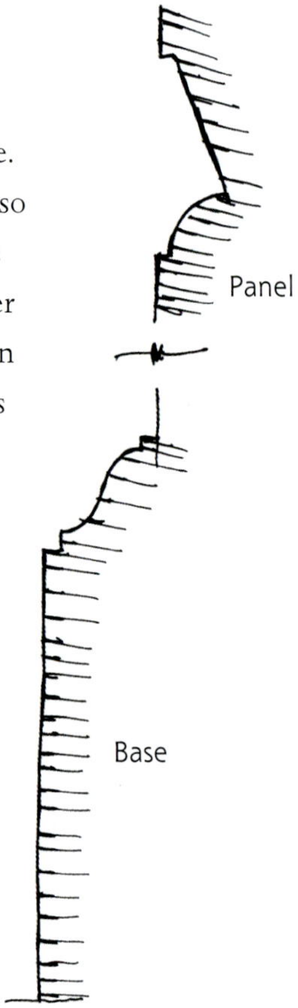

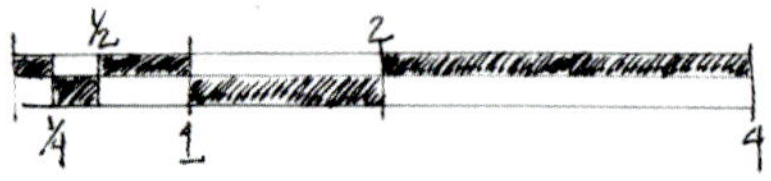

Fireplace Wall

The fireplace has no bolection molding around its face, which would commonly be seen in a house of this period. The firebox opening is framed on the side by pilasters that rise up through the cornice, which projects in correspondence with the pilasters' depth. The pilasters are very refined with entasis and stop-fluting (1), or flutes that are filled in at the bottom third of the pilaster height.

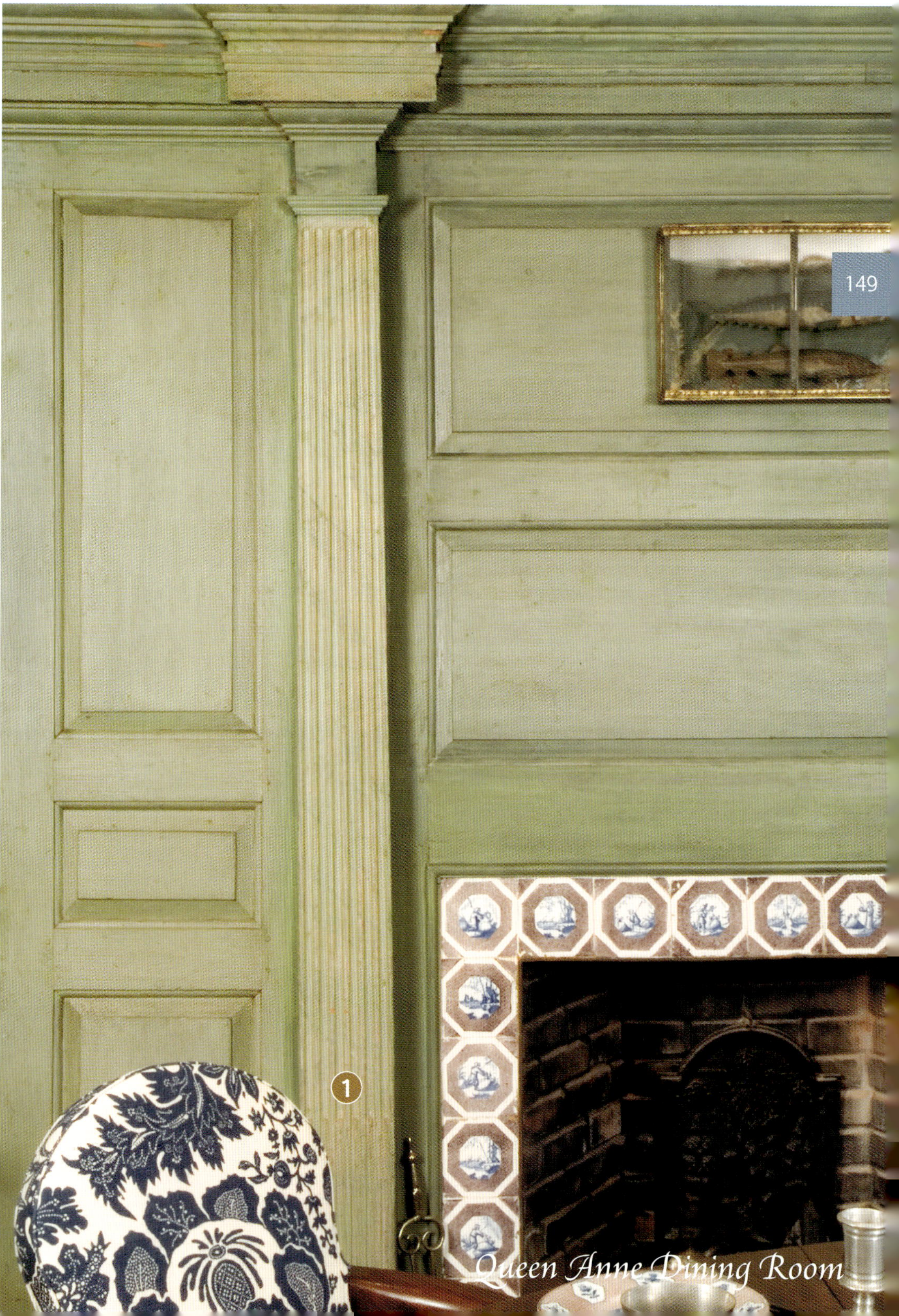

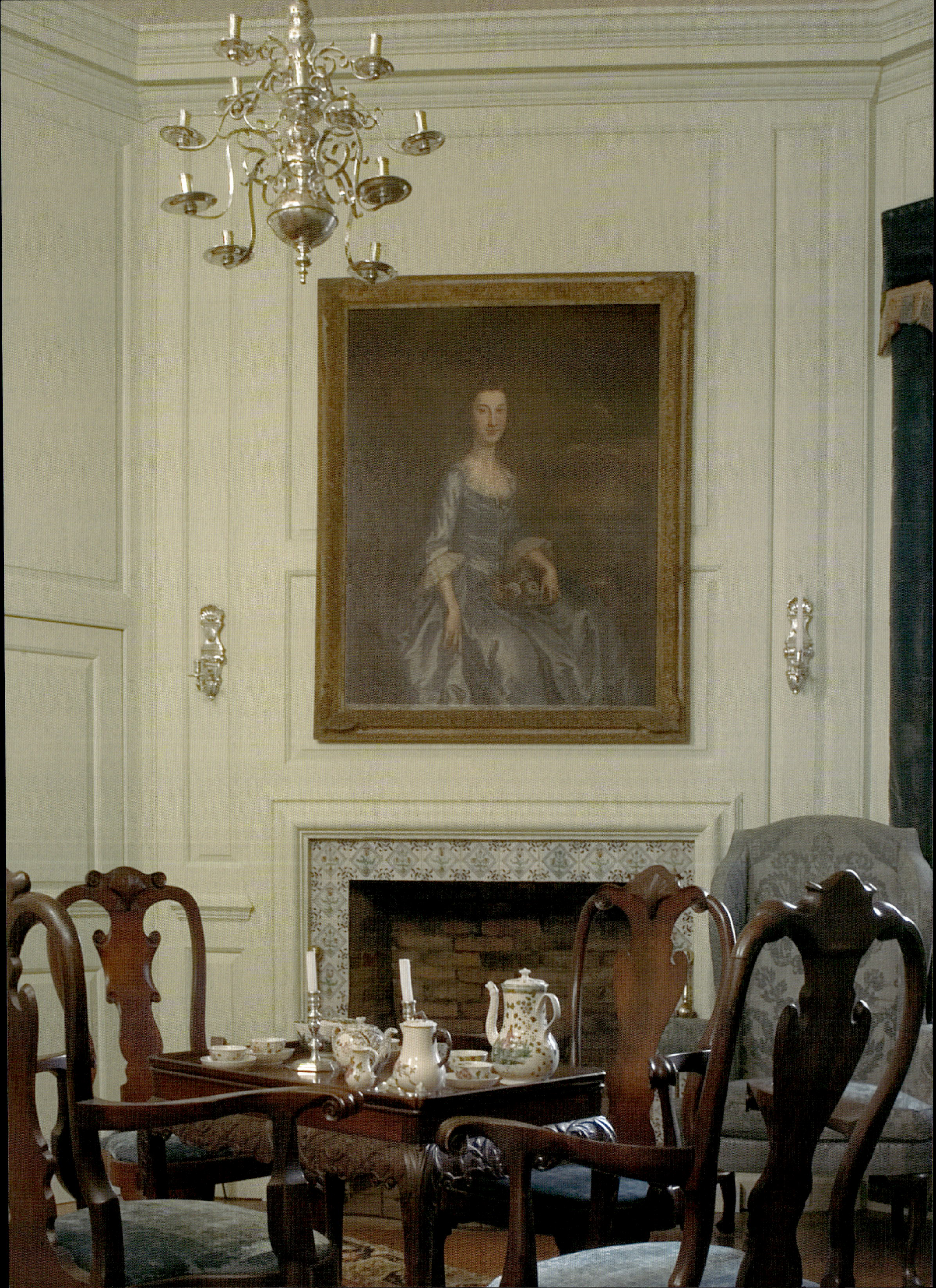

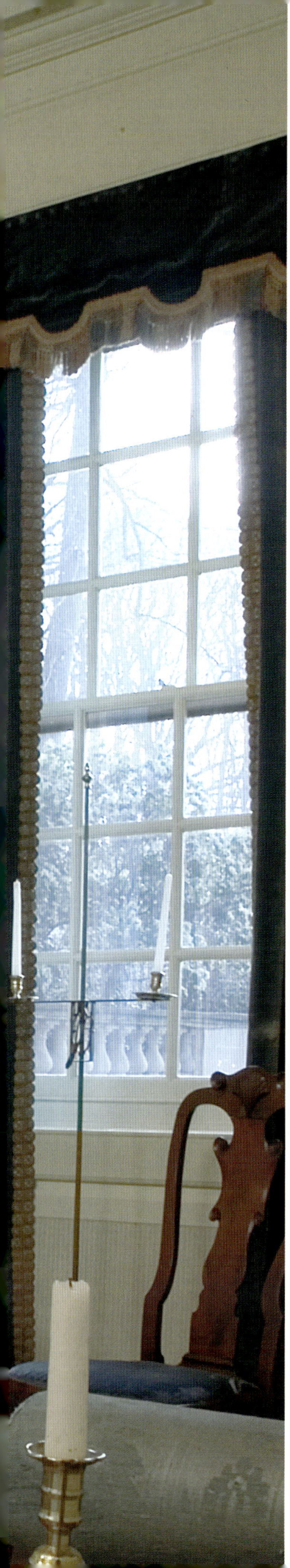

Readbourne Parlor

Centreville, Maryland, circa 1733

11'10" high by 16'10" wide by 15'4" wide

Readbourne Parlor is an early Georgian room at Winterthur created out of woodwork from the early eighteenth-century Queen Anne's County, Maryland, home of Colonel James Hollyday, a lawyer with influential ties and associations.

It is not known who designed and built Readbourne, but Hollyday had a brother and cousin with ties to building, and John Earle, a master builder who lived nearby, may have been involved. Queen Anne's County, Maryland, is one of the oldest areas of colonial settlement and was an active area at the time this house was built for a prominent family.

Readbourne Parlor is a room of graceful proportions, simple expression, and an arrangement of architectural elements common to its era.

The Readbourne Parlor's corner fireplace forms a welcome gathering spot in the room.

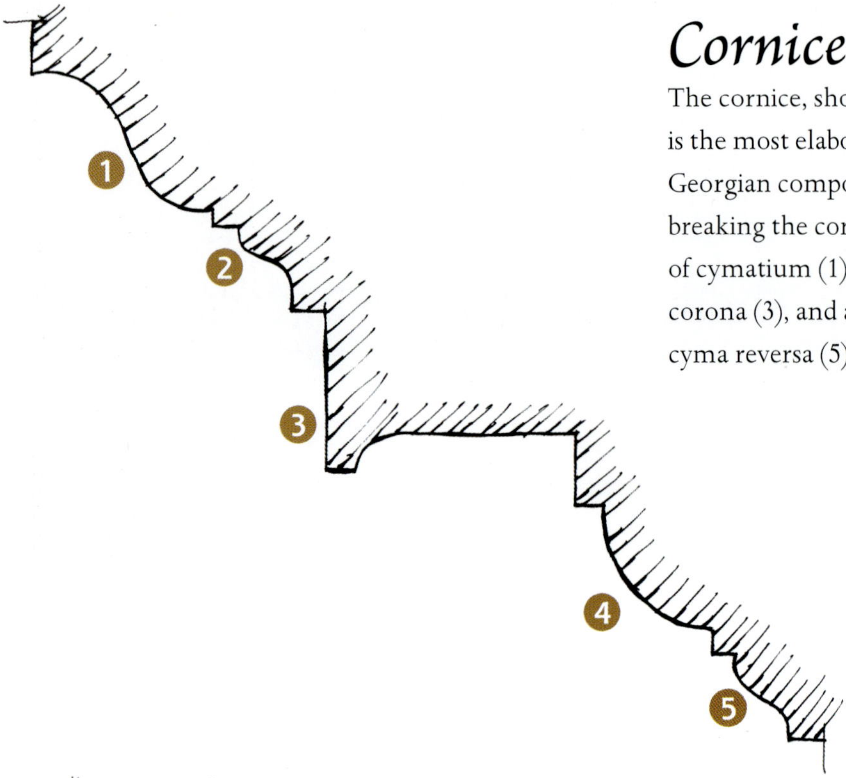

Cornice

The cornice, shown in the photo on the previous page, is the most elaborate molding element and a common Georgian composition. It is made up of three pieces, breaking the cornice into its simplest arrangement of cymatium (1) with its cyma reversa bedmold (2), a corona (3), and a bedmold formed of an ovolo (4) and cyma reversa (5).

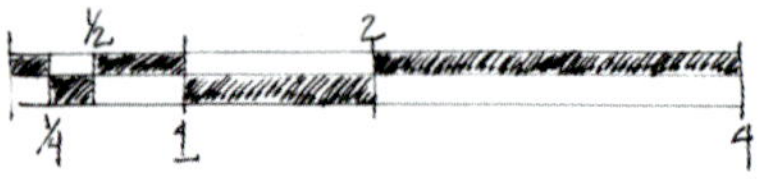

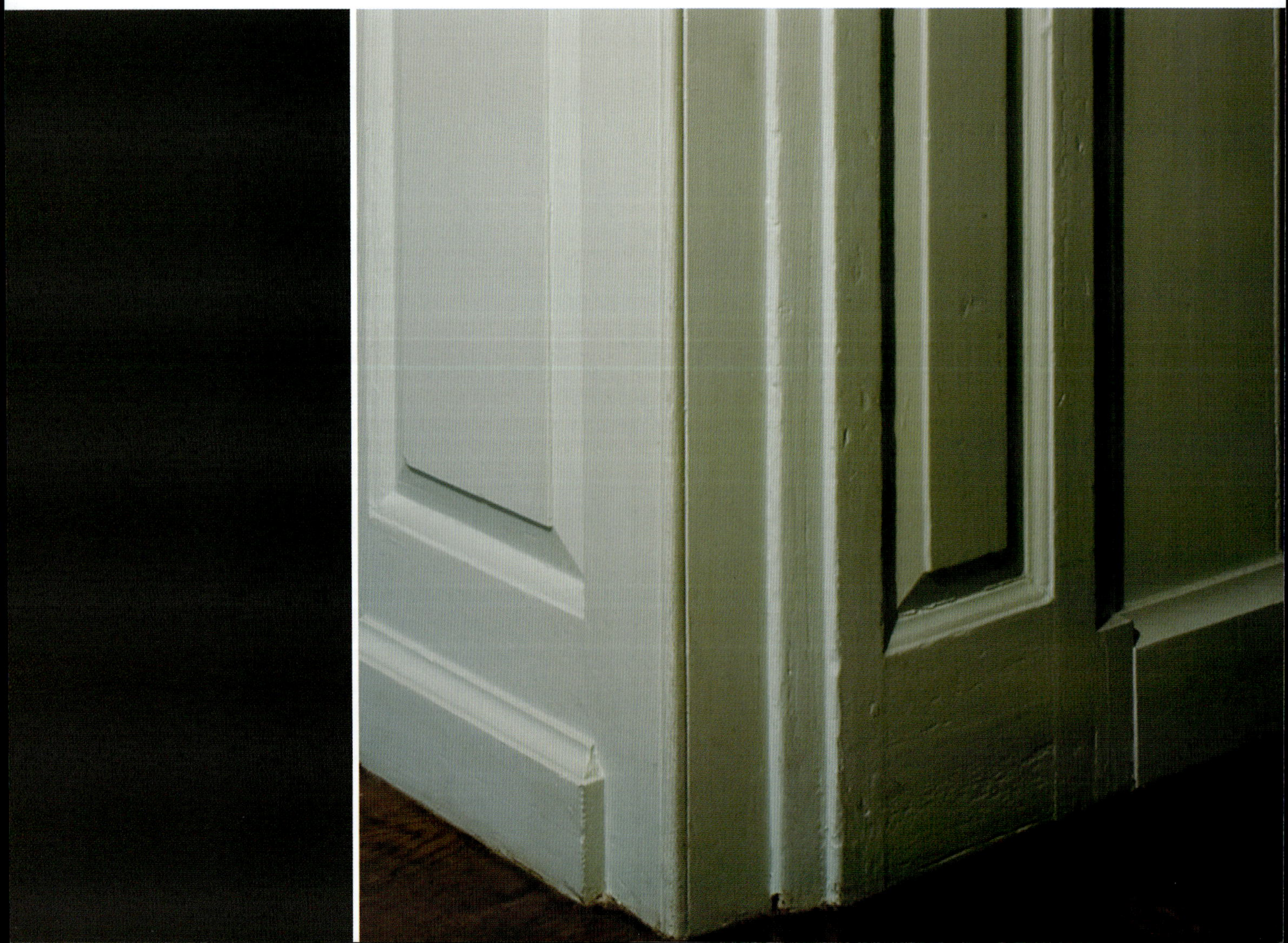

Fireplace Wall

The room's most interesting feature is the fireplace, situated at an angle in the corner (shown on the previous spread). A bolection molding surrounds the large firebox with two panels above.

The firebox is flanked by a lower panel in the dado level, a chair rail, and tall upper panel in the zone of the wall or column. This arrangement allows one to see the classical ordering of the room, and the proportions established here continue around the room.

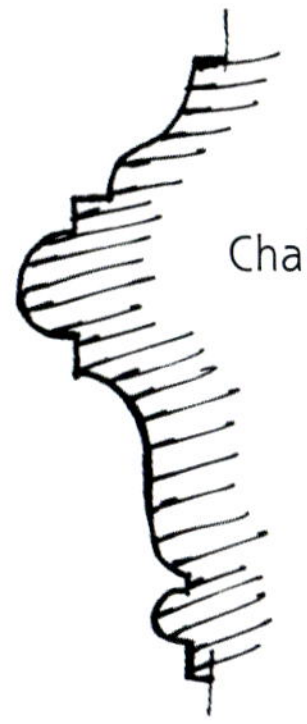

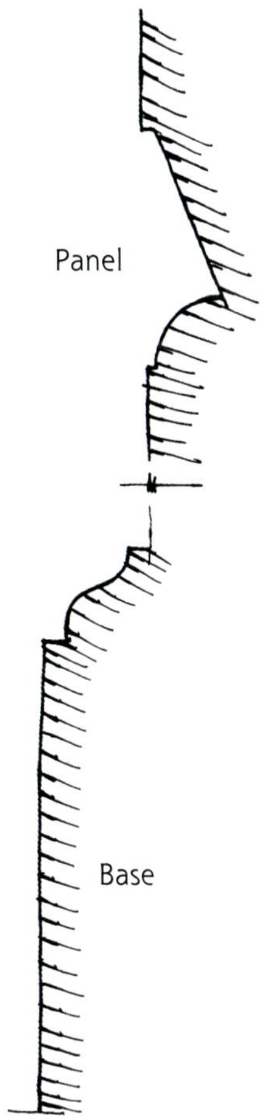

Base

As with other rooms of this period, the base is very simple, merely covering the joint between the wall paneling and the floor, and giving the slightest articulation of a base around the room. There is no formal architrave around the door or openings, just a simple bead.

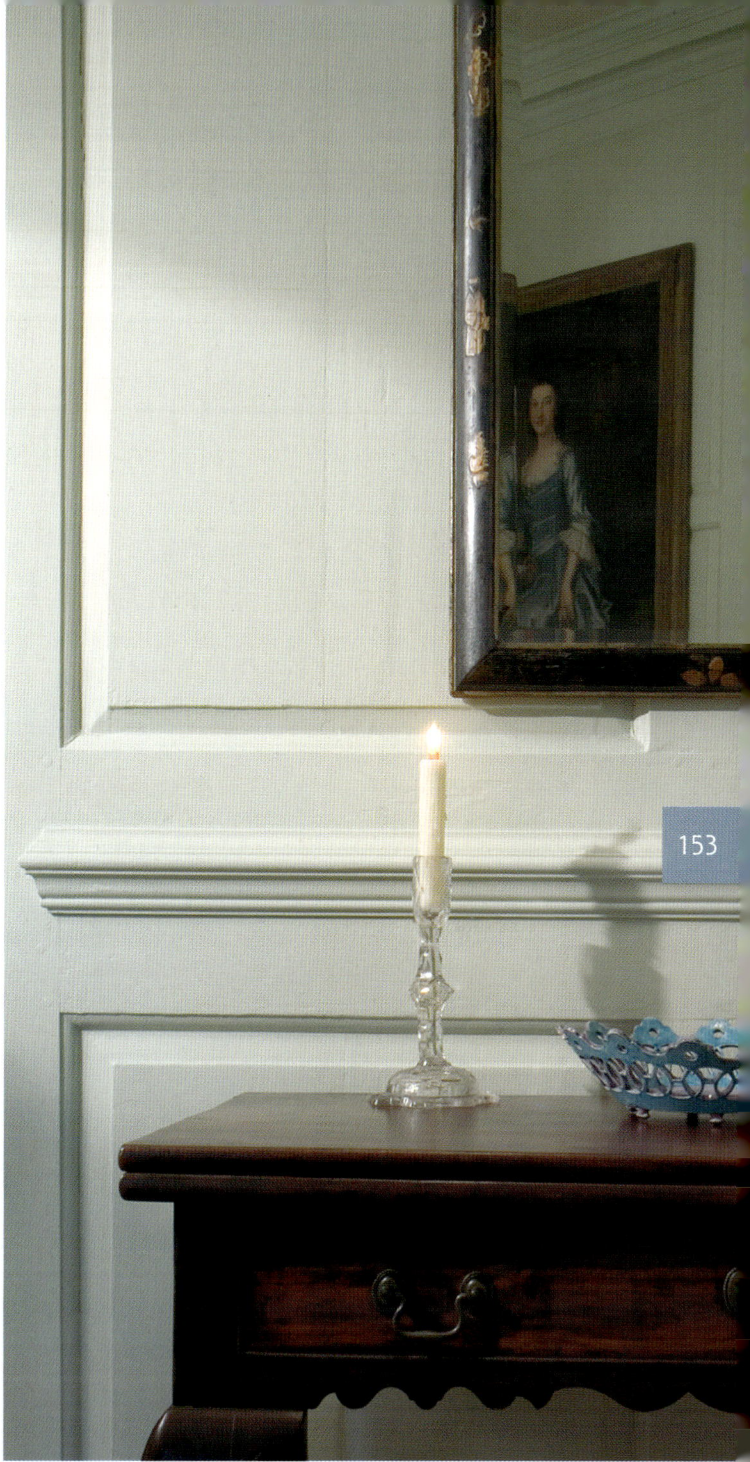

Readbourne Parlor

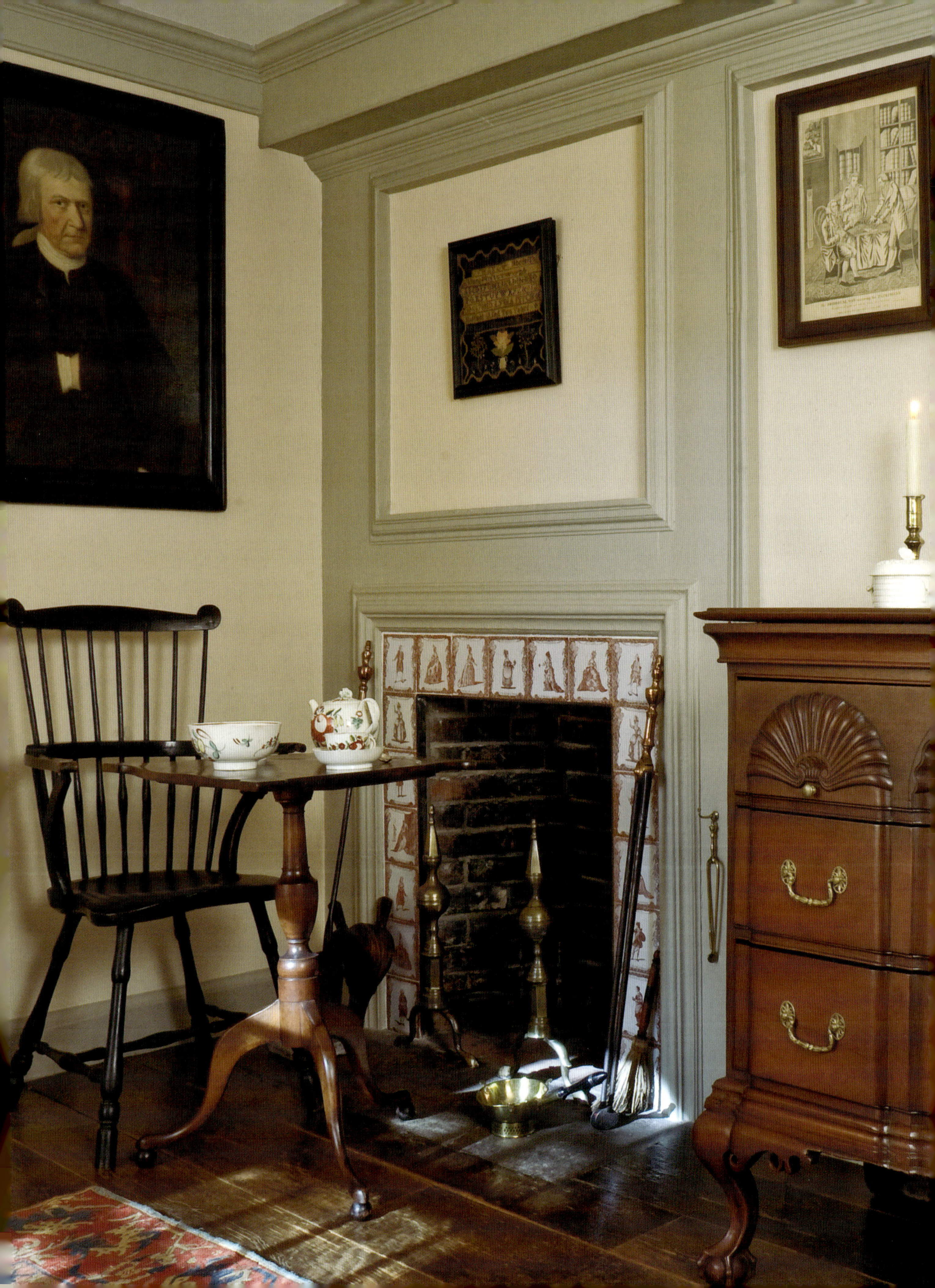

Simsbury Room

Goodwin House, Simsbury, Connecticut, 1760

7'3" high by 13'1" wide by 11' long

The woodwork for this small room comes from the Goodwin House, built in a small town near Hartford, Connecticut. Though simple, the Simsbury Room has an easy charm that is endearing. With its low ceiling, asymmetrical composition, and plain moldings, it shows how small and less-formal rooms can be articulated.

A ceiling beam is dressed up with panels on the bottom, a way of formalizing the room and integrating the functional structure with the design of the room. The low ceiling height was not uncommon in houses in the northern colonies, where maintaining warmth was important; indeed, the low scale creates an appropriate coziness.

Though the fireplace is off-center in the room, showing the tolerance for asymmetry typical in earlier colonial architecture, the broad open wall space to the right balances its weight. A panel below this, capped by a chair rail that becomes the panel mold surrounding the open plaster area, completes the balancing act.

An asymmetrically located fireplace creates a nice place for tea.

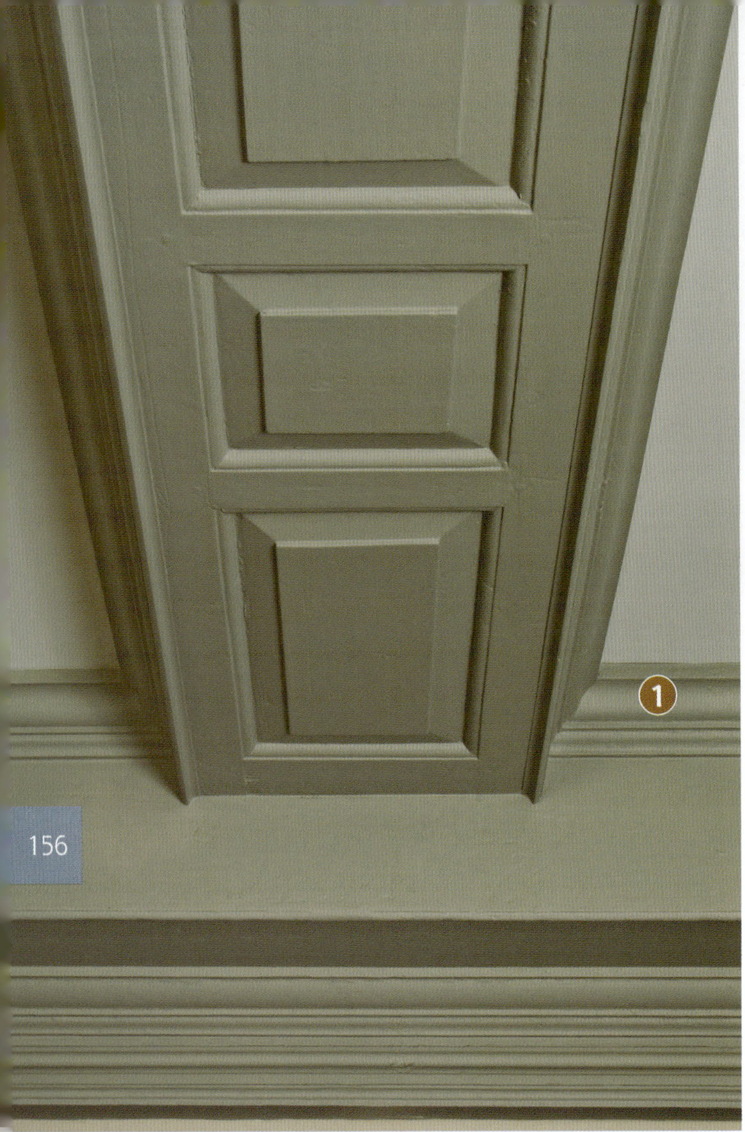

Cornice

The cornice in the room is essentially a decorated beam, capped with a simple cornice (1) at the juncture of the ceiling and beam.

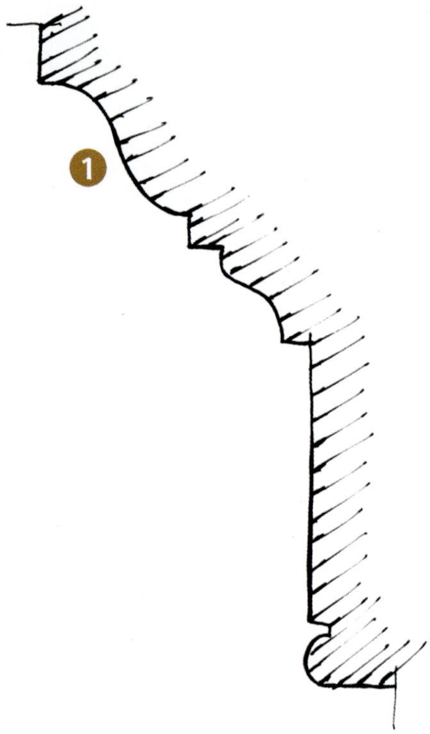

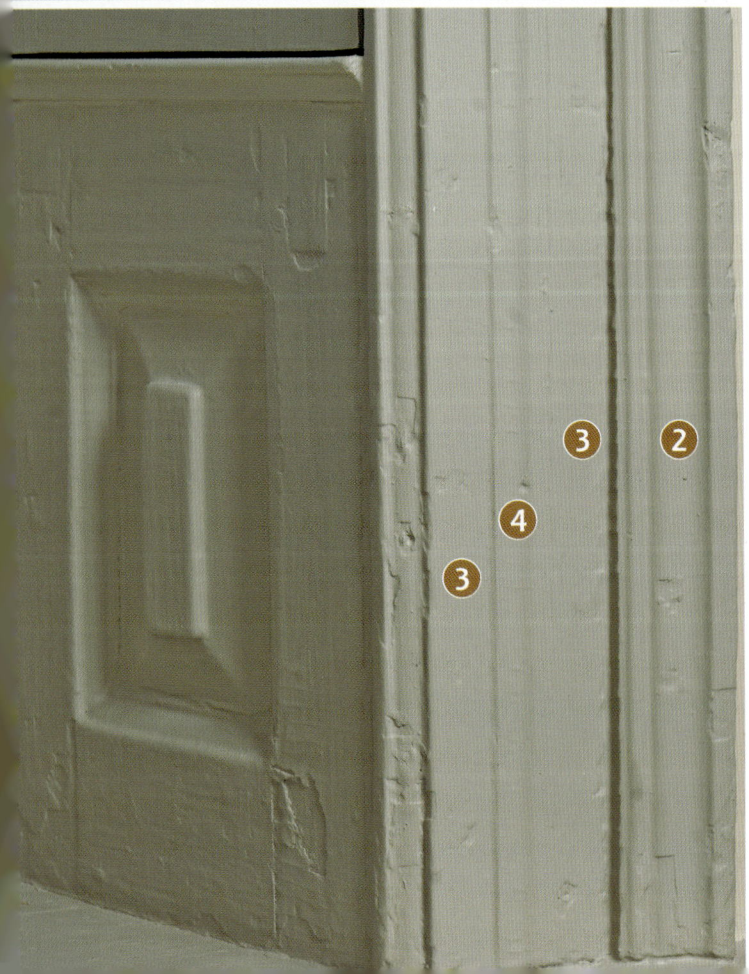

Architraves

The door architrave contains all of the elements of a classical architrave with a backband (2) formed of a cyma reversa and a bead and two fascias (3) separated by another cyma reversa (4). The same refined architrave surrounds a window opposite the fireplace. The depth of the wall allows for pocketing interior shutters and a window seat formed by the deep windowsill.

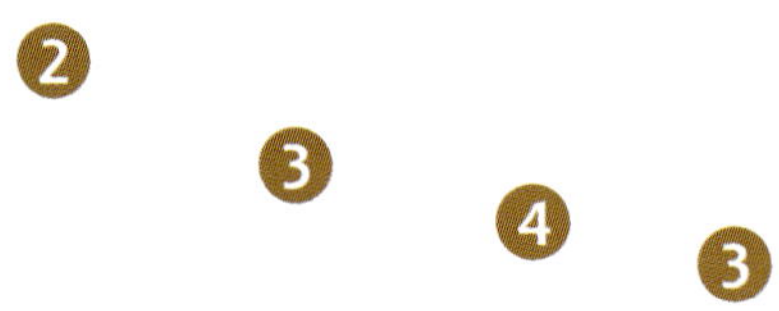

Door Architrave

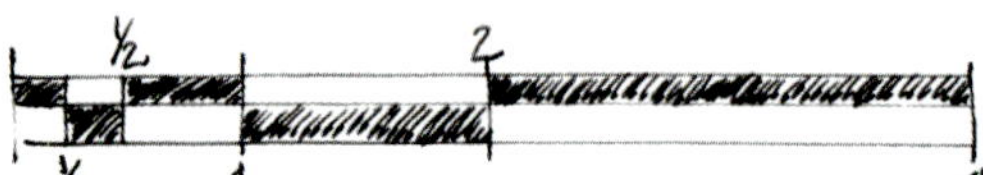

Chair Rails & Panels

In the Simsbury Room, the chair rail along the fireplace wall is just twenty-four inches high, much lower than in other rooms where the wainscot might typically be closer to thirty-six inches high. But the low height is perfectly proportioned to the low ceiling height.

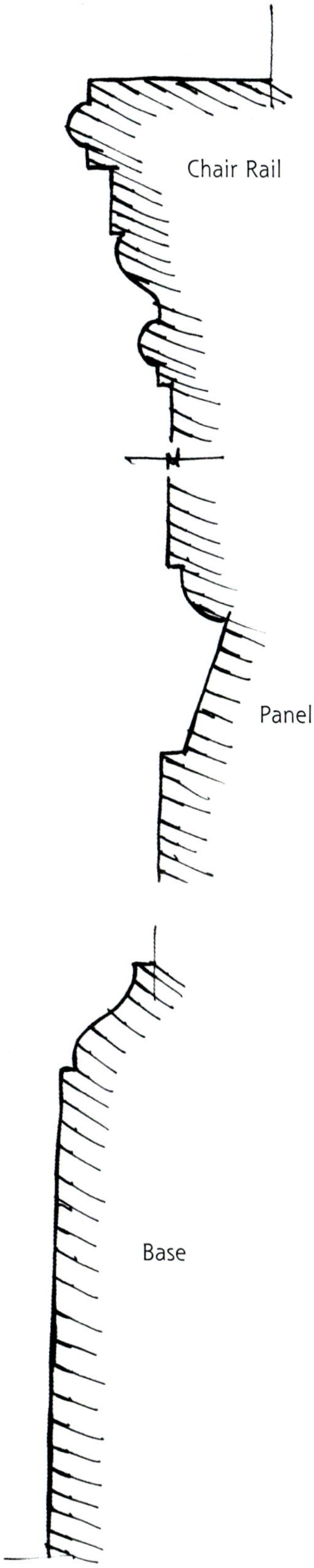

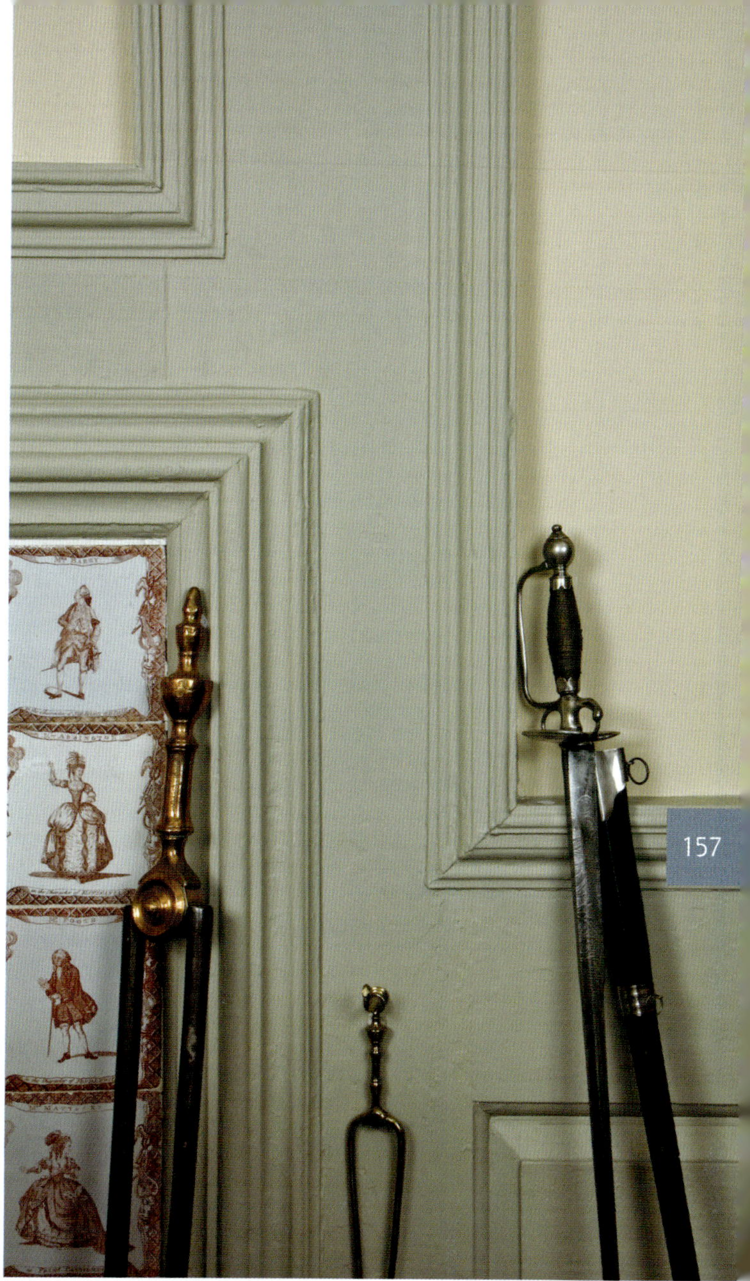

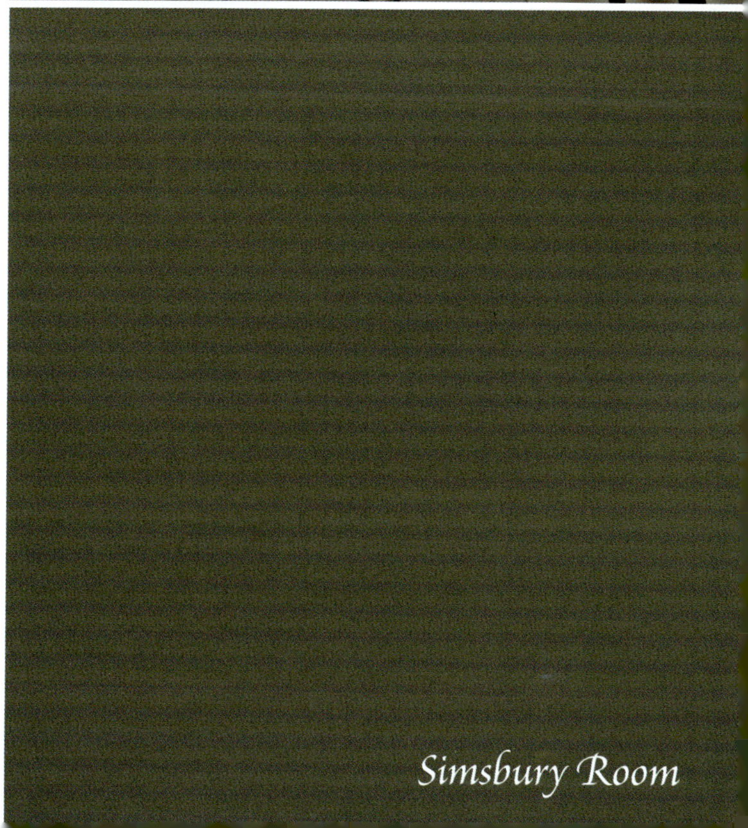

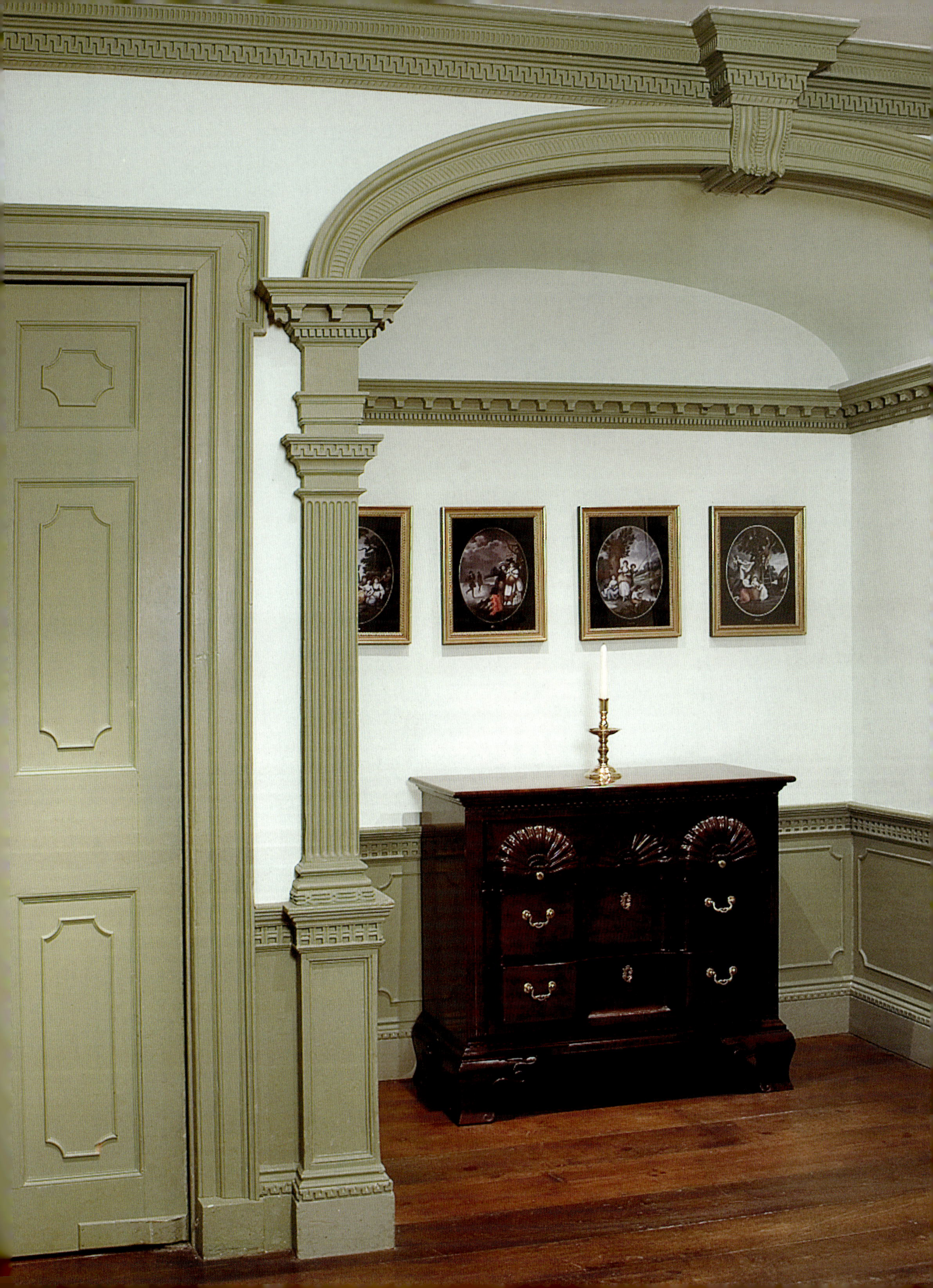

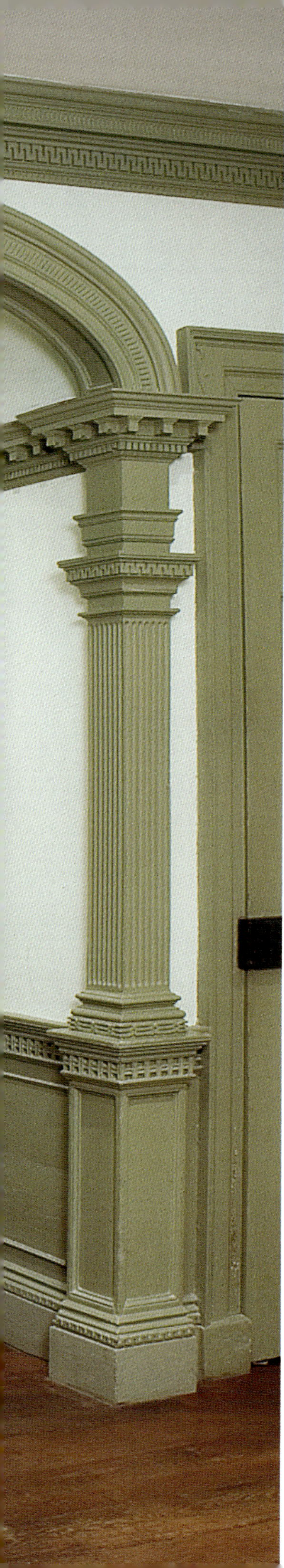

Somerset Room

Bowers House, Somerset, Massachusetts, circa 1800

8'9" high by 22'2" wide by 16' long

The Somerset Room was originally built as an addition to the home of Jerathmael Bowers. The parlor from that home, Bowers Parlor, was built earlier in a Georgian style and is also installed at Winterthur (page 46). Bowers made his money in commerce and trade, and it is possible the 1703 structure encompassed an already standing earlier residence. Bowers' son, John, made improvements to the house in the early 1800s, including the Somerset Room, before he eventually squandered his father's fortune.

In the Bowers' home, the Somerset Room served as the dining room. A fireplace on the short wall is balanced by a recess framed by an elliptical arch located on the opposite wall. In addition to its graceful proportions, the room has carefully wrought Federal details. The moldings are strongly linear but small in dimension, appearing delicate in scale. Various fretwork and dentil designs, as well as gouging, animate the surfaces and create a room of great intricacy.

Aspects of the room's design are possibly inspired by William Pain's *The Practical Builder*.

The Somerset Room's elaborate cornice is graced by fretwork and intricate carving. The elliptical arch balances a fireplace on the opposite wall.

Cornice

An otherwise canonic cornice is brought to life with three different ornamental motifs. First, the corona is textured with a repeating gouge detail with a small hole above (1). Beneath this, a dentil course is treated with fretwork dentils, sometimes called "Wall of Troy" dentils (2). These run in a meandering band under the corona. Supporting this is a row of small pyramids, or guttae (3). The combined effect of all three moldings and the differences in their rhythm and texture are highly refined and stunning in visual impact.

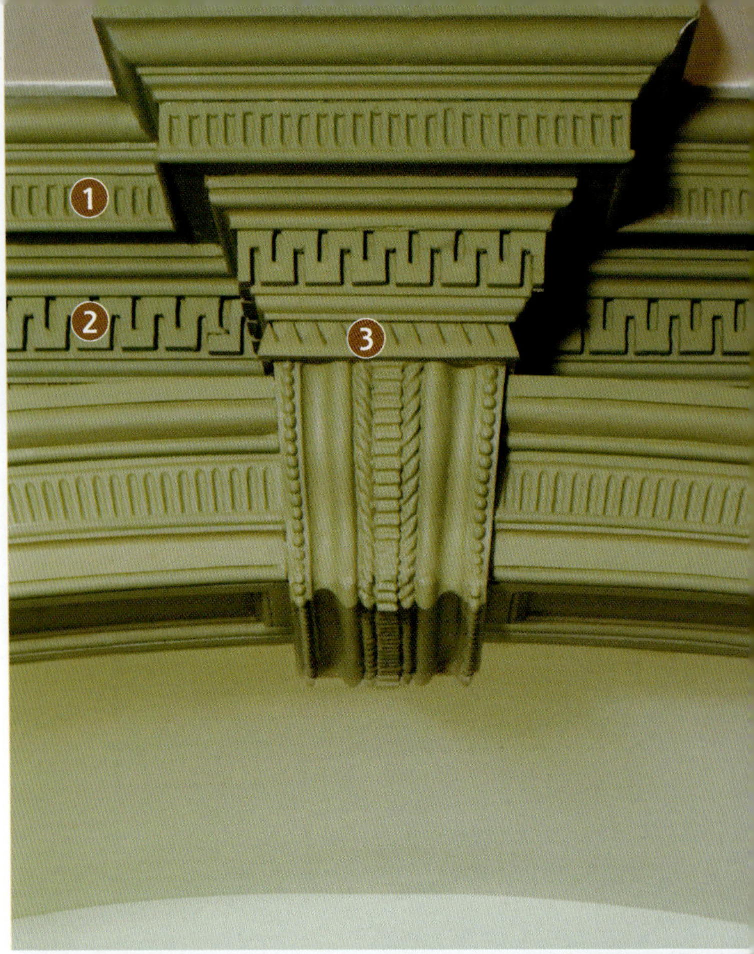

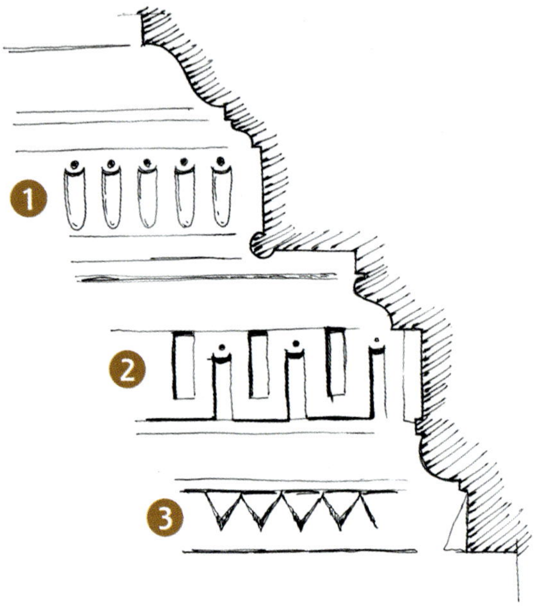

Patterns such as these from Pain's *Practical Builder* would have inspired craftsmen of the day as well as their patrons.

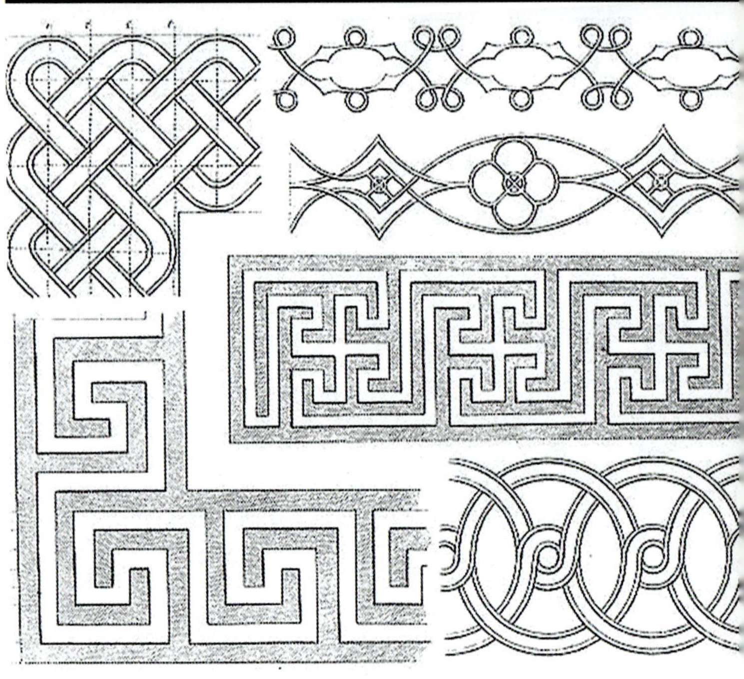

Architraves

The architraves around the doors and windows are delicately proportioned with repeated circular shapes. They are not decorated as elaborately as other moldings in the room, providing some relief from the other busy surfaces.

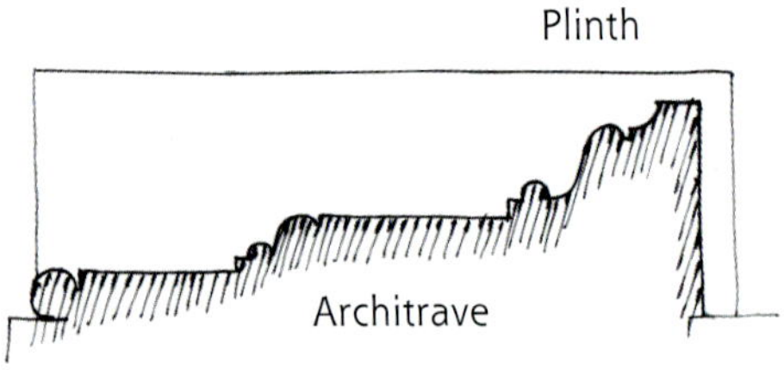

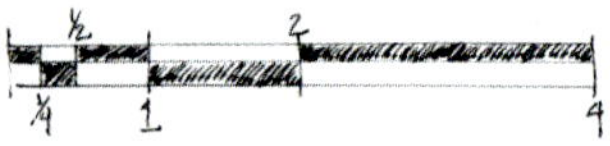

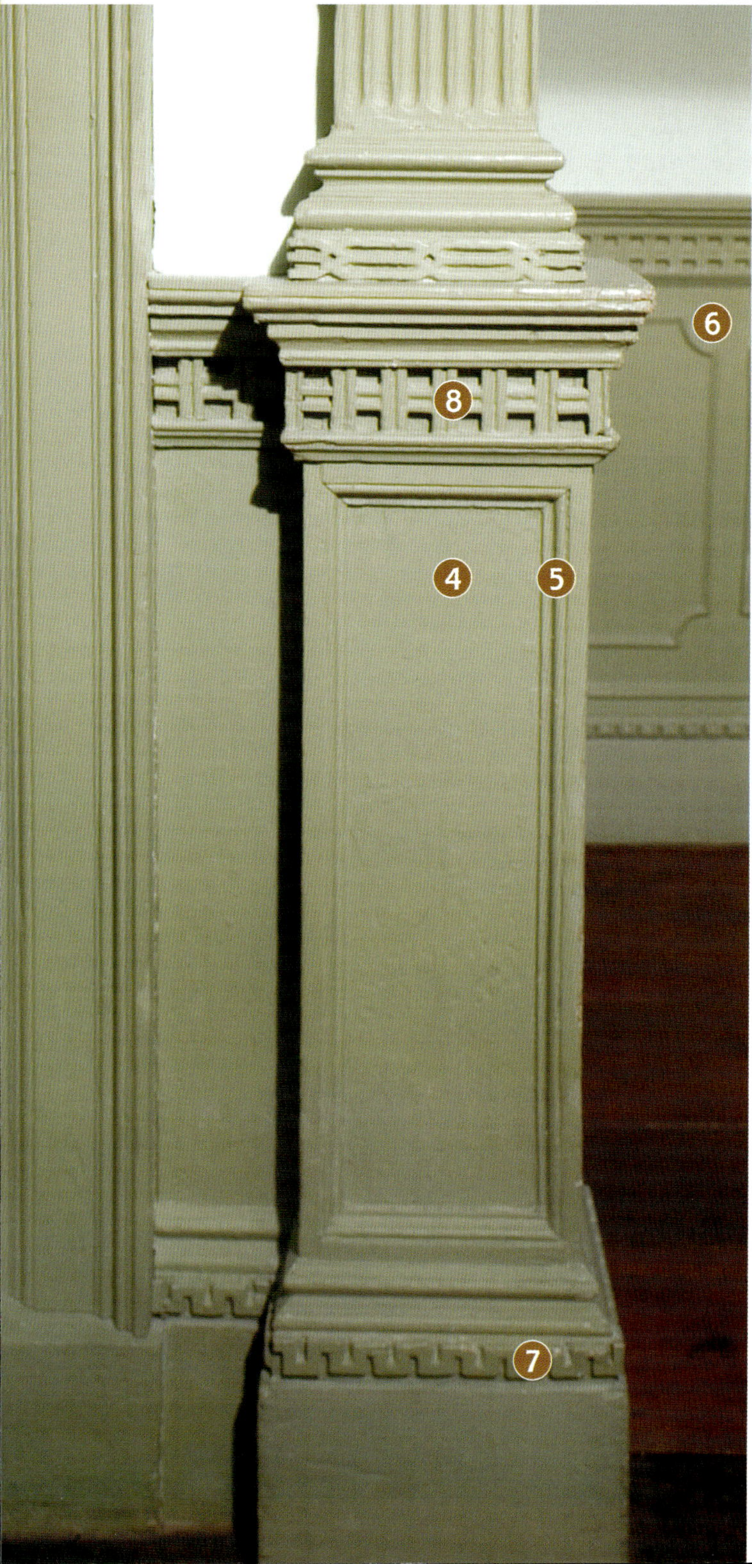

Wainscot

A wainscot wraps around the entire room. Common to the Federal style, the panels (4) are flat with an applied molding (5). Each corner of the molding curves inward (6), an exotic variation seen in rooms of this time and clearly shown on the photo on page 158. The base molding of the wainscot rises nearly seven inches, and its cap has a dentil band (7) reflecting the cornice above. The surbase is also ornamented with fretwork resembling small "H" figures marching around the room (8).

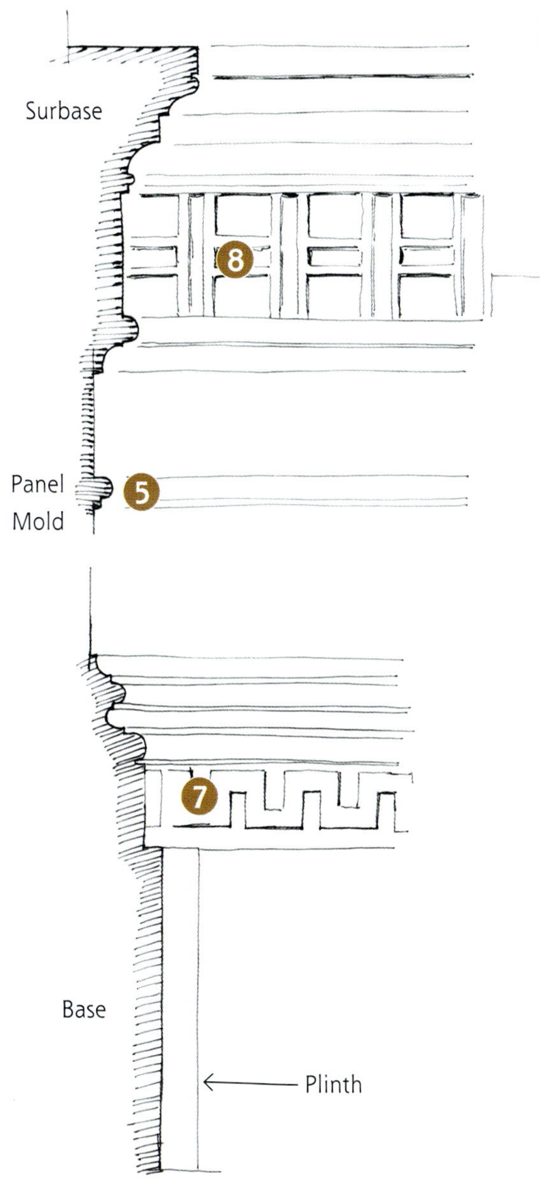

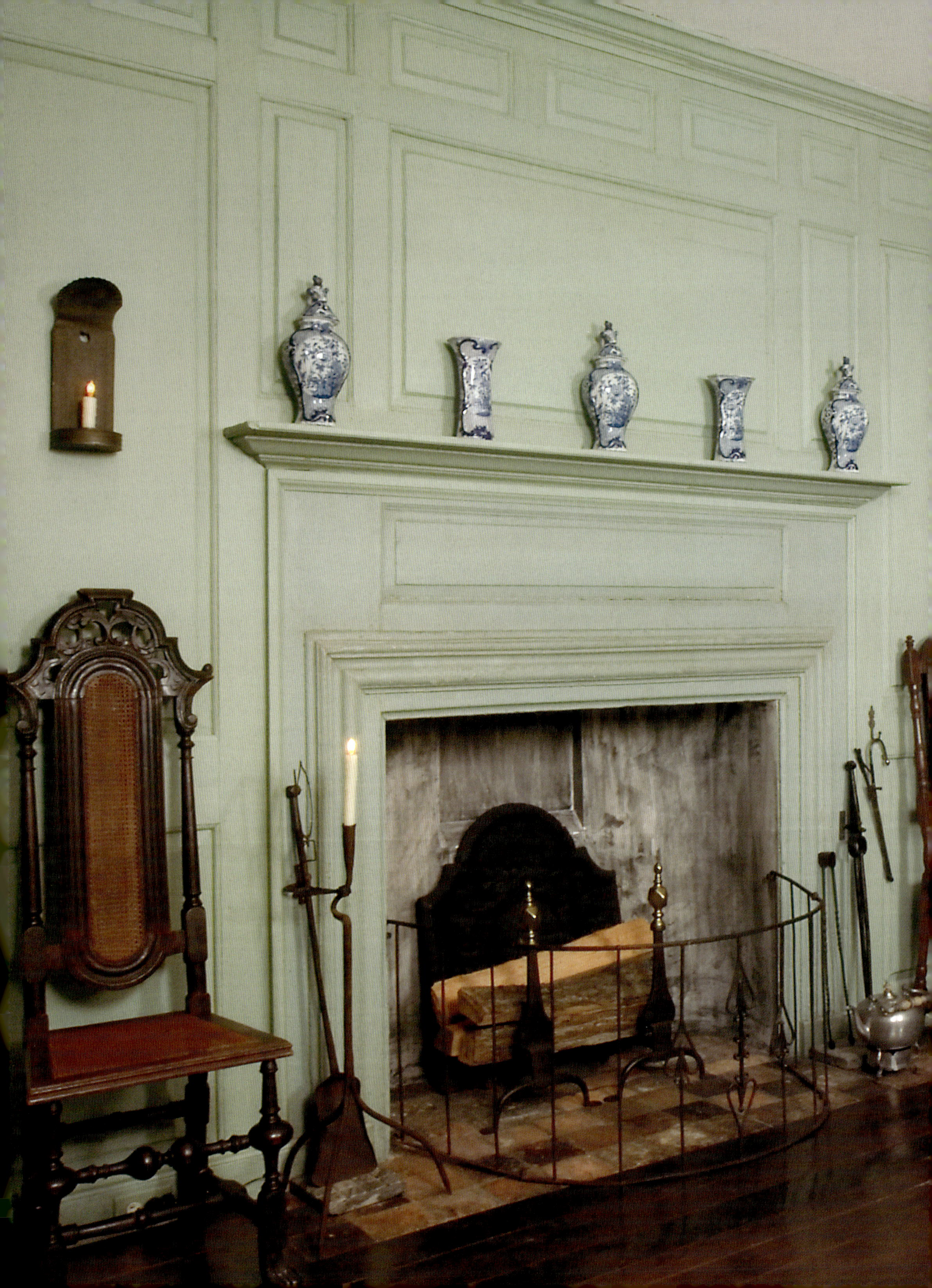

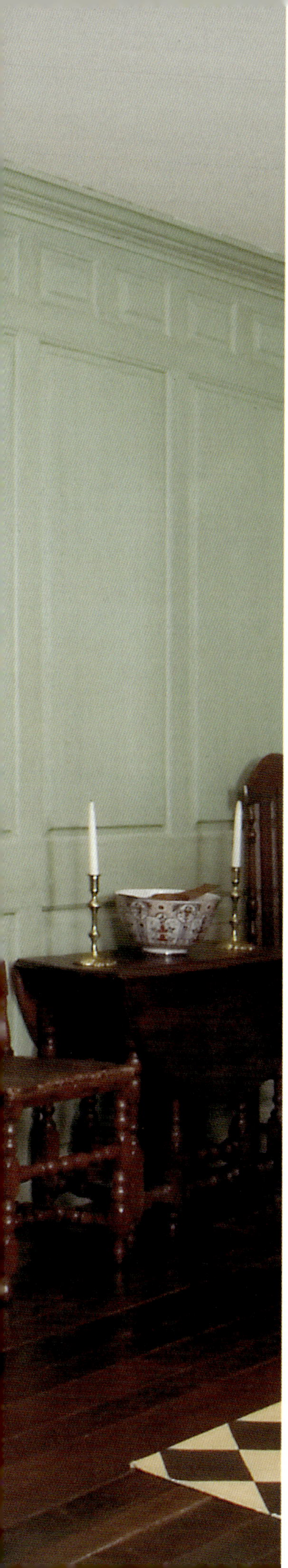

Tappahannock Room

Tappahannock, Virginia, circa 1740

9' high by 19'5" wide by 15' 8" long

Located along the Rappahannock River, between Washington, D.C., and Richmond, is the town of Tappahannock, Virginia—a thriving community in colonial America. One of the earliest houses in Tappahannock was a brick, one-and-one-half story structure built for Archibald Ritchie, a wealthy merchant. He enlarged his house along Prince Street in the mid-eighteenth century and added the woodwork that was used to create the Tappahannock Room at Winterthur.

The room's fully paneled walls are of note due to two characteristics that may be derived from Joseph Moxon's 1703 book *Mechanick Exercises; or, The Doctrine of Handy-Works*. The unique elevation, with the insertion of a small upper band, or frieze, of panels is uncommon, found elsewhere in Virginia only at Tuckahoe along the James River. Moxon's book describes this type of composition using frieze-like panels.

Additionally, the fully paneled walls rise smoothly to the ceiling with no surbase separating the dado from the wall, as was commonly used to both protect the wall from chairs and visually subdivide the room's height. However, the typical wall division into dado, surbase, and wall is hinted at with lower panels, a wide panel rail, and tall upper panels. This lack of surbase may also be attributed to Moxon, whose book states that a base and surbase are not always needed in a room of lower ceilings. Tappahannock's are a relatively low nine feet.

The entire ensemble forms a consistent skin around the room, imbuing it with a calm atmosphere.

The Tappahannock Room's small upper row of frieze panels is distinctive and unusual.

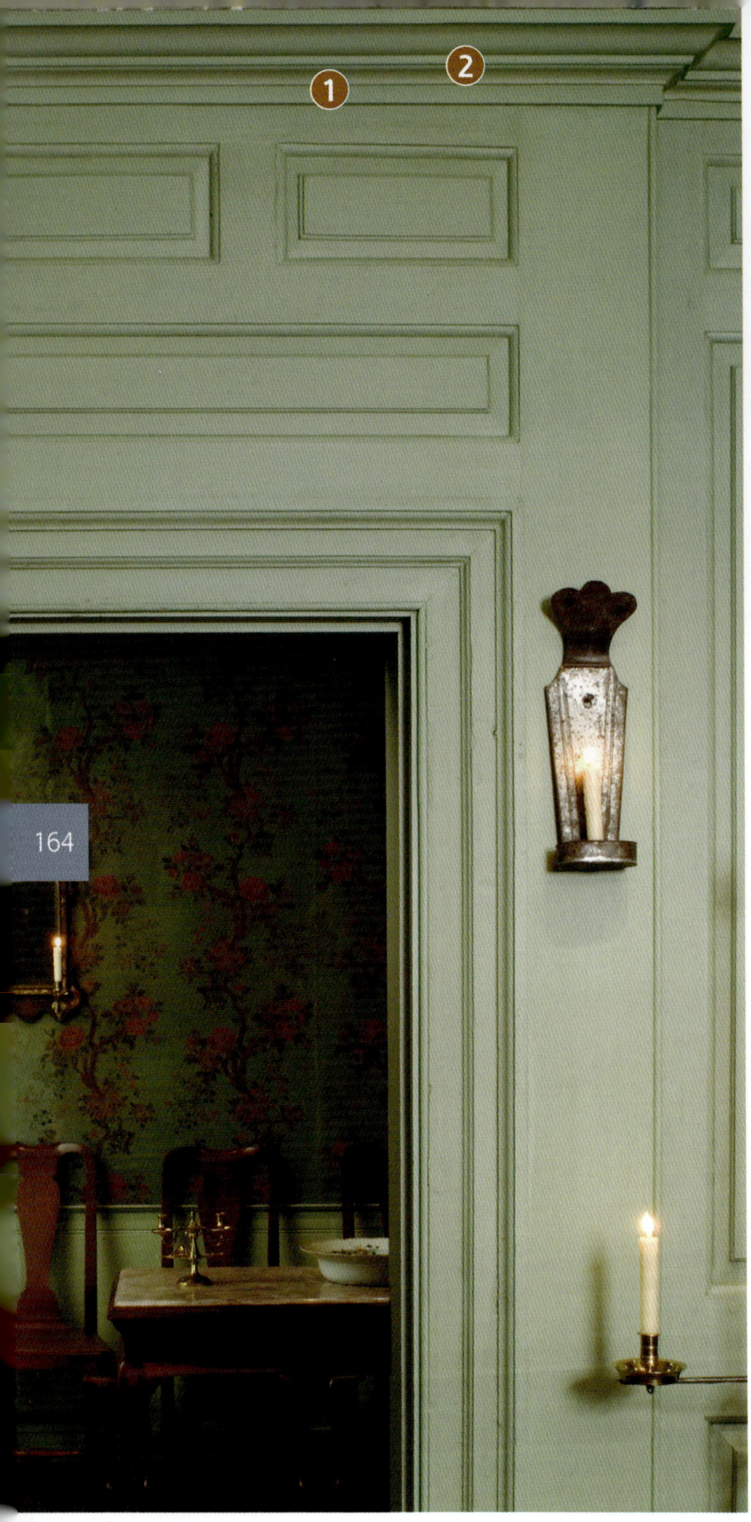

Cornice

The cornice's delicate scale corresponds to the subtlety of the panel composition and is assembled in the expected manner. A tall fillet (1) beneath the bedmold (2) transitions between the cornice and the wall.

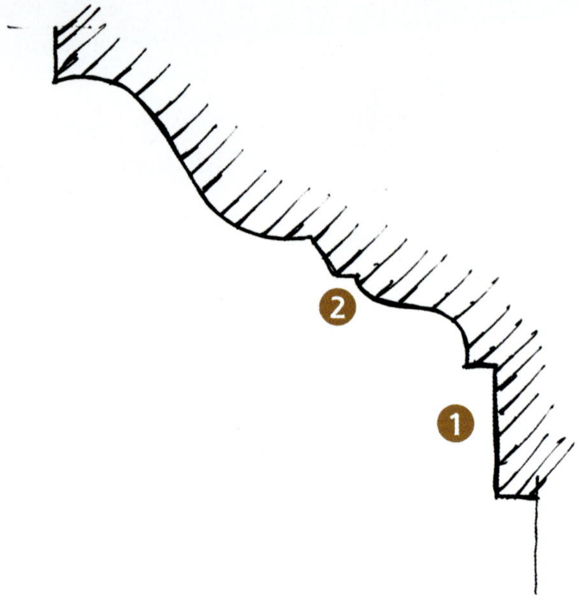

Architraves

The door architrave is an appropriately scaled six inches wide and two inches deep. Like the cornice and panel details, its composition is canonic with a backband (3), two fascias (4) separated by a molding (5), and a three-quarter round bead (6) at the jamb-side edge.

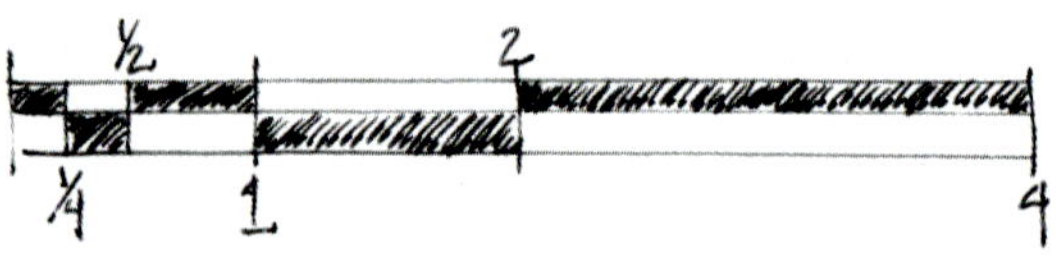

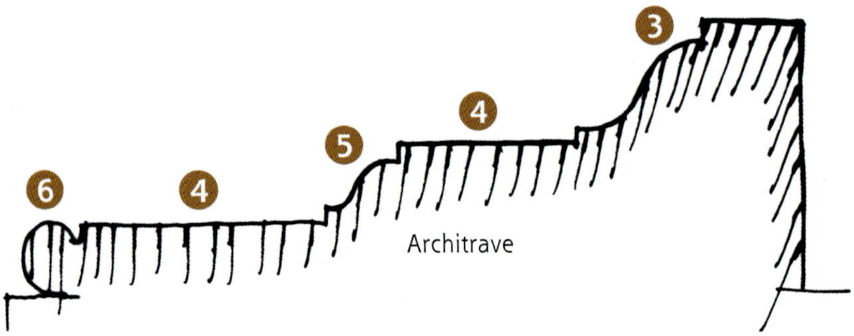

Panels & Base

The panels of the Tappahannock Room are both unique and typical. As previously mentioned, the frieze panels (7) at the top of the wall are not common; however, the panel details are: a narrow molding surrounding a beveled panel rises flush to the surface of the stiles and rails. More rarely, such as in the Gidley Room, bolection molding is used, and the panel sits above the surface of the stiles and rails. By varying the composition of panels and their details, different effects can be achieved. A room's height may be visually increased or decreased depending on the number and size of panels, or a wall may be made to feel smooth-surfaced and calm or sculptural and robust with different panel details.

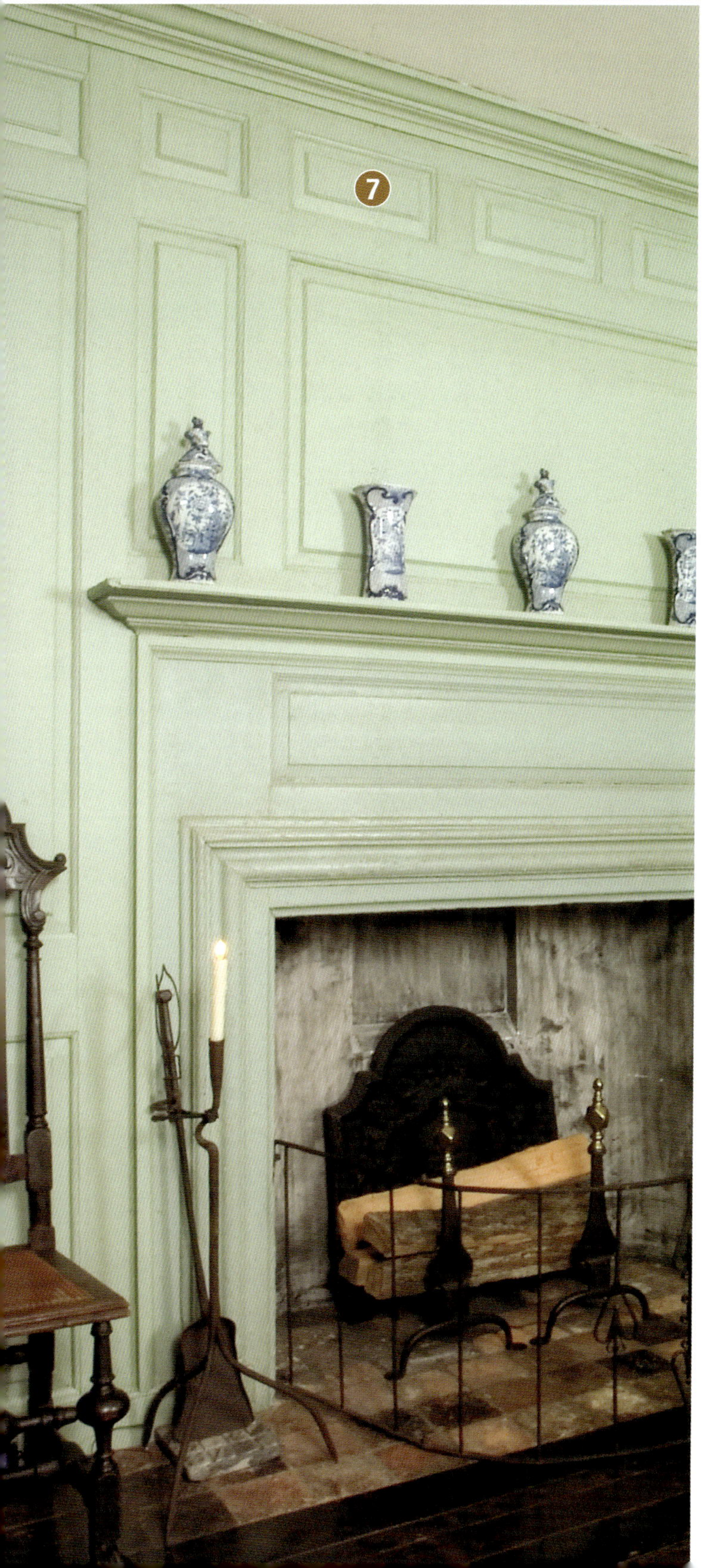

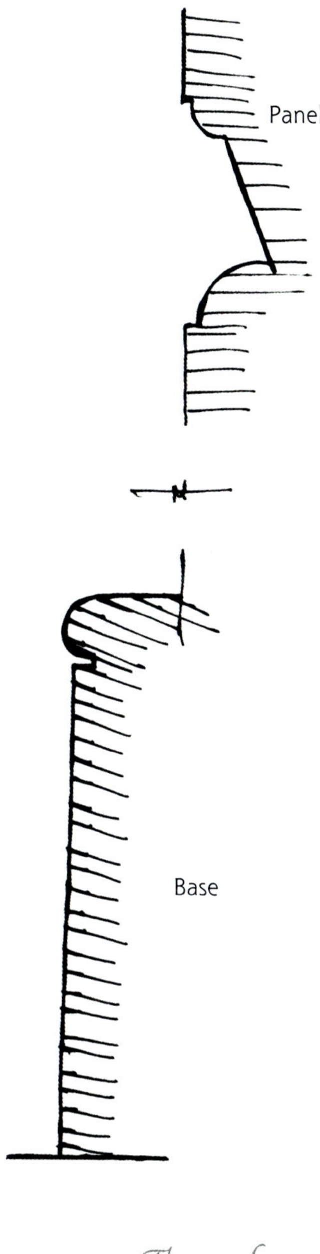

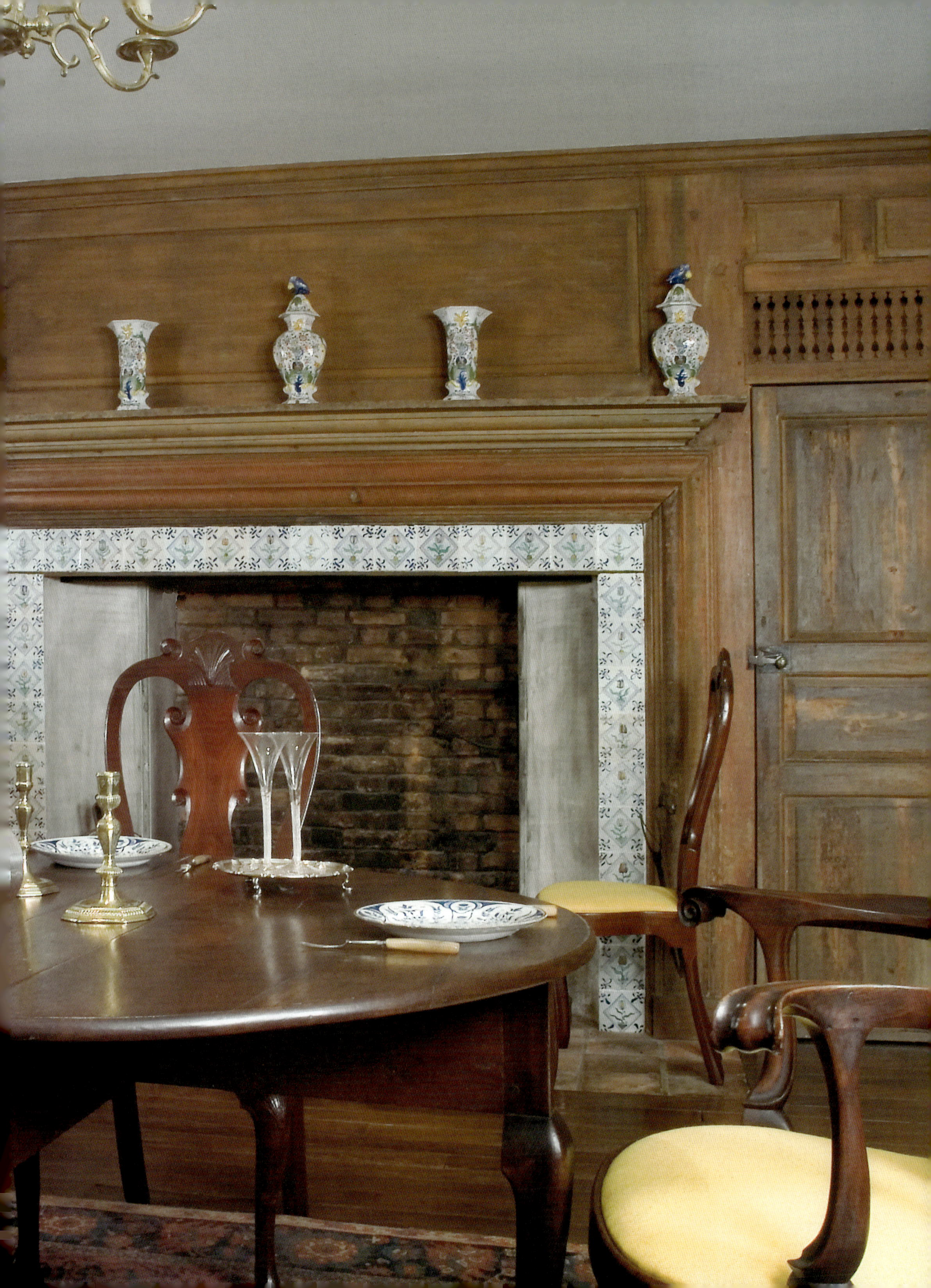

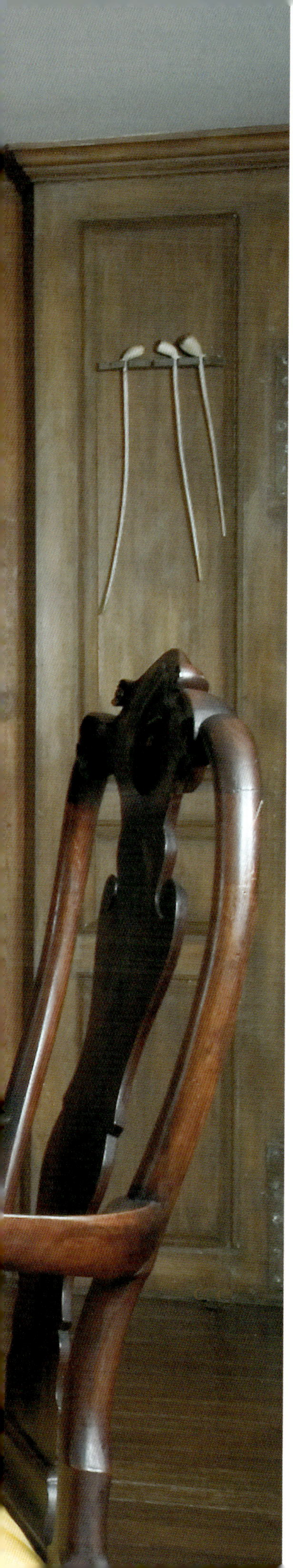

Vauxhall Room

Greenwich, New Jersey, circa 1725

The Vauxhall Room, one of the earliest Georgian style rooms installed at Winterthur, came from the Vauxhall Gardens home of Thomas Maskell, a mariner. He built his house near Greenwich, New Jersey. In the early eighteenth century, the port of Greenwich, a few miles up the Cohansey River from the Delaware Bay, was an important location for trade as it was one of three official entry ports for New Jersey.

Maskell's original two-story brick house with a later frame addition contained the woodwork that now forms the Vauxhall Room. The fireplace chimney projected into the room, its back integrated with the outside wall of the house. This helped to conserve the warmth generated by the chimney. In the spaces left on either side of the chimney, cupboards and a stair rising to the upper floor were built-in and unified by a paneled wall. The room's remaining three walls are not paneled, but covered in wallpaper.

On the room's long wall, a large firebox almost four feet tall dominates the elevation and once shed its warmth into the room. A bolection molding surmounted by a mantelshelf surrounds the firebox. As created here at Winterthur, two side cupboards have a fretwork vent above them, a detail common to the region and the period. The areas above the mantelshelf, cupboards, and doors are all paneled wood.

The Vauxhall Room focuses on a large fireplace set in a paneled wall.

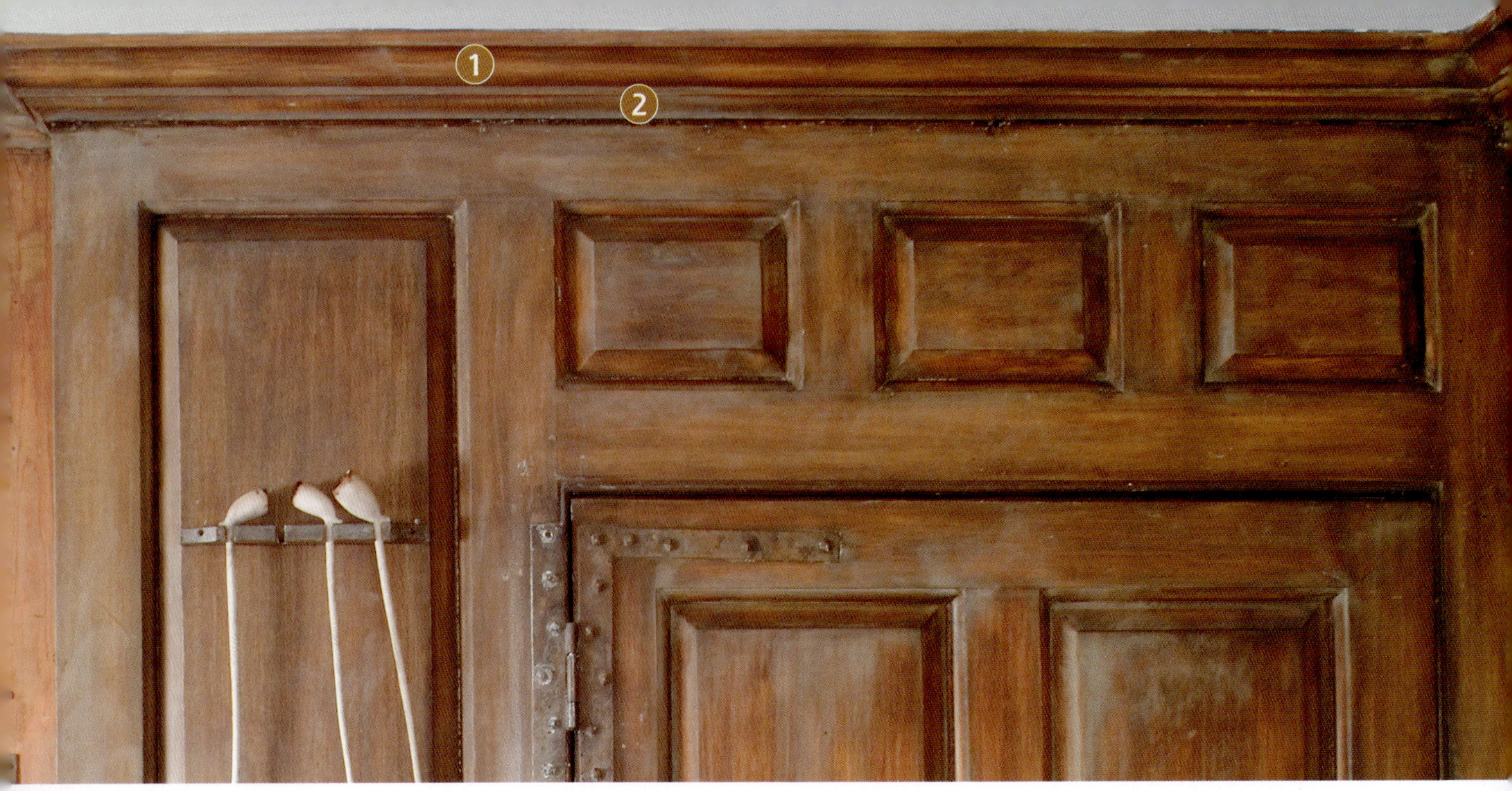

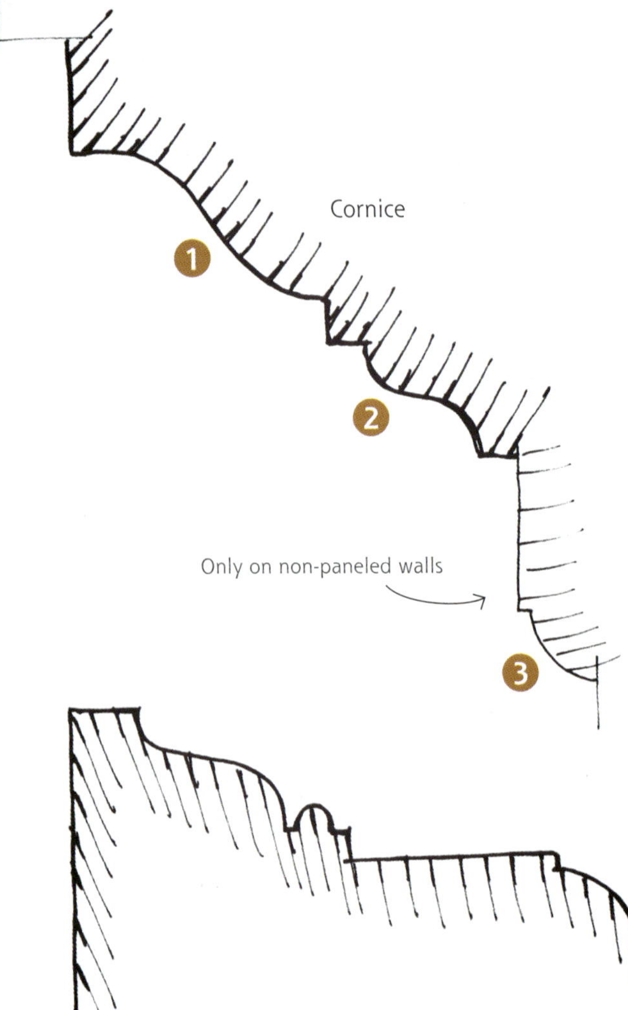

Cornice

A simple cornice made up of a cymatium (1) and bedmold (2) runs around the entire room. At the three non-paneled walls, an additional small molding appears (3). Like the baseboard, a cornice has both practical and aesthetic functions: it bridges the physical gap between the wall and ceiling, and it makes the visual transition between them.

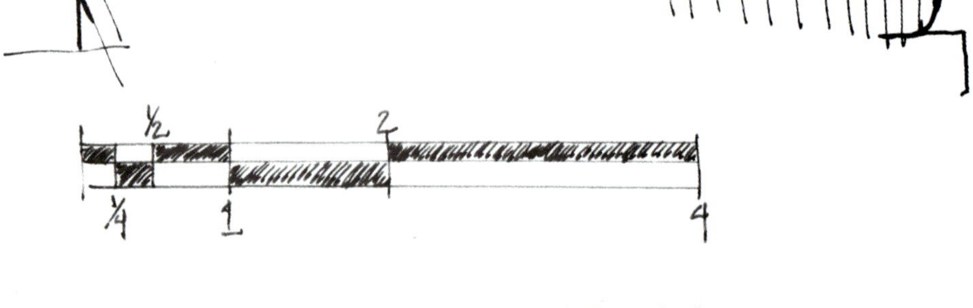

Architraves

The door architrave is large in comparison to the more restrained baseboard and cornice. It is five-and-a-half-inches wide and projects one-and-one-half inches into the room.

Base and Panel

The baseboard continues from the fireplace wall to the remainder of the room. It is simple—a tall plinth topped with a neat base cap, almost five inches high altogether. Baseboards are important aesthetically to unify a room and give it scale while also functionally hiding the joint between the wall and the floor.

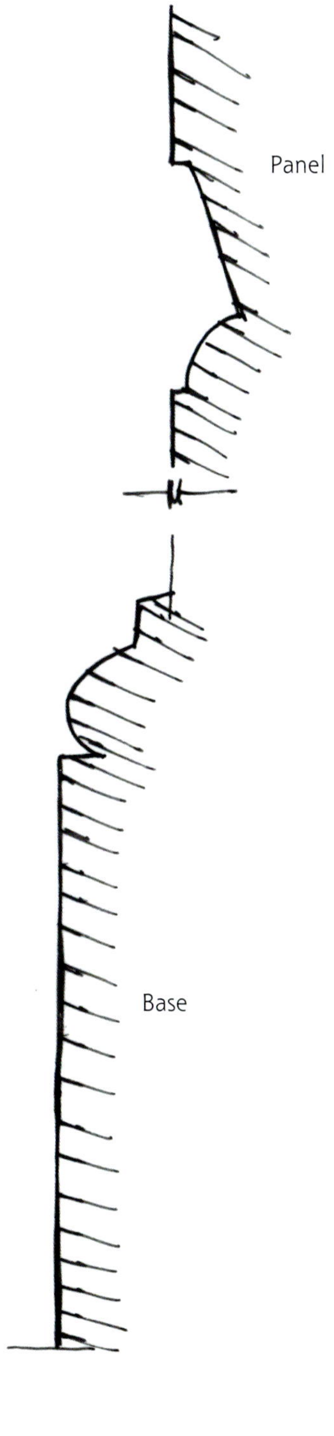

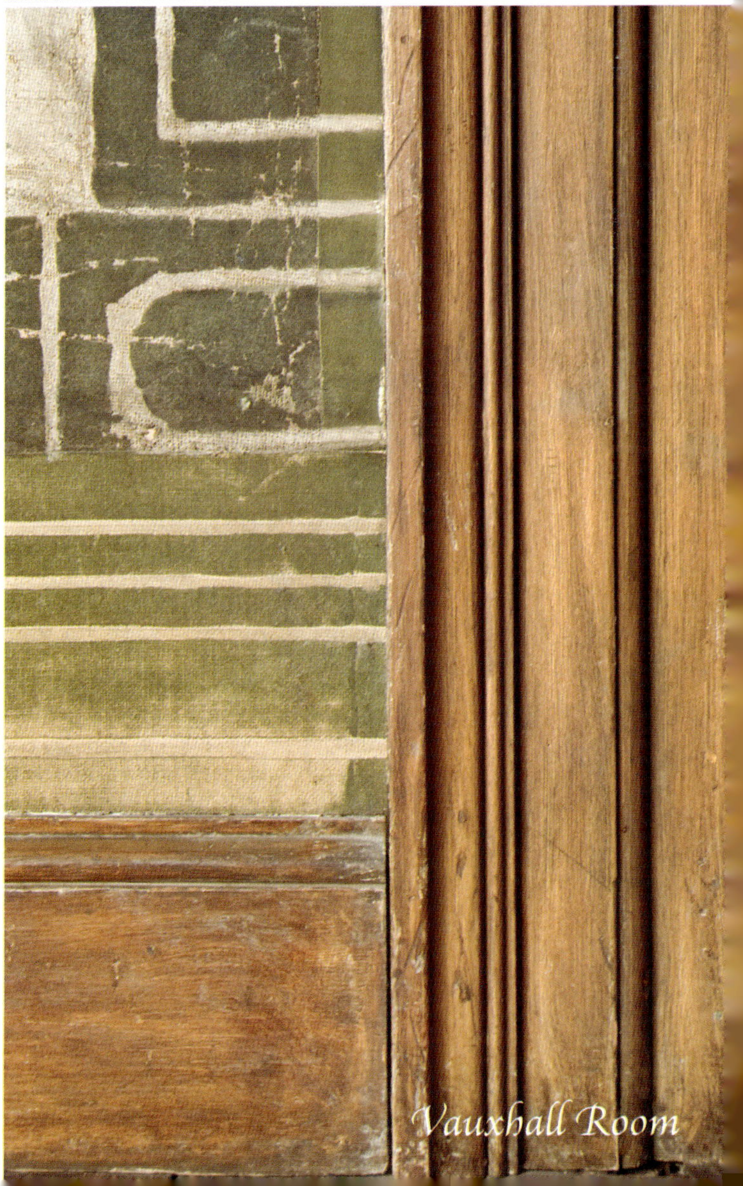

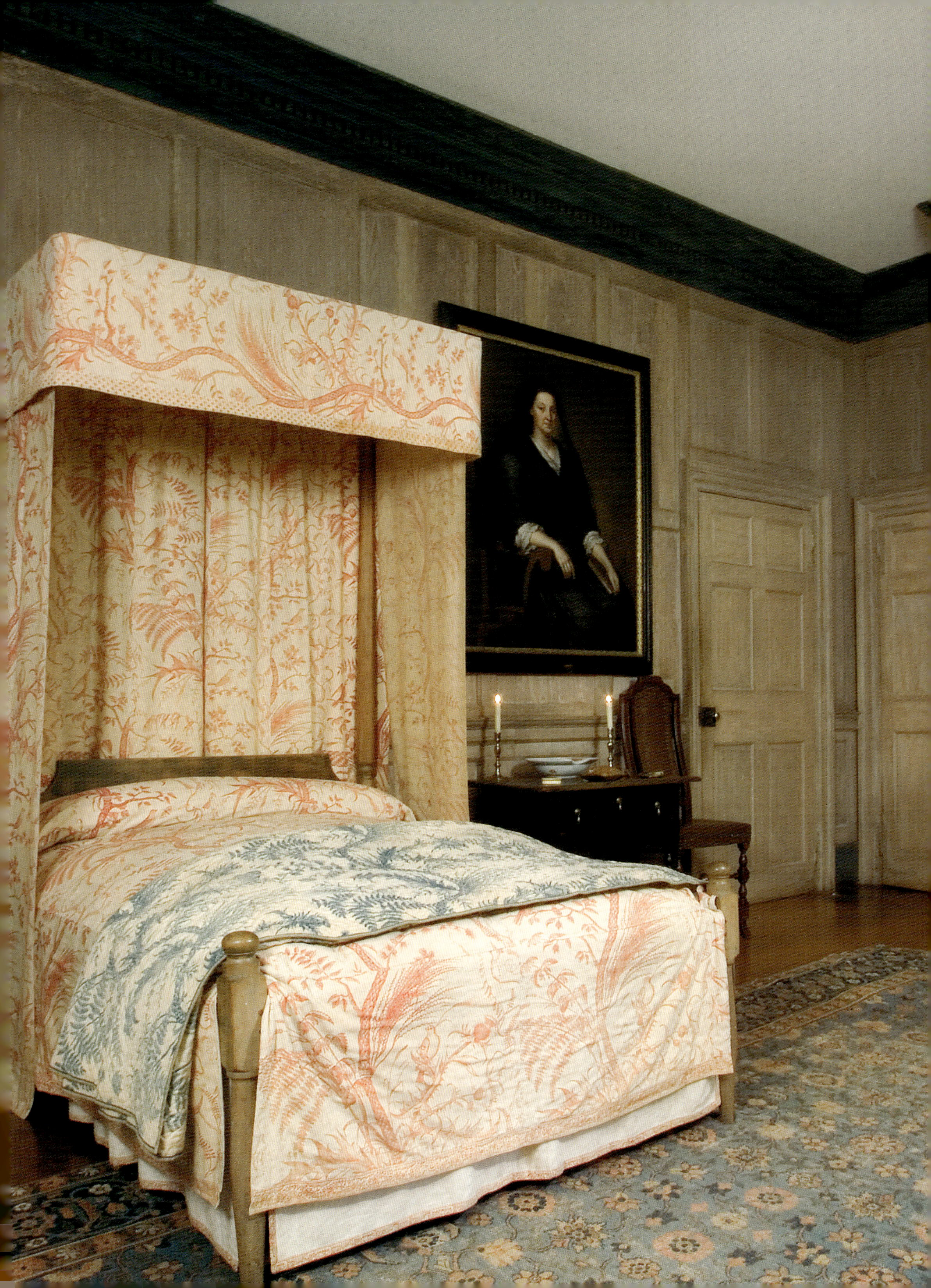

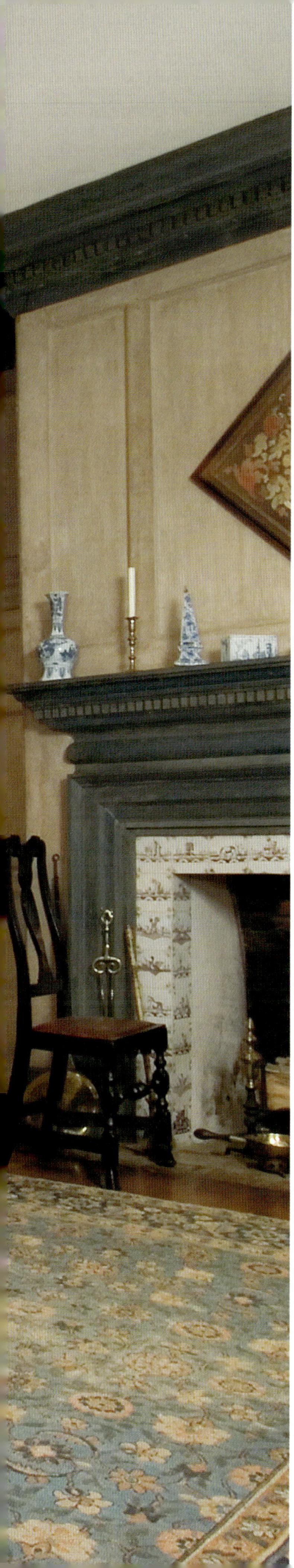

Walnut Room

Belle Isle Plantation, Litwalton, Lancaster County, Virginia, circa 1770

10'10" tall by 15'3" wide by 23'11" long

The Walnut Room comes from Belle Isle, a plantation on the Rappahannock River near the Chesapeake Bay. Mr. du Pont purchased eight rooms from Belle Isle, including the Lancaster Room (page 92), which also appears in this book.

Belle Isle was built for Thomas Bertrand Griffin, who inherited the land in 1761. He began construction in 1767, one year after his marriage to Judith Burwell. The Burwells, an influential family in Virginia, built the spectacular Carter's Grove on the James River, a National Historic Landmark near Williamsburg, Virginia.

The Walnut Room's generous volume is described by fully paneled walls and bold moldings. The paneling, which only appears natural, is painted in a faux bois finish. The wooden wall panels contrast with the dark blue tone of the baseboard, cornice, and mantel. It is a high-contrast color scheme different from other monochromatic Georgian style rooms and may be a twentieth-century invention.

The Walnut Room is an intriguing mix of Federal and Georgian details.

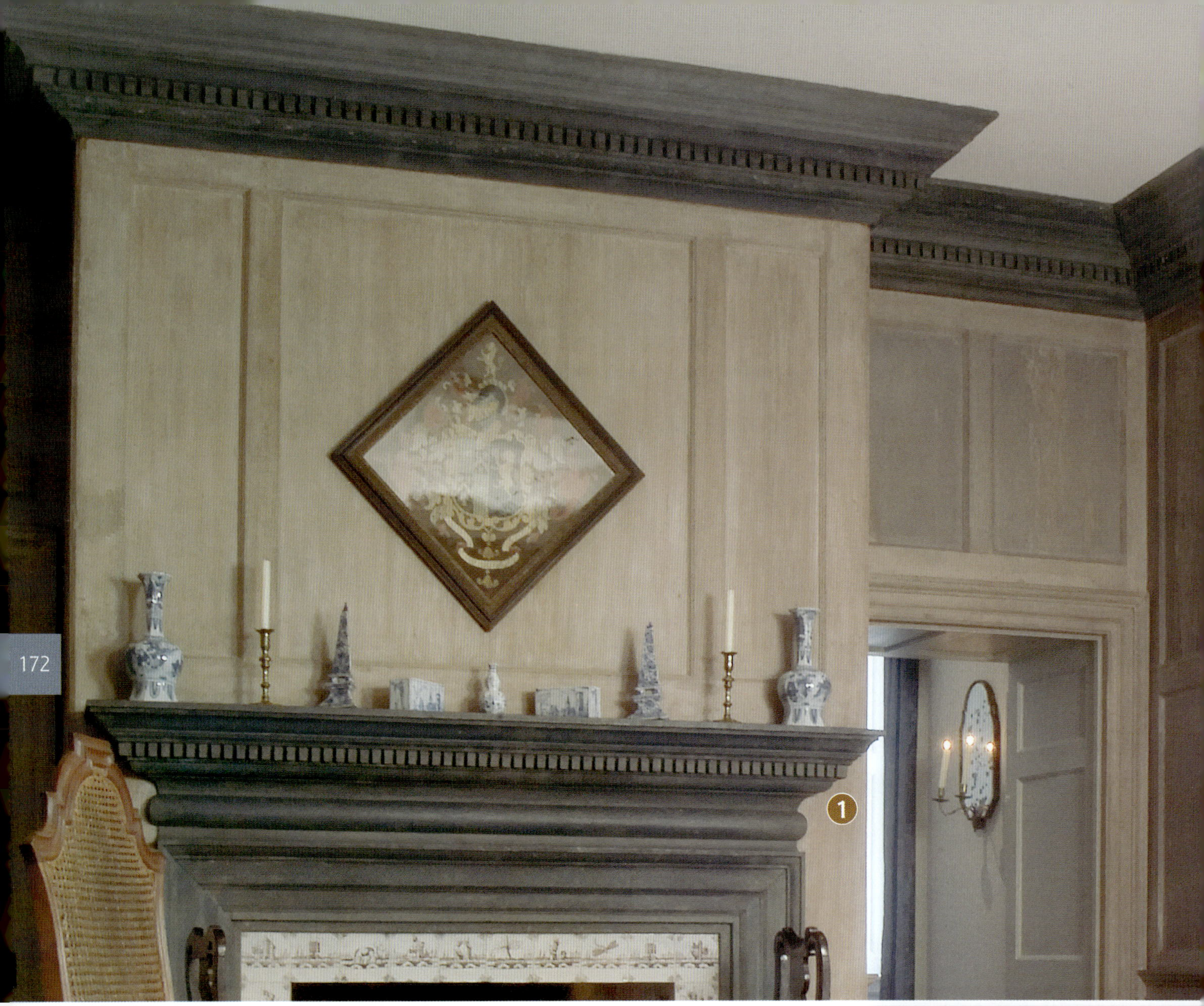

Fireplace Wall

At one end of the short wall, a chimney breast with its large fireplace projects almost three feet into the room. Symmetrically disposed doors balance on either side. The mantel is composed of common classical elements assembled with some unique touches. An architrave, rather than a bolection molding, frames the firebox. Above, a small frieze (1) made up of three parts—a cove, a pulvinated (bulging) middle section, and another cove—transitions to a cornice with its bedmold of dentils. The same cornice moldings used in the mantel are repeated in the room cornice.

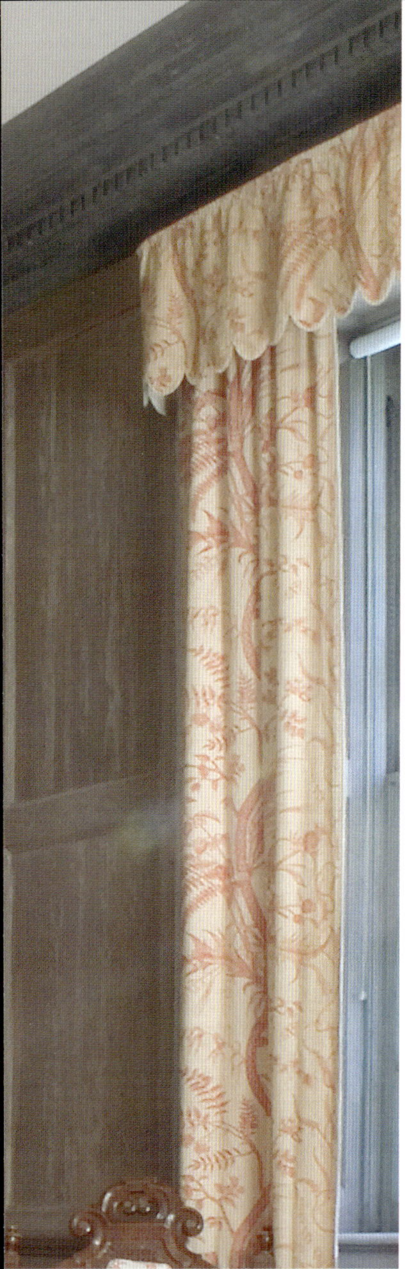

Cornice

The cornice is large and appears more so due to its dark color contrasting with the light wall color. It projects out more than ten inches and is equally tall. Despite its canonic molding shapes and assembly, it lacks a projecting corona beneath the cymatium (2), where one finds a cove molding (3) instead. The lack of a deeply projecting corona and its shadow line is an accommodation often made for interior conditions.

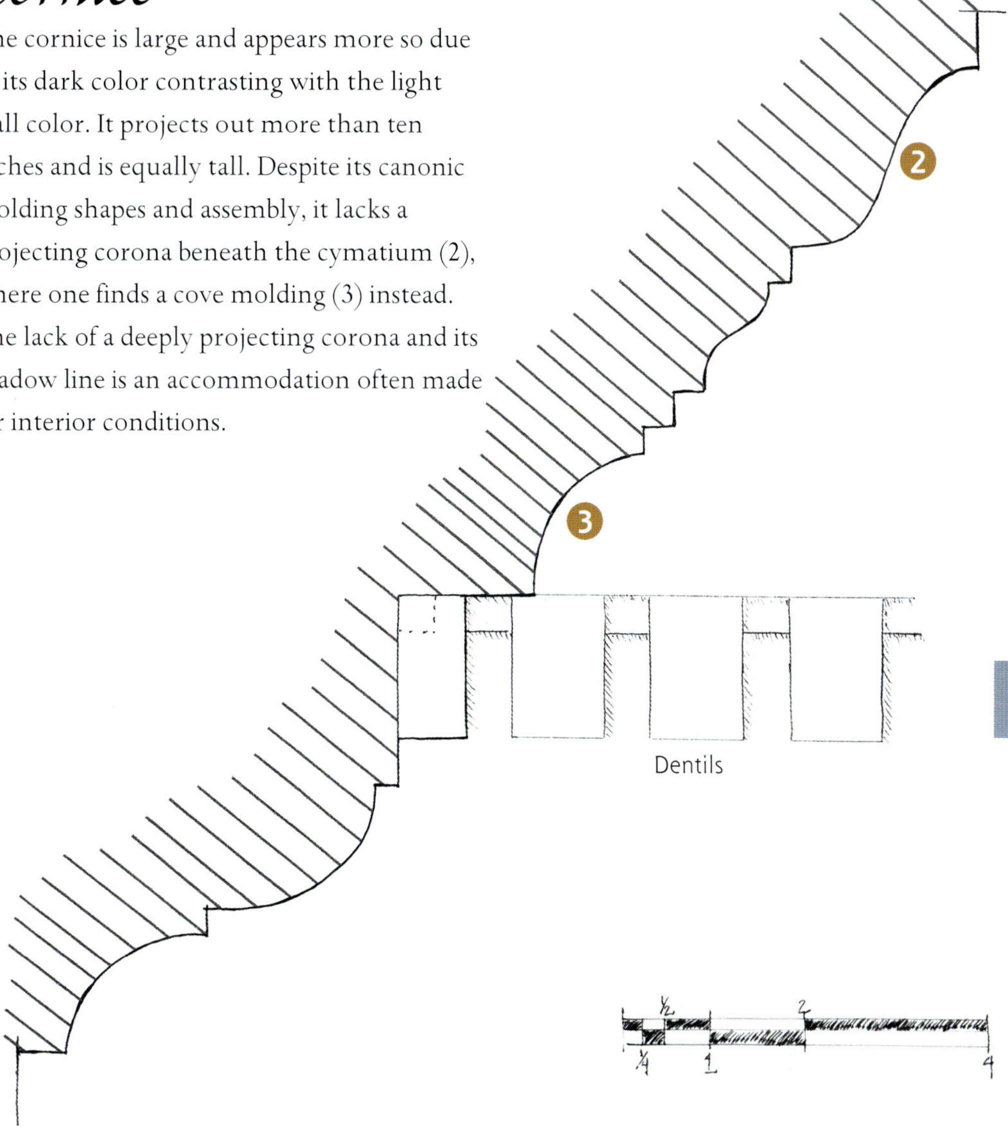

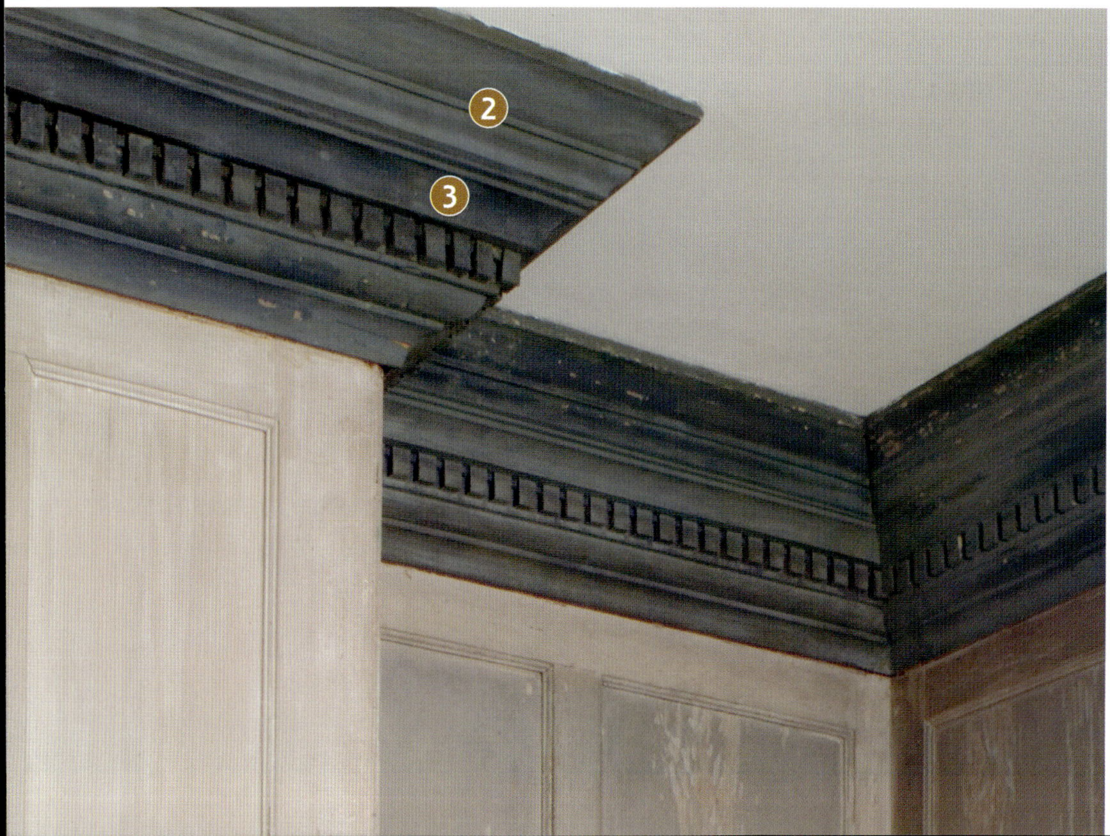

Walnut Room

Chair Rail, Panels, & Base

The paneling is different from what one commonly expects to see in Georgian paneling of the late eighteenth century. Rather than the field of the panel being raised, it is flat. There is one register of panels in the dado below the chair rail and two registers above, helping to counter the height of the room. The base is one of the tallest at Winterthur, yet it doesn't project as greatly as other Georgian style base moldings. Instead, it is topped with a simple base cap formed of a bead and a cove.

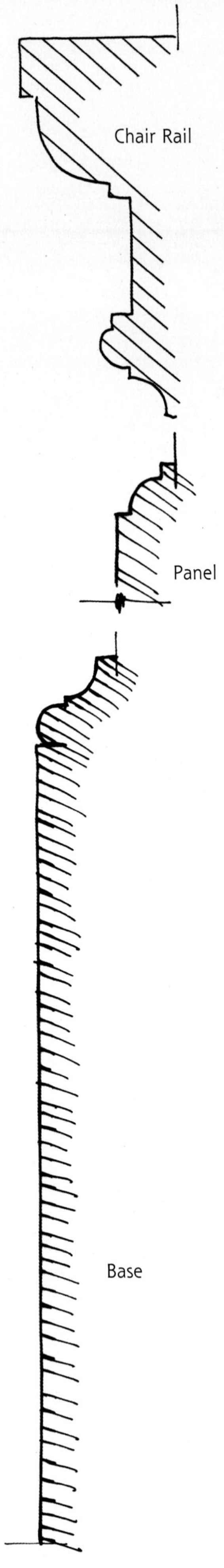

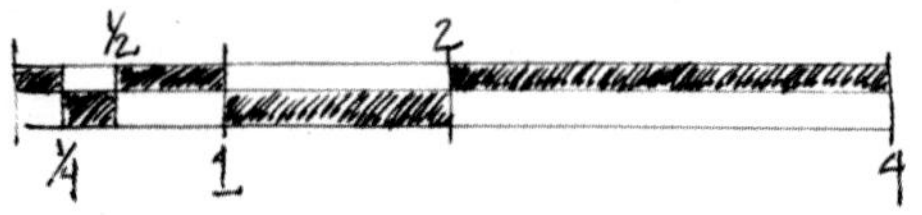

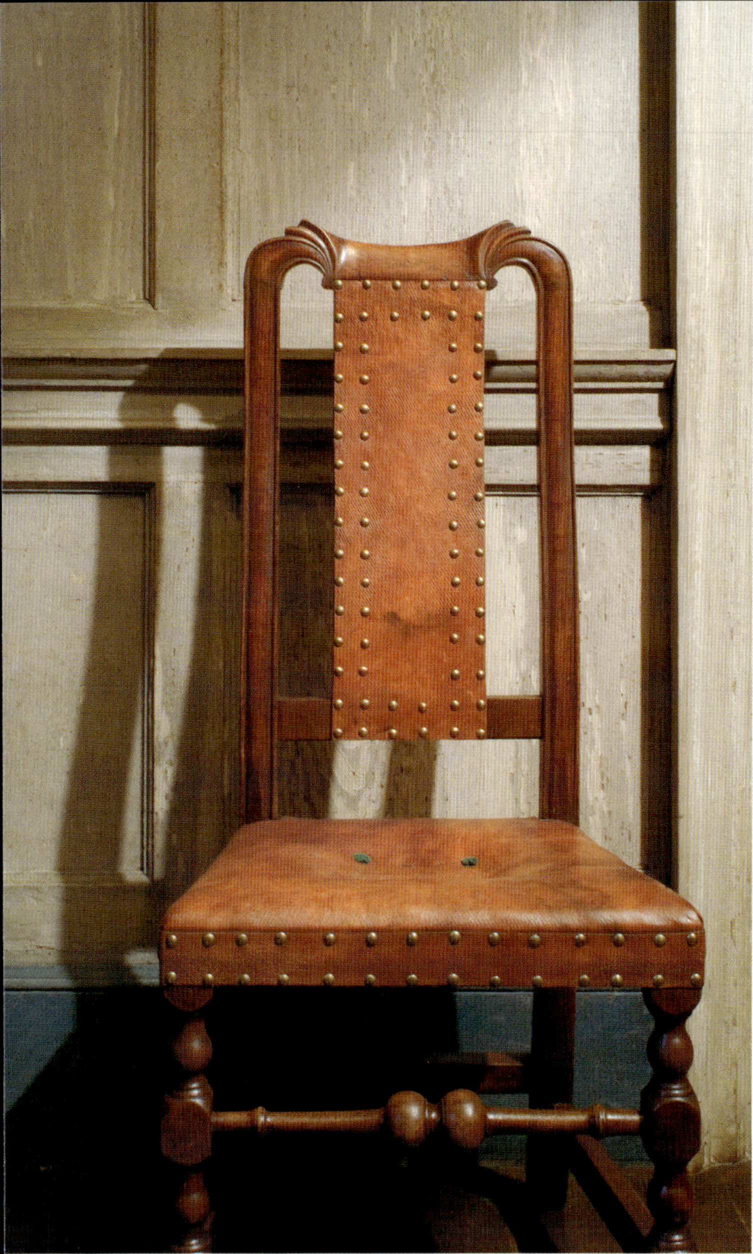

Architraves

The door architrave is a typical Georgian assembly with a large ovolo at the backband, but it utilizes a cove molding rather than a cyma reversa to separate the two fascias. This small choice keeps the door architrave in relation to the cove moldings found in the mantel and room cornice. The door architrave is similar in its large scale to the surbase, or chair rail, that wraps the room.

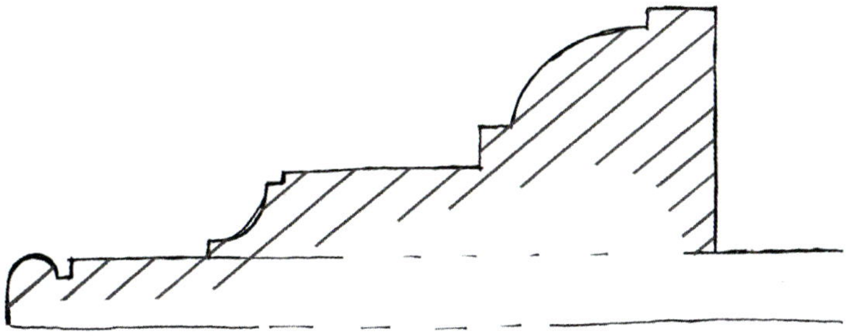

Architrave

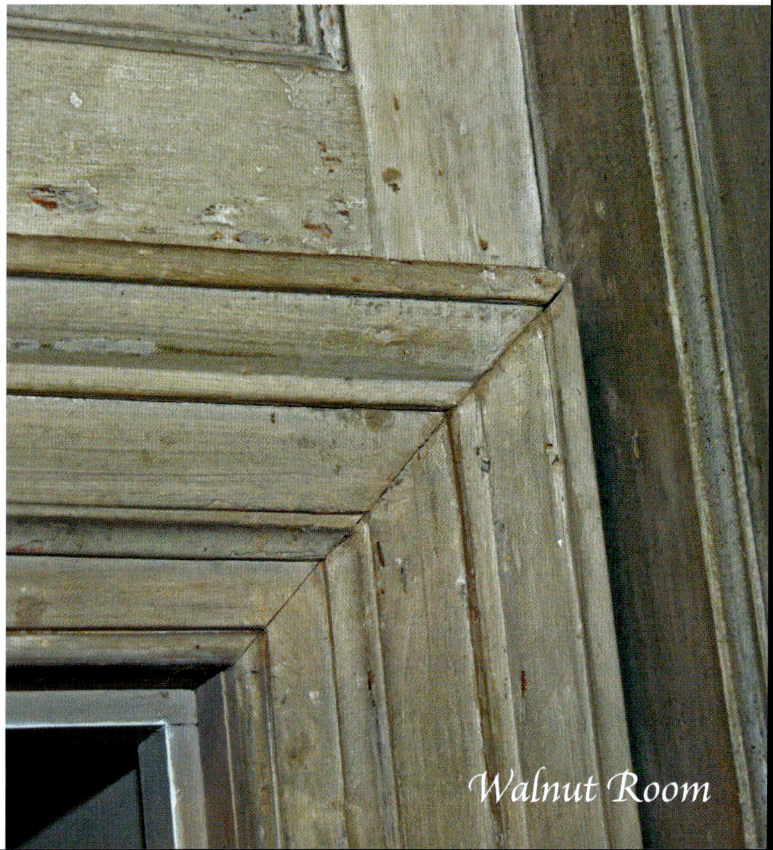

Resources

Traditional American Domestic Architecture
Recommended Resources for Further Study
Compiled by Christine G. H. Franck

Architectural Treatises

Alberti, Leon Battista. *On the Art of Building in Ten Books*, translated by Joseph Rykwert et al. Cambridge et al.: MIT Press, 1988.

Palladio, Andrea. *The Four Books of Architecture*. New York: Dover Publications Inc., 1965.

Serlio, Sebastiano. *The Five Books of Architecture*. New York: Dover Publications Inc., 1982.

Smith, Thomas Gordon. *Vitruvius on Architecture*. New York: Monacelli Press, 2005.

Vitruvius, Marcus Pollio. *The Ten Books on Architecture*, translated by Morris Hickey Morgan. New York: Dover Publications Inc., 1960.

Domestic Architecture

Architects Emergency Committee. *Great Georgian Houses of America, Vols I – II*. New York: Dover Publications Inc., 1970.

Axelrod, A. *The Colonial Revival in America*. New York: W. W. Norton & Co. Ltd., 1985.

Benjamin, Asher. *The American Builder's Companion*. New York: Dover Publications Inc.

Benjamin, Asher. *The Architect, or Practical House Carpenter* (1830). New York: Dover Publications Inc.

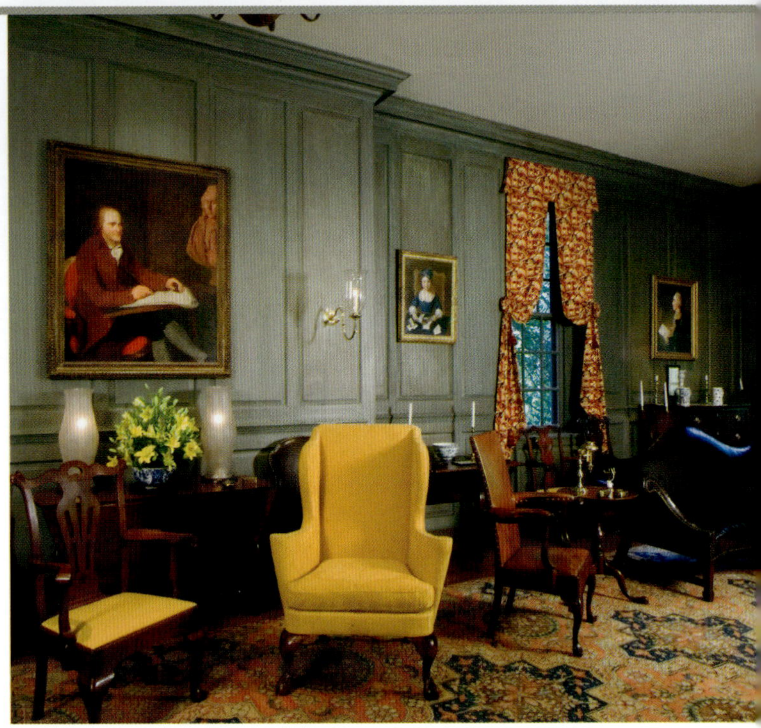

Curl, James Stevens. *Georgian Architecture*. London: David & Charles Publishers, 2002.

Garrett, Wendell. *American Colonial: Puritan Simplicity to Georgian Grace*. New York: Monacelli Press, 1995.

Garrett, Wendell. *Classic America: The Federal Style and Beyond*. New York: Monacelli Press, 1995.

Garvin, James L. *A Building History of Northern New England*. Lebanon, N.H.: University Press of New England, 2002.

Hamlin, Talbot. *Greek Revival Architecture in America*. New York: Dover Publications Inc., 1985.

Howard, Hugh. *Colonial Houses: The Historic Homes of Williamsburg*. New York: Harry N. Abrams Inc., 2004

Kimball, Fiske. *Domestic Architecture of the American Colonies and of the Early Republic*. New York: Dover Publications Inc.

Lafever, Minard. *Modern Builder's Guide*. New York: Dover Publications Inc., 1969.

Lafever, Minard. *The Beauties of Modern Architecture*. Da Capo reprint, 1968.

Lane, Mills. *Architecture of the Old South Series*. Beehive Press, various dates.

Morrison, Hugh. *Early American Architecture: From the First Colonial Settlements to the National Period*. New York: Dover Publications Inc.

Parissien, Steven. *The Georgian House in Britain and America*. New York: Rizzoli, 1995.

Stoney, Samuel Gaillard. *Plantations of the Carolina Low Country*. New York: Dover Publications Inc., 1990.

Wilson, Richard Guy. *The Colonial Revival House*. New York: Harry N. Abrams Inc., 2004.

General Books on Domestic Style

Massey, James and Shirley Maxwell. *House Styles in America*. New York: Penguin Studio, 1996.

McAlester, Virginia and Lee. *Field Guide to American Houses*. New York: Knopf, 1984.

McAlester, Virginia and Lee. *Great American Houses and Their Architectural Styles*. New York: Abbeville Press, 1994.

Morgan, William. *Abrams Guide to American House Styles*. New York: Harry N. Abrams, 2004.

Rifkind, Carole. *A Field Guide to American Architecture*. New York: New American Library, 1980.

Upton, Dell. *America's Architectural Roots: Ethnic Groups that Built America*. New York: Wiley, 1987.

Online Resources

Historic American Buildings Survey
http://memory.loc.gov/ammem/collections/habs_haer/

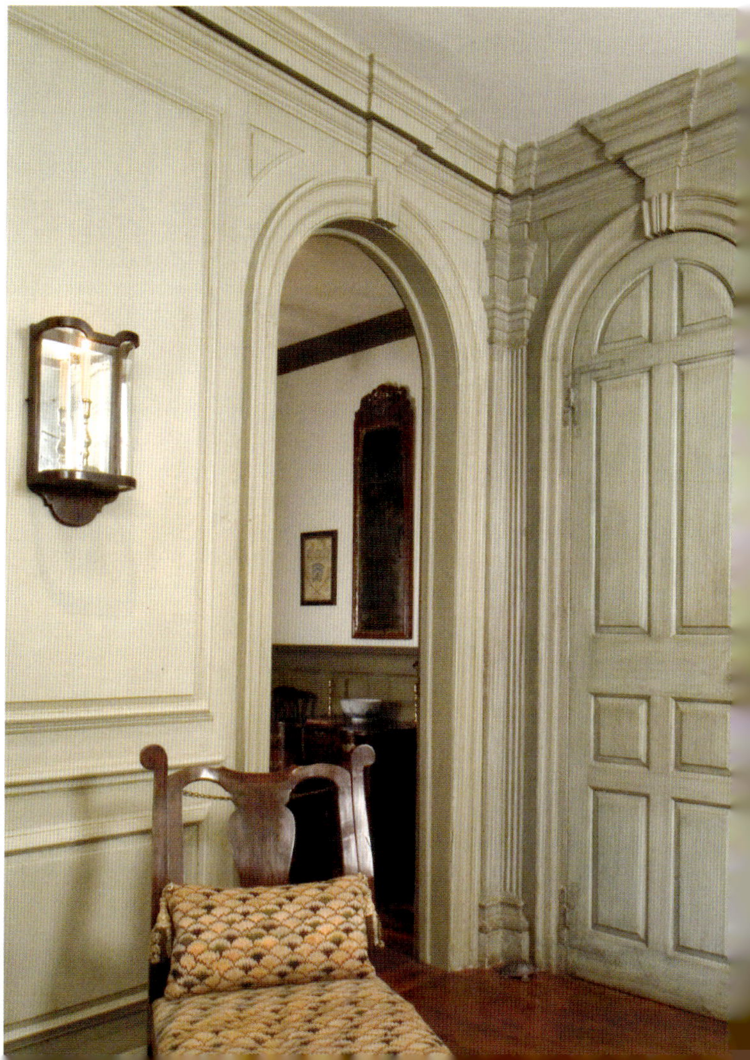

Index